Language
as
Articulate Contact

SUNY Series in
Speech Communication

Dudley D. Cahn, Editor

John Stewart

Language
as
Articulate Contact

Toward a Post-Semiotic
Philosophy of Communication

STATE UNIVERSITY OF NEW YORK PRESS

Production by Ruth Fisher
Marketing by Fran Keneston

Published by
State University of New York Press, Albany

© 1995 State University of New York

For information, address the State University of New York Press,
State University Plaza, Albany, NY 12246

Library of Congress Cataloging-in-Publication Data

Stewart, John Robert, 1941–
    Language as articulate contact : toward a post-semiotic philosophy
of communication / John Stewart.
        p.   cm. — (SUNY series in speech communication)
    Includes bibliographical references and index.
    ISBN 0-7914-2287-9 (acid free). — ISBN 0-7914-2288-7 (pbk. : acid
-free)
    1. Language and languages—Philosophy.   2. Semiotics.
3. Communication—Philosophy.   I. Title.   II. Series.
P106.S815   1995
401—dc20   94-7309
                                                                  CIP

10 9 8 7 6 5 4 3 2 1

To Lincoln Matthew Stewart
with gratitude for time and confirmation

CONTENTS

PREFACE

This work critiques one prominent account of the nature of language, the view that language is essentially a system of signs or symbols, and outlines an alternative that builds on the descriptions of language developed by Martin Heidegger, Hans-Georg Gadamer, Martin Buber, and Mikhail Bakhtin. The project began over twenty years ago. Working as a communication philosopher and theorist, I employed insights from Gilbert Ryle, J. L. Austin, and the Wittgenstein of the *Philosophical Investigations* to identify shortcomings in the accounts of language and meaning that were prominent among rhetoricians and communication theorists and teachers.[1] During this research, I became aware of the pervasiveness of semiotic conceptualizations of language and the degree to which these conceptualizations were unreflectively maintained, especially given Ludwig Wittgenstein's critique of picture theories of language, J. L. Austin's analysis of what he called the *descriptivist fallacy*, and Gilbert Ryle's analysis of linguistic meaning. Subsequent work clarified that, although ordinary language philosophers provided a useful critical perspective, their work did not point clearly toward a credible alternative. Later study of Martin Buber's philosophy of communication convinced me that any such alternative account of the nature of language would have to affirm its dialectic, collaborative, and oral-aural dimensions. Consequently, as I will argue, this alternative cannot be developed from either a semiotic foundation or from an analysis of what Austin and John Searle term *speech acts*.

A sabbatical in 1985 provided the opportunity to study at Boston College with Hans-Georg Gadamer, to read Heidegger with

ix

William Richardson,[2] to attend a lecture series by Jürgen Habermas, and then to visit the Buber Archives at Hebrew University and converse with philosophers, linguists, and pragmatics scholars there and at Tel Aviv and Haifa. These experiences confirmed my belief in the need for an alternative. This conviction has been intensified over the past seven years by postmodern writers' criticisms of representationalist epistemologies and theories of language. One of the hallmarks of philosophical discussions of postmodernism has been the argument that neither philosophy nor language represents or "mirrors" nature and that epistemological approaches that construe knowledge as representation are flawed. *Language as Articulate Contact* may in fact be described generally as a response from the perspective of communication theory to some central features of these postmodern critiques of representationalism.[3] My primary goal is to extend the postmodern critique of representation to semiotic accounts of the nature of language and to outline an approach to language that is responsive to this critique.

Therefore this work addresses concerns of not only communication theorists but also philosophers, linguists, and semioticians. Some readers may view such an interdisciplinary focus as inherently problematic. Questions may arise about which disciplinary perspective ought most appropriately to be figure and which should be ground, and whatever the resulting conceptual hierarchy, some readers are likely to be dissatisfied. Moreover, any author attempting such a project is vulnerable to criticism from disciplinary specialists.

But one problem with some current discussions of the nature of language is that they are not interdisciplinary enough. In philosophy, the Channel is still wide enough to prevent some scholars on each side from taking seriously the writings of their counterparts who work in a British analytic, hermeneutic, or phenomenological tradition. U.S. and European linguists and semioticians often express little interest in or familiarity with claims about the nature of language made by postmodern philosophers, and for the most part, the reverse is also true. The dialogic "translinguistics" produced by members of the Bakhtin circle is cited primarily by literary theorists, even though these works outline persuasive and, some would say, genuinely novel accounts of the nature of language and communication that could contribute to analyses by philosophers, linguists, and communication theorists. Efforts by followers of Austin and Searle to analyze "speech acts" for the most part ignore critiques by communication theorists of the efficacy of grounding an account of the inherently social process of language in the construct of individual intent and the narrow scope of a conceptualization of communication dependent on what has come to be known as the *conduit metaphor*.[4]

This is why any contemporary account of the nature of language adequate for its subject matter will have to be interdisciplinary. Toward this end, I include in this work discussions of not only Heidegger, Gadamer, Bakhtin, and Buber, but also Aristotle, Plato, the Stoics, and Augustine; Locke, Horne Tooke, and Humboldt; Saussure, Peirce, Cassirer, and the Wittgenstein of the *Tractatus*; Kenneth Burke, Vladimir Volosinov, Calvin O. Schrag, artificial intelligence theorists, and educators of the deaf. Of course, many additional authors have essayed the nature of language, and I do not offer this sample as exhaustive. My principles of selection are "the symbol model," which, as Chapter 1 explains, is a five-part description of the nature of language, and the alternative, post-semiotic account of the nature of language outlined in Chapter 4. The scholars from various disciplines whom I discuss have played especially prominent roles in the development of these two perspectives, and I juxtapose their writings in order to clarify the theoretical and practical commitments inherent in each.

Because my approach to validity or "truth" is hermeneutic, I do not argue that the account of language offered here is more "accurate" than semiotic accounts; that is, that it corresponds more closely to what language "really is." Instead, I argue that it is to be preferred, in Gadamer's words, because of what it comes to in its being worked out.[5] As this account is developed in the chapters that follow, I argue that, unlike the view it replaces, it is coherent, which is to say that its elements fit together in a plausible whole; that it captures a significant contemporary consensus among philosophers and communication theorists; and that it avoids many of the pitfalls and conceptual cul-de-sacs of semiotic accounts. I also contend that this perspective can be tested empirically through analyses of actual instances of living language in speech communication, and I offer some brief examples of such analyses.

Some reviewers with postmodern inclinations have questioned why I argue in this work for an *alternative*, post-semiotic account of the nature of language, rather than a *complementary* one. Given postmodern commitments to multiple readings, polysemy, and undecidability, one might expect my argument to lead toward a pluralist position, one that affirms the explanatory power, in various contexts and for various purposes, of a variety of semiotic and post-semiotic accounts of the nature of languge. But my account is not pluralist in this sense for two reasons. First, as I mention later, although I acknowledge the utility of semiotic analyses of some artifacts and actions, I do not believe that one can successfully lay out a semiotic account of *the nature of language*. The reason is that such accounts fail the tests of plausibility, coherence, and applicability just mentioned. And this leads to my second response: Along with many other postmodernists, I do not believe that *any* reading is as efficacious as any other. Criteria of coherence exist that can enable theorists to choose among competing philosophical and theoretical positions. Semiotic accounts of the nature of language are crippled by the serious problems of plausibility, coherence, and applicability that I develop throughout this work. The most important single one is the representational problem. To argue that language is fundamentally semiotic, one has to affirm some version of the claim that language—like knowledge or philosophy—does indeed somehow "mirror" something nonlinguistic—"thoughts," "signifieds," "meanings," or some other features of the "natural" or "objective" world. This claim, I argue, cannot be coherently developed, plausibly communicated, or effectively applied.

Another word about "method": I attempt to approach the works I analyze as a curious conversation partner who is focally interested in my interlocutor's explicit and, frequently, implicit view(s) of language. In other words, I approach this material as something of an ethnographer of the text, intent on letting it speak in its own voice. Often important aspects of the views embodied in an author's works surface not in axioms or theoretical propositions but in elaborations, discussions, metaphors, and examples. Sometimes even more subtle details of word choice, topic sequence, or evaluative intonation are evidence of the text's perspective on language. As a result, the reader will find more than the usual amount of quoted material in this book. Typically, I try to provide enough text for the reader to check my close reading against his or her own interpretations. These quotations thus function as data to support my claims about the views of the nature of language manifested in each text. I believe that only when one attends carefully to these sometimes extensive excerpts, can one recognize clearly what is distinctive about its view of the nature of language.

I hope it is also clear that, although I do not believe that one can give a coherent account of *language* as a system of symbols, I do recognize the profound usefulness of symbol vocabulary in discussing a variety of human artifacts and actions. It certainly continues to be useful to view flags and insignia as symbolic, along with certain locations, events, and characters in literature; objects, materials, and actions in rituals; and probably similar phenomena in dreams. Such symbols contribute significance to their human world because of what they point toward beyond themselves. The flag, whale, bread, or river, for example, directs the awareness and experience of those who perceive it to something that is other, distinct, and typically of more profound or nuanced meaning. Human language itself, however, is certainly not exclusively and, I argue, not even essentially made up of these kinds of phenomena.

Part I of *Language as Articulate Contact* consists of five chapters. The first demonstrates that prominent contemporary linguists, semioticians, sociologists, and communication theorists continue to view language as essentially a system of symbols. I describe the five theoretical commitments that are implicit in this characterization and explain how they interrelate. Then I argue that any account of the nature of language ought to be informatively applicable to paradigm instances of the phenomenon it purports to describe. One potential explanandum is the account itself; a characterization of language should explain the sentences or paragraphs in which the explanation is articulated. Another potential explanandum is the paradigm—although certainly not the only—instance of natural, living language; that is, conversation: two-person dialogue in real time. As Chapter 1 demonstrates, neither can be explained by the symbol model. In other words, despite the model's popularity, it fails two crucially important tests of application.

The conclusion of Chapter 1 previews the remainder of the work. As I note, Chapters 2 and 3 review the historical development of the symbol model from the pre-Socratics to the present to demonstrate how the model originated and grew and how various thinkers attempted to deal with its manifest shortcomings. These chapters reveal the presence of an unbroken thread from one set of early assumptions about the nature of language to the writings of linguists, sociologists, and communication theorists of the 1990s.

In Chapter 4 I propose an alternative, post-semiotic account of the nature of language articulated in terms that parallel the five commitments of the symbol model discussed in Chapter 1. This alternative is elaborated in Chapter 5 via a review of three complementary lines of research in hermeneutic philosophy, education of the deaf, and artificial intelligence. Each of these research programs develops an account of the nature of language that is similar, in some ways, to the account I build on postmodern philosophy in Chapter 4.

Part II consists of three chapters that employ the symbol model and the description of language as articulate contact as critical perspectives to analyze works by Vladimir N. Volosinov, Kenneth Burke, and Calvin O. Schrag. These chapters demonstrate how such analysis can reveal in works like these a basic tension between semiotic and post-semiotic accounts of the nature of language. They thus provide a way to interpret incomplete, inconsistent, or otherwise confusing sections or features of these works.

Acknowledgments

The College of Arts and Sciences and the Graduate School Fund of the University of Washington provided important support for portions of the research reported here. Hans-Georg Gadamer was an accessible and electrifying teacher, and William Richardson and the philosophy faculty of Boston College were hospitable and edifying. Mark Alfino of the philosophy department at Gonzaga University provided an especially useful review of the manuscript, and my comments on pp. 113–114 are a direct response to a question he raised. Dallas Willard introduced me to language philosophy over two decades ago at the University of Southern California. I have profited greatly from conversations with a number of colleagues, including Marcelo Dascal, Chip Hughes, Alan Scult, Michael Hyde, John Angus Campbell, and Carole Blair, and with many outstanding graduate students (now professionals in their own right), including Allen Clark, Sam Bradley, Paul Falzer, Karen Williams, Ken White, Susan Dyer, and Karen Zediker. Lisa Coutu also contributed research to Chapter 2. I owe the greatest intellectual debt, however, to Walter Fisher, who directed my doctoral work and then became the best kind of conversation partner and friend. Although he continues to question some of my claims, Walt generously participates in each conversation and responds to each essay with editorial acumen, intelligence, and love.

Part I

Language: A System of Symbols
or Articulate Contact?

Chapter 1

The Symbol Model and the Nature of Language

I sometimes look into the eyes of a house cat. What occurs is surely more than simply my projection. The returning look almost asks, "Can it be that you mean me? Do I concern you? Am I here for you? What is it about me?" The sun of reciprocity seems to rise, and then almost immediately to set. Feline eyes shift, and the twitch of ears and tail indicate that over there, brutish normalcy has resumed. I may continue to address the animal, but my glance is no longer *met.* [1]

Historically, many thinkers have characterized this kind of event as one of "understanding," which seems clearly to be part of my experience, but not of the cat's. Understanding, writes Hans-Georg Gadamer, is a fundamental endowment of humans, one that appears to distinguish us not only from domesticated pets but also from even our dolphin and primate cousins. Efforts to explain understanding almost universally rely on the construct "linguisticality" or "language." As Gadamer puts it, "above all, [understanding] takes place by way of language and the partnership of conversation."[2]

Efforts to describe language, in turn, typically exploit some version of the semiotic assumption that language is fundamentally a system of signs or symbols. For example, according to contemporary linguist Julia Kristeva: "The idea that the fundamental core of *la langue* resides in the *sign* has belonged to various thinkers and schools of thought, from ancient Greece through the Middle Ages and up to the present time. In fact, every speaker is more or less conscious of the fact that language symbolizes or *represents* real facts by *naming* them. The elements of the spoken chain—for the moment let us call them words—are associated with certain objects or facts that they *signify*.[3]

On this point, language scholars of various stripes concur with Kristeva. According to psycholinguist Charles E. Osgood, for example, it is important to answer the question "What is a Language?" to address such other important questions as "Do certain nonhuman animals 'have' a language? . . . When does a developing child 'have' a language? [and] How may languages have developed in the human species?" Osgood argues that the basic question can best be answered by enumerating six essential criteria, the fourth of which he calls *the semantic criterion*, which holds that the production of identifiably different and nonrandomly recurrent physical forms follows nonrandom rules of reference to events in other channels. "This criterion," Osgood explains, "implies that for anything to be a language it must function so as to *symbolize* (represent for the organism) the non-necessarily-*here* and the not-necessarily-*now*."[4]

Sociologist Norbert Elias also maintained that the distinction between symbol and reality is fundamental to human sense making. To understand virtually anything, Elias wrote, humans must be able to distance themselves from physical reality: "they must, as it were, mentally ascend to a level of synthesis above that of its existence here and now as a heap of matter." Various types of symbolic representations allow humans to do this, and languages are the most important. The need for communicable symbols "extends to the whole fund of knowledge of a language community and ultimately of humanity, including functions, situations, processes, and symbols themselves." In fact, "communication by means of symbols, which may differ from society to society, is one of the singularities of humankind. . . . One may rightly say that all this is obvious."[5]

Communication theorist Michael T. Motley accentuates the apparent obviousness of this claim about language as he begins his examination of the construct of intent with a review of "some extremely common, if not quite universal assumptions found in even the most elementary discussions of communication." The first of these virtually universal postulates is that "communication is characterized by symbolic behaviors, that is to say, that communication involves the transmission and/or reception of symbols." "Traditionally, *symbols* have been defined as signs arbitrarily related to their referents," he notes. And "the cognitive process of preparing a message for transmission to another requires, among other things, that we select signs from among a repertoire of possibilities. Signs thus selected and transmitted *function as symbols.*"[6]

Some language theorists set out to correct what they acknowledge are oversimplifications in semiotic characterizations of language and communication. For example, Umberto Eco attempts to articulate key features of what he calls a *general semiotics,* which embraces "text, semiosis, significant practice, communication, discourse, language, effability, and so on."[7] A central part of Eco's work is meant to "disentangle" the concept of sign "from its trivial identification with the idea of coded equivalence and identity" and restore the centrality of *interpretation* to what he calls the *semiosic process.* Eco demonstrates that the essential feature of the sign has been expressed in the antique formulation *aliquid stat pro aliquo,* something stands for something else. The symbol has been characterized similarly, he notes, although this construct typically foregrounds the vagueness and openness of *aliquo:* "with symbols and by symbols one elucidates what is always beyond one's reach" (p. 130). Using the example of a badge worn at one's buttonhole, Eco emphasizes that something is a sign or symbol "only inasmuch as it *does not stand for itself.* It does not stand for its molecular composition, its tendency to fall down, its capability of being packaged and transported. It stands for something which is outside itself" (p. 20).

Eco argues that the problem with the classic formula is that it obscures the importance of human interpretation in semiosis, where interpreting a sign means defining "the portion of continuum which serves as its vehicle in its relationship with the other portions of the continuum derived from its global segmentation by the content. It means to define a portion through the use of other portions, conveyed by other expressions" (p. 44). The outcome of this interplay among signs is the elucidation of reality, which Eco calls *the world* or "the pulp itself of the matter which is manipulated by semiosis" (p. 45). In the final chapter of *Semiotics and the Philosophy of Language,* Eco describes the "seven semiotic requirements" that actually make a sign a sign, the first six of which are aspects of the *aliquid stat pro aliquo* formulation and the seventh of which is the aspect of interpretation. Thus Eco's project to revise the oversimplified identification of semiosis with "the idea of coded equivalence and identity" ultimately reaffirms most features of historical analyses, including the ontological claim that in the process of semiosic representation, human meaning connects with "the pulp itself of the matter which is manipulated by semiosis." In other words, this prominent and influential effort to revise the philosophical foundation of semiotics—the concept of the sign—ultimately concludes that a sign is indeed, at its root, "something that stands for something else."

As these and other writers develop their views of the nature of language, substantive differences arise. Kristeva often relies on Saussure's *Cours de linguistic générale*, but she also distances herself from some of its conclusions. Elias rejects aspects of the Cartesian-Kantian analyses that inform many of the semiotic accounts of language that preceded his. Motley cites C. K. Ogden and I. A. Richards's classic, *The Meaning of Meaning*, but his view of communication moves significantly beyond the telementational, conduit-metaphor[8] perspective outlined in that work. Eco concurs at some points with Kristeva and Elias and disagrees with them at others. It is clear, in short, that semiotic accounts of language are not all of a piece; they differ in important ways, and each of these authors would accept some claims made in complementary writings and reject others.

The Symbol Model

Despite their substantive differences, however, these authors share some common commitments. These make up what I call the *symbol model*, the view that language is fundamentally a semiotic system, a system of signs and/or symbols.

Some language scholars who embrace a semiotic perspective explicitly avoid "symbol" terminology. They take pains to distinguish generally between signs and symbols and to differentiate among specific types of signs, for example, "decisigns," "natsigns," and "comsigns."[9] These scholars would argue that it is both imprecise and misleading to group semiotic programs together under the *"symbol* model" rubric. But as the citations from Osgood, Elias, and Motley indicate, and as will be further demonstrated in Chapters 2, 3, and 5, *symbol* is the term most frequently used by scholars in a variety of disciplines to characterize the basic nature of language. Scores of communication theorists, linguists, philosophers, semioticians, and others continue to argue that the human animal is distinctive because of its ability to "symbolize" and that human language is essentially a "system of symbols." Therefore I have chosen the term *symbol model* to label not only these programs but also those that foreground "sign" rather than "symbol" vocabulary, because both sets of approaches adhere in varying degrees to five interrelated theoretical commitments.

The first commitment of the symbol model is an ontological one. These accounts presume a fundamental distinction between two realms or worlds, the world of the sign and the signified, symbol and symbolized, name and named, word and thought, *aliquid* and *aliquo*. As I indicated, although writers have described significant—although sometimes contradictory—differences between signs and symbols, these two phenomena are ontologically similar because they are both primary semiotic units, which means that they are viewed as fundamentally different from whatever it is that they signify or symbolize.

Descriptions of the symbol model's two realms or worlds differ, and in some cases theorists argue that they are virtually indistinguishable or inseparable. But, once the semiotic assumption has been made, a basic structural a priori has been established, and even those who argue for inseparability must struggle to make their accounts of language coherent with what is often termed the *Janusfaced* character of language. I call this basic ontological claim the commitment to *two worlds*. It holds that there is a difference in kind between the linguistic world, or the world of "signifiers," and some other world, that of "things," "mental experiences," "ideas," "concepts," or some other "signifieds."

The four additional commitments that make up the symbol model follow from this one. Commitment 2 is the belief that the linguistic world consists of identifiable units or elements (e.g., phonemes, morphemes, words, utterances, speech acts) that are its atoms or molecules. The third commitment is the claim that the relationship between these units of language and the units that make up the other of the two worlds is some sort of representational or symbolizing relationship.[10] Commitment 4 is the belief that these ontologically distinct, representationally functioning units make up a system, the system called *language*. The final commitment asserts that language is a tool or instrument humans use to accomplish their goals. One central claim of this book is that some version of these five commitments is entailed by the decision to characterize language semiotically. In other words, I argue that *some version of these five commitments necessarily follows as a consequence of using "sign" or "symbol" vocabulary to describe the nature of language.*

Commitment 1: Two Worlds

These five commitments are interrelated in several ways. First, as I noted, the two worlds claim is most basic. As Chapter 2 demonstrates in detail, this claim embodies the ontology first established in pre-Socratic, Platonic, and Aristotelian formulations of the nature of language. The basic distinction between the linguistic world and the mental (nonlinguistic) world was embodied in the influential Aristotelian formula: "Spoken words are the symbols of mental experience and written words are the symbols of spoken words."[11] This became the medieval formula linking *aliquid* and *aliquo*. In Kristeva's words cited earlier, the distinction is between "language" and "real facts"; for Osgood, the two worlds consist of "physical forms" and "events in other channels" or present "symbols" and "the not-necessarily here and the not-necessarily now." Elias distinguished between "symbols" and "physical reality" or "a heap of matter"; and, for the most part, Motley is satisfied with the distinction between "symbols" and "referents." In places, Eco speaks of two different "portions of the continuum," but at others he distinguishes between the sign and "the world (the continuum, the pulp itself of the matter which is manipulated by semiosis)" (p. 45). This sample of perspectives illustrates some of the diversity that characterizes expressions of the commitment to two worlds.

Eco's is not the only work in which this commitment to two worlds appears to be modified or even rejected, only to resurface. Early in the *Cours* , for example, Saussure labeled the two phenomena *concept* and *sound image*, and claimed that both were psychological entities. But, as I demonstrate in Chapter 3, Saussure subsequently treated concept and sound image as ontologically distinct, both when he discussed the temporality of the latter and when he outlined the representational relationship between them. This set of moves is typical. Theorists who treat language semiotically sometimes acknowledge the potential problems created by their commitment to two worlds, but in virtually all cases, they postulate at one point or another a fundamental distinction between linguistic phenomena, on the one hand, and nonlinguistic phenomena, on the other.

Once the existence of two realms or worlds has been posited, and one wishes to carry on the conversation, one requirement for coherency is that the theorist explain the nature of each world—what each is made up of, looks, or sounds like. Most language scholars have approached this issue by beginning with analysis rather than synthesis, which has led them to identify the *units* that purportedly make up each world. Thus arises commitment 2, to some form of atomism. Then, once one has asserted the existence of two different worlds consisting of two different sets of units, coherency demands that one explain how units in one world relate to units in the other. This question has been answered with the claim that one set of units somehow *represents* (signifies, symbolizes) the other—commitment 3. At this point, language has been characterized as a semiotic system consisting of units in one world that in some way represent units in another—commitment 4. Given the existence in the human world of this more-or-less objective system, coherence then demands that one give an account of how humans relate to this system. Commitment 5 is a response to this question: Humans use the system instrumentally to accomplish their goals.

Commitment 2: Atomism

As I noted, the commitment to atomism is embodied in the decision to begin with analysis rather than synthesis, that is, to approach language by dividing it into units. This move has been popular since the first primitive pictographs isolated some visible features of notable events and the letters of the first alphabets designated specific sounds or phonemes. In each case, consequential decisions were made to mark some elements of communicative experience *and to ignore others.* For example, pre-Socratic Greeks graphically represented not only distinctions between closely related consonants such as /p/ and /b/, but also between related vowels such as /e/ and /æ/. But, although their system marked differences between voiced and unvoiced consonants and front, medial, and back vowels, it included no units to highlight the differences between, for example, a threatening greeting and a welcoming one or a serious question and an ironic one. Thus the atomism commitment has not only focused attention on parts rather than wholes, it has also highlighted some kinds of parts and ignored others with as much or more semantic and pragmatic importance. Although it would constitute another major project, it would be illuminating to trace the implications of these early choices through the history of theorizing about language.

The commitment to treat language atomistically has been most apparent in theorists' dependence on examples of single words to support their claims about the semiotic character of language. The literature is replete with claims that *horse, tree, ox, chair, table, cat, hat,* and *mat* are all paradigm examples of units of language that, when analyzed carefully, will reveal the basic character of language itself. At best, of course, these analyses can account for only some aspects of the operation of one category of language units, concrete nouns. To generalize from these to language itself, theorists have had to assume that concrete nouns were the paradigmatic units of language and that all other units can be compared to or contrasted with them. From at least Aristotle forward, abstract nouns, adverbs, prepositions, conjunctions, and so on have been analyzed in terms of or in ways parasitic on the analysis of concrete nouns. As Chapters 2 and 3 demonstrate, critics have noted the indefensibility of this way of proceeding, and as a result, especially in the twentieth century, some theorists have concentrated on phonemes, utterances, or speech acts. But these phenomena are also typically treated as discrete units that, in various combinations, make up language. In this way, commitment 2 persists even in some of the most recent accounts of language.

Commitment 3: Representational

The commitment to representationalism follows directly from the first two commitments. Given two worlds or realms, each made up of units, one is led to ask how units of one relate to units of the other. Familiar interpersonal experience has often appeared to offer a hint: Names represent individual persons; therefore, early theorists speculated, is it not probable that other words function similarly? Fortunately, it almost immediately became apparent to most theorists that it would be difficult to locate the "thing named" for many categories of words, including negative terms, articles, prepositions, and conjunctions. But unfortunately, rather than reexamining the basic assumption that words function representationally, scholars typically have looked for ways to salvage their semiotic analyses. As already noted, one strategy has been to argue that problematic words only represented by virtue of their connection with other, concrete and positive words. This strategy led to tortuous efforts to analyze "categorematic" and "syncategorematic" terms that peaked in the late Middle Ages. A second strategy has been to generate various kinds of entities for these problematic terms to represent, such as John Locke's "the absence of something," which, he postulated, was the representamen or thing named for the word *nothing*.[12] Early in this century Gilbert Ryle labeled this strategy *the 'Fido'-Fido fallacy*, because it holds that every meaningful expression must signify an extralinguistic correlate, as "Fido" signifies Fido.[13] But Ryle failed to point out that his criticism undermined not just referential theories of word meaning but all semiotic, representational accounts of language. Partly as a result, these accounts persist.

A third strategy has been to distinguish various kinds of representational relationships, including those that are logical, psychological, cultural, or communicative. Wittgenstein argued in the *Tractatus*, for example, that words were representations in the sense of the German term *Darstellung* ("model," "presentation," "exhibition"—a logical representation) but not in the sense of *Vorstellung* ("picture"—a sensory representation). But this distinction did not alter the basic structure of the symbol model. Virtually all contemporary dictionaries, encyclopedia, and glossaries define a symbol as *something that stands for or represents something else*.[14] And the claim persists in each articulated version of the symbol model that the representing unit from world$_1$ in some way stands for (signifies, symbolizes, represents) another unit from world$_2$.

Commitment 4: System

Theorists frequently overlook the significance of the fact that semiotic characterizations of language picture it as a system rather than either as an event or as a mode of human being. In Chapter 2 I review Wilhelm von Humboldt's nineteenth-century effort to redirect language scholarship by emphasizing that what was being studied was en*ergeia* or *activity*, not *ergon*, or *product*. I also note how Humboldt stopped considerably short of this goal. And even after his efforts, the inclination to treat language as a system has consistently hypostatized the process, frequently under the rationale that this is the only way to treat it systematically, objectively, or "scientifically." Again, Saussure's work exemplifies this tendency. He acknowledged distinctions among human language ability (*langage*), the system of language (*langue*), and speech (*parole*) and noted that historically, the actuality of *parole* always comes first. But he also insisted that linguists concentrate on *langue*, the system of language. One reason Saussure focused on language as a system was that he wanted to emphasize how each linguistic unit is meaningful only in relation to the other units making up its system. This insight was one of his primary contributions to modern linguistics and laid the foundation for structuralist theories of language and culture. But Saussure also restricted linguistics to the study of *langue* because, he claimed, it was the only phenomenon that was orderly enough and accessible enough to be studied *scientifically*.[15] This move perpetuated a subject-object relationship between linguists and language, and it is this feature of commitment 4 that, I believe, has significantly distorted subsequent language study.

Commitment 5: Tool

Explicit adherence to the tool commitment emerged relatively late in the development of the symbol model. Virtually all classical authors acknowledged that language is *used* in various ways. According to

Cicero, for example, there were three: to instruct, to delight, and to move hearers. But the modern and contemporary emphasis on language as an instrumental tool reflects the Enlightenment proclivity for subject-object explanations, similar to those reflected in the system commitment. Such analyses begin with the Cartesian *cogito* and the irreducible distinction between the human subject and the objects that subjects allegedly encounter, construct, and manipulate. From the perspective of commitment 5, language is one of the more-or-less objectifiable tools subjects use to accomplish their goals.

Historically, of course, the primary use of the language tool has been viewed as the communication of thoughts or ideas. Among others, Locke underscored the importance of the communicative function of language, and the eighteenth century theorist John Horne Tooke would not even grant "language" status to the solitary mental naming that some of his predecessors had analyzed. Horne Tooke argued that the fact that the purpose of language is "to communicate our thoughts" should "be kept singly in contemplation," but that unfortunately this fact "has missed all those who have reasoned on this subject."[16] As this commitment has been worked out, language has often been treated as an instrument uniquely available to humans and the primary reason for our superiority over all other animals.

I emphatically do not mean to claim that any contemporary language scholar explicitly accepts the simplistic word-idea relationship that Aristotle or Locke outlined or, Kristeva's comment notwithstanding, the notion that there is a one-to-one correspondence between word and thing, idea, response, or meaning. These simple referential versions of the symbol model have been fatally discredited by many modern and contemporary scholarly programs, including the analytic critiques of Wittgenstein,[17] Ryle,[18] Austin,[19] and Searle,[20] and the hermeneutic efforts of Heidegger,[21] Gadamer,[22] and other postmodernists. But as I noted in relation to Ryle's criticism of the " 'Fido'- Fido fallacy," the connection has not consistently been made between these discredited referential theories and the general practice of characterizing language as a semiotic system. In other words, many scholars appear not to recognize how some version of the symbol model inheres in every semiotic account of language or communication. This is because, when language and communication scholars adopt "sign," "symbol," and "symbolizing" vocabulary, they are led by this vocabulary toward positions strikingly close to the discredited referential versions of the symbol model.

As I also noted earlier, one of the primary goals of the following chapters is to support this claim. But before reviewing the conceptual history of the symbol model, proposing an alternative, and testing it, it may be useful to make explicit some other conceptual difficulties inherent in the symbolic view of the nature of language.

Some Limitations of the Symbol Model

The Reflexivity Problem

Although Kristeva focuses primarily on historical description, she discusses a number of language *practices*, including psychoanalysis, oratory, and literature. She notes that when discussing practices, the meaning of the term *language* does not correspond to that of the system described by grammarians. But, she maintains, all these practical applications do have in common "the fact of being a system of signs."[23] As a result, it would seem reasonable to expect that Kristeva's sketch of language as a system of signs should be applicable to the practice in which she engaged as she wrote it.

As noted earlier, Kristeva asserts, "In fact, every speaker is more or less conscious of the fact that language symbolizes or *represents* real facts by naming them. The elements of the spoken chain—for the moment let us call them words—are associated with certain objects or facts that they *signify*."[24] If we are to accept this account of the symbol model, we should be able to apply the view of language it presents to this instance of language itself. In other words, it should be possible to analyze these two sentences into the elements that are associated with certain objects or facts they signify. Moreover, if Kristeva has accurately captured part of the essential or basic nature of language, the process of applying her insight should reveal something coherent and nontrivial about (a) language or (b) this particular example of discourse. Let us, therefore, try applying Kristeva's analysis to her own two sentences.

If she believes that her analysis actually describes only "elements of the *spoken* chain," then it is inappropriate to examine these written sentences. Her writings clearly indicate, however, that she would agree that some version of the symbol model also applies to written language.

The units or elements of language, she argues, "are associated with certain objects or facts that they signify." But are they? In these sentences, the words *speaker, words*, and *objects* appear to support her contention. Although they are general labels, each appears to be associated with a potentially definable "object" that it could be said to "signify": *speaker*, with a human engaged in uttering; *words*, with utterance or discourse units surrounded by time or white space; and *objects*, with those features of the human environment that are visible, tangible, and stable. Some difficulties arise with this line of reasoning, due to the lack of consensus among grammarians and linguists over exactly what constitutes a *word*, and among philosophers about the technical definition of *object*. But if we avoid insisting on too much precision, there appears to be a rough and ready sense in which these words label, point to, or represent (signify) certain nonlinguistic entities.

This is, however, a very imprecise analysis for a topic this important. Moreover, it is difficult to apply this analysis to almost any other words in these two sentences. What objects or facts are signified by *in, every, is, or, of, the, that, symbolizes, real, naming, let, call, are, with, certain*, or *they*? For example, certainly no one would claim that some object is signified by the word *in*. But could it be said to signify a "fact"? May *in* be said to represent a certain state of affairs, for example, the state of affairs of being enclosed or delimited? Obviously this cannot be the case here, because *in* is functioning as part of the idiom *in fact*. Are we thus to conclude that Kristeva's claim applies only to nonidiomatic terms? And must we now look for an object or fact for the words *in fact* to signify? Where would such a search lead? Or is it more reasonable to conclude that Kristeva's claim about language in general cannot be applied to this specific instance of language?

Indexical terms, such as *the, that*, and *they*, present another set of difficulties. One central feature of such words is that they are context dependent, which means that unless the context is both specified and concrete, there could not possibly be any object or fact for them to signify. Problems arise partly because in actual sentences the context is frequently either incompletely specified or anything but concrete. In Kristeva's sentence, the antecedent of *they* is *words*, so, one would surmise, she would claim that *they signifies words*. This analysis would be neat and complete, were it not for two subsequent problems. The first involves the aforementioned difficulty of defining the term *words*. Because of this difficulty, the claim that this term signifies *words* does not constitute a claim about any clearly definable "object" or "fact," unless one is to conclude that the signified is the token (that is, this particular instance of the printed word) of *words*, in which case the claim is trivial. A second problem is that the claim that the word *they* "signifies" the word *words* amounts only to a grammatical or syntactic observation about how the two words are functioning. Nothing nontrivial can be claimed on this basis about "the world," "objects," "facts," or anything outside language.

What about the word *symbolizes*? Does this term signify a definable object or fact? Certainly not an object. So how might one describe the "fact" that "symbolizes" signifies by naming? Let us try, {the act of using an object or word to stand for something else}. It would be consistent at least with Wittgenstein's *Tractatus* to call the combined states of affairs described in these brackets a "fact." Moreover, one could conceivably argue that this is the fact that the term *symbolizes* signifies. In this analysis, Kristeva's claim is that the system of language (*la langue*) engages in the act of using words to stand for something else. In addition, language does this by *naming* these "real facts."

It is difficult to determine how to assess this claim. In the first place, it strains credulity to postulate that "language," which, recall, is an objectifiable "system," can itself perform the intentional act of naming. But it is even more difficult to comprehend what it could mean to say that the word *symbolizes* in this sentence (or perhaps in the system of language?) is functioning to represent the fact presented in brackets *by naming it*. A name designates ostensively. It points to the thing or person named. Does *symbolizes* function this way here? When one comprehends this part of these two sentences, is it because one has been pointed toward the act in brackets by being given its name?

As I noted earlier, difficulties such as these have been acknowledged for at least 2500 years. Aristotle identified precisely this problem with *of, the, that*, and *they*, and Ryle and many other twentieth-century language analysts have also highlighted these problems. But Aristotle's solution, and the solutions of many subsequent language theorists, have virtually all been centrally dependent on the very semiotic commitments that create the problem in the first place. When one attempts to test these commitments by *applying* the claim that language is made up of word units functioning representationally, one is led inexorably to questions like the ones raised here. Often the difficulty with these questions is not so much that they have one answer as opposed to another, but that one does not quite know how to go about answering them. How does one think about the object or fact allegedly signified by *in* or *is*? Could it actually be the case that words other than nouns represent by naming? It is easy to understand Wittgenstein's conclusion in the *Philosophical Investigations* that questions like these can emerge only when language "goes on a holiday." And yet philosophers, linguists, and other theorists continue to make assertions about the nature of language that cannot possibly be true of the very language used to make the assertions themselves.

The Natural Language Problem

On the one hand, it is completely reasonable to expect internal consistency in a philosophical or theoretical formulation. On the other hand, the practice of attempting to hoist a theorists on her or his own petard has a long, but not particularly distinguished history. The reader of this analysis of Kristeva's sentences may have the nagging sense that something slightly unfair has happened and, more important, that somehow the central issue has not really been addressed. As a result, I propose to shift focus to two instances of naturally occurring conversation.

Clearly, *any effort to define or characterize the nature of language should be informatively applicable to instances of language's natural occurrence.* The theoretical formulation, in other words, should apply readily and fruitfully to paradigmatic examples of its explanandum. It is equally clear that *the paradigmatic instance of language is conversation,* verbal-nonverbal exchange between humans in real time, either face-to-face or mediated by some electronic modality (e.g., telephone). This is the activity humans engage in characteristically, routinely, naturally, and constantly. Some version of it makes up the lion's share of most humans' personal and occupational lives.[25] Unfortunately, this point appears to have been lost on many language theorists, who concentrate instead on examples devised to support their arguments. Philosophers have typically generated armchair examples about the present king of France or the morning-and-evening star, and linguists and semioticians have speculated about whether green ideas sleep furiously and have attempted to analyze such pseudo-utterances as "Hello, Tom. This is Bill. I promise you that John will return the money." A typical recent analysis works with such examples as

Tom opened the door   Sam opened his book to page 37
Sally opened her eyes   The surgeon opened the wound.[26]
The carpenters opened the wall

Artificial constructions such as these can often clarify their authors' ideas, but they cannot test them. Like focusing on concrete nouns, the tendency to use only hypothetical examples has, I believe, contributed to the persistence of the symbol model despite its manifest inapplicability.

But a group of researchers who call themselves conversation or discourse analysts do examine discourse much closer to actual conversation. They use audio and sometimes video recordings to create detailed transcripts that embody a much fuller sense of living language than do examples generated by even the most creative armchair theorist. These scholars employ a variety of print conventions to indicate such nonverbal features of spoken language as vocal emphasis, pause, and overlapped speech. For example, capital letters designate emphasis, one or more colons indicate a prolonged sound or syllable, brackets enclose overlapped talk, and pauses are marked by either a dot or a count of seconds in parenthesis. Here are two brief transcripts by conversation analysts of naturally-occurring interchanges which should provide a reasonable test of the symbol model:

Example 1. Two College Students

1. John: So what do you THI::NK about the bicycles on campus?

2. Judy: I think they're terrible.

3. John: Sure is about a MIL:LION of 'em.

4. Judy: eh ⌈he:h ⌉
5. John: ⌊Duzit⌋ SEEM da you: there's a lot more people this year?

6. Judy: The ⌈re- ⌉ ye:ah, for su:re
7. John: ⌊Go-⌋   GOD, there seems to be a mILlion people

8. Judy: Yeah. (1.0) YE:ah, there's: way too many. I can't-at tIMEs the

9.   bicycles get so bad I just got off mi ⌈ne an ⌉ hh .h and gi(h)ve up!
10. John: ⌊Oh riLleh⌋

11. John: I unno when I DODGE one then I have to DODGE another one 'n

12.   its an endless cycle.

13. Judy: Yeah (1.0) oh they're TERrible.

14. John: 'S so many people.

15. Judy: Um hmm[27]

Example 2. Caller to Poison Control Center (Excerpt)

1. P.C.:   Poison Control = Can I help yo:u.

2. Caller: hhh Uh-yes I wz wondering- uhm could *Raid* hh
              uhm ( ) effect the

3.   bra:in permanently d'y'know.

4.   (0.3)

5. P.C.:   Oka:y C'n y' tell me the reason why y'wanna//
              know tha:t.

6. Caller: Well y'see uhm ( ) my husband sprayed this house
              that we have

7.   out in Romulus he- he- thought he wz being
              bugged. (0.2) suh he

8.   wen' out n' 'e got four cans ( ) of Raid. =

9. P.C.:   = What type of Raid.

10.   (1.2)

11. Caller: Gee I don' even know. = I ih-ih-j's says y'know ( )

12.   Raid like y know fer killing bugs. = uhm hhh I'm
              not even too

13.   sure which one he go:t. (0.4) N 'e got four cans 'a
              this 'n 'e

14.   spra:yed the whole house 'n carpeting rilly thick
              with this. hhh A:n

15.   then he uh:m (0.5) did it that morning but then
              he went t'back ( ) in

16.   the house like that afternoo:n, an he was in that
              house all day 'n

17.   all night. =

18.   P.C.: = How long ago was dis. =

19. Caller: = Now this here happened uh- Saturday morning, I gotta call from

20.   him ah- cuz he 'ed said he was seein' things 'n 'e was kinda acting

21.   weird, j'know.[28]

As the reader no doubt can sense, these transcripts capture something much closer to language as it actually occurs than the examples commonly used by philosophers, linguists, and semioticians to support their claims about the nature of language. Of course, this is "informal" language, which means, among other things, that it functions only partly in the service of "propositional content" or "truth value." The interlocutors are as engaged in making contact and negotiating their respective identities as they are in asserting. Questions are at least as important as answers, and pause, stress, and rhythm—and in Example 1, facial expression, proximity, gesture, movement, and various unmarked features of vocal intonation— contribute significantly to conversational outcomes. But if one is interested in language as it is lived, these examples are surely more paradigmatic than the hypotheticals typically discussed, and as relatively "spontaneous" and "natural" instances, they warrant close attention.

The reader may also sense what outcome will result from testing the symbol model by applying it to these examples. But without belaboring the obvious, I hope, let us ask whether the language displayed here appears to fit the description of the nature of language offered by those who characterize it as a system of signs or symbols functioning representationally and instrumentally.

As in Kristeva's prose, many of the concrete nouns in these examples appear to be accurately described by the symbol model. *Bicycles, campus, people, Raid, brain, house, Romulus, cans, bugs, carpeting*, and even *Saturday* or *Saturday morning* could all conceivably be thought of as language units that label, signify, represent, and in some cases even name objects or events in the interlocutors' nonlinguistic worlds. As I explain in Chapter 4, one could seriously question the extent to which several of these concrete nouns label "nonlinguistic" entities. For example what exactly "is" *Raid, Romulus, carpeting*, and *Saturday morning*? These questions notwithstanding, however, to acknowledge that these words may be thought of as signs or symbols of things is still to leave unexplained the majority of the words and phrases in these examples.

And it is much more difficult to generate coherent and useful insights by applying the symbol model to them.

For instance, consider just the first word of the first utterance in Example 1—*So*. What might this unit of language signify or symbolize? If a theorist committed to the symbol model agreed that this were a suitable unit to analyze, he or she might argue that this word represents John's desire or intent to introduce his question with something like the equivalent of *hence* or *therefore*. John begins his utterance this way to connect it with whatever preceded it, and he chooses the word *So* because of its informality. Thus the word symbolizes a "concept," "idea," or an aspect of the speaker's preceding emotional and mental state, and this state is specifiable, given the communicative context.

On its face, this account is plausible enough. But for it to be consistent with the two worlds commitment of the symbol model, the mental state must actually be specifiable and must be ontologically different from the word. Consider the first requirement: Is it specifiable? Could one describe a discrete mental state that actually could be said to precede the utterance of *So*, and that would be signified by this specific utterance? Certainly this task would be difficult. One first wonders how to describe this specific a mental state. Some mental states can be easily, if a bit loosely, characterized as, for example, the states of "feeling worried" or "intending to be on time." But how might one go about describing the mental state signified by John's utterance of the word *So* in this context? Perhaps one could characterize it as one of informal-transitional-introductory temporalizing or as encouraging-tentative-inclusive friendliness. But such abstract descriptions hardly satisfy the requirement to define the specific phenomenon that is the signified of this word. Note, also, how the effort to describe this specific "intent," or "concept" depends on a model of the mind that is probably indefensible. To accommodate the commitment to two worlds, one has to view the mind as a container of some sort filled with entities of very puzzling ontological status. To develop this kind of model, cognitive functioning has to be hypostatized in ways that clearly conflict not only with the results of current cognitive psychology and artificial intelligence research (see Chapter 5), but also with contemporary philosophical anthropology. Today, virtually every school child knows that the mind is not coherently describable as a container filled with the kinds of entities that are required by the symbol model.

What about the distinctiveness of this mental state? Is it clearly different in kind from the utterance that allegedly signifies it? And can it coherently be said to *precede* the utterance of *So* in such a way that *So* can *represent* it? One way to test whether this is the case is to ask if the same mental state could occur in the absence of this word. Is the mental state that is the alleged signified of *So* the same or different from the one that would accompany John's utterance in this context of *Hence* or *Therefore*? On the one hand, the answer seems simple. Because *So* is more informal than either *Hence* or *Therefore*, the mental states would obviously differ. On the other hand, to verify this response, one would have to be able to call up these mental states in the absence of these words or their synonyms and assess their relative formality—and their other distinctive features. But it is extremely difficult to determine how one might call up the mental state of, for example, informal-transitional-introductory temporalizing without the word *So*, to see (hear?) whether it is identical to or different from a closely related mental state. In fact, the problem is even more basic: How does one go about calling up mental states in the first place? And if one can in fact perform this activity, could a mental state that is "called up" for the purpose suggested here be identical to the mental state spontaneously experienced by John in this conversation? As "an example called up for purposes of analysis," would this mental state not differ from the original one? It is difficult to tell how even to begin to respond to such questions, and yet they are necessarily raised by the theoretical commitments that make up the symbol model.

A version of this same analysis could be applied to virtually any of the other words that are not concrete nouns or pronouns in these two examples. In utterance 1 of Example 1 this list includes *what, do, THI::NK, about, the,* and *on.* At least an additional 184 of the 282 words in these two instances of discourse could be similarly analyzed.[29]

But again, all this may seem a little silly. As I noted earlier, no contemporary scholar would seriously contend that one can specify any sort of one-to-one correspondence between specific signifier and specific signified. Surely the current understandings of language held by philosophers, linguists, semioticians, and communication theorists have progressed far beyond such a Lockean conceptualization. Contemporary scholars who subscribe to the symbol model might well argue that semiosis is basic to language, but they also insist that the process is much more complex and subtle than is implied by the simplistic analysis proposed and critiqued in the immediately preceding paragraphs.

For one thing, it is sometimes argued, individual words are not the units of signification in these examples. Phrases are, or idioms, or propositions, or sentences, or utterances. The signifier in line 1 of Example 1 is not the single word *So*, but *So what do you THI::NK* or perhaps the entire utterance, *So what do you THI::NK about the bicycles on campus?* This move appears to avoid the worst difficulties created by word-by-word analyses. But it does not solve the problem, because these difficulties simply resurface at another point in the analysis. The shift from words to word or sound groups does not do away with the requirement to identify the ontological status of the signified. Assuming that it is nonlinguistic, one must again treat it as some sort of mental or cognitive state. And it is obviously just as difficult to specify the mental state signified by the phrase or sentence as it is to specify the mental state signified by a single word. It is also just as difficult to argue that the mental state signified by a phrase or sentence is distinct from the words that allegedly signify or symbolize it.

But what if it is not nonlinguistic? Can this hoary ontological conundrum not be dissolved by simply acknowledging that both signifier and signified are of the same ontological status? Saussure made exactly this move when he specified that "the two elements involved in the linguistic sign are both psychological"[30] and when he emphasized that each linguistic unit is meaningful only in relation to the other units making up the circumscribed *system*. But, as I explain in more detail in subsequent chapters, there are two closely related reasons why the problem cannot be solved this way.

First, *one cannot coherently abandon a commitment to there being an ontological difference between signifier and signified while maintaining that a representational relationship exists between the two*. Representation, in other words, is a relationship that exists between two dissimilar phenomena. A symbol is something that stands for something *else*. A flag can represent a country; a graphic image— for example, a silhouette of a long-haired person wearing a skirt— can signify that a restroom is for women; an attorney can represent a client; and it can even be initially coherent to claim that a word signifies or symbolizes a thing, idea, or feeling. But a flag cannot *stand for* another flag, and a warning symbol cannot *signify* another warning symbol. Moreover, whenever one human represents another, he or she does so by virtue of the difference between them—one is elected and the other a constituent, or one is professionally certified for the service and the other in need of it. And no morpheme, word, or phrase can coherently be said to *stand for* another morpheme, word, or phrase. Even synonyms are mutually substitutable but not *representationally* related. As a result, it cannot make sense to claim both that two related phenomena are of the same ontological status and that the relationship between them is representational. If the purported relationship is a signifying or symbolizing one, then the phenomena need to be different in kind.

This coherency difficulty probably explains why theorists who claim at one point that signifier and signified are similar tend subsequently to treat them as ontologically distinct. And this is the second reason why the representational problem cannot be solved this way: This strategy presages a contradiction. Both Émile Benveniste and Kristeva make this point about the *Cours*. As Benveniste explains, "Even though Saussure said that the idea of 'sister' is not connected to the signifier *s-ö-r*, he was not thinking any the less of the *reality* of the notion. When he spoke of the difference between *b-ö-f* and *o-k-s*, he was referring, in spite of himself, to the fact that these two terms applied to the same *reality*. Here, then, is the *thing*, expressly excluded at first from the definition of the sign, now creeping into it by a detour, and *permanently installing a contradiction there*" (italics added).[31]

Saussure appears to have noticed this permanent contradiction, that is, that he could not maintain both his claim that *signifiant* and *signifié* were equally psychological and his commitment to there being a representational relationship between them. So later sections of his work acknowledge the necessity of the ontological difference. Eco's analysis cited earlier contains the same contradiction. At one point Eco speaks of the two aspects representationally linked by the sign as different "portions of the continuum," and subsequently he claims that one is linguistic and the other is part of "the world" or "the pulp . . . of the matter."

In short, protests that the two worlds commitment of the symbol model is no longer a part of serious language theorizing, and therefore that any attempt to test it against living language is irrelevant or unfair, can be sustained only if one ignores a substantial part of the significant contemporary literature in philosophy, linguistics, semiotics, and communication theory. "*Up to the present time*" (italics added), Kristeva writes, "every speaker is more or less conscious of the fact that . . . the elements of the spoken chain . . . symbolize or *represent* real facts by *naming* them." "Language," claims Osgood, functions "to *symbolize* (represent for the organism) the non-necessarily-*here* and the not-necessarily-*now*." The fact that symbols enable humans to distance themselves from "existence here and now as a heap of matter" is "obvious," according to Elias. And even as Eco resists the "trivial identification [of the sign] with the idea of coded equivalence and identity," he develops an account that is dependent on the same theoretical commitment that undergirds the "trivial" view he resists; namely, that language essentially involves the occurrence in an interpreting human being of a representational relationship between some *aliquid* and some *aliquo*. As subsequent chapters demonstrate, these citations are only a sample of the expressions of the two worlds commitment that influential scholars in several disciplines have made from ancient times through the past decade. The ontological difference basic to the symbol model is alive and well despite protestations to the contrary. And yet this feature of semiotic characterizations of the nature of language cannot coherently be applied to concrete instances of the phenomenon it purports to describe.

Before assessing the applicability of the remaining theoretical commitments, I want to remind the reader of the hermeneutic approach to validity that guides this critique. A realistic or idealistic approach would argue that the symbol model is "accurate" or "inaccurate," "true" or "false." It would do so by identifying the independently existing, specifiable phenomena against which one could juxtapose the model to determine how well the model captured or corresponded to these realities. To test the symbol model in this way, one would need a supply of words, representeds, and manifest relations between them. But the process of testing the first commitment of the symbol model in these examples has clarified that the model cannot be verified in this way, because the signified is generally unspecifiable. There is, in other words, a shortage of identifiable phenomena against which to test the model's correspondence, due primarily to the impossibility of maintaining a subject-object relationship with one's language. As a result, I argue, one would be well-advised to give up the correspondence criterion and instead to ask how coherent, plausible, and applicable the symbol model is. These are the questions that guide a hermeneutic validity test. As Gadamer puts it, from this perspective the hermeneutic theorist is interested primarily in what a model comes to in its being worked out.[32] A primary argument of this book is that the symbol model does not fare well as it is worked out and that the model has very limited applicability and equally limited plausibility and coherence. When those who propound it attempt systematically to trace out its implications and applications, they typically find themselves in one of several argumentative, theoretical, or philosophical cul-de-sacs, similar to those just encountered in the attempted analysis of *So*. And they are in good company; as Chapters 2 and 3 demonstrate, these intellectual and practical deadends have been occupied by some of the West's most respected thinkers. The problem, I argue, is not a lack of rigor or imagination. The problem is the model: Language cannot be coherently, plausibly, and usefully described as a system of symbols.

Efforts to test the other assumptions of the symbol model lead to a similar conclusion. As noted earlier, the atomism assumption pictures language as made up of identifiable units, often words. Leaving aside, for a moment, the difficulties of determining exactly what a word is, the bulk of the discourse in these two examples is both hearable and seeable as grammatically identifiable individual units. But several distinct utterances do not fit this pattern, for example "Duzit" (Example 1, line 5), "unno" (Example 1, line 11), "'s" (Example 1, line 14), "d'y'know" (Example 2, line 3), "ih-ih-j's" (Example 2, line 11), "t'back"(Example 2, line 15), and "j'know" (Example 2, line 21). How can the commitment to atomism be applied to elements that appear to be *combinations* of the basic units specified by the model? In addition, the brackets in Example 1 between lines 4–5, 6–7, and 9–10 indicate overlapped talk. Commitment 2 would indicate that Judy is simply saying "he:h" at the same time John is saying "Duzit," and is saying "-ne an" at the same time John is saying "Oh riLleh," and that one can appropriately understand this language by examining these individual words or individual sentences. But a conversation analyst would respond by repeating the argument outlined earlier against the efficacy of word-by-word or sentence-by-sentence analysis and for the claim that more is revealed in these instances of language by attending to the molar rather than the molecular units. Moreover, most conversation analysts would not treat the larger units as signifiers and thereby get caught in the search for signifieds. Instead, the claim might be made, for example, that the overlap as a whole is a significant (read "meaningful" or "notable") unit because all three talkovers are interruptions of the female by the male. Such analysis might also point out that Judy's "-hh.h and gi(h)ve up!" in turn 9 after John's overlap could be traceable in part to the fact of his overlap, not just to the previous words in her utterance or his locution "Oh riLleh." These are some features of this exchange that any attempt to analyze these examples as made up of individual units would leave unaccounted for. And this is the central difficulty created by the atomism commitment of the symbol model.

Especially by way of commitments 4 and 5, the symbol model pictures language as a system existing over against humans. According to this part of the model, persons manipulate the various language resources available to them to accomplish their conscious and unconscious goals. This part of the model has had considerable explanatory power. Various cognitive theories of message production or reception, for example, assume a representational and instrumental view of language consistent with the symbol model. Some of these theories have provided informative analyses of how cognitive plans get adapted to audiences or modified as a result of behavioral rehearsal and then expressed in a variety of communicator styles that are said to be external representations of these cognitive structures or processes. It has also proven useful for some analysts and critics to closely hear or read discourse to identify the implicit or explicit intent it manifests. But, because this part of the symbol model is also limited and distorting, these analyses also create virtually as many problems as they solve.

For one thing, living language includes many significant features not readily explainable following the cognitive-intent-to-linguistic-action structure of many versions of the symbol model. Consider, for example, some of the elements of rhythm and emphasis in Example 1. Across these fifteen turns at talk, John and Judy's discourse crescendos and decrescendos complementarily. John's first turn includes an emphasized or intense "THINK," while Judy's response is matter-of-fact in tone. John's second and third turns repeat the intensity level of turn 1 with "MIL:LION" and "SEEM." Judy's intensity builds in line 6 with "for sure," and then, in lines 8 and 9 it appears nearly to match John's intensity with "at tIMEs" and "an gi(h)ve up!" John continues the intensity in line 11 with DODGE, and Judy mirrors it in line 13 with the 1 second pause followed by "TERrible." Then both decrescendo in lines 14 and 15.

A symbol theorist who focused on these features of the language would typically characterize them as a series of outward manifestations of inward *intent* and might further distinguish between the interlocutors' "informative" intent (to say something about something) and their "communicative" intent (to have their discourse understood as functioning in this way). Thus one might speculate that the initial intent of John's somewhat overdrawn intensity is to cope with the apprehension that accompanies the need to find a talk topic, and Judy may intend to increase the comfort level of the interchange by joining John at his level of intensity. This analytical strategy, pursued by such theorists as John Searle and his followers, treats intent as originating in the message encoder.[33] Unfortunately, although this strategy offers some insights into communication, it also raises questions about where on the unconscious-to-conscious continuum a given intent resides, how one treats multiple and simultaneous intentions, what the relationship is between consciousness and intentions, and whether an utterance motivated by a given intention can reflexively or recursively affect that intention. Problems such as these lead some discourse analysts to conclude that conversation simply cannot be analyzed as "language of thought," as a series of external manifestations of internal process. For one thing, everyday talk is too complex, rapid, and yet, for the most part, successful to be explained by intent-to-action models. As Janet Bavelas and Linda Coates argue, "The problem with treating communicative behavior in conversation as mindful is that existing models of mindful behavior do not deal well with such precisely and rapidly improvised behavior."[34]

This is one reason why the strategy of analyzing conversation as governed by intent creates problems. Partly in response to these problems, other theorists treat intent from the perspective of the message decoder and typically replace *intention* with *attribution of intent*. The influential claim by communication theorists, Watzlawick, Beavin, and Jackson that "One cannot not communicate" frames intent from this perspective.[35] Although this move, too, has been fruitful, it also raises difficult questions about the relationship between decoder inference and the mental experience of the encoder. One wonders whether intent has much explanatory efficacy if it is simply treated as a projection, construal, or attribution by a listener. A third practice has been to limit intent to what is decidable from the interaction between the interlocutors. From this perspective, the antecedent conditions that purportedly prompt discourse exist not so much as cognitions in one or the other of the interlocutors' *minds* as in their *talk*. This functional or interactional approach focuses on observable behaviors as they are manifested within the context of a relationship and as part of a negotiated process. But interactional accounts of intent are also problematic. One disadvantage is that they appear to reduce meaning to behavior and thus change the question from "What does he or she mean?" to "What can his or her behavior be said to mean?"

Difficulties such as these have led some communication researchers to discard "intent" altogether. As Bavelas puts it: "it is perfectly reasonable to propose such intuitively appealing concepts as goal and intention, but the proponent takes on clear definitional and empirical obligations in doing so. If these obligations are not met, then there is the strong possibility that the apparently utility of the concepts is due solely to their slipperiness: Tautological concepts with surplus meanings . . . will always be 'right'—and therefore meaningless. It is no loyalty to such concepts to leave them in this state."[36]

Such are some of the theoretical and empirical issues raised by the system and instrumental commitments of the symbol model.

The central *philosophical* problem with these two commitments is that (along with several versions of the commitment to two worlds) they embody a Cartesian-Kantian, subject-object view of the nature of language. As I noted, this set of moves treats language as essentially a *tool* that humans employ strategically and tactically. But this picture has been subjected to strong criticism by a variety of twentieth-century philosophers. For example, Martin Heidegger argued that subject-object analyses of humans begin one giant step too far into the problematic, because, prior to any operations as subjects over against a more-or-less "objective" world, humans engage in a variety of everyday practices into which we are socialized but that *we do not represent in our minds.*[37] Heidegger labeled this process *being-in-the-world*; in Chapter 4, I call it *everyday coping*. The process consists primarily of the activities of interpretive involvement that constitute human existing. Sometimes humans experience themselves as conscious subjects relating to objects by way of intentional states such as desires, beliefs, intentions, and goals, but, as Heidegger argued, this is a derivative and intermittent condition that presupposes the more fundamental being-in-the-world, which cannot be understood in subject-object terms. This line of thinking has led not only Heidegger but also Neitzsche, Wittgenstein, Lyotard, Foucault, Derrida, Rorty, and other postmodern authors to build a broad consensus that calls for serious rethinking of subject-object analyses of human being. As Thomas McCarthy puts it, for many postmodern writers, "the epistemological and moral subject has been definitively decentered and the conception of reason linked to it irrevocably desublimated. Subjectivity and intentionality are not prior to but a function of forms of life and systems of language; they do not 'constitute' the world but are themselves elements of a linguistically disclosed world."[38]

In Chapter 4, I explain in more detail the subject-object bias of the symbol model and summarize criticisms of it to introduce a post-semiotic view of the nature of language.

Summary and Preview

Some influential contemporary philosophers, linguists, communication theorists, literary critics, and semioticians continue to treat human language as essentially a system of signs and/or symbols. As a result, their works implicitly or explicitly manifest, to varying degrees, the five theoretical commitments that make up the symbol model. Commitment 1 is to *two worlds*. The symbol model assumes that there is an ontological distinction between two realms or worlds, typically the linguistic and the nonlinguistic, and that language establishes a relationship between them. The second commitment is to some form of *atomism*, the belief that language, like "reality," is made up of identifiable elements or units. Commitment 3 is *representational*. It specifies that the relationship between units of language and units of the nonlinguistic world with which they are associated is some sort of standing-for relationship. The fourth is the *system* commitment, the belief that the units of language and the conventions that prescribe their use make up a unitary system. Commitment 5 is the belief that this system of language is used by humans *instrumentally* to accomplish their purposes and goals.

My argument is not that these commitments can or should be overlaid on the writings of symbol theorists. I mean to argue that they emerge due to the demands of coherency, which is to say that they are semantic and pragmatic outcomes of the initial decision to treat language semiotically. As a direct result of characterizing language as symbolic (or signic), one is led to adopt descriptors that are themselves "Janus-faced"; these descriptors entail that identifiable units symbolize or signify other identifiable units. This is simply part of "what it means" to claim that something is a symbol or sign. Signification and symbolization are also forms of representation, and as a result, semiotic characterizations of language are inherently representational. Because representation presumes ontological difference, the two worlds commitment follows from the choice of semiotic descriptors. Atomism and representationalness follow similarly; thus, the first three commitments of the symbol model do little more than explicate what is implicit in the terms *symbol* and *sign*.

The commitments to system and instrumentality follow in a similar way from the inclination not just to treat language semiotically, but to characterize it as a *system* of signs or symbols. As Humboldt and others have recognized, it makes a significant difference whether one treats language as a formed or created product or as a dynamic, fluid process. The former move hypostatizes what is lived as event and imports the subject-object distinction into language scholarship. Although this strategy undoubtedly allows the language scholar to proceed more "scientifically," it may also distort the phenomena of interest beyond recognition. Little can be learned about language as it is experienced by applying a paradigm that works best—and then only partially—for concrete nouns.

Chapter 2 traces the development of the symbol model from the origin of the Greek alphabet to Humboldt's *On Language*. I discuss the impact of some of the earliest decisions to abstract certain features of language and ignore others. Plato's accounts of the nature of language in *Cratylus* and the *Seventh Letter* are reviewed, along with Aristotle's formulation in *De Interpretatione* and other works. I show how the Stoics and Augustine modified some features of the Greek view they inherited, and how the speculative grammarians, especially Thomas of Erfurt, attempted to cope with some of the problems inherent in this approach. The chapter then briefly recounts the Port-Royalist version of the symbol model and John Locke's influential statement of it in 1690. I show how the same model was embodied in the efforts of Condillac, Rosseau, and Herder to account for the origins of language and in the other prominent eighteenth-century line of language scholarship, the attempt by John Horne Tooke and others to establish linguistics as a science. I end the chapter with a review of Humboldt, because he came closest to breaking with the symbol model.

Chapter 3 demonstrates how versions of the symbol model persisted through the nineteenth and early twentieth centuries. The chapter begins with a review of the Kantian effort to develop a comprehensive semiotic philosophy undertaken by the American pragmaticist Charles Sanders Peirce. Then I recap Saussure's theory of signs and the picture theory of meaning announced in Wittgenstein's *Tractatus*. The chapter concludes with an account of the version of the symbol model in Ernst Cassirer's philosophy of symbolic forms and the philosophy of reason, rite, and art developed at midcentury by Cassirer's American student, Susanne Langer.

Chapter 4 develops a post-semiotic perspective anchored in the claim that language should be viewed first and foremost as constitutive articulate contact. I review Heidegger's and Gadamer's accounts of the relationship between language and world and extend their argument to propose that the two worlds commitment be replaced by acknowledging that there is only one human world and it is linguistic. I argue that the paradigmatic site of language's occurring is in events of speech communicating and hence that any account of the nature of language should begin with this event and be informatively applicable to instances of it. I show how subject-object analyses cannot give an adequate account of this event, and thus instrumentalist models of language are inherently incomplete. I argue that language as a living event can best be understood by recognizing that its first business is contact. This contact is articulate in two senses; it generates distinctions and it occurs paradigmatically as oral-aural event. I connect the former claim about articulateness to recent work in cognitive science and the latter to work by

Volosinov, Bakhtin, Ong, Buber, and others on the nature and significance of orality. I also argue that because language is constitutive, it does not represent world but builds or develops it. I propose, in sum, that language can fruitfully be treated first and foremost as event, not as system; that this event embodies the distinctive dynamic of human being, which is understanding; that this ongoing process of understanding via languaging is the human's way of constituting world; that this understanding occurs in contact between persons, which is to say that the event is irreducibly dialogic; and that this understanding in contact is articulate, which means that it both accomplishes differentiation and occurs paradigmatically as oral-aural contact.

Chapter 5 reviews three diverse research programs that reinforce, in various ways, the view of the nature of language outlined in Chapter 4. The first is philosopher G. B. Madison's hermeneutics of intersubjectivity. The second is the research carried out by deaf educators who demonstrate the status of Sign (in the United States, American Sign Language, or ASL) as a full-fledged language. When juxtaposed against the work of educators committed to exclusively oral methods of deaf education, this research can also be seen as developing a view of language consistent with the one outlined in Chapter 4. Finally, I review some recent work in artificial intelligence that acknowledges the weaknesses in symbolic models of cognition and replaces them with a connectionist model. I show how scholars who are attempting to mediate between the symbolic and connectionist paradigms are applying a view of the nature of language that is also similar in important respects to my account of language as constitutive articulate contact.

In Part II, I illustrate the efficacy and usefulness of this post-semiotic view by analyzing from this perspective accounts of the nature of language developed by philosopher V. N. Volosinov (Chapter 6), literary critic Keneth Burke (Chapter 7), and philosopher Calvin O. Schrag (Chapter 8). Volosinov, a colleague of Bakhtin, begins his *Marxism and the Philosophy of Language* with a semiotic account and then, as he attends more and more closely to the centrality of "utterance," moves farther and farther away from the symbol model. Burke was a widely cited literary theorist and critic who prominently featured symbol vocabulary in his discussions of literature, society, language, and humanity. But Burke also highlighted features of language that go well beyond the operation of any "system of symbols." Similarly, Schrag, George Ade Distinguished Professor of Philosophy at Purdue, develops a decisively postmodern account of language, the coherency and adequacy of which is ultimately threatened by a residual commitment to some aspects of the symbol model. These chapters show how each author develops an account of the nature of language that, on the one hand, affirms its world-constitutive and relational potency and, on the other, treats it to some degree as a system of representational symbols. I argue that each of their attempts to give an account of the nature of language simultaneously rejects and accepts aspects of the symbol model. As a result, each account at some points illuminates the most subtle and distinctive features of living language and at other points repeats aspects of thoroughly discredited Aristotelian or Lockean formulations and thereby obscures central aspects of the dynamic it is designed to explicate.

This volume as a whole is meant to demonstrate how several interrelated lines of contemporary thinking call into question one prominent view of the nature of language, to encourage communication and language scholars to reflect on the adequacy of the symbol model and to argue that an adequate account of the nature of language must begin from the recognition that it is first and foremost articulate contact. The chapters making up its companion volume, *Beyond the Symbol Model: Reflections on the Nature of Language*, contain responses to this general problematic articulated by a number of philosophers, communication theorists, linguists, and semioticians. Together, these two volumes are designed to help carry on one contemporary conversation about human communication and the nature of language.

❀ Chapter 2

The Symbol Model
from the Ancients to Humboldt

No single book, much less one or two chapters, could comprehensively survey 2700 years of language scholarship. But it is possible in this space to trace how the symbol model summarized in Chapter 1 has functioned as one pervasive and prominent way of characterizing the nature of language. This chapter and the next complement—and rely on—histories of linguistics and grammar by R. H. Robins;[1] Thomas A. Sebeok;[2] Norman Kretzmann, Anthony Kenny, and Jan Pinborg;[3] Herman Parret;[4] G. L. Bursill-Hall;[5] Hans Aarsleff;[6] Julia Kristeva;[7] and D. S. Clarke, Jr.[8] But whereas these scholars trace developments within the history of linguistics and grammar, this chapter and the next review pronouncements about the nature of language that underlie or are presupposed by analyses of such grammatical and linguistic topics as the parts of speech, comparative phonologies, and linguistic universals. Thus these two chapters most closely parallel Roy Harris and Talbot J. Taylor's *Landmarks in Linguistic Thought*, which shows how the view they label *surrogationalism* has pervaded historical discussions of language.[9] Some linguistic historians and other subject-matter specialists may question my selection of theorists and be dissatisfied by the brevity of my discussion of each. But the historical survey in this chapter and the next is meant to be selective—its principal of selection is the symbol model—and to support the relatively narrow claim that versions of the symbol model have indeed prominently characterized language study from the pre-Socratics to the present. I begin with accounts of the nature of language which develop what seems to be the most obvious of all linguistic "facts," the ontological distinction between words and the world.

The Alphabet as a Representative System

Historians commonly identify the early Greek experience of wonder as the beginning of philosophical or theoretical thinking, at least in the West. But theorizing specifically about language appears originally to have been prompted by more pragmatic concerns, especially economics and historical preservation. The need for a bartering system apparently motivated the first of all known scripts, the cuneiform of the Sumerians. Clay tokens of exchange were created that were encased in small, hollow but totally closed podlike containers or bullae, with indentations on the outside representing the tokens inside. So, for example, seven indentations on the outside carried with them evidence of what was inside—seven clay shapes of cows or ewes. In this way the "symbols" on the bullae were always accompanied by their concrete significations.[10] Later, the first Mesopotamian attempts at grammatical analysis of the Sumerian language were apparently motivated by the desire to preserve a classical literature written in a language that was becoming obsolete at the time.[11] The first linguistic activity in India was also apparently conservatory; it began with the development of a written version of the oral Veda which probably occurred between the tenth and seventh centuries B.C. This document was designed primarily to preserve the Vedic heritage, which was required for recitations at the rituals that were a focal element of the culture.[12] Prior to these early instances of language scholarship, Chinese, Phoenician, and Aztec cultures had also employed various forms of written script.

But the Greeks were the first to translate these economic and conservatory impulses into a project with inestimable theoretical and even philosophical import when they devised the initial system that could be called an alphabet in the modern sense. The significance of the Greek alphabet, and the primary difference between it and earlier systems of script, is that it separately represented both vowels and consonants of the spoken language.[13] The inclusion of vowels was decisive. With this innovation, writes Walter Ong, "the Greeks reached a new level of abstract, analytic, visual coding of the elusive world of sound" and thereby "gave ancient Greek culture its intellectual ascendancy over other ancient cultures."[14] This achievement also had significant practical value to the Greek traders, diplomats, and colonizers who had to deal with their non-Greek-speaking neighbors, because it laid the groundwork for translation. It opened the door to language analysis and speculation that moved far beyond practical applications.

It is worth underscoring the sense in which this very first achievement of language scholarship was *representational*. Just as the indentations on the outside of the bullae were different in kind from and stood for what was inside, each character of the Greek alphabet was different in kind from and stood for a vowel or consonant sound. In fact, some of the earliest records of the development of the alphabet reveal an increasing effort to distinguish among various closely related phonemes so each could have its individual symbol or surrogate.[15] This direction of development is both plausible and coherent. As naturally social and articulate creatures, humans had doubtless been speaking and listening to one another since well before the advent of even the most primitive pictographs. These communicative experiences were lived primarily in the modality of sound and secondarily as experiences of sight, touch, smell, perhaps taste, and such combined impressions as timing, rhythm, and visual composition. The central importance of these communicative experiences to individual and group life was certainly obvious, as was the fact that it would be advantageous to have some way to preserve and pass on crucial features of them. The most direct way to preserve and pass on selected aspects of these communicative experiences was to capture, picture, or represent some of their primary elements—sounds—in a sight or visually based graphic system flexible enough to be broadly applicable. In this way the initial conserving impetus of language scholarship led to efforts that were fundamentally representational: letters of the first alphabet were designed to represent certain distinguishable phonemes.

But it is also worth underscoring two additional features of this earliest thinking about language. The first concerns the narrowness of this representational system and its inherent limitations. As I noted earlier, distinctions among vowels—/e/, /ɛ/, /æ/—were marked, as, for example, were those between voiced and unvoiced consonants—/p/, /b/. But many other significant features of the communicative experiences were omitted, including the complex and nuanced pitch variations that distinguish, for example, a sincere comment from an ironic or humorous one, and most other semantically important elements of speech rate, volume, and vocal quality. In addition, facial expressions and kinesic, proxemic, haptic, and chronemic features were also outside the scope of the alphabetic representation system, even though these elements were undoubtedly as important in ancient communicative experience as they are today. The change from a primarily aural medium to a primarily visual one was also consequential. As Ong emphasizes, "sound . . . exists only when it is going out of existence." In the lived experience of oral-aural communicating, one can seldom have all of even one word present at once. The written alphabet "implies that matters are otherwise, that a word is a thing, not an event, that it is present all at once, and that it can be cut up into little pieces."[16] Clearly authors of the first alphabet made many far-reaching decisions about which features of their communicative experiences to represent and which to leave outside the scope of the system they devised. One important rationale may have been that the omitted features appeared to be so content and context dependent that they could not be a part of an abstract *system*. Another might have been rooted in the obvious difficulty of identifying the units—Ong's "little pieces"—of such important aspects of the whole as communicative timing, proximity, and touch. Other decisions were, in a sense, made for these authors by the inherent differences between a visual medium and an aural one. But for whatever collection of reasons, the Greek alphabet, although revolutionary and of decisive intellectual importance, was a thin and partial abstraction which represented only some elements of the human communicative experience it was designed to capture.

A second important feature of alphabetization is that the process established a representational paradigm for thinking about language generally. As I noted, it seemed patently obvious—and still does—that writing represents speech. *But it did not necessarily follow that speech also represented something else—e.g., ideas or objects.* And yet early thinking moved in precisely this direction. It was only a short step from the creation of an alphabetic system for representing phonemes to the analysis of morphemes or words as similarly representational. The inclination to take this step was reflected in one of the first theoretical disputes that attracted the attention of most of the pre-Socratic authors of surviving texts or fragments about language, the dispute over *orthotes onomaton*, the correctness of words or names. Democritus, Protagoras, Prodicus, and Hippias all wrote on this topic, and Plato summarized many of their arguments in the dialogue *Cratylus*. In a sense these discussions extended earlier efforts to represent sounds with letters by focusing on the appropriateness or fidelity of the connection between words and the realities that they purportedly represented or "named." Importantly, the term *onoma* or "name" was a general one; many examples in extant texts discuss not only the labels for persons, things, and events, but also verbs and adjectives. Hence, one feature of the dispute was that it construed its object atomistically in that it was concerned with a variety of individual words as contrasted with sentences, propositions, utterances, or speech acts. Another feature of the dispute was that proponents of various views were frequently prescriptive. Protagoras, for example, wanted to correct the feminine gender of the Greek words *Mēnis*, "wrath," and *Pēlēx* , "helmet," so that the words themselves more closely resembled or represented that which they labeled.[17] In short, the primary goal of those who argued for "correctness" was to relate each name to some one thing that was the word's meaning, just as a person's name designates that one person and no other. As Kerferd summarizes the argument on this topic in Plato's *Euthydemus*, "To each segment of reality there belongs just one logos and to each logos there answers just one distinct segment of reality."[18] Only names that were characterized by this fidelity, this accurate link between the name and the thing named or meaning, were considered correct.

This way of looking at words generated obvious problems, because it required there to be some person or thing for each distinguishable word to name. These problems were also addressed in early Greek discussions of language. For example, writers struggled with the fact that this account deprived negative statements of meaning, because what is not (does not exist), cannot be named. For related reasons it raised difficulties with false statements and denials. One response to this problem—the one offered by Heraclitus—was to affirm that the world which words represent is filled with objective contradictions. This move allowed contradictions in language still to be understood as accurate representations of contradictions in the world and thus "correct." Another response, developed by Parmenides, was to distinguish the world of appearance from the world of being. A version of the Heraclitan response came to characterize the sophistic view. According to Kerferd, most Sophists maintained that "language as a whole must provide formulae for exhibiting reality, and the structure of language must exhibit the structure of things. But the world of experience is characterised by the fact that all or most things in it both are and are not. Therefore language also must exhibit the same structure. . . . Thought in the fifth

century B.C. was concerned . . . with the search for a one-one relationship between things and names, on the basis that the meaning
of any name must always be the thing or things to which it refers."[19]

Plato

Several of Plato's works contain portions of the earliest well-devel-
oped analyses of this problematic. He discussed related issues not
only in *Euthydemus*, but also in *Protagoras* and *Sophist*. But
Cratylus and Plato's *Seventh Letter* deal most directly with the representational nature of language. The dialogue *Cratylus*[20] recounts
the ongoing dispute over the correctness of names by tracing arguments among Socrates, Hermogenes, a follower of Parmenides, and
Cratylus, a philosopher who, according to Aristotle, came to mistrust
language so profoundly that he eventually communicated only with
gestures. The two primary accounts of the correctness of names discussed in *Cratylus* are the natural or mimetic and the conventional
or volitional. According to the former, names are naturally related
to or mimic that which they name—onomatopoeia is the most obvious example. The conventional theory Hermogenes championed in
the dialogue maintained the contrary view that the word-thing relationship is arbitrary, and according to Hermogenes, this meant that
it is subject to the speaker's own decisions and choices (384d).

Early in the dialogue Socrates argued that Hermogenes' volitional theory could not be correct, because it is incapable of distinguishing truth from falsity. If any word could be used arbitrarily to
name any thing, a speaker saying, "A horse has four legs" could be
speaking a private language in which *horse* is the name for what
we call "the human." Thus in this case the statement, "A horse has
four legs" would be false. Against this volitional view Socrates expressed the Platonic argument that "things are not relative to individuals"; they do not fluctuate "according to our fancy, but they are
independent, and maintain to their own essence the relation prescribed by nature" (386d–e). To speak correctly is thus to use names
in a proper way, and this means using them to divide up reality appropriately. Those names are correct that correctly *represent* what
they designate; just as a painter represents with color, speakers represent with names (424d–425b). According to Harris and Taylor, this
part of the dialogue constructed a two-stage theory of language: "The
primary names are built up by a mimetic process through combinations of sounds which copy the essential nature of the thing named,

and this mimetic process is based upon the physiological articulations of the individual sounds in question. Once these primary names are established, the repertory is then extended by combining them into meaningful compounds according to their primary senses."[21]

Having outlined this theory, Plato then had Socrates question it in a series of exchanges with Cratylus. One exchange concerned the different criteria of similarity that must be applied when comparing various names with their respective things named. Another line of argument cited the fact that some names are not reliable guides to the nature of the thing named. Socrates argued, "For if [the giver of names] did begin in error, he may have forced the remainder into agreement with the original error and with himself; there would be nothing strange in this, any more than in geometric diagrams, which have often a slight and invisible flaw in the first part of the process, and are consistently mistaken in the long deductions which follow" (436d). Socrates concluded that, if one can choose between learning about things "through the medium of names" or "from the things themselves," one would be wise to choose the latter.

In this dialogue, neither the natural nor the conventional theory emerged unscathed. Socrates concluded by urging Cratylus to "Reflect well and like a [hu]man" and not to accept either doctrine uncritically. But the dialogue evidenced Plato's commitment to representational thinking and the idea that truth is anchored in a world beyond language. Socrates did not counter Hermogenes' individualist account of the arbitrary nature of names by arguing that the community, rather than the individual, provides the standard for the correctness of arbitrary names, probably because this would have committed him to both a Sophist epistemology and a democratic politics. But, as I noted, he found other weaknesses in this account, and he also criticized Cratylus' mimetic or natural view of language because of its inherent vulnerability to error. Harris and Taylor argue that Plato rejected aspects of both doctrines to insist that "language reaches both beyond our opinions and beyond itself" to the world of forms or ideas which Plato described in subsequent writings.[22]

Perhaps the most explicit of these later writings is a section of Plato's *Seventh Letter*, written to the friends and companions of the deceased Syracusan Dion. Here, as a basis for his advice about how to live their lives without their dead friend, Plato summarized central features of his metaphysics, epistemology, politics, and view of the nature of language. "For everything that exists," he wrote, there are five classes of objects.

We have then, first, a name, second, a description, third, an image, and fourth, a knowledge of the object. . . . and we must put as a fifth entity the actual object of knowledge which is the true reality. . . . these four [names, descriptions, bodily forms, concepts] do as much to illustrate the particular quality of any object as they do to illustrate its essential reality because of the inadequacy of language. Hence no intelligent [hu]man will ever be so bold as to put into language those things which his reason has contemplated, especially not into a form that is unalterable—which must be the case with what is expressed in written symbols. . . . For this reason no serious [hu]man will ever think of writing about serious realities for the general public so as to make them a prey to envy and perplexity (342b–344c).

Clearly Plato did not entirely take his own advice. His writings that addressed the "serious realities" of language laid down the first detailed version of the symbol model. According to his account, sketched in his works and summarized in *The Seventh Letter*, there is a fundamental distinction between the linguistic (phenomenal) and the nonlinguistic (noumenal) world. The relationship between these two worlds is representational, in that language is made up of words that function to name aspects of this other reality. The question about the correctness of names is legitimate, because, as one commentator puts it, "language itself must submit to the test of whether the opinions it embodies—and conveys implicitly—are correct accounts of the structure and nature of reality."[23] For Plato, aspects of the noumenal world served as the primary designates or referents for names. To test language we must look beyond it to the Forms or Ideas to determine how well the words represent or symbolize aspects of that nonlinguistic world.

Aristotle

Plato's most distinguished pupil developed an approach to language that was similarly committed to the symbol model but that differed from his mentor's in part by elaborating an alternative version of this model. Throughout his corpus, Aristotle's extensive comments about language treated it as a natural phenomenon, as a conventional medium, and as an artificial composition and symbolic structure.[24] The natural basis of language (*logos*) is "voice" or "articulate sound" (*phonë*). Oviparous quadrupeds and birds have voices, but only humans have speech. "The minimum unit of significance is therefore voice considered as individual word."[25] Moreover, as Richard McKeon summarized, "Since language is the peculiar function of an animal who possesses a soul, that is, the imagination requisite for the imposition of meanings, as well as the special organs requisite for the production of voice, the marks of meaning may be found in the analysis of language as a symbolic structure or in the analysis of thought as expressed in language or in the analysis of things signified by thought."[26]

Aristotle briefed this view in the enormously influential second paragraph of *On Interpretation*, the classical statement of the symbol model: "Spoken words are the symbols of mental experience and written words are the symbols of spoken words. Just as all [humans] have not the same writing, so all [humans] have not the same speech sounds, but the mental experiences, which these [sounds] directly symbolize, are the same for all, as also are those things of which our experiences are the images" (16a). Here Aristotle codified the inclination simply to transfer the representational account of the link between writing and speech to the account of the link between spoken sounds and that which they purportedly represent. It is difficult to overemphasize the significance of this move. *Ancient experience with letters became the model or analog for ancient understanding of talk.* Because one phenomenon could apparently be explained representationally, it was assumed that the other, very different phenomenon could be explained similarly. But this crucial assumption was never articulated, let alone supported by argument.

For much of Western thinking, these lines and others in Aristotle's corpus established the pattern for treating language as fundamentally *semiotic*, that is, as made up of units that function as *symbols* (later treated as a type of *signs*). Pinborg notes that Aristotle had an impact on subsequent language scholarship that "cannot be overestimated. [Aristotle] created the frame within which the problems of language were to be discussed for the following centuries."[27] Harris and Taylor concur: "the Aristotelian view of language was incorporated lock, stock and barrel into the Western educational tradition which has shaped our own assumptions about linguistic 'common sense'."[28] As I will demonstrate in Chapters 3, 6, 7, and 8, many current accounts of the nature of language continue to be plagued by problems created by the underjustified inference that, just as written letters are representational, so are spoken sounds or words.

These lines from *On Interpretation* expressed a position that was different from Plato's in two ways. First, Platonic Ideas or Forms were not the ultimate sources of meaning. Rather, the "real world" as perceived by human senses anchored what language discussed. For Aristotle, the world was sense-able, and the connection between words and the world was indirect, mediated through the human mind or soul. The discourse expressed in sound and voice was symbolic of the passions of the soul, just as written discourse was symbolic of what is spoken. Second, although the mind stored "likenesses" of the things perceived, there was no mimetic relation between these likenesses and the words that symbolized them, as there sometimes was in Plato's account. The relationship between mental contents and words was purely conventional. "So," Harris and Taylor summarize, "the chain which connects words to the world is one which Aristotle divides into two sections. There is a section of natural, universal processes (linking the world via our sense perceptions to our mental representations of the world); and there is a section of conventional non-universal processes linking mental representations to language."[29]

As many scholars have noted, the Aristotelian corpus does not contain one work that systematically elaborates the view of the nature of language briefed in these lines of *On Interpretation*. Given that the only Greek word that can sometimes be translated as "language" (*logos*) is also translated "speech," "reason," "argument," "meaning," and "thought," this omission is not especially surprising. But there are important comments about Aristotle's view of language, not only in *On Interpretation* but also in his *Metaphysics*, his discussions of logic in the *Categories* and the *Prior* and *Posterior Analytics,* and his *Rhetoric* and *Poetics*. Without attempting to review all these comments, I want to highlight four ways Aristotle contributed to the historical development of the symbol model.

The first two have already been noted: Aristotle explicitly codified the model, and he introduced thought or thinking as a mediating process in the symbolic system. Spoken words symbolize mental experience and written words symbolize spoken words. A third contribution was to sharpen the analysis of the function of convention by foregrounding the importance of social or cultural agreement. This move altered the *orthotes onomaton* discussion. As a committed conventionalist and a thinker centrally concerned with change, Aristotle had to develop an explanation of what guaranteed the *stability* of a name. He wanted to explain what enabled the ordinary speaker to be confident that the name *Socrates* identified the same individual across time. The source of this stability, he argued, can be nothing other than convention, but this differs from Hermogenes' sense in *Cratylus* of one individual's arbitrary decision. Stability came from the decision being part of an ongoing social process with its own kinetic energy. This social process, however, was not simply a custom or habit, such as following a certain cycle of annual feast days. As Harris and Taylor summarize, "Naming-conventions, and their stability, are *necessary* if language is to be an expression of *logos* and human speech behaviour is to be that of a rational creature." And the differences among various languages do not raise questions about this stability, because "the important thing is not the sounds or letters the name is composed of, but the connection between the name and what it stands for."[30] This stability is both a reflection of and a requirement for human rationality itself. So this feature of language is a part of that which distinguishes the human as a rational animal.

The fourth way Aristotle developed the symbol model was to face directly—though not entirely satisfactorily—some of the problems created by the obvious existence of words that do not seem to symbolize any thing, such as adjectives, adverbs, conjunctions, prepositions, and articles. In *Poetics*, he called conjunctions and articles *nonsignificant sounds*, the former of which are "capable of combining two or more significant sounds into one" and the latter of which "mark the beginning, end, or dividing-point of a Speech."[31] He did not reconcile the obvious inconsistency between this claim and his global definition of words in *On Interpretation*. A second move was to develop what became his theory of consignification. As I note later, in the Middle Ages this theory evolved into a clear distinction between words that have referential meaning in their own right (*significantes* or categorematic terms) and words that are meaningful only when joined to words of the first kind (*consignificantes* or syncategorematic terms). Aristotle laid the groundwork for this theory in *Categories* when he distinguished between "simple" and "composite" signification. Simple words "signify substance, quantity, quality, relation, place, time, position, state, action, or affection."[32] Composite words signify only in combination with simple ones. This point was clarified in *On Interpretation* when he wrote of verbs, "A verb . . . is a sign of things said of something else. . . . And it is always a sign of what holds, that is, holds of a subject. . . . When uttered just by itself, a verb is a name and signifies something—the speaker arrests his thought and the hearer pauses—but it does not yet signify whether it is or not. For not even 'to be' or 'not to be' is a sign of the actual thing (nor if you say simply 'that which is'); for *by itself it is nothing, but it additionally signifies some combination, which cannot be thought of without the components*" (italics added).[33] Aristotle's theory of consignification was one central feature of his attempt to maintain a general, noun-based, semiotic account of the nature of language despite the obvious presence of many kinds of words that did not appear to symbolize or represent any identifiable thing. But as late-Medieval and early-Renaissance scholars discovered, this part of the Aristotelian approach was less than fully responsive to the inherent problems created by viewing language semiotically.

In short, Aristotle first articulated the basic formula of the symbol model, and although in some places he appeared to question aspects of it, most of his discussions of language were consistent with its basic assumptions. In *Sophistical Refutations* he even went so far as to claim that because "it is impossible in a discussion to bring in the actual things discussed: we use their names as symbols instead of them" (165a 6–8). Clearly Aristotle's analyses of language went well beyond the claim that there is a simple equivalence between units of discourse and things. His development of the symbol model was highly nuanced and, as I note later, one may argue that he actually introduced ideas that subsequent authors accused him of overlooking. But his most fundamental, and unfortunately most simplistically expressed account of the nature of language in the first sentences of *On Interpretation* served as the conceptual anchor for virtually all Western discussions of the nature of language from 400 B.C. through at least the eighteenth century.

The Stoics

One approach to language that contributed to the transmission—and to some degree the modification—of Aristotelian ideas was that attributed to the Stoics. In the third century B.C., an Athenian named Zeno was fond of posting himself near the *Stoa Poikile* or Painted Colonnade in the northwest corner of the agora so he and his followers could discuss philosophy. Because of their habitual gathering place, they came to be described as *men from the Stoa* or *Stoics*.[34] Zeno's primary concern was ethical. He wanted to establish principles to govern conduct and demonstrate that they were right. These principles depended on an understanding of the human as a rational animal in a physical universe. Zeno recognized the centrality of Aristotle's logic to an understanding of the human animal, but he was also aware that this logic presupposed the existence of the Greek language. He and his followers thus concluded that the study of language, the relationship between language and thought, and the relationship between language and reality were essential to understanding the system of thought Aristotelian logic revealed.[35] The fact that they conceived of the problematic as one concerning the *relationship* between language, on the one hand, and thought or reality, on the other, suggested that their account would likely maintain the semiotic focus established by Aristotle.

Almost nothing of Zeno's writing survives, nor anything by Cleanthes, Chrysippus, or his other early successors. Our knowledge of Stoic philosophy comes primarily from accounts by critics, especially Plutarch and Sextus Empiricus, and from comments by other proponents and opponents writing in Latin between about 100 and 300 A.D. Stoicism declined rapidly in the third century, but it continued to exert influence, especially among members of the Christian church determined to construct an intellectual structure for their faith.[36] One scholar claims that "it is generally agreed that the Stoic account of semantics is superior to and more sophisticated than the more influential one offered by Aristotle in the *De Interpretatione* (16a3–18)."[37]

One argument supporting this assessment is that Stoic discussions of the nature of language emphasized—some scholars would say introduced—a three-part distinction that subsequently pervaded language philosophy through at least the early twentieth century. It is the distinction among what is usually termed *signifier, signified*, and *object of reference*. Aristotle presaged this distinction by making mental contents mediators between words and things. But most commentators argue that the Stoic version of this insight was more explicit and more fully developed than Aristotle's. Sextus Empiricus summarized the Stoic distinction in these words:

> True and false have been variously located in what is signified (*to semainomenon*), in speech (*phone*), and in the motion of thought. The Stoics opted for the first of these, claiming that three things are linked together, what is signified, that which signifies (*to semainon*) and the object of reference (*to tynchanon*). That which signifies is speech ('Dion'), what is signified is the specific state of affairs (*auto to pragma*) indicated by the spoken word and which we grasp as co-existent with (*paryphistamenon*) our thought. . . ; the object of reference is the external existent, that is, Dion himself. Of these, two are bodies, speech and the object of reference. But the state of affairs signified is not a body but a *lekton*.[38]

The construct *lekton* is both one of the most problematic terms in Stoic philosophy and a key to understanding the Stoic version of the symbol model. The Stoics distinguished between merely uttering a noise and *legein*, which is to utter a noise in such a way as to represent a state of affairs in mind. By *lekton* they appeared to mean "what is said," where, as A. A. Long notes, "'what is said' covers 'statement' or 'state of affairs' signified by a word or set of words."[39] *Lekta* were apparently incorporeal existents that mediated between words and things. Some scholars claim that the presence of *lekta* makes the Stoic theory of meaning especially sensitive to a distinction Aristotle overlooked; namely, that between sense—what a word "says"—and reference—the mental picture it allegedly represents. This feature makes Stoic language theory similar to the late-nineteenth- and early-twentieth-century referential theories develped by Gottlob Frege, Rudolf Carnap, and others. In Frege's analysis the terms for the Stoic signifier, signified, and object of reference are *sign—sense—reference* and in Carnap's *designator—intention—extension*.[40] These elements are also highlighted in the widely cited popularization of Frege and Carnap, *The Meaning of Meaning* , authored in 1923 by C. K. Ogden and I. A. Richards. The triangular model that is the centerpiece of this book identified the three primary units of language as "symbol," (signifier), "act of reference" (signified), and "referent" (object).[41]

In Stoic language theory, each linguistic sign was indicative of a meaning that was said to subsist with a human thought. Zeno and other Stoics were concerned about the connection between words and reality, because this connection, they argued, makes words meaningful. Their understanding of "reality" was essentially materialist: "[T]o exist is, according to Stoic ontology, to be capable of prompting a rational presentation, one that can be articulated in speech. And to be capable of prompting such a rational presentation is to be a three-dimensional solid."[42] But these material existents are not meanings. In this sense, Stoic theory of meaning was intensional rather than referential. They viewed meanings as linguistic contents—*lekta*—isomorphically related to the respective signs on the level of expression. This is why Graeser argues that "it seems best to take the term *lekton* to mean 'what is said' or 'what is meant' rather than 'that which can be expressed'."[43] At the same time, he maintains, *lekta* in general "must not be identified with concepts qua psychical entities either"; they are "immaterial, [but] somehow objective and something others can grasp."[44]

As the discussions by Long and Graeser underscore, the Stoic construct *lekta* was both central to their theory of meaning and frustratingly elusive. For the purposes of this review, the Stoic discussions demonstrate how difficult it was for the first scholars attempting to give an explicit account of the nature of language to deal with the problem of the relationship between "words" and "the world" when this relationship was presumed to be fundamentally *representational*. Like others writing at the time, Stoic authors recognized that it was clearly unsatisfactory to continue to claim that words somehow represented things as proper names represent their bearers. It appeared more promising to think of the representational relationship as existing between words and some mental entities, but this move also created almost as many problems as it solved. Stoic writers apparently introduced the term *lekta* to cope with some of these problems by labeling the immaterial, nonconceptual, yet somehow objectively graspable entities that they had to create to have something for words to *represent*. But it was difficult for both Stoic writers and their critics—and it continues to be difficult for interpreters of Stoicism—to explain precisely what *lekta* were. The problem, I argue, lies primarily in the way the issue was defined, then and frequently now. Only when one begins with the assumption that language is a semiotic, representational system is one forced to discover or create some class of entities for units of language to stand for or represent. Hence, as Wittgenstein might say, this problematic needs to be dissolved rather than solved. The fly can be shown the way out of the fly-bottle when language is no longer viewed as representative of or a surrogate for aspects of "reality" or "the world."

The Bible and St. Augustine

But dissolving this problem is no easy task; one feature of the history of language scholarship that Wittgenstein certainly noticed is the obstinacy of the difficulties experienced by these earliest writers. Although they developed many new insights about the natural and the human world, the texts they relied on continued to treat language as a semiotic system. Among the most influential of these texts was the Christian Bible, and among the most influential Christian writers, especially between the third and the twelfth century, was St. Augustine.

The second chapter of Genesis contains the biblical account of God bringing to Adam "every beast of the field and every bird of the air" so Adam could *name* them.[45] This narrative was highly significant for several reasons. First, it made the creation of language second in primacy only to the creation of human life itself. In addition, this account foregrounded the decisive role of humanity in the development of language; here the human being took on the role Plato attributed to "the giver of names." Third, and of equal significance for our purposes, is the fact that this discussion of language turned its hearers' and readers' attention back to the concern with *orthotes onomaton*, the correctness of names. The fact that the beasts and birds were first created and then named underscored again that things (or beings) and names are of different orders of reality. Clearly the former can exist without names, but not vice versa. Moreover, names do not alter reality, because reality is already complete without them.[46] In this way the biblical account maintained the crucial two worlds assumption. Because the world of names is ontologically distinct from the world of things, correctness of names is to be desired, but "incorrect" names do not substantively affect the realities they name. This general doctrine, which is based on the two worlds assumption and focused on the process of naming, is what Harris and Taylor call *nomenclaturism* or, "in its more general form, *surrogationalism*" because it is "based on the assumption that the words we use are vocal surrogates (that is to say, substitutes) for meanings: the meaning is what the word 'stands for'."[47] In short, the account of the nature of language most prominent in the Bible is that language is fundamentally a system of *names*.

Genesis 2 described how Adam managed to name correctly by applying a version of the natural or mimetic view Plato reviewed in *Cratylus* as Adam called his helpmate *wo-man*, "because she was taken out of man." Later Adam named this woman, the mother of all living persons, *Eve* at least in part because the word resembles the Hebrew word for living (Genesis 2:22, 3:20).

The Bible mentions additional features of language beyond its naming character, but less prominently. For example, the narrative in Genesis 11 about the Tower of Babel notes both the power of communication and the power of naming. "The whole earth had one language and few words," the chapter begins. Its unified population found a plain in the land of Shinar and built a great city, complete with "a tower with its top in the heavens." This was the way these humans had of making "a name for [them]selves." God noticed both the tower and the power reflected in this linguistically unified act of of self-aggrandizement and decided that the independence breathed into humanity earlier in Genesis was not working out altogether satisfactorily. God's solution was not simply to destroy the tower or to rain down a plague of pestilence or disease but to "confuse their language, that they may not understand one another's speech." The human movement toward omnipotence ceased as humanity was scattered "over the face of all the earth," and to commemorate this event, the place was named *Babel* (compare the

Hebrew word *balal*, "confuse") "because there the Lord confused the language of all the earth."

Two significantly different observations about language are reflected in this narrative. As I mentioned, the first part of the story highlights the enormous power created by effective *communication*. The people were able to build the city and the tower *because* they "had one language and few words." Their unity enabled them to accomplish so much that God, so the story goes, was actually worried that "nothing that they propose to do will now be impossible for them" (Genesis 11:6). So God cut them down to size by simply confusing their language. In this way, the story positively and negatively illustrates the virtually limitless potential of effective communication and mutual understanding. But it also offers an account of why humanity speaks many different languages, and as it does so, the story echoes the earlier and later biblical reduction of language to *names* and *naming*. In this narrative humanity's power was clearly anchored in its general ability to communicate, not just to name, but one major point emphasized by the storyteller is that the place was named *Babel* because "there the Lord confused the language of all the earth," and the Hebrew term *balal* can be translated "confuse." So the point about the potency of effective communication shares center stage in the story with a comment on the correctness of a name. The historical tendency to reduce a comment on language as communication to an account of language as names is thereby reinforced.

Although differences among the languages spoken by various peoples are frequently acknowledged in the Old Testament, many subsequent references to language continue to foreground the definitive nature of names and naming.[48] In Genesis 16:11 an angel tells Hagar that she shall name her son Ishmael, meaning "God hears," "because the Lord has given heed to your affliction." God changes Abram's name to Abraham in Genesis 17:3–5 because he is to be father of a multitude. Isaac names one well Esek to commemorate the "contention" that occurred over it, another Stinah for "enmity," and a third Rehoboth, "broad places or room," to commemorate other related events (Genesis 26:19–23). When Moses speaks to God in Exodus, his central question is what to tell his people God's name is. "YHWH," God replies, which is connected with the Hebrew word for "to be." "Say this to the people of Israel, 'I AM has sent me to you'" (Exodus 3:14). By naming God with a *rhema* or predicate rather than an *onoma* or noun, Biblical narrators underscored not only the divinity of this being but also the differences between this God and all others with conventional *onoma* names.

New Testament accounts of language are predictably more sophisticated than those of the Old Testament. Volumes will continue to be spoken and written about, for example, the significance of translating *logos* as "Word" in John 1:1 and the disciples' speaking in tongues on the day of Pentecost (Acts 2:1–42). But the significance of names and naming persists. Luke reported Jesus assuring the seventy he had appointed, "rejoice that your names are written in heaven" (Luke 10:20). Gallio, proconsul of Achaia refused to adjudicate the dispute over the local Jews' condemnation of Paul, because it was "a matter of questions about words and names and your own law" (Acts 18:12–17). In his letter to the Ephesians, Paul reminded his readers that "every family in heaven and on earth is named" from God the Father (Ephesians 3: 15). And to the Hebrews Paul wrote, "When [Jesus] had made purification for sins, he sat down at the right hand of the Majesty on high, having become as much superior to angels as the name he has obtained is more excellent than theirs" (Hebrews 1:3–4).

Given this picture of language as fundamentally a system of names, it is not surprising to see surrogationalism prominently manifested in many biblical scholars' discussions of language. The most influential ancient codification of this view was developed in the fourth and fifth centuries by the prolific North African professor, pastor, presbyter, and bishop, Aurelius Augustinus. In his *Confessions*, Augustine narrated how the significance of words first dawned upon him as a child.

> My elders would make some particular sound, and as they made it would point at or move toward some particular thing. From this I came to realize that the thing was called by the sound they made when they wished to draw my attention to it. That they intended this was clear from the motions of their bodies, by a kind of natural language common to all races which consists in facial expressions, glances of the eye, gestures, and the tones by which the voice expresses the mind's state. Thus, as I heard words repeatedly used in their proper places in various sentences, I gradually learned to understand what objects they signified; and after I had trained my mouth to form these signs, I used them to express my desires.[49]

It is amusing to read such a confident adult account of what had to have been a much less solitary and much more complicated process than Augustine understood. It is also enlightening to contrast the writer's obvious awareness of the nonverbal complexities of these communicative events—"facial expressions, glances of the eye, gestures, and [vocal] tones"—with the simplistic view of language he deduced from these experiences—words signify objects ostensively. The view Augustine developed in subsequent writings was only slightly more sophisticated. For example, in *De Dialectica* he wrote, "A word is a sign of any kind of thing, which can be understood by a hearer, and is uttered by a speaker. A thing is whatever is sensed or understood or is hidden. A sign is what shows both itself to the senses and something beyond itself to the mind. To speak is to give a sign by an articulate utterance. By articulate I mean one that can be comprised of letters."[50]

Book II of *De Doctrina Christiana* begins with a definition of a sign as "a thing which causes us to think of something beyond the impression the thing itself makes upon the senses," and an explanation of the distinction between natural and conventional signs.[51] Conventional signs are designed exclusively to communicate: "Nor is there any other reason for signifying, or for giving signs, except for bringing forth and transferring to another mind the action of the mind in the person who makes the sign" (p. 35). Nonverbal gestures are signs, Augustine noted, but many more signs "pertain to the ears" rather than the eyes, "and most of these consist of words" (p. 35). "For words have come to be predominant among [humans] for signifying whatever the mind conceives if they wish to communicate it to anyone" (p. 36). Moreover, echoing Aristotle, "signs of words have been constructed by means of letters" (p. 35); written words are thus signs of spoken ones.

Augustine's rhetorical theory elaborated on this view of the nature of language. For example, he distinguished between literal and figurative signs by explaining that the former designate "those things on account of which they were instituted," for example the ox of *bos*, whereas the latter "occur when that thing which we designate by a literal sign is used to signify something else; thus we say 'ox' and by that syllable understand the animal which is ordinarily designated by that word, but again by that animal we understand an evangelist, as is signified in the Scripture, according to the interpretation of the Apostle, when it says, 'Thou shalt not muzzle the ox that treadeth out the corn' (p. 43). If a reader is confused by figurative signs, he or she "should study them partly with reference to a knowledge of languages and partly with reference to a knowledge of things" (p. 50). And the devout student must pay heed to the referents of significant signs: "[The person] is a slave to a sign who uses or worships a significant thing without knowing what it signifies. But [the person] who uses or venerates a useful sign

divinely instituted whose signifying force he [or she] understands
does not venerate what [is seen] and what passes away but rather
that to which all such things are to be referred" (pp. 86–87).

A recent summary of Augustine's account of the nature of language identifies in *De Doctrina Christiana, De Magistro,* and *De
Dialectica* sixteen theses or themes. For the purposes of this review,
the most significant are the following: Augustine believed that

1. Speaking is giving signs;

2. words are signs given in speech;

3. a sign is a thing employed for signifying something;

4. words are things whose sole employment is for signifying.

5. Every word is a sign;

6. every sign signifies something. . . .

8. Words convey thoughts, but it is unclear whether Augustine means that words signify the thoughts they convey or
   the things which are the subject matter of those thoughts
   (or both).[52]

Christopher Kirwan, the author of this account, notes that Augustine turned to the Stoic doctrine of *lekta* at one point in his writing to elaborate some features of his semiotic perspective. In *De
Dialectica* Augustine claimed that whatever is perceived from a word
by the mind is called a sayable (*dicible*, a neologism that Latinized
lekta). He also claimed that four elements "must be kept distinct:
word, sayable, saying, thing."[53] Augustine's development of this notion included the claims that a "sayable" (*lekta*) is perceived from a
word by the mind not the ears and kept shut up in the mind; it is a
conception of a word in the mind; it is not a word but what is understood in a word; it is what occurs in the mind by means of a word;
and it is a word perceived in advance of any vocal sound. Says
Kirwan, "It is hard to fit all these into a coherent account."[54] Here
the difficulty with the *lekta* construct surfaces again. The problem,
as Kirwan suggests, is that Augustine was trying to work with a
fundamentally problematic Stoic attempt to describe the incorporeal
entities that it was necessary to invent in order to have a
representamen for many of the linguistic units in their semiotic account of language.

Kirwan also highlights some distinctions between Augustine's
views and the views of those who preceded him. For example, he

notes that roughly a thousand years of philosophy before Augustine had produced much theorizing about the difference between "indicative" and "representative" signs. The former were said to cause something beyond themselves to come into thought or show something beyond themselves to the mind. The latter referred to certain structures and "the structures contained within the represented thing are matched by structures within its representation."[55] Kirwan argues that the representation theory is in some cases "not only plausible but true," but that such a theory is "not Augustine's . . . for him 'Sign' means 'indication'." Kirwan also attempts to clarify "what kinds of thing words signify," including "external objects," and "thoughts and wills." And he reviews Augustine's attempt to cope with the problem of identifying the signified of the obviously problematic term *nihil*.[56]

The primary point I want to make about Kirwan's analysis is that it operates consistently within the two worlds, atomism, and representational assumptions, and Kirwan does not always evidence a clear sense of the significance of this fact. Although he takes pains to distinguish *indicating* from *representing*, both the doctrine that words signify mental contents ("indicate") and the doctrine that they signify material structures ("represent") assume an ontological difference between sign and signified. This becomes apparent as one notes how the list of things that words allegedly signify is always a list of nonlinguistic entities—"external objects," the person Romulus, the city Rome, "thoughts," "wills," and so forth.[57] And, as Kirwan notes, Augustine breaks his sword on *nihil*, because he is unable to describe the (nonlinguistic) ontological status of the entity "nothing." Kirwan clearly acknowledges the insurmountable problems created by Augustine's account of the nature of language; the account, he writes, is "neither original nor profound nor correct."[58] But he also affirms the partial truth of the view that words "represent," and his argument about the distinction between "indicating" and "representing" fails to note the crucial similarity between these two positions. In the end, both Kirwan's praise for Augustine's view of language and his criticism operate from within a semiotic view of the nature of language.[59]

Medieval Speculative Grammarians

After Justinian closed the philosophical schools of Athens in 529, learning was under clerical patronage. Under the organizational scheme of the trivium and quadrivium, education focused first on language-related disciplines: grammar, logic, and rhetoric. But most writings were pedagogical or practical, and between 400 and 1100 most writing was based on Roman sources. As a result, virtually no significant contributions were made to Western thinkers' understanding of the nature of language between the sixth and the twelfth centuries.[60] At that point, with the rise of scholasticism, new developments began to occur. Language again became the focus of philosophical speculation, virtually all of which operated from firmly within the symbol model inherited from Aristotle, the Stoics, Augustine, and Aquinas.

Evidence of this dependence is reflected in a theoretical distinction that surfaced in several scholastic works, that between the *significatio* and the *suppositio* of a word. This distinction paralleled aspects of the Stoic division between *to semainomenon* and *to tynchanon*. Scholastic authors defined the *significatio* as the relation between the sign or word and what it signified, whereas the *suppositio* was the thing, person, event, and so on that the word may substitute for. Thus, according to Robins, "because *homo*, man, means [signifies] 'man', *homo* or *man* may stand for (*supponere*) Socrates, Guy Fawkes, or Harold Wilson. . . . This basic distinction comes up repeatedly, in somewhat different forms and with different interpetations, in such binary oppositions as meaning and reference, connotation and denotation, and intension and extension."[61] Clearly these discussions of *significatio* and *suppositio* elaborated but did not fundamentally alter Aristotelian and Stoic accounts of the nature of language. The symbol model persisted.

Several historians claim that the most interesting medieval discussions of language were found in the works of speculative grammarians or Modistae, a group of writers who described the "modes of signifying" (*modis significandi*) identifiable in language. These writers integrated the grammatical description of Latin as formulated by Priscian and Donatus with scholastic philosophy, which Aquinas had codified in his synthesis of Aristotelian ideas and Catholic theology. The Modistae were motivated by the conviction that simple descriptions of Latin, no matter how thorough, were superficial, because they did not investigate the causal bases of the various parts of speech.

Peter Helias, Roger Bacon, Martin of Dacia, and other authors developed modistic theory in the twelfth and thirteenth centuries, and then Thomas of Erfurt's work, *Grammatica Speculativa*, written about 1300, became the standard handbook of the modistic approach to language. This work reflected the conviction that the modes of signifying are not parts of the meaning of a word but parameters that specify how a word carries a meaning. For example, Thomas and other Modistae argued that the verb *currere*, "run," and the noun *cursus*, "a run," signify the same thing—running—but signify it in different ways. Therefore, they argued, the two words have different modes (ways) of signifying.

Grammatica Speculativa includes exhaustively detailed analyses of active and passive modes of understanding and signifying and of the nature and function of most the the common parts of speech. Thomas's commitment to two worlds is apparent, for example, when he defines the active mode of signifying as "the mode or property of the expression vouchsafed by the intellect to itself by means of which the expression signifies the property of the thing."[62] He defines the *noun* as "a part of speech signifying by means of the mode of an entity or determinate understanding" (p. 155) and then struggles mightily from within the symbol model to define non-substantive parts of speech in conceptually consistent ways. He defines a participle as "the part of speech signifying by means of the mode of being and nonseparation from the substance, or of union with the substance which is the same thing" (p. 241); an *adverb* as "a part of speech signifying by means of the mode of adjacency, which signifies its own essence by means of the mode of being and determines it in absolute terms" (p. 247); and a *preposition* as "the part of speech signifying by means of the mode of adjacency to some case form, linking it and referring it back to the act" (p. 265). The reader can judge for himself or herself whether Thomas's definitions are coherent and capable of being operationalized.

Michael Covington's description of Thomas's project underscores its commitment to the primary features of the symbol model: "The concept of modus signi*ficandi*," Covington notes, "was developed to explain the role of grammatical categories, such as part or speech, case, and tense, in the sign-meaning relationship *that links words to real-world objects*" (italics added).[63] Harris and Taylor concur with Covington when they note that the Modistae carried out "an essentially surrogationalist enterprise" that was designed to explain in detail how "language systematically reflects reality."[64]

Covington's graphic summary of Thomas of Erfurt's analysis of language illustrates the primary features of this surrogationalist account. This is illustrated in Figure 2.1. As this figure indicates, Thomas of Erfurt believed that a real-world object gives rise to a concept in the mind that is represented by a meaning in language. Simultaneously, various properties of the real-world object (*modi essendi*) are "coconceptualized" along with the object itself, which is to say that they are acted upon by the mind's

In the real world		MODI ESSENDI, properties of the object in the real world	RES the object in the real world
In the mind	MODI INTELLIGENDI ACTIVI, the ways the intellect can 'co-understand'	MODI INTELLIGENDI PASSIVI, properties of the object 'co-understood' by the intellect	CONCEPTUS the object as represented in the mind
In the language	MODI SIGNIFICANDI ACTIVI, the ways the word can consignify	MODI SIGNIFICANDI PASSIVI, properties of the object consignified by the word	SIGNIFICATUM the object as signified by the word

Figure 2.1 Ontology and the modes of signifying (Thomas of Erfurt)[65]

"modes of understanding" (*modi intelligendi activi*) to give rise to "modes of being understood" (*modi intelligendi passivi*). These in turn lead, through "modes of signifying" (*modi significandi activi*) on the part of the word as a linguistic element, to "modes of being signified (*modi significandi passivi*) in the word as actually uttered.[66] As the presence of the term *consignify* indicates, Thomas's account integrated the medieval thinkers' acceptance of Aristotle's distinction between *significantes* and *consignificantes* (cf. *categorematic* and *syncategorematic* terms). So, for example, use of the term *homo* to talk about "man" signifies a human being and, according to modistic terminology, the general features of humans are "consignified"; that is, signified along with the specific, lexical meaning.[67]

It is easy to be impressed by the complexity of Modistic analyses and at the same time dismayed by the difficulty of applying them to virtually any actual instance of language. Versions of this point, in fact, anchored the most damaging criticisms of the Modistae. The movement died because of the stark inadequacies of its account of the connection between language and "reality." For example, in 1333 Johannes Aurifaber argued that (1) "modes of signifying are not needed to explain why sentences are grammatical"; (2) "there is no empirical evidence for modes of signifying; they have no visible effect on the words in which they are supposed to inhere," and (3) "it is not possible to conceptualize one object under a variety of *modi intelligendi* as modistic theory requires."[68] William of Ockham argued similarly, and as a result of these attacks and others, the modistic movement had withered by the middle of the fourteenth century. Given the way this chapter of linguistic history died, one might hope that language theorists would have been ready to connect their analyses more closely to language as people live it rather than relying virtually exclusively on armchair examples of Latin references to Greek personages.

The Port-Royalists and Locke

Certainly Renaissance thinking moved in precisely this direction. Moreover, increasing interest in Hebrew, Arabic, vernacular languages, and those employed by natives discovered in the New World dramatically increased the complexity of language scholarship. But for the first several hundred years of the modern era, the most influential Western accounts of the nature of language continued to be dominated by what was basically a rationally rather than empirically based Aristotelian version of the symbol model.

One of these influential accounts was developed by Antoine Arnauld and Claude Lancelot, two monks at the Port-Royal Abbey in France. Arnauld and Lancelot were clearly pedagogical innovators. Their textbooks were written in French rather than Latin, so that their students could develop new knowledge on the basis of knowledge already possessed. Their *General and Rational Grammar* was also innovative in that it began from the claim that the primary function of language is communication. But this idea unfolded in what can now be seen as a predictable way, as the authors claimed that communication occurs only insofar as words mirror the structure of the thoughts being expressed. "This," they wrote, "is why the different sorts of signification which are embodied in words cannot be clearly understood if what has gone on in our minds previously has not been clearly understood, since words were invented only in order to make these thoughts known."[69]

The Port-Royal *Grammar* elaborated its authors' version of the symbol model in these words:

> It remains for us to examine the spiritual element of speech which constitutes one of the greatest advantages which [the hu]man has over all the other animals, and which is one of the greatest proofs of [the hu]man's reason. This is the use which we make of it for signifying our thoughts, and this marvelous invention of composing from twenty-five or thirty sounds an infinite variety of words, which although not having any resemblance in themselves to that which passes through our minds, nevertheless do not fail to reveal to others all of the secrets of the mind, and to make intelligible to others who cannot penetrate into the mind all that we conceive and all of the diverse movements of our souls.
>
> Thus words can be defined as distinct and articulate sounds which [humans] have made into signs for signifying their thoughts.[70]

The authors' point that words do not have "any resemblance in themselves" to thoughts clarifies their commitment to the two worlds assumption. The Port-Royal position on the representational nature of the link between words and thoughts had been clarified two years earlier in *The Art of Thinking,* which argued, "When one considers an object in itself and according to its own being, then he thinks of that object simply as a thing; but when he considers an object as representing some other object, then the first object is being thought of as a sign."[71]

One reason why the Port-Royalists' writings were so respected and influential was that they included an account of the nature of language grounded in a theory of the operations and contents of the mind. With the help of Pascal, Descartes, and Augustine, *The Art of Thinking* explained that a thought or proposition consists of two ideas joined by the mental operation of affirmation and judged to be similar or dissimilar. The subject noun stands for the first of these ideas, the predicate for the second, and the copula stands for the operation of affirmation. Thus the grammatical categories "subject" and "predicate" were shown to be categories of cognition. This account of the general properties of human thought emphasized, as Harris and Taylor note, that cognition was "independent of both language and experience." Moreover, this view that thought and language were ontologically distinct and that the former determined the structure of the latter was "one of the guiding principles of European linguistic thought for many decades following the publication of the *Grammar*."[72]

According to *The Art of Thinking*, upon hearing the articulate sounds that make up a word, one forms an idea of the sounds that evokes another idea, which is that of a particular thing. This second idea is the meaning of the word. For example, "The rainbow is taken as God's sign that he will never again destroy the human race by flood. Whether or not the rainbow is a real thing, the rainbow remains a sign of God's promise so long as the idea of a rainbow excites in us the idea of God's promise."[73] Thus there are four terms involved in this analysis: two material (the sounds and the thing) and two spiritual (the idea of the sounds and the idea of the thing, the former of which evokes the latter).[74]

The Port-Royalists' commitment to the symbol model eventuated in some some rather unusual claims about the nature of language. One was that there was actually only one verb, the third person singular present indicative of the verb *to be*; that is, *is*. Other words ordinarily classified as verbs, they argued, are in fact combinations of *is* and some other part of speech having the function of a noun. So, for example, when one says *Sum homo*, "*sum* not only signifies the affirmation, but also includes the signification of the proposition *ego*, which is the subject of this proposition. The diversity of these significations joined in the same word is that which prevented many otherwise very astute people from properly understanding the nature of the verb, because they did not consider it according to what is essential to it, namely affirmation, but rather according to . . . relationships which are accidental to it *qua* verb.[75] This doctrine, among others in the Port-Royalist corpus, may be understood generally as one unfortunate consequence of their commitment to the symbol model, and more specifically as a reflection of their determination to treat the structure of language, conceived as a Cartesian *res extensa*, as in some way isomorphic with the structure of certain *res cogitans*.

One final feature of the Port-Royal works that is germane to this review is their commitment to producing a general, rationally anchored analysis that was not weakened or cluttered by being applied to non-Indo-European tongues or atypical linguistic constructions. The *Grammar* does not attempt to give an account of any language based only on convention; it focuses only on those determined by what Arnauld and Lancelot took to be the rational structure of thought. The authors of the *Grammar* argued that "It is a maxim that those who work on a living language must always keep sight of the fact that those modes of speech which are authorized by a general and uncontested usage ought to pass as legitimate, even if they are contrary to the rules and internal analogy of language. On the other hand, one ought not to adduce them in order to cast doubt upon the rules and disturb the analogy of languages.... Otherwise, he who will linger only on these aberrations of usage, without observing the foregoing maxim, will cause a language to remain forever uncertain, and lacking any principles, it will never be able to be determined."[76] This passage may be read as one of the first explicit commitments in the modern age to treating language "scientifically," where science is viewed as the activity of abstracting and generalizing from experience to establish immutable rational principles. Later, such influential writers as Saussure strongly affirmed this orientation.

The movement toward a scientific treatment of language was enhanced by John Locke's efforts to integrate, among other influences, Descartes's epistemological focus, Bacon's analysis of the four idols and his account of the place of semiotics in the sciences, and Hobbes's empiricism into what has been called "the first modern treatise devoted specifically to philosophy of language."[77] Locke's view of language was not novel; in fact, it owed at least as much to Aristotle and the Stoics as it did to Descartes, Bacon, and Hobbes. But for over a century and a half after its first publication in 1690, Locke's *Essay Concerning Human Understanding* exerted almost as much influence over language scholars as Aristotle's comments in *On Interpretation* had exerted centuries earlier. Part of the reason was that Locke dedicated portions of all four books of the *Essay* to explicit and detailed comments on the nature of language. In addition, this work was the first to establish the new epistemological orientation of semantics, which was subsequently worked out in numerous Enlightenment treatments of logic. For these and other reasons, Hans Aarsleff claims, "the history of the *Essay* was in large measure the history of modern thought, of the eighteenth century."[78]

Locke's central thesis was that words signify ideas. As he saw it, the reason humans need such signs is obvious. First, humans require ideas to cope with the concrete and abstract furniture of the world: "since the things the mind contemplates are none of them, beside itself, present to the understanding, it is necessary that something else, as a sign or representation of the thing it considers, should be present to it: and these are ideas."[79] But ideas are of limited value to both individuals and groups of humans until they are recorded or communicated. And these actions require another set of signs to represent ideas, just as ideas represent things. As Locke expressed this notion, "The use [humans] have of . . . [words] being either to record their own thoughts,for the assistance of their own memory; or, as it were, to bring out their ideas, and lay them before the view of others: words, in their primary or immediate signification, stand for nothing but *the ideas in the mind of him that uses them . . .*" (III.2.2).

At many points of the *Essay* Locke expressed this claim as a general one, applicable to all kinds of words. In other places he excepted propositional connectives, the copula, the word *not*, and syncategorematics, as if they did something other than "signify ideas." Even as he excepted these categories of words, however, he treated them semiotically. Syncategorematics (for Locke, adverbs, prepositions, and conjunctions), for example, were not "names of ideas in the mind," but were "made use of to signify [NB] the *connexion* that the mind gives to ideas, or to propositions, one with another" (III.7.1). As an example, Locke listed five "relations the mind gives" to the propositions joined by *but*. One was "a stop of the mind in the course it was going, before it came quite to the end of it." Another was "a supposition in the mind of something otherwise than it should be" (III.7.5). Locke seemed clearly to conceive of these significates as kinds of mental entities—perhaps with something like the ontological status of the Stoics' *lekta*—locatable "in the mind." And just as things and qualities were the entities that nouns and adjectives "stand for," these phenomena or entities called *relations* or *connexions* were signified by syncategorematics. So in the *Essay* as a whole, Locke treated language as a system of various categories of words that, in different ways, signify or stand for various phenomena.

His commitment to this semiotic perspective, when combined with his rejection of the notion of negative ideas, led Locke to devise a curious solution to the problem of identifying what negative terms signify. Terms such as *insipid, silence,* and *nihil,* he wrote, "stand not directly for positive ideas, but for their absence. [These words] denote positive ideas, v. g. *taste, sound, being,* with a signification of their absence" (II.8.5). And later, "All [these] negative or privative words . . . signify no ideas . . . but they . . . signify their absence" (III.1.4). Locke's example in Book II is the shadow of a man, which he discusses as an entity made up of "the absence of light." It is difficult to determine how one might extend this example to identify in practice something substantive that could qualify as the "absence" of being, sound, or taste. In fact, one may legitimately wonder whether Locke's claim that the signification (or perhaps the referent) of the word *silence* is "the absence of sound" substantively improves Heraclitus' or Parmenides' attempts to deal with this same problem. Like the earlier writers, Locke encountered these difficulties primarily because of his commitment to the symbol model.

Much of Locke's *Essay* was dedicated to outlining the various ways that language fails to conform to what he saw as its true nature. Words, he wrote, are *arbitrary* signs of the ideas they stand for; the act of uttering a word as the vocal sign of a given idea is a *voluntary*—and hence infinitely variable—act; and this act is performed by a unique *individual.* Thus, although the primary purpose of language is to be a vehicle of thought, that is, to transmit ideas from one mind to another, the system is inherently flawed. As Locke explained, "every [hu]man has so inviolable a liberty, to make words stand for what ideas he [or she] pleases, that one has the power to make others have the same ideas in their minds, that [one] has, when [one] use[s] the same words that he[or she] does" (III.2.8). His primary solution to this problem was to apply his approach to definition. One should begin, he argued, by recognizing that, although many efforts at communicating involve complex ideas, each complex idea is analyzable into simple ideas and there is little danger that the names for simple ideas will be understood differently by different individuals. So the speaker's task is to analyze each complex idea into its simple units and use these to ensure clear communication. As his critics noted, Locke did not show how to guarantee that each analysis of a given "complex idea" will break it down into exactly the same "simples." Nor did he tell whether or how one may be certain that someone else signifies the same idea one has in mind by a given word or name.

As was the case with his intellectual forebears, Locke was not unaware of some of these problems. But, again like them, his fundamental commitment to a semiotic view of the nature of language effectively undermined his ability to respond to such criticisms. Instead he was led to argue in the first chapter of Book III of the *Essay* that a renewed commitment to etymology could solve the communication problems created by ambiguous signifying and symbolizing. Locke argued,

> It may also lead us a little towards the original of all our notions and knowledge, if we remark how great a dependence our words have on common sensible ideas; and how those which are made use of to stand for actions and notions quite removed from sense, have their rise from thence, and from obvious sensible ideas are transferred to more abstruse significations, and made to stand for ideas that come not under the cognizance of our senses; v.g. to *imagine, apprehend, comprehend, adhere, conceive, instil, disgust, disturbance, tranquillity*, &c., are all words taken from the operations of sensible things, and applied to certain modes of thinking. *Spirit*, in its primary signification, is breath; *angel*, a messenger: *and I doubt not but, if we could trace them to their sources, we should find, in all languages, the names which stand for things that fall not under our senses to have had their rise from sensible ideas* [italics added]. By which we may give some kind of guess what kind of notions they were, and whence derived, which filled their minds who were the first beginners of languages, and how nature, even in naming of things, unawares suggested to [humans] the originals and princples of all their knowledge . . . (III.1.5).

In this part of Locke's account, Plato's "giver of names" or the Bible's "Adam" has become "nature" or "the first beginners of languages." A version of either Platonic mimesis or Aristotelian similarity between perception and meaning has been imported to account for the connection between "name" and "sensible ideas." The promise that drove both the dispute over *orthotes onomaton* and the advice in *On Interpretation*—that humans can actually achieve the ideal of telementational communication—has maintained its allure. And Locke "doubted not" that language problems could be solved by clarifying precisely which parts of the *world* were historically first *represented* by which *words*.

Some recent attempts to rehabilitate aspects of Locke's account of the nature of language reveal how insidiously the symbol model can pervade theorizing about these matters. Norman Kretzmann, for example, argues that Locke's semantic theory is much more subtle than many of his critics have recognized. For one thing, Kretzmann claims, passages in the *Essay* give reason to believe that Locke did not require a discrete idea to serve as the signification of every meaningful word. Locke distinguished, Kretzmann argues, "between a name's signification and what the name was used to refer to,"[80] so that some words represent ideas and others represent *objects*. John Jenkins quotes Kretzmann with approval, arguing that the latter has demonstrated that Locke "was obviously aware of the important connection between words and things and of the role of the objective world as providing a public checking procedure for our correct use of language." This shows, writes Jenkins, that "Locke's was not the simple-minded theory of language which many of his commentators have assumed."[81] But neither Kretzmann nor Jenkins appears to recognize that both the "naive" and the "sophisticated" construals of Locke's theory assume the distinction between two worlds. As is by now apparent, whether one argues that words represent ideas or that words represent objects, one is assuming an ontological difference between the linguistic and the nonlinguistic worlds and a representational relationship between them. In this way, the claim that words represent objects is problematic in exactly the same ways as is the claim that words represent ideas.[82]

Two Eighteenth Century Developments

Locke's *Essay* prompted a great deal of interest in language among eighteenth century European intellectuals. Between about 1740 and 1775, one prominent group of these writers invested considerable energy in speculations about the origins of language. Etienne Bonnot, Abbé de Condillac, and Jean-Jacques Rosseau were two primary contributors to the effort that culminated in 1771 when Johann Gottfried Herder won the Prussian Academy's prize with his *Abhandlung über den Ursprung der Sprache*. Then late in the century John Horne Tooke combined twin commitments to political nationalism and scientific empiricism with Locke's beliefs about the value of etymological analysis into an account of the nature of language that, while ultimately unproductive, was nonetheless influential.

Condillac devoted the second part of his *Essai sur l'origine des connoissances humaines* to a discussion of language. Although he praised Locke, he argued that, to grasp the fundamental principles of both language and mind, one must inquire into their origins in the state of nature. His primary claim about the natural distinction between humans and other animals was expressed early in the *Essai*. The key, as for so many writers before Condillac, was the connection (*liaison*) between words and what they signify. *Brutes* can represent an object in their brains only becase the image of it in their brain is closely connected with the object present. "But as soon as a [hu]man comes to connect ideas with signs of his [or her] own choosing, we find ... memory is formed. When this is done, he [or she] begins of him [her]self to dispose of his [or her] imagination, and to give it a new habit. For by means of the signs which [one] is able to recall at pleasure, [one] revives, or at least is often capable of reviving the ideas which are connected with them."[83]

Language began naturally, with the expression of emotions in gestures. Then humans substituted articulate sounds for gestures: "Indeed, how would a word become the sign of an idea, if this idea could not be shown in the language of gesture?"[84] So the first language consisted of concrete nouns for simple objects, and then the system became increasingly abstract. But association or connection remained focal; humans associated ideas involuntarily and voluntarily, and "language is the most palpable example of the connections we form voluntarily."[85] Thus Condillac's account is another that rests on the claims that language is a system of individual words, that there is a difference between words and what they are "about," that words signify, represent, or stand for that which they are "about," and that humans use words to accomplish their goals. Moreover, the primary goal of the human use of language was communication, which both Locke and Condillac conceived of as telementational—consisting of the transfer of ideas. The analysis of language thus conceived was considered to be necessary for any thorough understanding of human beings.

Hans Aarsleff argues that "Rosseau and his contemporaries took Condillac for granted, while later generations have tended to remember only Rosseau."[86] Like Condillac, Rosseau believed that language began with concrete nouns that had "natural" relations with their referents and that in turn were interconnected with very few grammatical distinctions or constraints. The fact that contemporary language bore little resemblance to its beginning "in the state of nature" could be explained by its movement farther and farther away from its true source or origins. Ernst Cassirer emphasized that these arguments were scarcely more than repetitions, not only of Condillac but also of Giambattista Vico's claim that all the original words "were monosyllabic roots, which either reproduced a natural sound by ono-matopoeic, or immediate expressions of emotion, interjections of pain or pleasure, joy or grief, surprise or terror."[87]

Rousseau spent much of the first five chapters of his *Essay on the Origin of Language* describing how forms of expression evolved from gestures to poetic or "figurative" spoken words and then to words representing ideas. Without benefit of any data from descrip-tive linguistics, he argued that one can learn about spoken languages by studying forms of writing, and that the most primitive languages depict objects; moderately developed languages are made up of "signs of words and of propositions"; and the most highly civilized languages are based on an alphabet that represents spoken sounds.[88] Language developed differently in southern and northern climates, he also claimed, because of the different climatological and physical con-straints on human associations in the two regions. The overall goal of his *Essay* was to trace the etiology of the human condition from a state of nature through institutional forms to civil society. The de-velopment of language corresponded for Rosseau to successive stages of social organization, from savage to barbaric to civilized. The ear-liest languages were the most immediate and spontaneous and the latest most generalized and conventional. In short, his account added little to earlier versions of the nature of languge, but it was employed in a distinct project of social criticism subsequently developed espe-cially by Romanticists.

Essay on the Origin of Language was also the title of J. G. Herder's prizewinning submission to the Prussian Academy. After a lengthy introduction replete with acknowledged "digressions," Herder argued in this work that language originated when one of the first human's reasoning abilities enabled him or her to single out a "distinguishing characteristic" that identified some nearby ob-ject, for example, a lamb that was distinguished by its bleating. As the human named this characteristic, "human language [was] in-vented!" "The sound of bleating perceived by a human soul as the distinguishing mark of the sheep became, by virtue of this reflec-tion, the name of the sheep, even if [the human's] tongue had never tried to stammer it. He [she] recognized the sheep by its bleating: This was a conceived sign through which the soul clearly remem-bered an idea—and what is that other than a word?"[89]

In his *Essay*, Herder acknowledged not only Condillac and Rousseau but also several other German, French, and English writers who had pursued his topic. Sometimes in support, but more often in contrast to their claims he argued (a) that language is a human invention, not a divine one, (b) that language had to be an individual, not a social invention; (c) that language and thought are indissolubly bound together—"*ratio et oratio!*" (p. 121); (d) that sound, rather than sight or touch, is the primary sense modality that gave rise to language, and words for soundless objects or events are based on words from hearable ones; (e) that verbs were created first (e.g., the lamb's bleating) and nouns developed from them; (f) that poetry is older than prose; and (g) that "language, from without, is the true differential character of our species as reason is from within" (p. 127).

For the purposes of this review, it is important to note how the assumptions of the symbol model are present in Herder's essay, but not conspicuously. His most basic claim is that human reason is uniquely able to overcome "the pressure of sensuousness" that overwhelms all nonhuman animals and thus to acknowledge a "distinguishing characteristic," and that "the first act of this acknowledgment results in a clear concept," which is immediately "marked" with a sign that is the first word (p. 116). The human "recognized [the lamb] humanly when it recognized and named it clearly, that is, with a distinguishing mark" (p. 117). Thus the yet-unspoken name or mark appeared to be of a different order of reality from the distinguishing characteristic that it stands for: A word (name) is the sign of a concept. But Herder's proto-Romantic orientation—he was known as "the teacher of Goethe and the disciple of Hamann" (p. 167)—and the scholarly context surrounding his essay led him to emphasize features other than language's systematicity or the connection between words and the world, features that had centrally occupied earlier writers. As a result, this line of eighteenth century language inquiry increased the prominence in the literature of such topics as the interconnection between language and thought, the individual vs. social nature of language, and the significance of the fact that language is primordially aural rather than visual. Important treatments of all these topics appeared later in Wilhelm von Humboldt's work.

In many ways, the other eighteenth-century development that influenced subsequent language theorizing could not have been more different from the speculations about the origin of language proffered by Condillac, Rousseau, and Herder. But the symbol model was still basic to both lines of thinking. Echoing Locke, John Horne Tooke began Part I of his major work, *The Diversions of Purley*, with the claim that "The purpose of language is to communicate our thoughts." Horne Tooke would not even grant "language" status to the solitary mental naming that Herder analyzed. For Horne Tooke, the communicative principle, which, he argued, should be "kept singly in contemplation, has missed all those who have reasoned on this subject."[90]

The Diversions of Purley was cast as a dialogue, and Horne Tooke began his argument with a criticism of earlier accounts of the nature of language that appears to have been motivated by his dissatisfaction with the simplest versions of the *symbol model*. The main problem, he wrote, is that others have reasoned that "Words are the *signs* of *things*. There must therefore be as many sorts of words, or parts of speech, as there are sorts of *things*. . . . For words being the *signs* of things, their sorts must necessarily follow the sorts of the things *signified*" (pp. 18, 21). But, his interlocutor insisted, you are forgetting that "Modern Grammarians" acknowledge words to be not the signs of things but "the signs of ideas." "This has not much mended the matter," Horne Tooke replied; "the nature of Language has not been much better understood by it. . . . The very same game has been played over again with *ideas*, which was before played with *things*" (pp. 23, 24).

Horne Tooke claimed that all previous scholars had been confused about how words signify because they had overlooked the fact that language has two aims: The first is "to *communicate* our thoughts: the second, to do it with *dispatch*" (p. 27). Especially because of this second central aim, only some words are immediately either the signs of things or the signs of ideas; the others "are merely *abbreviations* employed for dispatch, and are t*he signs of other words*"(pp. 26–27, italics added). Here Horne Tooke introduced an idea that could conceivably have moved his theorizing decisively away from the two worlds assumption. Signs and symbols were commonly defined as entities that represent or stand for something *else*, not for entities identical to the signs or symbols themselves. So it is possible that he was making no distinction here between a linguistic and a nonlinguistic world. Had Horne Tooke developed this claim that words simply signify other words, he would have had to explain what it might mean for one kind of entity to "stand for" or "represent" another of the same kind of entity. This is because, as I noted in Chapter 1, when the ontological difference is removed, the coherence and force of the "representing" or "standing-for" relationship seems also to dissolve. As it turned out, however, Horne Tooke faced neither this promise nor this challenge, because he did not develop his argument in this post-semiotic direction. According to his analysis, some words signify things, some signify ideas, and the remaining ones indirectly, through other words, also signify either signs or ideas.

Horne Tooke argued that only two sorts of words are necessary for communication—nouns and verbs—and all other words are actually abbreviations. His analysis of the noun followed Locke: "it is the s*imple* or *complex*, the *particular* or *general sign* or *name* of *one* or *more Ideas*" (p. 52). From nouns he moved to general explanations of the article, interjection, the word "that," and conjunctions. Then he spent the remaining 384 pages of volume 1 of *Diversions of Purley* reviewing prominent English authors' uses of conjunctions, prepositions, and adverbs to identify precisely their "manner of signification." This exhaustive etymological research was dedicated to demonstrating, as Harris and Taylor summarize, that "in the final analysis, the meaning of every word, regardless of its part of speech, is given by the simple idea(s) for which it stands, directly or through abbreviation. . . . Any word which does not stand directly for a simple idea should in principle be traceable to one or more other words which do."[91]

Thus Horne Tooke's work is significant not only because it was, in Britain, the most widely discussed language theory at the end of the eighteenth and the beginning of the nineteenth centuries. It was also motivated in part by its author's partial recognition of the very difficulties in earlier accounts of the nature of langue that I have attempted to highlight in this review. Moreover, Horne Tooke employed a form of empirical research, rather than relying primarily, as did most of his continental contemporaries, on speculation. In the final analysis, however, he reaffirmed the central features of the symbol model rather than breaking free from them.

Wilhelm von Humboldt

This chapter ends with Humboldt, because he was the first influential Western language scholar to have one foot firmly planted in both semiotic and post-semiotic approaches to language. On the one hand, Humboldt articulated the intimate connection between language and world and thus opened the door much more widely than Horne Tooke did to a radical reconsideration of the two worlds assumption underlying the symbol model. Humboldt himself did not fully move through this door, but, as I will clarify in Chapter 4, his work suggested to Hans-Georg Gadamer some of the insights that allowed Gadamer, following Heidegger, to propose a genuinely post-semiotic account of the nature of language. On the other hand, Humboldt developed the post-semiotic features of his thinking in tension with clear commitments to aspects of the symbol model. As always appears to be the case with intellectual paradigm shifts, Humboldt's revolutionary claims were parasitic on and constrained by the very insights he nearly overcame.

Humboldt's major philosophical work, *On Language*, was written as the introduction to a three-volume analysis of the language of the Kawi, who inhabit an island in what is now part of Indonesia. Humboldt was a true polyglot, having thoroughly learned Greek and Latin in school, adding Basque in his early thirties, and then intensively studying the languages of Central America, Sanskrit, North American Indian languages, Chinese, Polynesian, Malayan, and Kawi, which was a mix of Sanskrit and Malayan. This breadth of knowledge enhanced the credibility of his claims about the nature of language. At the same time, it is important to note that his research was not empirical in the sense of being based on observation and firsthand experience; it was anchored entirely on the written materials he could collect in his study.[92]

Three features of Humboldt's work especially illustrated his recognition that language cannot be satisfactorily characterized as a semiotic system. The first was the claim for which he is perhaps best known. To pursue linguistic research successfully, Humboldt argued, "We must look upon language, not as a dead *product*, but far more as a *producing*. . . . Language . . . in itself . . . is no product (*Ergon*), but an activity (*Energeia*). . . . in its true and essential meaning . . . we can . . . regard, as it were, only the totality of this speaking as the language. . . . language proper lies in the act of its real production. . . . The break-up into words and rules is only a dead makeshift of scientific analysis."[93] This was the first explicit attempt by a prominent modern western philosopher of language to argue that scholars should focus not on the *system*—of phonemes, morphemes, words, propositions, and so forth—but on the *activity* of "languaging," not on the "product" but on the "producing." As I have noted, the early decision to treat language as a system was one factor that enhanced the attractiveness of semiotic analyses and focused language scholars' attention on the relationship between words and the world. Humboldt articulated the beginning of a genuine alternative to this approach.

A second crucial argument he advanced was that the "first element" of language is "articulated sound." Aristotle acknowledged a version of this point, and as this chapter has indicated, several other authors noted that speech initially manifests oral-aurally. But other writers typically focused on phonemic subunits rather than discursive or narrational sound. Humboldt argued that "the constant and uniform element in this mental labour of elevating articulated sound to an expression of thought . . . constitutes the *form* of language" (p. 50). "It is therefore self-evident," he continued, "that, in order to obtain an idea of the form of a language, we must first of all attend to the real nature of the *sounds*" (p. 52). Humboldt's treatment of sound introduced an important social element into his account of the nature of language: "But mental cultivation, even in the loneliest seclusion of temperament, is equally possible only through language, and the latter requires to be directed to an external being that understands it. The articulate sound is torn from the breast, to awaken in another individual an echo returning to the ear" (p. 41).

This comment about sound points toward a third, equally important claim. Like Herder, Humboldt saw language and thought as absolutely interconnected. He wrote: "Language is the formative organ of *thought. Intellectual activity,* entirely mental, entirely internal, and to some extent passing without trace, becomes through *sound,* externalized in speech and perceptible to the senses. Thought and language are therefore one and inseparable from each other. But the former is also intrinsically bound to the necessity of entering into a *union* with the verbal sound; thought cannot otherwise achieve clarity, nor the idea become a concept. The inseparable bonding of *thought, vocal apparatus* and *hearing* to language is unalterably rooted in the original constitution of human nature, which cannot be further explained" (pp. 54–55). Hans Aarsleff underscores the importance of this claim, especially in relation to the symbol model, when he emphasizes that, for Humboldt, language was not an "epiphenomenal outward manifestation or garb of thought for the utilitarian purpose of communication." It was not a "nomenclature of tags for concepts that had been offered ready-made to the mind by . . . perception." Moreover, language was not "like a tool-box with discrete instruments and parts designed for particular tasks." Thus language was "not merely designative; it is not representation."[94] As the pages of this chapter have demonstrated, most of Humboldt's intellectual forebears believed that language *was* precisely all these things—an outward manifestation of thought, a nomenclature for concepts, an instrument or tool for communicating. But Humboldt saw language differently; in Gadamer's words, "He recognized that the living act of speech, verbal energeia, is the essence of language, and thus overcame the dogmatism of the grammarians."[95] Thus, to the degree that Humboldt maintained the commitments expressed in these quotations, his work must be seen as a genuine departure from semiotic analyses of the nature of language.

On the other hand, at least three corresponding features of Humboldt's analysis reveal a continuing commitment to aspects of the symbol model. First, alongside and in tension with his description of the intimate connection between languaging and thinking, Humboldt often expressed the conviction that units of language represent or stand for units of cognition or "thoughts." For example, he claimed, "For the *intent* and capacity to *signify*, and not just in general, but specifically by presentation of a *thought*, is the only thing that constitutes the articulated sound, and nothing else can be stated to describe its difference from the *animal cry*, on the one hand, and the *musical tone* on the other" (p. 65). A few pages later he even more explicitly manifested a commitment to two worlds as he wrote, "By words we understand the signs of particular concepts. . . . If we picture language as a second world, that [the hu]man has objectified . . . from the impressions he [or she] receives from the true one, then words are the sole objects therein for which the character of individuality must be retained, even in form" (p. 70). And later, "Even for [physical objects that are plainly perceivable by the senses], the word is not the equivalent of the object that hovers before the sense, but rather the conception thereof through language-production at the particular moment of finding the word. . . . For language never represents the objects, but always the concepts that the mind has spontaneously formed from them in producing language . . . " (p. 84). In his discussion of the pause he noted, "the treatment of *sound-unity* thereby becomes a symbol of the particular *conceptual unity* desired"(p. 110). He called "the most primary essence of language" "articulation and symbolization" (p. 145). And finally, in the summary of his account of the nature of language Humboldt repeated that articulated sound, one of the two "constitutive principles" of language became the "actual *creative principle* in language" *because* of "its perpetual symbolizing activity" (p. 214). Clearly Humboldt was influenced by earlier semiotic analyses of language. At times he distinguished between the linguistic world and "the true one"; he claimed that a word "represents . . . concepts"; and he saw words as "symbols."

Second, although Humboldt's description of sound gave a social cast to his treatment of language, he, like other Romanticists, ultimately saw language as an individual activity rather than an interaction or transaction. Early in *On Language* he referred to language as "the organ of inner being,"(p.21), and his descriptions of the formative power of language upon thought focused on individuals rather than dyads or groups (e.g., pp. 54–55). He argued that, although language develops socially, "quite regardless of communication between [hu]man and [hu]man, speech is a necessary condition for the thinking of the individual in solitary seclusion"(p. 56). Perhaps the clearest expression of this belief surfaced in section 21 where he wrote, "*Language*, in the isolated word and in connected discourse, is an *act*, a truly creative *performance of the mind*; and in every language this act is an individual one, proceeding in a way that is determined from every angle" (p. 183). And in the book's summary he reiterated that the development of language proceeds in the human "from the unfathomable depth of . . . *individuality*, and from the *activity* of the forces within him [or her]." This development depends upon the energy "from [the human's] entire *mental individuality*," and the first constitutive principle of language thereby developed is "the *inner linguistic sense*" (p. 215). According to Aarsleff, the idea that "brings all the basic aspects of language into single focus" in Humboldt's work is "the privacy of language. Because the ideas in anyone's mind are radically private and because words are about those ideas, there can never be any assurance that one person's meaning is the same as another's" (p. xxviii).

So far as the nature of language is concerned, a third semiotic feature of Humboldt's theorizing is less prominent and less significant than the first two. But socially and politically it bears noting. Several critics have accused Humboldt of racism because of his argument that Sanskrit, Greek, and Latin are clearly superior languages to Chinese, Arabic, and those spoken by North and South American natives. Some have even found echoes of Humboldt's treatment of the "national character of languages" in the doctrines of Nazism.[96] For the purposes of this review, the important point about Humboldt's argument about the hierarchy of languages is that he determined the superiority of one language over another in part by assessing their respective abilities to *represent thoughts* fully and unambiguously.

In his chapter on the "character of languages," Humboldt emphasized that he viewed "character" as different from structure, he believed that it is most evident in the literary monuments produced by speakers of a language; and he was convinced that character was reflected best in the "spirit" of what is spoken and written. But he also claimed that the superiority of the character of one language over another was due in part to the language's ability to clarify and refine concepts (p. 151), accurately reflect the individuality of its speakers (p. 158), and provide for "a maximum *individualization of the object*, attainable only by penetration into every detail of sensory conception, and by the utmost concreteness of presentation" (p. 160). In other words, character also had to do with a language's ability to represent thoughts and things fully and accurately. As a language matures, he argued, "The youthful efflorescence of the language in its sensuous aspect becomes concentrated more upon its suitability for the *expression of inner thoughts*" (p. 166). This development reflected his belief that "the true field of differing word-value is the designation of *mental concepts*" (p. 167). In his summary, Humboldt responded to his critics by insisting that his account of the hierarchy of languages was not meant to reflect on the intellectual capacity of any peoples. A "more *imperfect language*," he claimed, is "initially proof only of the smaller *impulse* the nation has directed" to "elaborating *thought* by means of *sound*," "without implying any decision as to its other *intellectual merits*" (p. 217). Any "impartial scholar" can recognize, he concluded, that in these ways Sanskrit, Greek, and Latin are superior.

The reader may decide for himself or herself whether Humboldt responded adequately to the charges of racism. My primary point is that, viewed from the perspective of the symbol model, there is clearly a tension in Humboldt's account of the nature of language, because commitments to both a semiotic and a post-semiotic view of the nature of language characterize his work. With the help of Rousseau, Herder, and others, Humboldt recognized, on the one hand, that the limits of one's language are indeed the limits of one's world and that language therefore is more than simply a surrogational medium or a means of representing objects or ideas. But he came to these ideas through the semiotic analyses that preceded him and thus, understandably, his development of them is parasitic on those analyses.

The next chapter demonstrates that, despite Humboldt's sometimes radical insights, several influential nineteenth- and twentieth-century language scholars who followed him continued to treat language as primarily a system of symbols. Then Chapter 4 clarifies how Heidegger, Gadamer, and others have extended some of Humboldt's work into the beginnings of a genuinely post-semiotic treatment of the nature of language.[97]

❀ Chapter 3

Twentieth-Century Versions
of the Symbol Model

The previous chapter offered a narrative of various writers' discussions of the nature of language. As with any story, its materials were purposively selected, in this case to make a plausible argument that many influential scholars from at least the fifth century B.C. to the midnineteenth century characterized language as a system of symbols. The present chapter argues that several prominent twentieth-century philosophers of language have continued this practice.

A number of scholars have also departed from it. Important post-semiotic lines of language study have been developed in this century, but for the most part I postpone comment on them until Chapter 4. It is also true that the authors discussed here have addressed important issues that are beyond the scope of this chapter. My goal here is simply to demonstrate that the model of the nature of language identified in Chapter 1 continues to figure prominently in the thinking and writing of language scholars. This means that influential works continue to manifest a commitment to two worlds, a tendency to treat language as a system made up of units that function representationally, and an inclination to characterize language as an instrument or tool.

Like Chapter 2, this one is arranged roughly chronologically. It begins with C. S. Peirce, an American philosopher who wrote from the late 1860s to the first decade of the twentieth century. Then I comment on Peirce's Swiss contemporary, Ferdinand de Saussure, and follow that with descriptions of the views of the Wittgenstein of the *Tractatus*, Ernst Cassirer, and Cassirer's student Susanne Langer.

Charles Sanders Peirce

After completing two degrees at Harvard in 1859 and 1863, Peirce began delivering lectures on logic in the late 1860s. He worked part-time for the Coastal Survey and concentrated on lectures and essays until 1879, when he was appointed as a lecturer in logic at Johns Hopkins. His tenure there ended abruptly in 1884, and from then until his death in 1914 he wrote and lectured prolifically, often while barely subsisting materially.

Peirce has been called "the most profound native intellect to have appeared in the United States."[1] He envisioned his lifework as Kantian in scope, the establishment of a systematic foundation for a system of first philosophy. In fact, Christopher Hookway claims that, like Descartes and Kant, Peirce "wanted to provide a demonstration that, if we conduct our inquiries properly, we can obtain knowledge of an objective reality."[2] It is impossible to adequately characterize a program of this breadth and depth in a few pages. But I believe it is possible to identify one conviction Peirce held throughout his productive life, a conviction directly relevant to this analysis.

Peirce's entire project began with his theory of signs, and he was said to have inherited virtually the entire historical analysis of signs sketched in the previous chapter. He was intimately familiar not only with Greek and Roman sources but also with Ockham, Hobbes, Locke, and Horne Tooke.[3] Late in his life Peirce himself testified that "it has never been in my power to study anything,—mathematics, ethics, metaphysics, gravitation, thermodynamics, optics, chemistry, comparative anatomy, astronomy, psychology, phonetics, economics, the history of science, whist, men and women, wine, meteorology, except as a study of semiotic."[4] The combination of Peirce's intellectual power, the scope of his project, and the centrality of his theory of signs makes him, along with Saussure, the founder of modern semiotic.[5]

In the context of this review, the most important question to ask about Peirce's theory of signs is whether and, if so, how he distinguished between the linguistic and the nonlinguistic world. This is a difficult question to answer simply, partly because his ontology changed over the course of his life and partly because his statements about the human experience of the objective world—especially those discussing the categories of "firstness, secondness, and thirdness"— are often obscure to the point of impenetrability.[6] Clarke makes the important point that semiotic, for Peirce, was a logical discipline not an empirical one,[7] which could lend credence to the argument that, in the final analysis, Peirce was concerned only with the cognitive-perceptual world consisting of structures of thinking. It is also true that, in his 1905 paper, "What Pragmatism Is," Peirce argued that pragmatism shows how "almost every proposition of ontological metaphysics is either meaningless gibberish . . . or else is absurd."[8] This comment could support the claim that Peirce offered no explicit metaphysics or ontology. But such a conclusion would be misleading; Peirce frequently discussed problems created by the "nominalism" of some of his forebears, and at various times he characterized his own program as both "realist' and "idealist." Moreover, in the middle of his career he laid out a version of his own metaphysics, especially in a series of five papers that appeared in *The Monist* during 1891–1893.[9]

Hookway concludes from an analysis of these papers in the context of Peirce's other writings that Peirce

> believes that we know about objects which are not just states of our own minds, and, through his theory of perception, holds that we are directly aware of external objects. Ordinary empirical objects are real, and their character is independent of the will or opinion or any agents or inquirers.
>
> . . . Far from our cognitive constitution being *constitutive* of the nature of reality, rather, one task of logic is to invent a logical language which can be proved to be adequate to the description of a reality whose nature is given independent of the resources we have for describing or investigating it.[10]

In other words, Hookway concludes that for Peirce there was an objectively real world distinguishable from cognitions and language, and that a primary task of the philosopher or logician was to increase the degree to which the latter represent or faithfully correspond with the former.

Peirce's position on the two worlds question was clarified in his accounts of the primary construct in his philosophy, the Sign. Several definitions appear in the eight volumes of his collected papers, the most frequently cited of which is the deceptively simple, "A sign, or *representamen*, is something which stands to somebody for something in some respect or capacity."[11] He also wrote that "A *Sign* is anything which is related to a Second thing, its *Object*, in respect to a Quality, in such a way as to bring a Third thing, its *Interpretant*, into relation to the same Object, and that in such a way as to bring a fourth into relation to that Object in the same form, *ad infinitum.*"[12] In a letter to Lady Welby, Peirce reiterated, "I define a Sign as anything which is so determined by something else, called its Object, and so determines an effect upon a person, which effect I call its Interpretant, that the latter is thereby mediately determined by the former."[13]

Importantly, Peirce did not simply argue that there are two orders of reality, signs and not-signs; he did not treat cognition as a dyadic relation between knowing mind and object known.[14] Rather, he emphasized that *the process of semiosis connects the objective world with the world humans inhabit.*[15] Signification or semiosis, he argued, is a triadic relationship, among object, sign, and cognition, not simply a dyadic one between a knowing mind and an object or sense-datum. So any identifiable thing—a rock, animal cry, or building in the natural or built world, a flag, carved shape or other artifact, a linguistic word or document—may function as a sign when it is both determined by its object and at the same time determines a cognitive effect upon a person. And for humans this process of signification is ongoing and pervasive, because "all thought is in signs."[16]

Because of his insistence on the triadic nature of the relation, one could be led to believe that Peirce envisioned *three* worlds: one made up of objects, another of signs, and a third consisting of interpretants or cognitions. But this would also be misleading, because, as I noted, for Peirce semiosis is a *process*, which means that a sign is not a special kind of phenomenon. Instead, any phenomenon that *functions* semiotically, that is, to link object and interpretant, is "being" a sign. So, for example, a tree trunk from which bark has been stripped may function when perceived by a hiker as a *sign* of the deer that stripped it. If the hiker subsequently diagrams in a notebook the route she followed that day, and places a special mark where she found the stripped bark, the mark in the notebook would then be the sign, and the stripped bark itself—which was earlier a sign—would then be the *object* signified by the mark. In the latter case the given "reality" is simply that—an object—and in the former case the same "reality" is a sign.

But the important point for this review is that the familiar distinction between *two worlds* underlies this triadic analysis. In the first case the "object" bark determines the "interpretant" or cognition about deer, and in the latter case the "object" mark determines the cognition about bark sighting and bark interpreting. But the fundamental distinction between "object" (World$_1$) and "cognition" (World$_2$) persists. Signs function, primarily causally, to link aspects of "reality" with particular mental "interpretants."

This distinction was underscored by Peirce's conviction that it is always possible to misunderstand a sign. There is a difference, he claimed, between a correct interpretation of a sign and one that is ungrounded. This is because of the way signs mediate between reality and our cognitions. Understanding means *accurately* grasping some aspect of reality, which is to say that the phenomenon functioning as a sign determines or "causes" an interpretant that *corresponds appropriately* to the sign's real-world object. Misunderstanding occurs when the interpretant fails in some way to correspond with reality. Clearly this account of misunderstanding as failure-to-correspond is coherent only if one presumes a distinction between the cognitive and the objective worlds, the very distinction necessary for one to *correspond* with the other.

Peirce identified three primary ways signs connect object and interpretant and labeled the three as types of signs: icons, indices, and symbols. An icon signifies by virtue of its similarity to its object. Examples of icons are maps, diagrams, and blueprints. An index signifies ostensively, by pointing to or being causally related to its object, as a bullet hole is a sign of the bullet that caused it or a fossil is a sign of the past life it pictures. Some words, for example demonstrative and personal pronouns, are also indices because "they call upon the hearer to use his [or her] powers of observation, and so establish a real connection between [the] mind and the object; and if the demonstrative pronoun [*this/that*] does that—without which its meaning is not understood—it goes to establish such a connection; and so is an index."[17] In contrast with both icons and indices, a symbol signifies conventionally, by virtue of social agreement. In a passage that reinforced the two worlds commitment inherent in his view of symbols, Peirce wrote, "All words, sentences, books, and other conventional signs are Symbols . . . Any ordinary word . . . is *applicable to whatever may be found to realize the idea connected with the word*; it does not, in itself, identify those things. It does not show us a bird, nor enact before our eyes a giving or a marriage, but supposes that we are able to imagine those things and have associated the word with them."[18] Thus the symbol does not "show us" the aspect of reality (e.g., the bird) it symbolizes as, in a sense, an icon does. Rather, the symbol triggers an imaginative cognition of that which it symbolizes.

Given the pervasiveness of culture in every human endeavor, Peirce noted that there are few if any pure icons or indices; most signs are at least partly symbolic. But he believed that this three-part distinction could nonetheless be maintained, and subsequent Peircean categorizations of, for example, "qualisigns," "sinsigns," "legisigns," and "dicisigns," were dependent on this primary trichotomy.

Language constitutes the most important system of signs. As Fisch puts it, "It goes without saying that [for Peirce] words are signs; and it goes almost without saying that phrases, clauses, sentences, speeches, and extended conversations are signs. So are poems, essays, short stories, novels, orations, plays, operas, journal articles, scientific reports, and mathematical demonstrations."[19]

Like many other modern and contemporary theorists, Peirce struggled with the ontological commitments entailed by his conviction that semiosis definitively characterized all thought and language. He was clearly aware that his fundamentally and thoroughly representational analysis raised difficult questions about the representer ("sign"), the represented ("object"), the representation ("interpretant"), and the representing ("semiosis"). But rather than reconsidering his initial presupposition, Peirce attempted to construct a complicated system of logically necessary relationships between the objective world and human understanding of it. As he wrote to a friend five years before he died, "My idea of a sign has been so generalized that I have at length despaired of making anybody comprehend it, so that for the sake of being understood, I now limit it, so as to define a sign as anything which is on the one hand so determined (or specialized) by an object and on the other hand so determines the mind of an interpreter of it that the latter is thereby determined mediately, or indirectly, by that real object that determines the sign. Even this may be thought an excessively generalized definition."[20]

In the final analysis, Peirce's complex and nuanced program embodied most of the same beliefs that Locke expressed. This became Peirce's version of the symbol model: There are two worlds, one made up of objective reality and the other of cognitions. To a considerable degree, the nature of language can be understood by breaking it down into individual words that, in at least nine different ways, cause cognitive representations of aspects of objective reality. The adequacy of these representations is a function of how well they correspond to the realities they signify. And humans employ the resulting system in their efforts to understand the world in which they live.

Peirce applied this model very broadly, and scholars from a range of disciplines continue to be influenced by his work. Many mathematics educators, historians of science, logicians, cultural anthropologists, theologians, linguists, psychiatrists, sociologists—especially symbolic interactionists—and virtually all semioticians view Peirce as a seminal thinker.[21] His ontological or metaphysical thinking clearly cannot be reduced without remainder to the ideas I have reviewed here. But it is equally clear that Peirce did elaborate and apply a perspective on language that was consistent with the symbol model.

Ferdinand de Saussure

Saussure was born in Geneva the year Peirce was a Harvard sophomore and died one year before Peirce's death. Partly because Saussure's primary work was published posthumously, neither apparently influenced the other. As I noted, however, the two are generally identified together as the founders of modern semiotic. Peirce is credited for elaborating a general theory of signs whereas Saussure developed the first thorough account of the *linguistic* sign in its modern conception.[22]

From the perspective of this discussion, perhaps the most important section of Saussure's *Cours de linguistic générale* is Part I, Chapter 1, "Nature of the Linguistic Sign," which he began with an argument against the view that language is a nomenclature. Roy Harris, the most recent translator of the *Cours*, claims in both the introduction to his translation and in the final chapter of *Landmarks in Linguistic Thought* that in this chapter of the *Cours* Saussure effected a "Copernican revolution" in Western thinking about language.[23] This revolution, claims Harris, was anchored in Saussure's rejection of the notion that words name aspects of the nonlinguistic world or "stand for" something else of a nonlinguistic nature. Saussure, says Harris, saw as profoundly misconceived the doctrine of "surrogationalism," which is the belief that units of language are surrogates for something else. For Saussure, Harris argues, the reverse was true: the "human's understanding of reality came to be seen as revolving about their social use of verbal signs."[24]

The first part of Harris's claim, that Saussure argued against viewing language as a nomenclature, is firmly grounded in the text of the *Cours*. After the seven-chapter Introduction and two-chapter Appendix, the first words of Part I, Chapter 1 challenged exactly this view of language. Saussure noted that the conception that words are names assumes that ideas already exist independent of words. Moreover, this conception does not clarify whether the name is a vocal or psychological entity and it "leads one to assume that the link between a name and a thing is something quite unproblematic, which is far from being the case."[25]

But the next lines, in which Saussure began to develop his antinomenclature argument, raise questions about how thoroughly he was committed to the "revolutionary" perspective Harris identifies. The final sentence of the first paragraph reads, "None the less, this naive view contains one element of truth, which is that linguistic units are dual in nature, comprising two elements." Saussure argued that both these elements are psychological, "and are connected in the brain by an associative link. This is a point of major importance. A linguistic sign is not a link between a thing and a name, but between a concept and a sound pattern" (p. 66). The text of the *Cours* includes at this point a diagram of an ellipse horizontally divided in half, with the top half labeled *concept* and the bottom half *sound pattern*. The arrows on the diagram indicate that the associative link between the two halves can go in either direction, from concept to sound pattern or from sound pattern to concept. Saussure's final point in this section was that he reserved the term *sign* for the whole made up of concept and sound pattern, and that he preferred the terms signification (*signifié*) for concept and signal (*signifiant*) for sound pattern.

These eight paragraphs begin to reveal the pervasive influence of the symbol model in Saussure's thinking, because here *Saussure's rejection of surrogationalism or nomenclaturism was vitiated by his continued insistence that language is bipartite or semiotic.* In other words, his determination to replace one semiotic conception of language—the idea that words are fundamentally names—was undercut by his decision to put in its place another semiotic conception—the idea that language is made up of signs, each of which links concept (*signifié*) with sound pattern (*signifiant*).

This movement in the direction of the symbol model continued in the next section of this chapter of the *Cours*. Here Saussure argued that the "first principle" of semiology is that each sign is arbitrary, which is to say that there is "no internal connexion, for example, between the idea 'sister' and the French sequence of sounds s-ö-r which acts as its signal. The same idea might as well be *represented* by any other sequence of sounds" (pp. 67–68, italics added). As is clear from these lines, immediately after claiming that the relationship between concept and sound pattern can go in either direction, Saussure argued that the latter *represented* the former. But how does this claim affect the earlier one? Is a representational relationship actually reversible? Could Saussure coherently have written that "the *idea* 'sister'" *represented* "the French sequence of *sounds* s-ö-r"? Or, as he continued the paragraph, could he have argued coherently that on one side of the French-German border the concept "ox" *represented* the sound pattern b-ö-f and on the other side of the border the same concept *represented* the sound pattern o-k-s? These questions are puzzling primarily because a representational relationship is, in fact, not reversible. A word may be said to represent a concept, but not the other way around. So the first point at which Saussure appears to move away from the two worlds commitment of nomenclaturism—his argument that the relationship between concept and sound pattern is reversible—is at least rendered ambiguous by his subsequent argument that the latter *represents* the former.

Saussure's tendency to emphasize the representational character of the sign, not only on these pages but also, for example, on pp. 12, 15, 71, and 112, raises another issue that I briefly raised both in Chapter 1 and in my discussion of Horne Tooke's *Diversions of Purley*: What can it mean for one phenomenon to *represent* another of the same ontological status? As I noted, early in Chapter 1 of the *Cours*, Saussure appeared to avoid any commitment to two worlds by claiming that both concept and sound pattern were of the same ontological status in that they were both psychological phenomena. This is undoubtedly part of what led Harris to identify his position as "revolutionary." But when Saussure also claimed that signs are representational, he introduced a serious problem. As I argued earlier, one can easily envision a tree "representing" a forest and a flag "representing" a country, but what could it mean for a tree to "represent" another individual tree, a flag to "represent" another flag, a word to "represent" another word, or a concept or idea (psychological phenomenon) to "represent" another concept or idea? Two individual words or psychological entities could be said to be "synonymous" or "interchangeable," but can one coherently be said to "represent" the other? "As I argued earlier, "representation" labels a relationship between two ontologically distinct phenomena. Saussure appeared to overlook this feature of a representational relationship. As a result, his effort to transcend simplistic versions of the word-to-world relationship was again thwarted by his adoption of semiotic ways of thinking and speaking.[26]

The other major point Saussure made in section 2 is that he preferred the term *sign* to *symbol*. The reason, he wrote, is that "signs" are always arbitrary, but "symbols" are not. "They show at least a vestige of natural connexion between the signal and its signification. For instance, our symbol of justice, the scales, could hardly be replaced by a chariot" (p. 68). Although the example appears apt, it is interesting to note that Saussure's claim about this defining feature of the *sign* was precisely the same as Peirce's claim about the defining feature of the *symbol*. *Symbol* is what it is because it is arbitrary, claimed Peirce, whereas icons and indices are types of signs that are not wholly arbitrary. On the contrary, argued Saussure; *sign* is the arbitrary term. It would have been helpful had the two writers offered some evidence and reasoning to support their claims about these absolutely central constructs, but they did not. Both appealed only to "common sense."

Additional questions about Saussure's commitment to the symbol model may be raised regarding section 3 of his Chapter 1, where he introduced the notion that the linguistic signal, but not the concept or signification, is auditory in nature. This means, he wrote, that the signal "has a temporal aspect, and hence certain temporal characteristics: (a) *it occupies a certain temporal space*, and (b) *this space is measured in just one dimension*: it is a line" (pp. 69–70). This "fundamental principle" clearly distinguished the signal or sound pattern from the concept or signification. It made the former a different sort of phenomenon, a different kind of reality. Moreover, the section continued, this feature becomes apparent "immediately when [signals] are *represented* in writing and a spatial line of graphic signs is substituted for a succession of sounds in time" (p. 70, italics added). It is unmistakable that here Saussure saw a clear ontological difference between signal and signification.

These paragraphs lead one to ask several questions related to those I have just raised. First, what is the effect of this argument about the *difference* between *signifiant* and *signifié* on Saussure's insistence that concept and sound pattern are ontologically the same; that is, both psychological? How can concept and sound pattern be ontologically similar (identical?), although only one "occupies . . . temporal space"? Does this "fundamental" feature of temporality not make the sound pattern different in kind from the concept? Or did Saussure believe that both were "psychological" even though one occupied temporal space and the other did not? Was Saussure distinguishing between atemporal psychological realities and temporal ones? If so, can such a distinction be maintained?

Second, what, if anything, is suggested about Saussure's pattern of thinking by his claim that written language—perhaps even individual letters ("graphic signs")—*represent* "a succession of sounds"? He developed this point in Chapter 6 of his Introduction, "Representation of a Language by Writing." The primary point of this chapter was that the proper object of study for linguistics is not writing but the spoken word; linguists who privilege writing are committing the same error as believing "that in order to find out what a person looks like it is better to study his photograph than his face" (p. 25). So the linguist must distinguish between "sounds and letters" and recognize that "the sole reason for the existence of the latter is to represent the former" (pp. 24–25). Here Saussure's understanding of the relationship between writing and speaking was the same as the one Aristotle outlined in the second sentence of *On Interpretation*. Is it possible that Saussure sometimes thought of the relationship between sound pattern and concept as an analogue of this representational relationship—despite his initial rejection of nomenclaturism?

Clearly Saussure's discussion of "The Nature of the Linguistic Sign" attempted to move beyond the view that there is a simple relationship between words and objects or concepts. But it is equally clear that aspects of the symbol model continued to surface in his thinking to the extent that Harris's claim that Saussure effected a "Copernican revolution" in linguistic thought is probably overstated.

Some references outside the important first chapter of Part I also reinforce the impression that Saussure's thinking continued to be indebted to the symbol model. Regarding commitment 2—atomism—the *Cours* is replete with examples of single words from French, English, German, Greek, Proto-Indo-European, and other languages. His discussion of the analytic unit that is the proper focus of the science of linguistics concluded that it is *"a segment of sound which is, as distinct from what precedes and follows in the spoken sequence, the signal of a certain concept"* (p. 102). And in reference to the symbol model as a whole, twice in the Introduction he described a language as "a system of distinct signs corresponding to distinct ideas" (pp. 10, 15).

On the other hand, much of Saussure's discussion cannot be summarized in symbol model terms. For example, alongside his treatments of *signifié* and *signifiant* as ontologically distinct, one must remember the compelling two-sides-of-one-sheet-of-paper metaphor. As he wrote,

A language might also be compared to a sheet of paper. Thought is one side of the sheet and sound the reverse side. Just as it is impossible to take a pair of scissors and cut one side of the paper without at the same time cutting the other, so it is impossible in a language to isolate sound from thought, or thought from sound. To separate the two for theoretical

purposes takes us into either pure psychology or pure phonetics, not linguistics.

Linguistics, then, operates along this margin, where sound
and thought meet. *The contact between them gives rise to a
form, not a substance (p. 111).*

Moreover, although he relied extensively on single words as
examples, Saussure claimed that he did so only because "we cannot
have direct access to concrete entities and linguistic units" (p. 112).
Linguistics is like history, he claimed, in that it has no "immediately
perceptible entities. And yet one cannot doubt that they exist, or that
the interplay of these units is what constitutes linguistic structures"
(p. 104). These basic units, he argued, are oral-aural, anchored in
sound (e.g., p. 15). In addition, when he discussed the role of language in relation to thought, he did not treat it as a simple matter
of the former representing the latter. Saussure characterized the connection as "a somewhat mysterious process by which 'thought-sound'
evolves divisions, and a language takes shape with its linguistic units
in between those two amorphous masses. One might think of it as
being like air in contact with water" (p. 111). Throughout his work
he emphasized the systemic nature of language, the degree to which
each element depends for its definition and meaning on surrounding elements (e.g., pp. 86–87). And he emphasized that language is
"social in its essence" (pp. 19, 77) rather than simply psychological,
on the one hand, or objective-empirical, on the other.

In sum, Saussure grounded his discussions of linguistics as a
branch of semiology on a set of claims about the nature of language,
and these claims embodied some important aspects of the symbol
model. Although he appeared to recognize the need to escape a commitment to two worlds—which is probably why he initially defined
both *signifiant* and *signifié* as psychological entities—he reverted to
two-worlds thinking when he discussed the temporality of the sound
pattern, a "fundamental" feature not characteristic of concepts. His
position on commitment 2, atomism, vacillated. His theoretical statements affirmed the difficulty of identifying individual units and the
primacy of sounds rather than words, but his examples were consistently of individual words. Regarding commitment 3, Saussure
was unable at least part of the time to resist characterizing the relationship between concept and sound pattern as representational.
He did treat language as a system (commitment 4), but his view of
what this meant differed significantly from what *system* meant to
his symbol model forebears. He emphasized the interdependent and
processual features of any given language system and rejected the

notion that language is a system people instrumentally employ (commitment 5). These features of his analysis were particularly important to those who developed versions of "structuralism" from his ideas.[27] Although it is beyond the scope of the present work, it would be instructive to trace the extent to which the aspects of the symbol model that persisted in Saussure's work have been those most emphasized by his semiotician followers.

Ludwig Wittgenstein's
Tractatus Logico-Philosophicus

In one of the very few works focused on relationships between Saussure and Wittgenstein, Roy Harris describes one way the two were similar. Early in their careers, both Saussure and Wittgenstein affirmed the accuracy of nomenclaturism, although in the works for which each is primarily known, Harris argues, both reject the claim that language is made up of units that stand for, name, or are surrogates for units of thought or objective reality. At the same time, Saussure and Wittgenstein differed on what Harris calls the *biplanar character of the linguistic sign*. As was demonstrated earlier, Saussure affirmed this important vestige of nomenclaturism, surrogationalism, or the symbol model. The Wittgenstein of the *Philosophical Investigations*, on the other hand, rejected it in toto.[28] On the first page of the *Investigations*, Wittgenstein aimed his antinomenclaturist argument at St. Augustine's report in the *Confessions* about how he learned language, which I cited in Chapter 2. But, Harris points out, Wittgenstein's actual target was not the simplistic proto-theory St. Augustine outlined but the complex and nuanced accounts developed by Gottlob Frege, Bertrand Russell, and Wittgenstein himself in the *Tractatus Logico-Philosphicus*.

The *Tractatus* presents a detailed picture theory of language that has been the subject of countless scholarly interpretations.[29] I will not attempt another interpretation of the work's complexities here. I am interested only in the basic ontology of the *Tractatus* and the degree to which it embodies the five commitments that make up the symbol model. This can be clarified, I believe, by reviewing and then commenting on a sample of excerpts from the first four sections of the work .

The *Tractatus* is divided into individually numbered propositions, and the connections among propositions are indicated by the numbering system. So propositions $n.1$, $n.2$, $n.3$, and so forth are comments on proposition n; propositions $n.m.1$, $n.m.2$, and so forth are comments on proposition *n.m.*; and so on. I quote each proposition in its entirety, and ellipses indicate where I have omitted propositions.

1	The world is all that is the case
1.1	The world is the totality of facts, not of things . . .
2.04	The totality of existing states of affairs is the world. . . .
2.05	The totality of existing states of affairs also determines which states of affairs do not exist.
2.06	The existence and nonexistence of states of affairs is reality. . . .
2.063	The sum-total of reality is the world. . . .
2.12	A picture is a model of reality
2.13	In a picture objects have the elements of the picture corresponding to them. . . .
2.15	The fact that the elements of a picture are related to one another in a determinate way represents that things are related to one another in the same way. . . .
2.161	There must be something identical in a picture and what it depicts to enable the one to be a picture of the other at all. . . .
2.17	What a picture must have in common with reality, in order to be able to depict it—correctly or incorrectly—in the way it does, is its pictorial form. . . .
2.18	What any picture, of whatever form, must have in common with reality, in order to be able to depict it—correctly or incorrectly—in any way at all, is logical form; that is, the form of reality. . . .
2.19	Logical pictures can depict the world. . . .
2.21	A picture agrees with reality or fails to agree; it is correct or incorrect, true or false. . . .
2.223	In order to tell whether a picture is true or false we must compare it with reality. . . .
3	A logical picture of facts is a thought. . . .
3.1	In a proposition a thought finds an expression that can be perceived by the senses. . . .

3.12   I call the sign with which we express a thought a propositional sign. And a proposition is a propositional sign in its projective relation to the world. . . .

3.14   What constitutes a propositional sign is that in it its elements (the words) stand in a determinate relation to one another. . . .

3.2   In a proposition a thought can be expressed in such a way that elements of the propositional sign correspond to the objects of the thought.

3.201   I call such elements 'simple signs', and such a proposition 'completely analysed'.

3.202   The simple signs employed in propositions are called names.

3.203   A name means an object. The object is its meaning. ('A' is the same sign as 'A'.) . . .

3.22   In a proposition a name is the representative of an object.

3.221   Objects can only be *named*. Signs are their representatives. I can only speak *about* them: I cannot *put them into words*. Propositions can only say *how* things are, not *what* they are. . . .

4   A thought is a proposition with a sense

4.001   The totality of propositions is language

4.002   . . . Language disguises thought. So much so, that from the outward form of the clothing it is impossible to infer the form of the thought beneath it, because the outward form of the clothing is not designed to reveal the form of the body, but for entirely different purposes. . . .

4.01   A proposition is a picture of reality. A proposition is a model of reality as we imagine it.

4.011   At first sight a proposition—one set out on the printed page, for example—does not seem to be a picture of the reality with which it is concerned. But neither do written notes seem at first sight to be a picture of a piece of music, nor our phonetic notation (the alphabet) to be a picture of our speech.

And yet these sign-language prove to be pictures, even in the ordinary sense, of what they represent. . . .

> 4.0311 One name stands for one thing, another for another
> thing, and they are combined with one another. In this
> way the whole group—like a tableau vivant—presents
> a state of affairs.[30]

The *Tractatus* presents Wittgenstein's version of his logical atomism. As is indicated in these excerpts, important distinctions are
made among things (*Dinge*), objects (*Gegenstände*), states of affairs
(*Sacheverhalte*), and facts (*Tataschen*). Roughly, things are synonymous with objects, objects can be combined to make up states of affairs, and states of affairs can be combined to make up facts. But a
single object or thing can also be a state of affairs and a single state
of affairs a fact. So every state of affairs is a fact, but not conversely,
and the same relationship obtains between objects and states of affairs. When he noted in 2.05 that "the totality of existing states of
affairs also determines which states of affairs do not exist," he made
the ontology exhaustive by "covering" all that can either exist or not
exist. The various references to "the world" (*Die Welt*) and "reality"
(*Wirklichkeit*) also manifested Wittgenstein's commitment to laying
out an exhaustive, complete system. And, as is apparent from 2.18
forward, this system was a logical one whose interconnections are
necessary not contingent.

As is apparent from 2.12 forward, the *Tractatus* asserted that
the relationship between language and the world is a *picturing* one.
Wittgenstein's detailed account of this pictorial relationship is referred to as his *theory of symbolism,* and it is developed to match
this version of his ontology.[31] He argued that there was often an immediate correlation between the elements of a picture and the objects they represent, and in this case the picture *depicts* (*abbilden*)
reality. He employed the notions of pictorial form and logical form
(see, e.g., 2.17 and 2.18) to indicate how and what a picture represented. So, for example, he indicated that "for depiction, the form of
a fact must be projected on the logical space of states of affairs picturing the way a set of represented objects are supposed to stand to
one another."[32]

Beginning at 3.1, Wittgenstein developed his argument that
propositions are word pictures. In 3.12 he labeled a "sign (*Zeichen*)
with which we express a thought a propositional sign." This section
developed the argument that the world is made up of things standing in determinate relationships to one another, and that a proposition expresses a sense by indicating that things stand to one another
in certain determinate relationships. Robert Fogelin's summary of
section 3.2 clarifies how thoroughly the *Tractatus* laid out a version

of at least the symbol model's commitments to two worlds, atomism, and representationalism:

> The proper elements of a proposition Wittgenstein calls "simple signs" or "names" (3.201 and 3.202). . . .As *simple* signs, they are signs that admit of no further analysis via other signs. They are rock-bottom on the side of language. As *names*, they represent things. Furthermore, this rock-bottom level of language locks into the rock bottom level of the world:
>   3.203 A name means an object The object is its meaning. Thus the *pictorial relationship*, which we first examined with respect to pictures in general, is now established through an immediate correlation between the simple signs of the language (names) and the simple entities of the world (objects).[33]

In 4.002, Wittgenstein indicated why he was driven to lay out a logically perfect language. Everyday language "disguises thought" to the extent that "it is not humanly possible to gather immediately from it what the logic of language is."

Numerous critics have shown why this logically perfect language was anything but. For example, Edna O'Shaughnessy detailed some of the weaknesses in the notion that elements of the sign stand for elements in the signified: "Take the phrase, "the river" in "The river is long." For what could it stand? The river? But then, since all words in the sentence stand for an object, for what does "long" stand? The river too? But this is absurd. Shall we say then that "The river" stands for the river without its length, and "long" stands for its length? . . . Or shall we say that "The river" stands for the river with all its properties and "long" stands for its length, i.e., one of its properties? . . . Clearly a "stand for" account of the function of the words in a sentence will not do."[34]

Several scholars have also made the point that one can get a clear sense of what Wittgenstein himself understood as weaknesses in the view of language expressed in the *Tractatus* by examining the first 137 sections of his posthumously published *Philosophical Investigations*, which are dedicated primarily to demolishing his earlier account. As I noted, the later work began with an attack on the view of language sketched in Augustine's *Confessions*. The *Investigations* characterized this view as "primitive, "appropriate for only this narrowly circumscribed region" of language, and productive of a "haze" or "fog" that makes clear vision of language impossible. Wittgenstein also showed how numerous instances of everyday communicating cannot coherently be explained with this picture theory.[35]

It is apparent that when he wrote the *Investigations* Wittgenstein no longer believed that the essence of human language is that words stand for things and that sentences are combinations of such words picturing, in their combination, how objects are combined.

Allan Janik and Stephen Toulmin argue that the *Tractatus* included both an extended effort to develop a version of the symbol model and a clear acknowledgment of its profound limits. They claim that sections 1 to 6.375 work out Wittgenstein's representational theory of the relationship between language and the nonlinguistic world, and that the final four pages of the *Tractatus* affirm that any such representational theory ignores most of what should be of serious interest to the philosopher. The *philosophy* of the *Tractatus*, they argue, "aims at solving the problem of the nature and limits of description" or picturing. Wittgenstein's *worldview*, on the other hand, "expresses the belief that the sphere of what can only be shown must be protected from those who try to say it."[36]

Janik and Toulmin's reading, which emphasizes Wittgenstein's ethical interests, minimizes the fundamental differences between the perspective of the *Tractatus* and that of the *Philosophical Investigations*. It also clarifies how what might be viewed as the philosophical naiveté of Wittgenstein's early work matured during his years as a professor at Cambridge into an effort to deal with language as discursive and situated, an effort that led away from atomism, reductiveness, and representationalism and toward his account of language games. In short, these authors make a persuasive case for viewing Wittgenstein as a language theorist who pushed the symbol model to its limits, abandoned it, and turned to "ordinary" discourse because of its status as the paradigmatic site of language's occurring. Wittgenstein's nonrepresentational, post-semiotic accounts of this occurring continue to stimulate important theorizing and research.

Ernst Cassirer's and Susanne Langer's Symbolic Philosophies of Language

Because Cassirer was born fifteen years before Wittgenstein and died six years before him, chronology would appear to dictate that his comments on the nature of language be discussed before Wittgenstein's. I review them in this order, however, for two reasons. First, volume 1 of Cassirer's *Philosophy of Symbolic Forms*[37] was published two years after the appearance of the *Tractatus* and Cassirer's most influential English work, *An Essay on Man*,[38] did not appear until twenty-three years later. The second reason is conceptual: under the influence especially of Humboldt, Cassirer developed a philosophy of language, that although nineteenth century in style, was designed in large measure to overcome the versions of representationalism that dominated Aristotle, Aquinas, Locke, and even the Wittgenstein of the *Tractatus*. In this sense his vision was considerably more contemporary than the early Wittgenstein's. But Cassirer's alternative to what he called *copy theories* of language was itself thoroughly representational, and he anchored his approach in notions of "symbolizing" and "the symbol" that rendered not only his philosophy but also Susanne Langer's development and application of it, at least as semiotic as it was post-semiotic. Thus, Cassirer's and Langer's works embody a midtwentieth century version of the symbol model, and they also strain against this conception in some important ways.

Like many neo-Kantians, Cassirer envisioned his project as universal in scope; he wanted to analyze the forms and methods of all human thought, including the methodology of history, all forms of creative expression, and even prescientific human thought and imagination as revealed in language and mythology. The general nature of representation and the specific nature of language were central concerns in this project. Cassirer developed his views of symbolizing and language most explicitly in volumes 1 and 3 of his *Philosophy of Symbolic Forms*—entitled respectively, *Language*, and *The Phenomenology of Knowledge*—and in Chapters 2, 3, and 8 of *Essay on Man*. These works were epistemologically focused, but they rejected the Cartesian view that knowledge could involve unmediated contact between subject and object. Cassirer's was an epistemology of mediation; he argued that knowledge is generated as human consciousness spontaneously and continuously transforms all sense data or experience into meaning. These meanings mediate all human contact with objective reality. The operation of these mediating forces enables the human to live "not merely in a broader reality; he lives, so to speak, in a new *dimension* of reality. There is an unmistakable difference between organic reactions and human responses."[39] Moreover, humans live in this world of meaning whether they are engaged with myth, art, or science. In all arenas of human life, even the most basic relations of time, space, thinghood and the attribution of qualities are structures or forms mediated by the special operations of consciousness. As Cassirer summarized his project in the introduction to *The Phenomenology of Knowledge,* "The Philosophy of Symbolic Forms is not concerned exclusively or even primarily with the purely scientific, exact conceiving of the world; it is concerned with all the forms assumed by [the hu]man's understanding of the world. It seeks to apprehend these forms in their diversity, in their totality, and in the inner distinctiveness of their several expressions. And at every step it happens that the "understanding" of the world is no mere receiving, no repetition of a given structure of reality, but comprises a free activity of the spirit" (p. 13).

For the purposes of this review, Cassirer's most consequential decision was to conceive of and label this transformative process characteristic of human consciousness as representational and "symbolizing." Given hindsight, there could have been other choices; had he been writing today he might have been inclined by others' work to label the process *understanding, interpreting, sense making, information-processing, meaning making,* or even *minding.* None of these terms would necessarily have imported the representational, semiotic baggage that accompanies the label *symbolizing.* But Saussure's conviction that consciousness was, in fact, essentially representational made *symbolizing* the appropriate term. Unfortunately, this choice also helped prevent him from accomplishing his goal of overcoming the central weakness of the views of knowledge and language he inherited.

He called this central weakness "the naive *copy theory* of knowledge." This theory essentially treated words as objective copies of the objects they represented, and its primary weakness, Cassirer argued, was that it ignored those *subjective* features that, Kant had demonstrated, were a part of all language.[40] At the very beginning of the first volume of *The Philosophy of Symbolic Forms* Cassirer announced his intention to overcome this theory by substituting for it the recognition that "The fundamental concepts of each science, the instruments with which it propounds its questions and formulates its solutions, are regarded no longer as passive images of something given but as *symbols* created by the intellect itself."[41] Later in the chapter he explained how he believed symbolizing was fundamentally different from copying: "When, for example, we link a given intuition or idea with an arbitrary linguistic sound, we seem, at first sight, to have added nothing whatever to its content. And yet, on closer scrutiny, the content itself takes on a different 'character' for consciousness through the creation of the linguistic sign; it becomes more definite. Its sharp and clear intellectual 'reproduction' proves to be inseparable from the act of linguistic 'production' (pp. 106-107).

Here Cassirer employed the basic distinction between reproduction or representation and production or constitution that I introduced in Chapter 1 and will develop in Chapter 4. He clearly recognized that human knowledge at least partially *constitutes* rather than simply *representing* the forms of "the known," and that language distinctively *produces* rather than simply *reproducing* its "content" or subject matter. But he appeared to overlook two features of representation or reproduction. The first was that it is incommensurable with constituting or producing. To reproduce or "represent" a phenomenon is somehow to produce or present it *again*. Whether one conceives of the process as *vorstellen*, representing visually or spatially, or *darstellen*, representing logically (Cassirer's consistent choice), the construct involves one phenomenon presenting some other phenomenon again in another form. Producing or constituting, on the other hand, means bringing a phenomenon into being ab initio. These are clearly ontologically distinct processes. In any given case, there can be only one "first" production; every other version of the phenomenon must necessarily be derivative and parasitic. Thus the creation is ontologically different from the re-creation. As a result, it cannot be coherent to argue that both occur simultaneously. So Cassirer's claim that the two processes are "inseparable" in language at least demands explanation, explanation that Cassirer did not provide.

The second fact that, like some of his forebears, Cassirer appeared to overlook is that when he decided to characterize this dynamic as a representational, symbolizing one, he thereby imported into his system crucial features of the very "copy theory" he was trying to overcome. Consider, for example, the argument Cassirer made for calling the process *symbolizing*. Signs and symbols he argued, "belong to two different universes of discourse: a signal is part of the physical world of being; a symbol is part of the human world of meaning." They differ in that a signal or sign "is related to the thing to which it refers in a fixed and unique way;" Pavlov's dogs were responding to signs. But "a genuine human symbol is characterized not by its uniformity but by its versatility. . . . For this variability and mobility there is apparently no parallel in the animal world."[42] So like Peirce (but unlike Saussure), Cassirer believed that the most important feature of a symbol is that it is arbitrary—"versatile," "variable," and "mobile." Importantly, Cassirer conceived of this variability or arbitrariness as characterizing *the kind of relationship that holds between symbol and symbolized*. So argumentative necessity led Cassirer, as it had led theorists before him, from the construct "symbol" to the feature "arbitrariness" and thence to the need to specify what was "arbitrarily" related to what. For Cassirer the answer was that the "sense" or meaning was related arbitrarily to the "sensuous." This move raised the question of exactly how the former was related to the latter, which is a version of the same question that stumped the theorists who tried to specify how a linguistic "copy" was related to its "original." But Cassirer apparently did not notice this problem. In any case, he certainly did not respond to it. Instead, he treated this basic assumption of his Philosophy of Symbolic Forms as relatively unproblematic. As Carl Hamburg summarized, "Here a definition of the symbol-concept is given by way of the two terms of the 'sensuous' on the one hand and the 'sense' (meaning) on the other, and a relation between the two, which is most frequently referred to as 'one representing the other'."[43] Hamburg emphasized the mediated or triadic nature of the relationship among symbol (*ein Sinnliches*), mind (*Geist*) and meaning (*Sinn*), noted Cassirer's debt, through Charles Morris, to C. S. Peirce; and then concluded that Cassirer's theory of the symbolically mediated character of reality, "far from standing in need of ingenious philosophical demonstrations, merely formulates, on a level of highest generality, a semiotic function which, in various modifications, is assumed as a matter of fact by all who, within the legitimate contexts of their respective branches of investigation, inquire into the nature of physical, artistic, religious, and perceptual 'objects.'[44] For Hamburg, in other words, Cassirer's program was obviously semiotic and just as obviously right. I agree with the former conclusion. Regarding the latter, I want to reiterate that, insofar as it was semiotic, it raised some of the same questions about what represents what as were raised by the "naive copy theories" it was designed to correct.

This same problem surfaced again as Cassirer contrasted art and science in *Essay on Man*. Like other symbolic forms, he argued, art is not "the reproduction of a ready-made, given reality . . . it is not an imitation but a discovery of reality." Moreover, he maintained, "we do not . . . discover nature through art in the same sense in which the scientist uses the term 'nature.' Language and science are the two main processes by which we ascertain and determine our concepts of the external world. We must classify our sense perceptions and bring them under general notions and general rules in order to give them objective meaning. . . . The work of art in like manner implies such an act of condensation and concentration" (p. 183). Here, language and science are "abbreviations of reality" whereas art is an "intensification of reality." But, as Hazard Adams points out, the problem is that this kind of talk suggested that both rely on the same "ready-made, given reality" that Cassirer had already rejected.[45] So at one point Cassirer appeared to reject two-worlds thinking, but immediately thereafter he appeared to embrace it.

Cassirer's outline of the purported stages of language development provided another example of the difficulties that were created by his commitment to features of the symbol model. He argued consistently that, because representativeness or the *Darstellungs-funktion* is the sine qua non of linguistic meaning, the relation of "word" to "thing" and the nature of the truth relation in general were fundamental problems of any philosophy of language. "The function of language," he wrote, "Is not to copy reality but to symbolize it."[46] Language develops this symbolizing function, he maintained, through three stages: the mimetic or copy stage, the analogical stage, and the symbolic stage. In the first stage no real distinction is made between verbal sign and the thing to which it refers; the word is the thing. Onomatopoeia is an example. In the second stage, he argued, the relation between word and thing is analogical; for example, differences between front and back vowels correlate—at least in some languages—with expressions of lesser and greater distance. The third developmental stage is symbolic, and its defining feature is that the relation between word and thing is arbitrary.[47] Cassirer attempted to support the first two parts of this analysis with examples from comparative linguistics. But his argument is hardly convincing, nor could it be, given the level of generality of his claim. Moreover, he was unwilling or unable to provide similarly empirical examples of the "variable" or "ambiguous" representational relationship that, he argued, marks the third, symbolic stage. Instead, he reverted to such broad brushstrokes as the following:

> even where language starts as purely imitative or "analogical" expression, it constantly strives to extend and finally to surpass its limits. It makes a virtue of necessity, that is, of the ambiguity inevitable in the linguistic sign. For this very ambiguity will not permit the sign to remain a mere individual sign; it compels the spirit to take the decisive step from the concrete function of "designation" to the universal and universally valid function of "signification." In this function language casts off, as it were, the sensuous covering in which it has hitherto appeared: mimetic or analogical expression gives way to purely symbolic expression which, precisely in and by virtue of its otherness, becomes the vehicle of a new and deeper spiritual content.[48]

This kind of vague speculation did nothing to support Cassirer's empirical claim about the three developmental stages. He was forced to offer this kind of elucidation, however, by the difficulty of specifying exactly what phenomena the *Darstellungsfunktion* connected in the symbolic stage, that is, what specifically constituted "symbol" and "symbolized." As this review has demonstrated, several of

Cassirer's intellectual forebears had broken their swords on this same problematic.

On the one hand, then, Cassirer frequently characterized language in terms reminiscent of the symbol model and the "copy theories" he resisted. In volume 1 of The Philosophy of *Symbolic Forms* he evidenced his commitment to two worlds when he identified one of his topics as "the intellectual symbols by means of which the specialized disciplines reflect on and describe reality" (p. 77). "We find indeed," he wrote later, "that, beside and above the world of perception, all these spheres produce freely their own *world of symbols* which is the true vehicle of their immanent development." (p. 87). "From the moment when [the hu]man first turns his [or her] attention to it," he subsequently argued, "the world of language assumes for him [or her] the same specificity and necessity, the same 'objectivity' as the world of things" (p. 107). Cassirer praised Plato's analysis in his *Seventh Letter* "because for the first time it fully recognized a basic principle essential to all language. All language as such is 'representation'; it represents a specific 'meaning' by a sensuous 'sign'" (p. 125). He began chapter 1 of volume 3 of *The Philosophy of Symbolic Forms* with the claim, "We find that all theoretical determination and all theoretical mastery of being required that thought, instead of turning directly to reality, must set up a system of signs and learn to make use of these signs as representatives of objects" (p. 45). He argued that animal cries are not meaningful as are human symbols because they are not "correlated as signs with definite things and happenings in the outside world" (p. 109). And in *Essay on Man*--and other writings—Cassirer cited accounts of how Helen Keller and Laura Bridgman learned language to demonstrate that *"everything has a name*—that the symbolic function is not restricted to particular cases but is a principle of *universal* applicability which encompasses the whole field of human thought" (p. 54).

On the other hand, many of Cassirer's comments about language specifically resisted the inclination to reduce it to a system of symbols. This was especially true virtually every time Cassirer referred to Wilhelm von Humboldt's work. In the Introduction to volume 1 of *The Philosophy of Symbolic Forms,* he credited Humboldt not only with the insight that language is *energeia* rather than *ergon* but also with the recognition that the fundamental language event is oral-aural, and hence that it combines what had historically been treated as the subjective and the objective (pp. 92–93, 174). He quoted with approval Humboldt's argument that "languages are not really means of representing the truth that has already been ascertained, but far more, means of discovering a truth not previously known."[49] A page later he affirmed the accuracy of Humboldt's claim that people "do not understand one another by relying on the signs for things, nor by causing one another to produce exactly the same concept, but by. . . striking the same key in each other's spiritual instrument."[50] In Volume 3 of *The Philosophy of Symbolic Forms*, he attributed to Humboldt the insight that language is more than an instrument or tool, because "by the same spiritual act through which [the hu]man spins language out of him[her]self he spins him[her]self into it: so that in the end [one] communicates and lives with intuitive objects in no other manner than that shown [one] by the medium of language."[51] And Cassirer repeated Humboldt's argument that "the spiritual meaning of speech can never be fully appreciated if we consider solely the objective factor in it—if we take it as a system of signs serving solely to represent objects and their relations" (pp. 50, 206–207).

In short, there was a tension in Cassirer's work created by his belief, on the one hand, that Humboldt was right about the world-constituting ("productive") function of language, and his determination, on the other, to analyze language as a representational, symbolic ("reproductive") system. Hazard Adams notices this tendency in both Cassirer's analyses of art and his accounts of science. "He teeters on the edge of a copy theory," Adams claims. Moreover, "Cassirer's rhetoric leads to a plea for a recognition of the necessity of a culture of interlocking forms, but his language threatens to give away the gains he has made and to revert to a theory of naïve representation."[52]

This fundamental ambivalence was, for the most part, missed by Harvard philosophy professor Susanne K. Langer who, in the 1940s and 1950s, attempted to develop a theory of art based on Cassirer's philosophy of symbolic forms. Although her larger project has been viewed by many as fundamentally flawed,[53] Langer strongly influenced the views of language propounded by at least three decades of communication theorists.[54] Langer eschewed Cassirer's commitment to an idealistic interpretation of reality while affirming the accuracy of his analysis of symbolic transformation. "The triumph of empiricism in science is jeopardized," she wrote, "by the surprising truth that *our sense-data are primarily symbols.* . . . [T]he edifice of human knowledge stands before us, not as a vast collection of sense reports, but as a structure of *facts that are symbols* and *laws that are their meanings.*"[55]

Langer emphasized more than did Cassirer the "profound difference" between symbols and signs. Signs "indicate" or "announce," she wrote, whereas symbols "represent" or "remind." Symbols "let us develop a characteristic attitude toward objects *in absentia*, which is called 'thinking of' or 'referring to' what is not here" (p. 37). Symbols are "not proxy for their objects, but are vehicles for the conception of objects. . . . and it is the conceptions, not the things, that symbols directly 'mean'" (p. 61). Instead of treating symbolizing as an inherent feature of human consciousness, Langer described it as a uniquely human "need," which is "the essential act of mind [taking in] more than what is commonly called thought" (p. 45). The brain, she argued is constantly "actively translating experiences into symbols, in fulfillment of a basic need to do so" (p. 46). She called this process "symbolic transformation" and argued that "speech is, in fact, the readiest active termination" of this basic process. But it is only one termination; symbolic transformation also manifests in ritual and art.

"The logical theory on which this whole study of symbols is based," wrote Langer," is essentially that which was set forth by Wittgenstein . . . in his *Tractatus Logico-Philosophicus:* 'One name stands for one thing, and another for another thing, and they are connected together. And so the whole, like a living picture, presents the atomic fact (4.0311)" (p. 75). It is therefore not surprising that she defined language as "primarily a vocal actualization of the tendency to see reality symbolically" (p. 99). After a lengthy discussion of evidence from feral children, she concluded that language "is essentially an organic, functioning *system*, of which the primary elements as well as the constructed products are symbols" (p. 120).

These quotations should suffice to demonstrate Langer's indebtedness to the symbol model. She explicitly affirmed her commitment to two worlds, atomism, representationalism, and systematicity. Her position on the instrumentality commitment is less clear. She conceived of symbolic transformation as natural and spontaneous, and hence, one could conclude, not completely governed by intent or instrumentality. But she also argued that symbolic transformation "makes elaborate communication with others possible" (p. 48); she insisted that "any item that is to have meaning must be *employed* as a sign or symbol" (p. 55); and she argued "that *language is the only means of articulating thought*" (p. 81). So at least part of the time, Langer appeared to treat language as a tool used to communicate thought.

Langer's analysis was used to support the claims of many mid-century communication theorists that, as two of them put it, "whenever we say anything orally acoustic symbols stimulate the audience, and stand for our ideas. . . . Words are symbols for meanings since they stand for ideas."[56]

Langer's work embodied one state-of-the-art expression of the symbol model in the mid-twentieth century. Although she relied heavily on Cassirer, she also credited not only Aristotle, Bacon, and Locke but also Peirce, Wittgenstein, Carnap, and Russell. Like several of these authors, she attempted to develop a grand theory and to anchor it in an analysis of the nature of language that was thoroughly imbued by the symbol model.

As I noted in Chapter 2, communication theorists and other language scholars continue to develop and attempt to apply semiotic conceptions of the nature of language. Although, as the next two chapters will demonstrate, arguments for a post-semiotic view of language continue to emerge in both theoretical and empirical works, the symbol model, too, is still alive and well. I will review three more prominent instances of its influence in Part II, as I apply the analysis laid out in Chapter 4 to the works of V. N. Volosinov, Kenneth Burke, and Calvin O. Schrag.

It should be apparent at this point, however, that the symbol model is one clearly identifiable thread running through the history of Western thought about language, from the earliest attempts to analyze and preserve aspects of communicative experience to the most recent claims about the "obvious," "manifest," and "unquestionable" fact that, whatever else it may be, language is a semiotic system.

❀ Chapter 4

Language as Constitutive Articulate Contact

My argument has been that symbolic and other semiotic accounts of the nature of language embody five interrelated theoretical commitments. The first is that there is an ontological distinction between two realms or worlds, typically the linguistic and the nonlinguistic, and that language establishes a relationship between them. Some theorists attempt to obviate problems created by this claim by arguing that signifier and signified are indivisible, or that they have the same ontological status. But by the time their account of language is complete, in all cases examined here, some version of the two worlds distinction has resurfaced. The second commitment is to the belief that a thorough and coherent account of the nature of language can and should break it down into units—typically words, phonemes, morphemes, or sentences—and the third is that the relationship that exists between the units of World 1 and units of World 2 is representational. This representational commitment is what ultimately keeps a wedge driven between the two worlds of commitment 1, because one entity of a given ontological status cannot coherently be said to "represent" another entity of the *same* ontological status. Thus the two worlds, atomism, and representational commitments are tightly linked. Symbol model accounts also typically embody commitments to the claims that the units of language

103

and the rules that prescribe their use make up a coherent system and that humans use this system instrumentally to accomplish their purposes and goals.

As the previous two chapters demonstrated, classical accounts of the symbol model first appeared in the West in Greek and Roman treatises. These were elaborated during the Middle Ages and culminated in the seventeenth and eighteenth centuries in works by John Locke and his followers. Locke has served as a convenient foil for a number of nineteenth- and twentieth-century accounts that attempt to repair some of the most obvious problems inherent in this account of language. But some influential contemporary descriptions of language still embody all five commitments of the symbol model, and at least one 1976 essay even argues that Locke's theory was far from "simple minded" and should serve as a guide to current thinking.[1] The presence of this kind of essay, along with the arguments by linguist Julia Kristeva, semiotician Umberto Eco, sociologist Norbert Elias, and communication theorist Michael Motley, which were reviewed in Chapter 1, demonstrate that the symbol model is alive and well today.

But, as Chapter 1 also demonstrated, this model fails a crucial test: It breaks down when it is applied to even a simple example of the primary phenomenon it purports to describe. Most theorists concur that the paradigmatic instance of language is conversation, verbal-nonverbal exchange between humans in real time. Audio and video taping enable this phenomenon to be captured and reduced, more or less completely, to a print or electronic text which can be analyzed. Efforts to apply the symbol model to such texts founder, because it becomes almost immediately apparent that (a) living language cannot simply or clearly be divided into signifying units that stand in some representational relationship with their alleged signifieds, (b) living language is not reducible without remainder to a system made up of atoms or molecules and rules for their combination, and (c) humans do not live in a subject-object, instrumental relationship with the tongue they routinely speak.

These and other problems have led a number of contemporary philosophers to question the efficacy of the symbol model. Martin Heidegger argued, for example, that although "the entire structure of sign relations . . . has remained the standard for all later considerations of language, . . . the essential being of language is Saying as Showing" and that "its showing character is n*ot based on signs of any kind*"(italics added)."[2] Hans-Georg Gadamer agrees when he criticizes the semiotic "*concept of language* that modern linguistics and philosophy of language take as their starting point," because it inadequately captures "the language that lives in speech."[3] Gadamer emphasizes that from his perspective, language "is no longer a system of symbols or a set of rules of grammar and syntax"[4] and that "as long as [language] is even conceived as a symbolic form, it is not yet recognized in all its true dimensions."[5] Working from a significantly different tradition, Soviet language philosopher and literary theorist Mikhail Bakhtin affirmed similarly that "the utterance (speech product) as a whole enters into an entirely new sphere of speech communication . . . which does not admit of description or definition in the terms and methods of linguistics or—more broadly—semiotics," especially because "semiotics deals primarily with the transmission of ready-made communication using a ready-made code. But in live speech, strictly speaking, communication is first created in the process of transmission, and there is, in essence, *no code*" (italics added).[6]

In other words, at least three prominent contemporary philosophers working from at least two distinct traditions call for a post-semiotic account of the nature of language, an account that minimally would efface the traditional distinction between language and communication and seriously question the concept of language-as-code. But these philosophers do not develop an alternative that is responsive to the aporias created by the symbol model. For the most part, their works are more critical than constructive and their discussions of alternative accounts of the nature of language are generally sketchy. The purpose of this chapter is to begin to formulate such an alternative, and in the remaining chapters I elaborate it, first by discussing its connections with some related theorizing and then by testing it in application.

The Human World

The tendency of semiotic accounts of language to distinguish, for the most part implicitly, between two worlds alters the historical sense of the term *world* as the *single* coherent sphere that humans inhabit. Historically, humanity's general and primary sense of *world* appears to have developed out of the varieties of the cosmological myth that arose in Babylonian, Egyptian, Chinese, and Andean civilizations.[7] For example, as John Angus Campbell observes: "For the ancient Egyptian or Sumerian, the astrophysical universe was patterned on the analogy of human society, and human society was patterned on the analogy of the astrophysical universe. Reality was a community of beings in which similarity prevailed over difference. The resulting world picture was hierarchical, consubstantial, cyclical, and compact.[8] Campbell argues that the Hebrew and then the Greek historical epochs were marked by significant substantive changes in "world pictures," that is, in the hierarchical, consubstantial, cyclical, and compact similarity features that framed the understanding or sense making of members of these cultures.

In Greece, philosophy began, as Aristotle noted, with "wonder" at the world being as it is. Such wondering led to the Greek concept of *cosmos*, which labeled the state into which human habitation changed the primordial chaos. When human involvement transformed chaos into cosmos, the result was a more or less ordered whole, a condition of coherence and a degree of harmony, accompanied by a further sense of wonder at the human's inhabiting it. This whole was labeled *world,* and the term came to mean the *coherent sphere that humans inhabit.*

In the early twentieth century, the most influential account of this construct was Edmund Husserl's description of the *Lebenswelt* or *life-world,* a "universe of what is indubitable in principle."[9] Husserl emphasized that, because humans inhabit it, the life-world can never be completely objectified, and he maintained that the coherence of this indubitable universe is accepted and responded to, rather than being constructed or otherwise achieved: "Pregiven nature—the domain of the life-world—corporeal nature [is that] which is familiar to the ordinary [hu]man in everyday life and which he [or she] can get to know 'in more detail' but which he [or she] simply has no reason to single out and consider in a coherent way in its abstract unitary character, as natural science proposes to do."[10]

Alfred Schutz and Jean-Paul Sartre elaborated their own versions of this Husserlian "world," but Martin Buber and Hans-Georg Gadamer developed accounts most apposite to my emphasis here. Both of the latter philosophers exploited the distinction made in German between the nonhuman's *Umwelt*—environment or surround— and the human's *Welt* or world. Buber held that, "An animal . . . perceives only the things which concern it in the total situation available to it, and it is those things which make its *Umwelt*. . . . [But] It is only [the hu]man who replaces this unsteady conglomeration . . . by a unity which can be imagined or thought by him [or her] as existing for itself. . . . With [t]his human life, a world *[Welt]* exists."[11] Buber also underscored that humans do not exist in a subject-object relationship with their world: the human *inhabits* this coherent sphere. "An animal in the realm of its perceptions is like a fruit in its skin; [the hu]man is, or can be, in the world as a dweller in an enormous building which is always being added to, and to whose limits he [or she] can never penetrate, but which he [or she] can nevertheless know as one does know a house in which one lives—for [one] is capable of grasping the wholeness of the building as such."[12]

Gadamer concurs with Buber that the human, "unlike all other living creatures, has a 'world,'" for other creatures are simply embedded in their environment and do not have a relationship to it. He also concurs that the human has an "orientation toward" this realm that enables one "to keep oneself so free from what one encounters . . . that one can present it to oneself as it is."[13] But both also argue that the human is not in a subject-object relationship with his or her world. Rather, the human's world frames or contextualizes his or her understanding, and although it is "oriented toward" or "grasped" as a coherent whole, one's world cannot be reduced without remainder to an object of consciousness.

This general sense of the construct "world" has also been employed by scholars outside the ambit of philosophy. For example, John Shotter is one contemporary social psychologist who describes human understanding or sense making in "worldly" terms. Shotter begins by arguing that "we owe our being as we understand it" to "the world of our everyday social life," a world "consisting not only of socially constructed institutions, continually reproduced (and transformed) by the accountable activities occurring within them, but also of a larger social process out of which such institutions arise."[14] Shotter explicitly links understanding and world when he argues that people do not typically explain their actions by reference to their ideas, knowledge, or "to anything in their heads," but by reference to the contents of their *worlds*, and that "these are the terms in which the people themselves would account for their actions if pressed to justify them."[15] This is another expression of the point that one *inhabits* a world that *frames* understanding.

In short, Buber, Gadamer, Shotter, and others clarify that part of what it means to be a human is to dwell in a more-or-less coherent sphere describable as a "world." To say this sphere is "coherent" is just to say that it is understood or understandable, that it hangs together in a relatively unified complex into which all the parts more or less completely fit. Even claims that the human world is chaotic, incoherent, or "ineffable" characterize it as to some degree describable and hence understandable. Thus this sphere frames or contextualizes all human understanding or sense making. Everything experienced as meaningful is experienced as part of this world. Importantly, humans do not construct this world individually; we experience much of it as a given, an ordinarily taken-for-granted sphere into which we are born and acculturated and that we inhabit.

Although some questions are being raised in research with primates and dolphins, most theorists currently believe that humans are the only beings whose existence could be said to be "worldly" in this sense. Other animals exist in an "environment" or "surround" that lacks the sense of wholeness and coherence that routinely characterizes the human world.

This description of human understanding as worldly can be viewed as little more than an elaborated paraphrase of Heidegger's claim that understanding is Dasein's way of being.[16] Gadamer explained his mentor's insight: "*Understanding* is not a resigned ideal of human experience . . . nor . . . a last methodological ideal of philosophy in contrast to the naiveté of unreflective life; it is, on the contrary, the *original form of the realization of Dasein*, which is being-in-the-world. . . . Understanding is Dasein's mode of being.[17] In other words, humans are characteristically understanders, beings whose way-of-being is to understand, to construct sense, significance, meaning, and coherence. And humans accomplish this understanding situated in a *world*.

Because *world,* thus understood, is the sphere that humans inhabit, *there can be nothing outside of it.* The human world consists of everything that affects us and everything we affect. Humans cannot depart from their "worlds" or even project themselves into ontological outer space. All human activity and experience is historical (to employ a temporal frame), situated (to employ a spatial frame), thematic (to employ a topical frame), and relational (to employ a cultural, social, interpersonal frame), and the resulting multidimensional sphere is our "world." *Thus there cannot be two worlds.* "World" is the Ur-structure, the irreducibly primary site of human being.[18]

Language and World

This understanding of the construct "world" significantly alters the relationship between language and world that is prominent in the symbol model. As I have already noted, semiotic perspectives postulate that persons (subjects) use units of language to signify, symbolize, or somehow represent aspects of the (objective) world. But almost seventy years ago, Heidegger demonstrated how this kind of subject-object analysis of humans begins one giant step too far into the problematic, because it overlooks a more primordial kind of human understanding. As Herbert Dreyfus explains, "Since Descartes, philosophers have been stuck with the *epistemological* problem of explaining how the ideas in our mind can be true of the external world. Heidegger shows that this subject/object epistemology *presupposes a background of everyday practices into which we are socialized but that we do not represent in our minds* [italics added]. Since he calls this more fundamental way of making sense of things our understanding of being, he claims that he is doing *ontology*, that is, asking about the nature of this understanding of being that we do not *know*—that is not a representation in the mind corresponding to the world—but that we simply *are*."[19]

In other words, Heidegger noticed something that humans "are" and "do" prior to operating as subjects on objects. He observed that we are immersed in what might be called *everyday coping*: For the most part "without thinking," we make our way about, grooming and eating, operating vehicles and other machinery, avoiding or connecting with people around us, engaging in personal and professional transactions. These are all examples of our being-in-the-world. As a result of acculturation and upbringing, we more or less successfully, and yet in large part "mindlessly," *accomplish* this everyday coping. Sometimes, as Dreyfus notes, we "experience ourselves as conscious subjects relating to objects by way of intentional states such as desires, beliefs, perceptions, intentions, etc., but [Heidegger] thinks of this as a derivative and intermittent condition that presupposes a more fundamental way of being-in-the-world that cannot be understood in subject/object terms."[20]

Heidegger himself explains the distinction between derivative and intermittent conditions such as "knowing" and the more primary being-in-the-world in these words: "Knowing is now not a comportment that would be added to an entity which does not yet "have" a world, which is free from any relation to its world [i.e., a Cartesian cogito]. Rather, knowing is always a mode of being of Dasein on the basis of its already being involved with the world. The basic defect of epistemology is just that it fails to regard what it means by knowing in its *original* [italics added] phenomenal datum as a way of being of Dasein, as a way of its in-being, and to take from this basic consideration all the questions which now begin to arise on this ground."[21]

So from Heidegger's perspective, the person is not first and foremost a *cogito* employing reason to connect and disconnect with objects around it, but is first and foremost a situated interpreter, understander, or sense maker engaged in everyday coping.

But this understander does not cope alone; Dasein is thoroughly relational not individual, social not psychological. As Heidegger put it, "As being-in-the-world, Dasein is at the same time being with one another—more rigorously, 'being-with.'"[22] He emphasized that this human quality of being-in-the-social-world is irreducible. It is not that humans first "are" and then "behave in relation to" or "respond to" the people and things around them. Instead, as Heidegger explained: "The phenomenological statement, 'Dasein as being-in-the-world is a being-with with others,' has an existential-ontological sense and does not intend to establish that I in fact do not turn out to be alone and still other entities of my kind are on hand. If this were the intention of the stipulation, then I would be speaking of my Dasein as if it were an environmental thing on hand. . . . Being-with signifies a character of being of Dasein as such which is co-original with being-in-the-world. . . . This character of being-with defines the Dasein even when another Dasein is in fact not being addressed and cannot be perceived as on hand. Even Dasein's being-alone is only a deficiency of being-with."[23]

The specific relationship between language and world becomes evident when one recognizes that *the paradigmatic site of everyday coping is language.* This is the primary point of Heidegger's often-quoted claim that "Language is the house of Being. In its home [the hu]man dwells. Those who think and those who create with words are the guardians of this home. Their guardianship accomplishes the manifestation of Being insofar as they bring the manifestation to language and maintain it in language through their speech."[24]

But as his mention of "speech" suggests, Heidegger does not mean by *language* the *system* that the symbol model highlights. Richard Rorty agrees with Heidegger that approaches that reduce language to the status of a system reify the living process.[25] They need to be replaced with the recognition that, as philosopher Donald Davidson puts it, "there is no such thing as a language, not if a language is anything like what philosophers . . . have supposed. . . . *We must give up the idea of a clearly defined shared structure which language users master and then apply to cases*" (italics added).[26] Rorty shows how Heidegger and the Wittgenstein of the *Philosophical Investigations* basically agree on this point. When Heidegger claims that "language" is the paradigmatic site of everyday coping and self-interpretation, he means that Dasein accomplishes these projects in events of speech communicating. In Heidegger's words, "Discourse as a mode of being of Dasein qua being-with is essentially *communication.*" Moreover, as understood in this formulation, communication is emphatically "not a matter of transporting information and experiences from the interior of one subject to the interior of the other one. It is rather a matter of being-with-one-another becoming manifest in the world, specifically by way of the discovered world, which itself becomes manifest in speaking with one another."[27]

As I observed earlier, Bakhtin affirmed a closely related view of the irreducibly speech-communicative nature of language that has been sketched by Wittgenstein, Heidegger, Davidson, and Rorty. Bakhtin insisted that any philosophy of language must begin from the recognition that its subject matter is not an abstract system, because "language is realized in the form of individual concrete utterances (oral and written) by participants in the various areas of human activity."[28] When language is acknowledged to be this kind of phenomenon, Bakhtin argued, it becomes clear why it cannot be reduced to a system of signs or symbols, and thus cannot be described or defined using the terms and methods of linguistics or semiotics. Bakhtin described the connections between one's world and concrete events of verbal-nonverbal speech communicating especially poignantly when he wrote: "Everything that pertains to me [i.e., my world] enters my consciousness, beginning with my name . . . through the mouths of others (my mother, and so forth), with their *intonation*, in their emotional and value-assigning *tonality* [italics added]. I realize myself initially through others; from them I receive words, forms, and tonalities for the formation of my initial idea of myself. . . . Just as the body is formed initially in the mother's womb (body), a person's consciousness awakens wrapped in another's consciousness."[29]

Thus these authors describe how human worlds are collaboratively constructed (modified, developed, razed, reconstructed) in speech communicating. This is not to say that interlocutors usually or even typically *agree* or *concur* in their world constructing. Conflict is obviously pervasive and significant. But it takes two (or more) to disagree, and thus conflict, too, is necessarily relational, mutual, and in this sense collaborative. Even humans working at cross purposes—Arabs and Israelis, blacks and Afrikaaners, liberals and conservatives, Democrats and Republicans, plaintiffs and defendants—are collaborating. Humans naturally and characteristically accomplish everyday coping in collaborative speech communicating. In an effort to remove any vestiges of a subject-object orientation, this dynamic might be termed *worlding,* a process that *happens in address-and-response, in speaking-and-listening, that is, in verbal-nonverbal talk.* The locution *worlding in talk* is admittedly awkward, but it does point toward the ontological, relational, mundane, and speech communicative characteristics of these events.

The view of the relationship between person and world sketched by these thinkers is especially well-articulated in Gadamer's works. The thoroughly post-semiotic quality of Gadamer's perspective was noted as early as 1969 when Richard Palmer wrote, "Fundamental to Gadamer's conception of language is the rejection of the 'sign' theory of the nature of language."[30] Gadamer's writings verify Palmer's observation. From Gadamer's perspective, semiotic, subject-object analyses of language are inherently distorted, because "Language is not just one of [the hu]man's possessions in the world; rather, on it depends the fact that [the hu]man has a *world* at all." Humans are the only creatures for whom "the world as world exists," and this world depends on language.[31] Gadamer explains the connection between everyday coping or worlding and dialogue or conversation as follows:[32] "language has its true being only in dialogue, in *coming to an understanding*. This is not to be understood as if that were the purpose of language. Coming to an understanding is not a mere action, a purposeful activity, a setting up of signs through which I transmit my will to others. Coming to an understanding as such, rather, does not need any tools, in the proper sense of the word. *It is a life process in which a community of life is lived out* [italics added]. . . . for language is by nature the language of conversation; it fully realizes itself only in the process of coming to an understanding.[33]

In short, to be human is to engage in the life processes of coming to an understanding (everyday coping), processes that paradigmatically occur in conversation and are also carried out in reading and writing. Even when engaged in intractable conflict, humans are collaboratively constructing or negotiating their worlds in verbal-nonverbal address-and-response.

There is a clear distinction between this account of the relationship between language and world and the account present in the symbol model. This view emphasizes that understanding is a mode of being manifested in concrete events of conversing and that ultimately these *events* are what the term *language* labels. Thus the traditional distinction between language and communication is materially altered, or even effaced. No longer is the former simply an instrument used to accomplish the latter. In other words, language is no longer understood simply to be an abstract system of semiotic units instrumentally employed by humans pursuing the goal of communicating. Instead, it is acknowledged that humans engage in understanding ("worlding") linguistically, and that this verbal-and-nonverbal languag*ing* is synonymous with the complex process that some philosophers and many theorists call *human com-*

munication or *communicating.*[34] As a result, efforts to analyze syntactic or semantic aspects of what has been viewed as the "system" of language need to be broadened to acknolwedge both the indivisible interrelationships between the verbal and the nonverbal and the inherently relational nature of events of articulate contact.

Clearly this view of the relationship between language and world is incommensurable with the claim that language functions by connecting individual phonetic, morphemic, syntactic, or semantic units with the thoughts, things, ideas, or meanings they represent. Why incommensurable? Could not a pluralist or eclectic theorist embrace aspects of both this view and the symbol model? Especially if one is working from a generally postmodern, and hence polysemic perspective, what is problematic about the claim, for example, that "partially constituted" humans periodically make instrumental use of language?

The problem is that this rejoinder embodies a equivocal sense of *language* that is ultimately fatal for coherence. From the perspective being developed in this chapter, language (read "events of languaging") is (are) *constitutive*, which, as P. Christopher Smith puts it, means that "What is, is there first *in* an ever spreading, ever self-transforming speaking of it."[35] In this view, features of human worlds do not first exist and then get spoken or written of; they *come into being in talk*. Of course, no individual initiates this process; each of us is born into a family that, in the context of its culture and speech community, bequeaths us a world that, as we mature, we more- or less-substantively alter. Thus human worlds are not constituted *de novo*, but from what we inherit.

It is centrally important to recognize, however, that *the same phenomenon cannot be both constitutive and representational or instrumental.* Language cannot be coherently treated as simultaneously a world-constituting, characteristically human *way of being*, and as a *system* that is instrumentally employed by *already*-constituted humans to represent aspects of their worlds and accomplish other goals.

The constitutive and representational-instrumental views are incommensurable, in other words, because the former treats languaging as a primary human event and the latter treats it as a secondary or derived undertaking. Insofar as languaging is a way of being, humanity gets accomplished in or by way of this process or complex of events. Human worlds get, as it were, verbally and nonverbally spoken and listened into being. But the claim that language instrumentally represents, assumes the *prior* existence of humans who are already-constituted and capable of intending and representing. It also presupposes the existence of worlds which are objectively given and thus capable of being intended and represented. Thus, one may argue either that humans come-into-being linguistically, or that they are already "in being" and then subsequently "use" language. But both claims cannot be part of one coherent view of the nature of language. Humboldt recognized this fact nearly a century ago when he distinguished between treating language as *ergon* and treating it as *energia*. Heidegger and especially Gadamer extended Humboldt's analysis while avoiding most of his rationalistic and romantic inclinations; theirs is a philosophy not of language as a structure or system but of "languaging": understanding in events of speech communicating.

Thus if one views language as a constitutive mode of being, then it must continue to be this kind of phenomenon at those moments when humans are allegedly "making instrumental use of it." When one says, for example, "Please hand me that book," it certainly appears that one is simply *using* individual words to "make a request" and "refer to an object." For the scholar or student interested in the nature of language, it would seem to follow that the phenomenon under scrutinty could indeed be said to be a *representational system*. But when one is interrogating *the nature of language*, what seems plausible in this case turns out to be indefensible. One primary reason is that, "Please hand me that book" is, as Bakhtin emphasized, a *response* to elements of the discourse that frames it, and its discursive antecedents and consequents make up some small part of a world-constituting conversation or dialogue. The thinker interested in how the nature of language is evident in these discursive events cannot coherently argue that, at the moment of this single utterance, language is systematic and representational, and at some other moment in the dialogue, it is constitutive. The claims are incommensurable, because *one cannot make instrumental use of the constitutive mode of one's being-in-the-world.* Such an undertaking would involve a process analogous to lifting oneself by one's bootstraps. It would require one to treat in a subject-object way that which one *inhabits.* It would require language to be at the same time both constitutive and representational, and this is an equivocation fatal for coherence.

Therefore, it is clear why Gadamer concludes that, "if we stick to what takes place in speech," we recognize that "it is obvious that an instrumentalist theory of signs which sees words and concepts as handy tools has missed the point of the hermeneutical phenomenon."[36] As he explains this is one of the primary inadequacies of "the *concept of language* that modern linguistics and philosophy of language take as their starting point." And, he argues, this is also the specific problem with Cassirer's account of language as "symbolic form."[37] Accounts such as Cassirer's fundamentally misconstrue the relationship humans have to their language. As Gadamer elaborates, "Language is by no means simply an instrument, a tool. For it is in the nature of the tool that we master its use, which is to say we take it in hand and lay it aside when it has done its service. That is not the same as when we take the words of a language, lying ready in the mouth, and with their use let them sink back into the general store of words over which we dispose. Such an analogy is false because we never find ourselves as consciousness over against the world and, as it wore [sic], grasp after a tool of understanding in a wordless condition. Rather, in all our knowledge of ourselves and in all knowledge of the world, we are always already encompassed by the language that is our own."[38]

In other words, one cannot be in a subject-object relationship with the very feature that characterizes one as human.

Language as Constitutive

I titled this alternative to the symbol model "Constitutive Articulate Contact." My rationale for the first term, *constitutive*, emerges from the connections just outlined between and among world, understanding, language, and human being. First, to constitute is to produce rather than to reproduce or represent; to compose, form, or establish. As I noted, language as speech communication functions constitutively, not de novo, but in the context of what is inherited. Thus, languaging is the way humans "do" understanding and, in the process collaboratively "build," "remake," or "modify" worlds.[39] To be a human is to be an understander, which is to engage in processes of coherence building or sense making, processes that occur communicatively and that enable humans to constitute, maintain, and develop the worlds we inhabit.

No human understanding occurs outside this dynamic; this is the implication of Gadamer's claim that *"Being that can be understood is language."*[40] On the one hand, this formulation simply restates the argument that has already been made about the relationship between language and world: "that which comes into language is not something that is pregiven before language; rather, the word gives it its own determinateness."[41] In other words, language, as Rorty or Davidson might put it, does not mirror reality; it constitutes it.

On the other hand, Gadamer's insight also underscores the fact that linguisticality pervades the human world, that *all* human understanding is linguistic or speech communicative. This is a more consequential position to embrace. How can it be said that the entire rainbow of human emotions, for example, or the overwhelming presence of some works of art or dance are *linguistic*? Do these phenomena not transcend the boundaries of language? Certainly emotions and aesthetic experiences often cannot be described in words. So what could it mean to say that they are "linguistic"? What kind of new nominalism is being proposed here?

Gadamer responds to this line of questioning by distinguishing between human *meaning* and its sedimentation in language *systems*.[42] The human world, he reminds his reader, is a world not of things but of *meaning*. One's neighborhood, for example, is what it is (means what it means) not because of its number of persons per block but because of one's comfort or discomfort, preference or resistance, enjoyment or distress with its population density and other features. One's occupation is what it is (means what it means) not because of the number of hours worked, pay scale, number of days vacation, or ethnicity of one's superior or subordinate, but because of one's satisfaction or dissatisfaction, pride or disappointment, security or insecurity with hours worked, dollars earned, and so forth. The same can be said about all dimensions of our lives, from our relationships with our parents and children, to what it means for us to wear a certain pair of shoes. Humans live in a world of meaning.

The sense or meaning we make of things grows, in turn, out of our cultural, social, and interpersonal experiences—the values into which we are socialized as infants and children, the preferences we develop as we mature, the criteria we learn to apply. These cultural, social, and interpersonal experiences are what constitute linguisticality, because, in Gadamer's words, "language has its true being only in dialogue, in *coming to an understanding*."[43] In short, (a) our fundamental work as humans is the work of understanding, (b) this work is accomplished in concert with others, that is, communicatively, and (c) this communicative coming to understanding is, as noted earlier, what is meant by *language*. Thus, although one may not be able satisfactorily to label an emotion or to capture an aesthetic experience in a sentence or paragraph, linguisticality nonetheless pervades these experiences of meaning. The fact that one isolates a given state of being as "an emotion," an object as "a work of art," and a response to it as "overwhelming" or "ineffable" all reflect cultural categories and criteria of understandability that one has learned communicatively. Thus, these features of one's "wordless" experience are *linguistic.* The sense, "I can't put this into words" is a *linguistic* sense, and the conviction that one's inability constitutes a "failure"—or perhaps a "success"—is also accomplished or negotiated linguistically. Similarly, one can only determine that his or her available vocabulary choices are insufficient descriptors by applying criteria one has learned communicatively, so this feature of "nonverbal" experience is also linguistic. And this account could be extended: One's basic categories of sense making develop in communicative life, and this is what it means to say that they are linguistic. This is why, as Gadamer puts it, "Language always forestalls any objection to its jurisdiction. Its universality keeps pace with the universality of reason," and "there is no point of view outside the experience of the world in language from which it could become an object."[44]

Importantly, however, this account of the universality of linguisticality is neither nominalist nor relativist. For one thing, the human's world is not relative in the sense that there is some absolute "world in itself" against which it could be compared so that, in Gadamer's words, "the right view from some possible position outside the human, linguistic world could discover it in its being-in-itself."[45] Mundane understanding acknowledges that mountains, trees, walls, and furniture are not simply "made of language." Every view of "world" includes the affirmation of facticity or existence separate from the viewer. But it is important to remember that each world view includes this *as an acknowledgment or affirmation,* as an element of the world being affirmed. Facticity is a common feature of all worldviews save that of the solipsist, but it is not itself a "fact" separate from any view of the world. Whatever truth the affirmation of facticity enjoys is due to coherence and consensus not correspondence. No Archimedean observation post is available to render "relative" all worldviews that are allegedly dependent on other, less secure vantage points.

Equally important, this account is not relativist, because humans do not have free rein to constitute whatever world they prefer. As I have already noted, the reason is that, just as we do not have a subject-object relationship with language, we also do not live in such a relationship with our world. We are subject-to it as much as we intentionally construct it, or, in Gadamer's words, *"That language and world are related in a fundamental way does not mean, then, that world becomes the object of language."*[46] To say we inherit and inhabit the world is to say in part that we are constrained by it to at least as great a degree as we constrain it. The "it" that constrains us and which we constrain, however, is *world* not "reality" or "brute data,"[47] and this is to say that "it" is linguistic in the sense already explained (that is, it is achieved communicatively).

Heidegger used the phrase *undergoing an experience* to describe this dynamic. "When we talk of 'undergoing' an experience," he wrote, "we mean specifically that the experience is not of our own making; to undergo here means that we endure it, suffer it, receive it as it strikes us and submit to it. It is this something itself that comes to pass, happens."[48] Gadamer makes this same point when he argues that the concept of "play" is a clue to an ontological explanation of the process of understanding. He begins with the process of understanding a work of art and contends that a subject-object account of this process is unsatisfactory, because the view that an "aesthetic consciousness" confronts an art object "does not do justice to the real situation." Rather, understanding is an event of play, and "the mode of being of play does not allow the player to behave toward play as if toward an object." One reason is that "players are not the subjects of play, instead play merely reaches presentation (*Darstellung*) through the players."[49] When one is fully engaged in play, one is caught up into a dynamic over which one does not have full control; agency (individual determination) is at least balanced by—if not subordinate to—what happens *to* one. "This suggests a general characteristic of the nature of play that is reflected in playing: all playing is a being-played."[50] Obviously, however, that which "plays" the baseball player is not the "brute fact" or "objective, non-human reality" of the game, but baseball as a collaborative human accomplishment.

Gadamer fleshes out this sense of being played when he contrasts two German terms for "experience," *Erlebnis* and *Erfahrung.* The former labels an experience one "has" of something. This notion, he claims, dominated classical and romantic aesthetic theory and led to the treatment of aesthetic experience as a grasping of "the infinite whole."[51] *Erfahrung,* on the other hand, is the term for experience as something one undergoes or is subject to. This kind of experience cannot be repeated or replicated, because we cannot reconstruct all the conditions surrounding an event we do not control. It follows that this kind of experience "is experience of human finitude." The person with this experience knows that he or she is "master neither of time nor the future. . . . Real experience is that whereby [the hu]man becomes aware of his[/her] finiteness."[52]

Conversation is one common event which is characterized by this dynamic of play or *Erfahrung.* In Gadamer's words: "We say that we 'conduct' a conversation, but the more genuine a conversation is, the less its conduct lies within the will of either partner. . . .

Rather, it is generally more correct to say that we fall into conversation, or even that we become involved in it. . . . Understanding or its failure is like an event that happens to us."[53]

In a parallel way, the dynamic of worlding is constrained—and sometimes even determined—by the forces of culture, tradition and context. Worlding in talk is not an entirely relative or context dependent event, because cultural, ethnic, and family history help to define available meaning options, and individual experience helps frame interpretation. Thus there is a continuing tension between the repeated and the unrepeatable, between law and surprise. But this dynamic is nonetheless constitutive. Understanding is the human's way of being, and language is our way of understanding. By engaging both proactively and responsively in the play of language events, humans participate in the constituting of the coherent spheres we inhabit. And the paradigm of this dynamic is conversation.

Language as Paradigmatically Articulate Contact

The *articulate contact* part of the label for the alternative view of the nature of language I am proposing highlights two central features of the constitutive linguistic events I have just described. First, they are events of contact, which is to say that they are dialogic not monologic, communicative not psychological, social not individual. I noted earlier the centrality of this feature in Heidegger's thinking. It is also focal in Gadamer's observations that dialogue is "the original phenomenon of language,"[54] that "language has its true being only in dialogue,"[55] and even more simply, that "Language, for me, is always simply that which we speak with others and to others."[56] Of course, Gadamer's primary interest as a hermeneutician is in the contact between interpreter and *text,* but because he recognizes that "the hermeneutical problem is basically the same for oral and written discourse,"[57] his account of the fundamentally dialogic nature of language is apposite here.

Gadamer emphasizes that when one focuses on dialogue, one leaves behind "any starting point in the subjectivity of the subject, and especially in the meaning-directed intentions of the speaker."[58] Interpersonal speech communicating does not merely produce a "reification of intended meaning"; rather, one becomes involved in a process of collaborative construction. One's prejudices are put at risk, in part by the mere presence of the other. One enters what Gadamer terms *the midworld (Zwischenwelt) of language*, the event of collaborative coherence construction or understanding that results in the text being a *Zwischenprodukt*.[59] This dynamically collaborative dimension of language and of the text, writes Gadamer, is inaccessible to the methodology of the linguist, who wants to "shed light upon the functioning of language as such," but who does not "enter into the discussion of the topic that is spoken of in the text."[60] However every case of understanding "remains dependent upon communicative conditions that, as such, reach beyond the merely codified meaning-content of what is said."[61] In short, it is clear from several of his texts that Gadamer clearly recognizes the significance of the fact that human language occurs *between* understanders, in their contact.

Discussions of the nature of language produced by members of the Bakhtin circle focus on this same definitive feature of contact. As I also noted earlier, a central claim Bakhtin and his followers made is that language is *irreducibly responsive*, that every instance of language, each linguistic phenomenon, somehow *responds* to the language that frames it. In Volosinov's words, "Any utterance—the finished, written utterance not excepted—makes response to something and is calculated to be responded to in turn."[62] Word, he wrote, "is precisely *the product of the reciprocal relationship between speaker and listener, addresser and addressee*" (p. 86). Because of this defining feature, he insisted, *"the actual reality of language-speech is not the abstract system of linguistic forms, not the isolated monologic utterance, and not the psychophysiological act of its implementation, but the social event of verbal interaction implemented in an utterance or utterances.* Thus, verbal interaction is the basic reality of language" (p. 94). On the grounds of this claim, Volosinov labeled *fundamentally erroneous* the theory of understanding "that underlies . . . the whole of European semasiology" because "its entire position on word meaning . . . excludes active response in advance and on principle" (p. 73).

Bakhtin also highlighted the importance of responsiveness in his work. Because "the speaker is not Adam," he wrote, his or her language inevitably meets those of the conversation partners or other familiar viewpoints, world views, or opinions. The basic unit of language is the utterance, and "an essential (constitutive) marker of the utterance is its quality of being directed to someone, its *addressivity*."[63] This means that "each utterance is filled with echoes and reverberations of other utterances to which it is related by the communality of the sphere of speech communication. . . . Each utterance refutes, affirms, supplements, and relies on the others, presupposes them to be known, and somehow takes them into account" (p. 91). The "true essence" of "the event of the life of the text,"

Bakhtin concluded "always develops *on the boundary between two consciousnesses, two subjects*" (p. 106).

Buber echoed Gadamer's and Bakhtin's claims about language as contact. In *I and Thou* Buber identified the human world as "twofold in accordance with the two basic words [humans] can speak," words that are relational in that they are "not single . . . but word pairs": I-It and I-Thou.[64] In a subsequent essay, Buber's point about the relational quality of language was stated even more explicitly: "The fundamental fact of human existence is neither the individual as such nor the aggregate as such. Each, considered by itself, is a mighty abstraction. . . . The fundamental fact of human existence is [hu]man with [hu]man. . . . It is rooted in one being turning to another as another, as this particular other being, in order to communicate with it in a sphere which is common to them but which reaches out beyond the special sphere of each."[65]

In another essay Buber argued that he concentrated on the spoken word in part because it "does not want to remain with the speaker. It reaches out toward a hearer, it lays hold of him [or her], it even makes the hearer into a speaker."[66]

These authors and others elaborate the truism that the human is a social animal by clarifying how the paradigmatic event of uniquely human understanding is the event of *contact*—Gadamer's "conversation," Volosinov's "social event of verbal interaction," Bakhtin's "speech communication," and Buber's dialogue occurring in spokenness between persons. Any adequate account of the nature of language must affirm this defining feature: language happens in the human nexus.

As I suggested before, this is clearly not to say that all events of contact are friendly or that they all lead to agreement. Articulate contact is hostile as often as it is welcoming; Gadamerian conversation includes conflict; Bakhtin's speech communication incorporates critique, and Buber's dialogue often occurs between opponents. The point is not that there is always a friendly resolution of differences but that meanings are collaboratively coconstructed. Boxing matches, political campaigns, and even wars are exactly as coconstituted as weddings, national celebrations, and peace agreements.

The contact that characterizes all these language events is *articulate* in two senses. First, it is differentiated rather than compact. According to philosopher of history Eric Voegelin, the central direction of the development of human consciousness, both phylogenetically and ontogenetically, is from the compact "primary experience of the cosmos" to the "differentiated experience of existence."[67] This is the distinction between the contact of a hug or caress and the contact of a conversation; the former is compact and the latter differentiated. Human understanding centrally involves depicting differentiations, making distinctions, or categorizing; in fact, according to George Lakoff, contemporary cognitive science views this process "as the main way that we make sense of experience."[68] As Lakoff and others show, one approach to describing the unique power of human understanding is by tracing how such categories or distinctions as temporality, spatiality, family resemblance, polysemy, generativity, and metonymy turn the "blooming, buzzing confusion" we would experience without language into something *articulate*.

The second sense in which the events of contact that constitute language are "articulate" is that they are paradigmatically oral-aural. To articulate in this sense means to *pronounce* clearly and distinctly, to speak in ways that enhance understanding. Humboldt linked these two senses of *articulate* when he wrote: "*Articulation* rests upon the power of mind over the vocal organs, to compel them to deal with sound in accordance with the form of its own working. The point at which form and articulation meet, as in a binding medium, is that both divide their domains into *basic parts* ["categories"] whose assembly does nothing but form such wholes as bear within them the striving to become parts of new wholes. *Thinking*, furthermore, demands collection of the *manifold into unity*. The necessary marks of the *articulated sound* are therefore a sharply apprehensible unity, and a character that can enter into specific relationship with any and every other articulated sound imaginable" (p. 66).

This view of the centrality of articulated sound is supported by studies of human development, which indicate that the human's first senses through which contact normally occurs are sound and touch. After only twenty weeks in utero, the auditory apparatus of the normal human fetus is structurally comparable to that of an adult, and responses to sound are clearly part of normal fetal behavior.[69] Perinatal studies also underscore the importance of the acoustic environment of the fetus. One researcher argues, for example, that most of the unhealthy infants in his study were born to "catastrophic" mothers who were characterized by the ways they provided "interference with the accustomed rhythms of the fetus, causing disharmonic, repeated arrythmic *discontinuity in his [or her] acoustic vibratory environment*" (italics added).[70] Before the maturation of visual contact, the normal infant can recognize the sounds of its mother's and caregivers' voices, and as the infant matures, sound develops as its most economical and flexible contact modality.

Studies of orality indicate that this aspect of human development is one in which ontogeny recapitulates phylogeny. For example, Eric Havelock describes the significance of the development of human culture from sound-focused primary orality to sight-focused literacy: "In primary orality, relationships between human beings are governed exclusively by acoustics (supplemented by visual perception of bodily behavior). The psychology of such relationships is also acoustic. The relation between an individual and his [or her] society is acoustic, between [the individual's] traditions . . . law. . .government. . . . Recognition, response, thought itself, occur when we hear linguistic sounds and melodies and ourselves respond to them, as we utter a variant set of sounds to amend or amplify or negate what we have heard."[71]

Walter Ong, Adam Parry, Marshall McLuhan, and Alexander Luria have also fruitfully elaborated on the fact that humans distinctively accomplish contact oral-aurally. Ong offers especially thorough descriptions of the distinctive acoustic features of orality. For example, he notes that "sound exists only when it is going out of existence. It is not simply perishable but essentially evanescent, and it is sensed as evanescent."[72] As a result, in primarily oral cultures, "language is a mode of action and not simply a countersign of thought," and these oral peoples "consider words to have great power. Sound cannot be sounding without the use of power."[73] Orality also makes language essentially communicative: "An interlocutor is virtually essential: it is hard to talk to yourself for hours on end. Sustained thought in an oral culture is tied to communication."[74] Ong and other scholars describe how education in primary oral cultures exploits the biologically based power of rhythm and how new information is taught by inserting it into an ongoing repetitive acoustic pattern. Parry especially emphasizes the connection between acoustic mechanics and oral consciousness, and subsequent scholars have attempted to test this profound thesis about the relationship between language as speaking and thought.[75] It now appears that sound is a more prominent feature of human worlding than the visual bias of much of Western scholarship has heretofore acknowledged.

I am arguing, in short, that *to characterize language as articulate contact is both to affirm that languaging* (participating in language events as just described) *accomplishes the differentiated understanding that characterizes developed human being and to note that oral-aural sound is the paradigmatic modality of languaging.* As the second section of the next chapter clarifies, deaf people are not excluded from this analysis. Recent research on Sign, the language of the deaf, demonstrates that it too can be accurately characterized as constitutive articulate contact. Both conceptual and empirical studies conclude that contact is clearly the primary raison d'être for Sign and therefore that Sign cannot be adequately described as simply a system of symbols.[76] Moreover, this research concludes that Sign fully qualifies as a language in its own right and that, although it exploits sight rather than sound as its primary modality, it uses time in ways that are parallel to oral-aural speech communicating.[77]

To summarize, this account of language as constitutive articulate contact affirms that (a) language should be treated first and foremost as event, not system (as "languaging"); (b) this event embodies the distinctive dynamic of human being, which is understanding; (c) this ongoing process of understanding via languaging is the human way of constituting world ("world-building-and-rebuilding" or simply "worlding"); (d) this understanding occurs in contact between persons, which is to say that the event is irreducibly dialogic or interpersonal; and (e) this understanding-in-contact is articulate, which means both that it accomplishes differentiation or categorization and that it occurs paradigmatically as oral-aural contact.

The Two Accounts Compared

The differences between the symbol model and the view that language is constitutive articulate contact can now be clarified by contrasting the theoretical commitments embodied in each. First, the symbol model begins from the basic claim that there is a distinction between two realms or worlds, generally the "linguistic" and the "nonlinguistic." The post-semiotic view of the nature of language outlined here begins from the claim that there can be only one kind of human world, a pervasively languaged kind. Importantly, this is not to say that one sits on, drinks coffee from, or drives "language," or that if one walked far enough across a room, "words" would bloody one's nose. As I noted, all but solipsists acknowledge the existence of facticity separate from human perception and interpretation. But this facticity, as such, is not a part of any *world*. As Charles Taylor explains, there are no "brute data," if by *brute data* one means "data whose validity cannot be questioned by offering another interpretation or reading, data whose credibility cannot be confounded or undermined by further reasoning."[78] Data are encountered or experienced as situated, related to other data making up a world. This is to say that they are always interpreted, which means they are languaged. World, the Ur-structure of understanding, emerges from human contact, both with facticity and with other humans.[79] Each nonsolipsistic affirmation of facticity occurs as an acknowledgment that makes up part of the world being affirmed. And this affirmation is cultural, social, and interpersonal, because it is anchored in the speaker's or writer's linguistic tradition and addressed to his or her interlocutor(s). To put the point in other words, world is always world-for, and the beings "for" whom it is, are relational beings, ones formed, as Bahktin put it, "wrapped" in others. This one relational world of meaning is the irreducibly primary site of human being.

Second, the symbol model treats language as composed of identifiable units or elements, whereas the post-semiotic alternative focuses more holistically. The account of language as constitutive articulate contact offered here is premised on the conviction that synthesis can contribute at least as much to an understanding of language as analysis. Minimally, discourse critiques should move as the traditional hermeneutic circle prescribed, from whole to part and back again to the whole. Little purpose is served by focusing one's explicative energy exclusively on reducing language to its atoms. Of course, distinctions are still useful and important, but they can be made, for example, among types or functions of events rather than between individual elements. The anchor for understanding languaging should be the contact event as its participants live it.

Third, the symbol model embraces a representationalism rooted in the Cartesian-Kantian distinction between subject and object. This post-semiotic alternative treats language as constitutive or productive of (necessarily partial, tentative, and changing) ways of understanding rather than reproductive of cognitive states, things, or other units of language. This means that language is primary rather than secondary, that speech communicating is a principal not a surrogational dynamic. Friendly and hostile talk, conversation, address and response, and dialogue produce worlds; they do not simply reproduce or represent them.

Fourth, the symbol model treats language as a system, whereas the alternative described here treats language as event. Insofar as language is viewed as constitutive articulate contact, it is more fruitful for theorists and researchers interested in human communication—a category that includes most of those in the human sciences—to concentrate on "languaging," "interacting," or "transacting"[80] rather than on the system communicators are allegedly employing. This focus is preferable, especially because the so-called system of language cannot coherently be conceived as existing separate from, and in an object-to-subject relationship with, humans communicating. One implication of this concentration on event is that the traditional distinction between language and communication is significantly altered. Although it is still clearly useful to talk about individual languages, the term in such phrases as *the nature of language* or *language is a distinctive feature of humans* becomes synonymous with *communication* (or better, communica*ting*). Thus questions like, "How is language operating here?" or "What features of the speaker's or writer's language contributed to this outcome?" call for responses that clarify how interlocutors collaboratively constructed meaning in their verbal-nonverbal discourse.

Finally, the symbol model treats language as a tool or instrument humans use to accomplish their goals. This account of language as constitutive articulate contact, on the other hand, is predicated on the conviction that such an instrumental view is incomplete and misleading, primarily because humans cannot live in the subject-object relationship with language that the tool analogy requires. It seems to me that Gadamer is profoundly correct to remind us that we do not engage in speech communication essentially—or even partially—by taking the words of a language that are lying ready in our mouths, uttering them, and then letting them sink back into the general store of words in our linguistic armentarium. "Rather, in all our knowledge of ourselves and in all knowledge of the world, we are always already encompassed by the language that is our own."[81] Therefore it is most fruitful to treat language as the primary way humans be who we are and as a dynamic we are subject to or used by at least as much as we "manipulate" or "use." Here the view of language comes full circle. Insofar as world is linguistic, we *inhabit* or live in our language; we do not simply use it as a tool.

Conclusion

I argued in Chapter 1 that the symbol model cannot provide a coherent account of most living language, that it breaks down when applied to actual speech communicating. The reader might legitimately ask for a demonstration that the alternative proposed in this chapter fares better. How might this account of language as constitutive articulate contact inform, for example, our understanding of the brief excerpt from the dialogue between two college students about bicycles on campus? Recall that the partial text of this conversation looked like this:

EXAMPLE 1. Two College Students

1. John: So what do you THI::NK about the bicycles on
campus?

2. Judy: I think they're terrible.

3. John: Sure is about a MIL:LION of 'em.

4. Judy: eh ┌─he:h ─┐
5. John: └─Duzit─┘ SEEM da you: there's a lot more
people this year?

6. Judy: The ┌─ re- ─┐ ye:ah, for su:re
7. John: └─ Go-─┘   GOD, there seems to be a
mILlion people

8. Judy: Yeah. (1.0) YE:ah, there's: way too many. I can't- at
tIMEs the

9.   bicycles get so bad I just got off mi ┌── ne an ──┐
hh .h and gi(h)ve up!   │   │
                                             │   │
10. John: └── Oh riLleh ─┘

11. John: I unno when I DODGE one then I have to DODGE
another one 'n

12.   its an endless cycle.

13. Judy: Yeah (1.0) oh they're TERrible.

14. John: 'S so many people.

15. Judy: Um hmm[82]

Douglas W. Maynard, the conversation analyst who cites this
example of talk, finds in it several features of John and Judy's articulate contact that would not be apparent if he were to treat this
language simply as the systematic use of symbols. Maynard focuses
on the operation of a strategy he calls a *perspective-display sequence.*
Conversation partners use this strategy, he argues, to adapt a personal opinion to their listener's frame of reference. The strategy consists of first soliciting the other's opinion and then producing one's
own report in a way that takes the other's into account. In the first
three lines of the example, John provides a "perspective-display in-
vitation," to which Judy replies, and then John offers his opinion as

supportive of the perspective he has already elicited from her. Maynard argues that this conversational strategy can enhance the amount of agreement or consensus expressed in a conversation, and it is especially "pertinent to situations where cautiousness in giving reports and opinions seems warranted."[83]

Maynard points out that this excerpt includes a second perspective display sequence that builds upon the first. It begins at line 5 and ends at line 7. Subsequently, Judy produces a brief personal narrative in lines 8–9 telling how bicycles—the topic of the conversation—affect her. Then John's second story in lines 11–12 runs parallel with Judy's. He too has had to avoid bicycles to escape being a victim. Thus, *the kind of character* [italics added] that the teller of the first story is in hers is the same that second narrator is in his."[84] Maynard also notes that the stories work even though (because?) they are generic rather than specific. They both use such framing devices as "at times" and "when" to mark the experiences they narrate as typical rather than unique.

Finally, Maynard underscores the significance of the fact that John and Judy produce parallel second stories. The two could demonstrate understanding and agreement with statements of appreciation or approval. But a second *story* of the kind produced here *exhibits* a similar experience. "And," Maynard continues, "to the degree that coparticipants orient to a shared experience (of 'victimization,' for instance), it is relationally significant, in that it constitutes an accomplished 'intimacy,' if only momentary, that is a product of participants systematically pursuing talk that reveals their similarity."[85] But, John and Judy handle their victimization differently; Judy gets off her bike and "gives up," whereas John keeps dodging bikes in an "endless cycle." So John and Judy smoothly, subtly, but nonetheless poignantly display in this brief exchange both how they are different "characters" and how they are alike.

Clearly Maynard is able to develop several insights from outside the symbol model. In this brief excerpt, he finds evidence about the relationship displayed between the individual and the social, the dynamics of narrative collaboration, the discursive development of subject matter ("bicycles"), and the achievement of intimacy, without getting caught up in any effort to analyze "signifiers" and "signifieds." In fact, I would argue that he notices what he does in this discourse *because* he recognizes that these interlocutors are coconstructing the world they share in their aural-oral contact. John and Judy both produce bicycle stories that are "wrapped in" the other's parallel story, a clear example of *collaborative* construction. The complementary crescendo-decrescendo of the emphasized words—THI::NK, MIL:LION, SEEM, GOD, mILlion, and so on—that I discussed in Chapter 1 reveals another level of the interlocutors' intimacy, one embedded in the aural-oral dimensions of intonation, emphasis, and facial expression. Each speaker displays a world open to the other's participation, and both positively affirm the other's involvement in their worlds. In short, the symbol model collapsed in the attempt to use it to explicate the first word in turn 1, whereas aspects of the post-semiotic account offered in this chapter prove useful for elucidating several ways this talk is operating syntactically, semantically, and pragmatically.

Of course, the symbol theorist might not be interested in the relationship between the individual and the social, the dynamics of narrative collaboration, the discursive development of subject matter, or the conversational achievement of intimacy. Dozens of other questions could be asked about this discourse, and many of them focus on phonemes, morphemes, or phrases; on syntactic structures; or on individual word choices. One might wonder why semiotic and post-semiotic language scholars can not just agree to coexist, with those committed to the symbol model using it to pursue their questions and those who view language as constitutive articulate contact applying their own perspective?

On the one hand, I firmly believe that coexistence is the best possible likely scenario. I recognize that neither this chapter, nor this book—nor the book of essays planned to follow it[86]—will alter the scholarly practices of most of those committed to the symbol model.

On the other hand, I am less than fully satisfied by the eclecticism featured in this scenario. I would respond to the question about coexistence by appealing to the same criterion outlined in Chapter 1. Any model of language, if it is to be judged coherent and useful, should be informatively applicable to paradigm cases of the phenomenon it is designed to elucidate. Even most symbol theorists agree that language occurs paradigmatically as speech or speech communication. But the symbol model cannot be informatively applied to these events. This is one reason why I am skeptical about coexistence, eclecticism, or theoretical pluralism when what is at issue is the understanding of the basic nature of language itself.

Another reason for not embracing both the symbol model and this post-semiotic alternative is that the fundamental assumptions grounding the former have been thoroughly questioned in a wide range of contemporary scholarly works by Wittgenstein, Austin, Ryle, Heidegger, Gadamer, Derrida, Bakhtin, Rorty, and many others. In light of several of these critiques, for example, one simply cannot responsibly maintain a commitment to Cartesian-Kantian epistemology and its concomitant representationalism. It is no longer possible simply to affirm that philosophical language—or some other type—does, after all, "mirror nature." Similarly, after the philosophical work of Gadamer and Bakhtin and the anthropological studies of Dell Hymes,[87] Clifford Geertz,[88] John Gumperz,[89] and others, one can no longer affirm that language is simply a tool. We clearly live in something other than a subject-object relationship with our language. And to the degree we inhabit it, it cannot be a tool. This is another other argument against coexistence or theoretical pluralism.

Thus this chapter has argued initially that it is conceptually and practically useful to treat language first and foremost not as a system but as a kind of human event, as "languaging" or speech communicating. Second, this kind of event is the site of human being, the dynamic that distinguishes us as understanders from even our closest primate, whale, and dolphin cousins. Third, this ongoing, collaborative engagement in understanding via languaging is the human's way of constituting world ("world building and rebuilding" or simply "worlding"), when *world* is understood as the sphere of coherence we inhabit. Fourth, this understanding is negotiated; it occurs in contact between persons, which is to say that these events are irreducibly dialogic or interpersonal. Finally, this understanding in contact is articulate, which means both that it accomplishes differentiation or categorization and that it occurs paradigmatically as oral-aural contact.

In her 1993 speech accepting the Nobel Prize for Literature, poet Toni Morrison remarked, "Oppressive language does more than represent violence; it is violence; does more than represent the limits of knowledge; it limits knowledge."[90] Morrison's comment reflects an understanding of what is ultimately at stake here. Semiotic accounts of the nature of language permit discourse to be disconnected from its ethical and ontological consequences. This post-semiotic account permits no such disconnection; it points toward the intimate connection between human speech communicating and human being.

In the next chapter I review three diverse lines of scholarship that provide support for the account of the nature of language I have outlined here. Then, in Part II, I apply this view of language as constitutive articulate contact as a critical tool to illuminate features of three influential treatments of language and its consequences.

❀ Chapter 5

Diverse Friendly Bedfellows

Primarily because language is a central topic in virtually all reflective thinking about humans, and because each discussion of language presumes at least an implicit view of its nature, scholars in a variety of disciplines have pursued research programs that address the issues discussed in this book. Recently, several of these scholars have also offered explicit accounts of the nature of language that parallel or echo central aspects of the account developed here. This chapter reviews three such programs: from philosophy, the hermeneutics of intersubjectivity proposed by Gary B. Madison; from deaf education, the arguments of those who believe deaf persons should be encouraged to use Sign or ASL (American Sign Language) rather than being limited to lipreading or using invented, orally based language systems; and from artificial intelligence, the case for a connectionist rather than a symbolic model of human cognition.

I briefly review each program here, first to illustrate how scholars working from very diverse perspectives and reading, for the most part, disconnected literatures have arrived at some conclusions about the nature of language that are similar to those I argue for. At first glance, one would not expect hermeneutics, deaf education, and artificial intelligence to be closely related. But aspects of these lines of inquiry which are motivated by such dissimilar goals and informed by such dissimilar bodies of "evidence" and "data" actually do converge, to a considerable degree, in their views of language. The second reason for reviewing these programs is to thicken, via comparison and contrast, the post-semiotic description of language that has been developed in Chapters 1 and 4. In its similarities and differences with the view presented in this book, each program contributes to an understanding of language as constitutive articulate contact.

The Symbol Model and the Hermeneutics of (Inter)Subjectivity

Gary B. Madison is professor of philosophy at McMaster University and on the graduate faculty at the University of Toronto. Madison labels his central project *a poststructuralist phenomenology,* and several of his focal interests are suggested by the title of his 1990 collection of essays, *The Hermeneutics of Postmodernity* and its dedication, "To Paul Ricoeur and Hans-Georg Gadamer, from whom I learned what is vital. . . . "[1] Madison embraces much of postmodern thought, but unlike many postmodernists focused on deconstruction, he does have a story with a plot to tell, albeit a plot that is, as he puts it, "devoid of metaphysical closure" (p. ix). As major elements of this plot unfold, Madison's interest in language as a kind of articulate contact becomes increasingly evident.

Madison defines what he means by *postmodern* by contrasting it with the "epistemological and foundationalist" tradition that "originates with Descartes and which has perpetuated itself up to and into the twentieth century" (p. x). Modernism's primary feature, he writes, is its desire to achieve "a basic, fundamental knowledge . . . of what is . . . by turning inward into the knowing subject him[her]self (conceived of either psychologistically or transcendentally), where it seeks to discover grounds which will allow for certainty in our 'knowledge' of what, henceforth, is called 'the external world'" (p. x). Modernism's central methodological conviction, argues Madison, is that a thinker may come to know reality via true *representations.* In fact, Madison emphasizes, *"Representationalism* has been the name of the game from Descartes up to our twentieth-century positivists and analysts" (p. x). The two central products of modern thinking are "the notions of subjectivity and a fully objective, determinate world—the essential business of the 'knowing subject' ([the hu]'man') being that of forming true 'representations' of so-called objective reality" (p. x). Postmodernism is the attempt to spell out the consequences of the end of modernism, thus conceived. In contrast to some postmodernist writers, Madison affirms that his program is neither relativist nor nihilist. Also unlike many other postmodernists, he locates the beginnings of postmodernism in Husserl and finds Merleau-Ponty and Gadamer to be among its most lucid and productive expositors.

Given this orientation, it is not surprising that Madison frequently focuses his philosophical efforts on the nature of subjectivity—which he discusses in terms of "the mind-body problem"—and on connections between subjectivity and language. In "Merleau-Ponty and Postmodernity," for example, he begins with the perennial, even essential philosophical question, "What does it mean to be a subject who is conscious of his [or her] own existence as a subject" (p. 57)? Since antiquity, Madison points out, this problem has tended to be approached as a problem of the union of body and soul; "the mind-body problem (as we now call it) has been debated without letup by philosophers—without much success, it must be admitted" (p. 57).

During the modern period from Descartes to Sartre, Madison argues, inquiry into this problem was plagued by a dualism that resulted in the alienation of subject from object, psychic from corporeal, and thus the human from nature. "A consciousness which is alienated from itself is a consciousness which is split within itself, and such a consciousness, as we know from Hegel, is an unhappy consciousness" (p. 58). A central task of postmodern philosophy is to address this unhappiness, and Madison believes that Edmund Husserl paved the way for this effort. Madison traces Husserl's effort to show that the so-called objective world is not self-sufficient but relative to consciousness and grounded in transcendental subjectivity. This effort to overcome the subject-object split was taken up by several of Husserl's followers who were dissatisfied with other conclusions he reached. Among them, Maurice Merleau-Ponty argued that, although Husserl laid the groundwork, his "transcendental idealism was still a form of subjectivism" and thus still a prisoner of the subject-object duality (p. 60). Merleau-Ponty attempted to show that "there is absolutely no dualism between me and my body, between this body that in fact I am and the world which it inhabits and animates, and between me and the other" (p. 60).

Especially in his later work, which was published in the 1950's and early 1960's, Merleau-Ponty turned in this project to a reconsideration of *language*. He began by identifying a new anchor construct for the analysis of subjectivity, the *flesh*. In Madison's and Merleau-Ponty's words, the flesh is "neither the objective body nor the body which the soul thinks of as its own, the flesh is rather the sensible itself, 'the sensible in the twofold sense of what one senses and what senses.' The flesh is the formative milieu of both the corporeal and the psychic, of object and subject; it is the undivided Being (*l'Être d'indivision*) existing before the consciousness-object split."[2] The discovery of the flesh led Merleau-Ponty to a "complete reconstruction of philosophy" which was accomplished by a "complete reconstruction" of language. The claims he made about language seemed at that time extravagant. He asserted, for example "that language has us and that it is not we who have language," and in this way Merleau-Ponty effaced the prominence of the speaking subject in favor, as Gadamer would later put it, of a language that "speaks us."

Merleau-Ponty also linguistically—in fact, communicatively— redefined subjective *rationality*. He claimed that human beings are rational, not because, in Madison's words, "what they say and do has a transcendent guarantee in things, but simply because of the fact that, despite all the differences which set them apart, they can still, if they make the effort, communicate with and understand one another" (p. 70). For Merleau-Ponty rationality was a matter of "taking the risk of communicating."[3] Madison concludes that by approaching the subject as unified and linguistic, Merleau-Ponty did not "solve" the mind-body problem, but that he did contribute significantly to its unraveling.

Madison himself takes a significant step toward further unraveling this problem in "The Hermeneutics of (Inter)Subjectivity, or: The Mind-Body Problem Deconstructed."[4] He describes at the beginning of this essay how the problem has been approached as a metaphysical and epistemological one, and he argues that postmodern thought frees us, with respect to this question, "to break out of the epistemological circle, out of the metaphysical enclosure altogether" (p. 158). But, he emphasizes, not to nihilism. In response to those postmodernists who proclaim "the death of [the hu]man," Madison argues, "Can one, knowingly and in good conscience, say 'I do not exist'? Who would believe you if you said that to them? . . . Subjectivity is a fact, as indubitable as the fact that I exist, *ego sum*" (p. 159).

One insight postmodernism affords is that it is fruitless to ask about this subjectivity the metaphysical question, *what* the self or subject is. The only answer to this question is that it is some sort of *thing* or substance, and this is exactly how modern thinkers were led into vicious epistemological circles and metaphysical *aporias*. As Neitzsche clarified, the misleading genius of modernism was to approach this question via polar thinking, by attempting to contrast the self or subject with its opposite. But postmodernism offers a way out of thinking determined by the traditional polarities or doublets—appearance-reality, sensible-intelligible, material-immaterial, becoming-being, time-eternity, contingent-necessary, fact-essence, and matter-spirit. Where to?

Says Madison: *"Why can we not say that the self is simply a characteristic that we associate with those animate organisms referred to as humans? A characteristic of that most characteristic of human actions, pursued incessantly both in public and private, in wakefulness and in sleep—I refer to speech"* (p. 160, italics added). To paraphrase in a way that foregrounds links with Chapter 4, Madison argues that the way to overcome the mind-body problem and its accompanying paradoxes is to extend Merleau-Ponty's analysis—with the help of Gadamer—to the point where the self is conceived of as *the being constituted in the actions of speech.* He thus points toward a praxical linguistic ontology, an account of the human subject as speaker. For him it would appear that the event of speech is constitutive of humanity in almost exactly the same way that I argue it is.

But there is a difference. By *speech* Madison means "an action, the action of speaking about itself" (p. 160). Quoting psychoanalyst Roy Schafer, Madison continues, "The self is not an observable datum, since it is not any kind of *thing* at all, but it nonetheless is, in Schafer's words 'an experiential phenomenon, a set of more or less stable and emotionally felt ways of *telling oneself* about one's *being* and one's continuity through change.' In short, as he says, 'the self is a kind of telling about one's individuality' (italics added).[5] Here I would argue that Madison is led astray by Schafer in two ways. First, Schafer's formulation preserves a subject-object distinction by characterizing speaking as the action of one's speaking *about* itself. Insofar as this speech is *about* self, it makes the subject into a commentator on something external, other, distinguishable, and separate. In this way this formulation resuscitates the subject-object distinction and the concomitant perennial problem of accounting for how a being of one (subjective) sort can comment accurately or truthfully about a being of another (objective) sort—just one of the problems inherent in subject-object analyses. Second, Shaefer's formulation here is monological rather than dialogical, in that speech is construed as an (intentional) *action* performed by one speaker, rather than as a transaction occurring *between* interlocutors. This feature is reinforced when Madison cites with approval linguist Emile Benveniste's assertion that, *"I* refers to the act of individual discourse in which it is pronounced. . . . The reality to which it refers . . . is in the instance of discourse in which *I* designates the speaker that the speaker proclaims himself as the 'subject'."[6] In short, here Madison develops the view that it is the individual, *one*self who constitutes himself or herself in speech.

A few paragraphs later Madison appears to counter this interpretation when he adds, "it must not be thought that the grammatical self-referential discourse in which the self constitutes itself for itself as a self is a free-floating *monologue*, that the self is whatever it fancifully tells itself it is" (p. 162). The process is dialogic, he asserts, even though he claims that it is a reflexive one consisting of "the self pursu[ing] a conversation with itself" (p. 162).

Before describing how Madison attempts to cope with the apparently paradoxical claim that an essentially monological event can somehow be dialogic, I want to highlight two other features of his analysis that echo the description of language as constitutive articulate contact in Chapter 4. For one thing, he affirms as a basic principle of that form of postmodernism called *philosophical hermeneutics*, that, as Gadamer expresses it, "Being that can be understood is language." With regard to the question of subjectivity, Madison claims, this principle can be reformulated as "*The self that can be understood is language*" (p. 161). By this he means that the social or personal reality in question is inseparable from language; it "requires language in order to be told what it is, and it cannot properly be said to 'be' a self outside this telling" (p. 161). As this quotation indicates, Madison also conceives of language as processual rather than substantive, as "telling" rather than "system." I find Gadamer's reformulation of Heidegger's claim that language is the house of Being to be exactly as significant as does Madison and in virtually exactly the same way.

In addition, Madison concurs with Chapter 4 that this hermeneutical reconstruction of the self does not simply create a new kind of linguistic idealism. A metaphysician resisting Madison's analysis of the self might argue that this account makes the self into nothing but a matter of words, something empty of any "reality." As Madison points out, it is true that from this perspective the self is not a metaphysical substance or essence. But this does not mean the self is simply a matter of words. The phenomenological hermeneuticist does not say that the I is "nothing but" a linguistic construct, but rather (a) that it is essentially a process of becoming, and, (b) in Madison's words, that it "constitutes itself in and by means of language, by, as I said above, narrating itself"

(p. 164). He summarizes, "The language that we speak is neither, as the structuralist and poststructuralist types would maintain, a formal system of pure 'signs,' closed in upon itself and expressing nothing other than itself, nor is it, as various analytic philosophers of language would have it, a mere means for 'expressing' something completely other than itself, Thoughts (as Frege would say) or Things—language neither 'refers' to 'extra'-linguistic reality nor does it merely 'express itself'; language is the way in which, as humans, we *experience* what we call reality, that is, the way in which *reality* exists for us (p. 165).

Madison's dissatisfaction with semiotic conceptualizations of language parallels mine, and his account of the ontological dimension of languaging is very close to the one outlined in Chapter 4.

But there nonetheless remains a revealing point of difference between Madison's view and the one developed in this book. It centers on our different treatments of *contact*. Madison argues that experience is the raison d'être of language or discourse and that the "heart" or "inner *dynamis*" of experience is "desire . . . desire of the desire of another consciousness" (p. 165). The *aim* of communication, he contends, is "ultimately, to captivate the attention of our interlocutors. . . . In order to fascinate, captivate, seduce that other regard, that other desire, to make it desire our desire, we make of our living body a speaking body" (p. 166). So Madison's account becomes a form of dialogue defined by one interlocutor's purpose, intention, goal, or "aim." Madison acknowledges the centrality of contact in the business of speaking selves into being, but for him the contact is functional or instrumental. One's communicative behavior is prompted by one's antecedently experienced "desire," which leads (causes?) one to attempt contact with another. Thus the contact is strategically designed to perform an in-order-to function, and it can be planned, executed, and assessed with reference to this outcome.

I would argue, by contrast, that this reciprocally constitutive contact is not simply the outcome of one speaker's "aim," but is first and foremost the situation in which humans find themselves as they accomplish everyday coping. Sociality, in other words, is a given of the human condition, not a product of human making. We are born into an ongoing conversation—more accurately, a complex of ongoing conversations—that we observe, avoid, enter, sometimes contribute to, and, ultimately exit at death.[7] We inherit this communicative condition as part of our legacy as humans. We do indeed have the ability to choose some conversation partners and topics over others and to make some contributions—or attempt some distractions—rather than others. In these and other ways we can significantly enhance or diminish the quality of the contact we experience. But the contact itself is more our birthright than our project.

I agree with Madison when he writes, "What then is the self? It is a function of the conversation with other similar, desiring selves, a function of the self-reinforcing narratives they pursue together in their occasional, casual conversations as well as those more serious ones which last to all hours of the night" (p. 166). Along with Gadamer, however, I understand this dynamic as less under the control of "aims" and "desires" and more a mutual, reciprocal, inescapably collaborative way of being that emerges as our characteristically human coping is influenced by what Gadamer would call the *specific traditions* through which we grow. We are "spoken by" communicative languaging at least as much as we "speak" it.

I also differ subtly with the final point Madison makes as he addresses Gadamer's claim that "Only through others do we gain true knowledge of ourselves."[8] What can it mean from this hermeneutical perspective, asks Madison, to say that our stories, narratives, or histories are "true" or "not true"? Certainly not that they have truth value by conforming to or *representing* some objective, extralinguistic reality. But this is not to say that truth is entirely relative, Madison emphasizes. First, we must recognize that, as hermeneuticists concerned with what people *do*, we should speak adverbially, of "being in the truth." And, Madison writes, "We are in the truth when we are true to ourselves" (p. 169). This means our narratives are true when they are adequately coherent and when we are able, in our rewritings and retellings, to take up with greater subtlety of narrative all the "data" that we have already made use of and their interpretations. Our narratives are "in the untruth" or "inauthentic" when they are unable to do so (p. 169).

In response to Madison's formulation, I would argue that the "truth value" of accounts that emerge in everyday coping is determined conversationally or communicatively, not primarily with reference to the selves narrating or the histories of their data constructions. True narratives or true claims are those that withstand the test of articulate response; they are those that do not melt in the crucible of controversy. Madison and I would probably agree that human truth is situated and context dependent. For a time it was indeed "true" that the earth was flat, and then that the earth was a sphere. Now it is "true" that the earth is an oblate spheriod wobbling slightly on its axis, and this truth is also bound to change as its implications and limitations are made the subject of serious conversations. Closer to our concerns, it was true for several decades that Marxism had a significantly positive impact on life in Russia and the Ukraine. It may be true today that the overall social and political legacy of Marxism in these countries has been negative. Again, whatever truth this latter formulation enjoys will emerge in informed interaction. So truths change, but not willy-nilly. And the primary constraints that distinguish true from false claims are the constraints of serious conversation. True assertions must be coherently *responsive* to the claims that form their conversational context. For example, if one tries to address a question that has not been asked, one's discourse may well be heard as incoherent. Topicality is also constrained by conversational rules and expectations. Astrologers and astronomers do not—and in an important sense cannot—converse seriously with one another, because they are engaged in fundamentally different conversations. In short, I would argue contra Madison that relativism is constrained not primarily by the selves or histories of those narrating but by the interlocutors' shared understanding of what counts as response-able conversation. Specifically, these constraints could probably be described as a combination of something like Grice's conversational maxims,[9] and the situationally appropriate, content-specific coherency demands.

In sum, as a postmodern philosopher interested in the mind-body problem, Gary B. Madison finds in Husserl, Merleau-Ponty, and Gadamer support for a position very close to the account that develops out of my interest in interpersonal communication, Heidegger, Gadamer, and Bakhtin: "The self that can be understood is language." More specifically, the self is "simply . . . the characteristic . . . *speech*." This does not make selves into whatever words people utter, because "language" and "speech" are not the semiotic, representational systems described by linguists, semioticians, and philosophers of language. Rather, language is first and foremost an event of contact, *the* world-constituting event of human contact. "Language is the way in which, as humans, we *experience* what we call reality, that is, the way in which *reality* exists for us." Madison and I differ in our descriptions of how this contact is dialogic, and in our analyses of how competing claims are adjudicated and how truth value is assessed. But our very different trajectories still converge on very similar accounts of the nature of language. The following section of the chapter reviews another philosophical and pedagogical trajectory that converges with this one.

The Symbol Model and Deaf Education

(by John Stewart and Susan K. Dyer)

Sociologist Vito Signorile believes that "there are some significant things for students of language to find in the world of the deaf."[10] And indeed there are.

In 1755, Charles Michel Abbé de l'Epée began the first free school for the deaf in the world, in Paris. Shortly thereafter another school for deaf children was launched in Germany by Samuel Heinicke.[11] The French taught using the gestural signs that members of the deaf community had developed as they communicated among themselves and with their hearing family members and friends. The German school, on the other hand, relied on purely oral instruction emphasizing lipreading and vocalization, an approach designed primarily by hearing teachers. Thus from the beginning, educators of the deaf have used markedly different approaches, and with little acceptance on either side of the other point of view. Proponents of these approaches have engaged in a heated dispute referred to as the communications debate, the war of methods, or the oral/manual controversy. In books, articles, conference presentations, and advertisements for educational programs, scholars and teachers have argued over which is the most appropriate communication methodology for educating deaf learners—oral or manual. Over the past two decades, these two approaches to deaf education have further divided into three. Oralist educators continue to proscribe the use of any form of sign language for instruction and emphasize the teaching of lipreading and vocalization. Especially in the English-speaking world, the manualist camp has split into those advocating a philosophy of total communication or combinism and those educators advocating bilingualism. The former group favors the use of invented sign language systems in combination with spoken English. Bilingualists, on the other hand, educate deaf students using their natural signed language and teach English as a second language.[12] The orientations of these groups are summarized in Table 5.1.

Today, the majority of scholars and researchers concerned with deaf education continue to focus their efforts on identifying the most appropriate communication methodology. But how does the controversy among deaf educators relate to this book's concerns? As Susan K. Dyer demonstrates, the primary difference between the educators' approaches lies not in pedagogy but philosophy. Dyer argues that the three current educational approaches are anchored in

Table 5.1. Current Approaches Taken by Educators of the Deaf

ORALISM	COMBINISM	BILINGUALISM
Spoken English used as language of instruction.	Speech and invented sign systems used as lang. of instruction.	ASL* used as language of instruction. Goal is fluency in ASL *and* English.
ASL prohibited.	ASL prohibited.	Invented systems prohibited.
Emphasis on speech.	Emphasis on English.	Emphasis on subject matter.
Emphasis on lipreading.	Emphasis on lipreading	Lipreading only after literacy in English
Residual hearing development is *necessary* for speech.	Residual hearing development is *encouraged* and often *necessary*.	Residual hearing development is *encouraged*.
Almost no deaf teachers.	Approximately 14% teachers are deaf.	Goal is 100% deaf teachers.
English taught as first language.	English taught as first language.	English taught as second language.

*American Sign Language or Sign

two contrasting views of the nature of language.[13] This is the feature that makes them relevant here.

The approach to deaf education originally developed in France privileges the nonoral gestures, facial expressions, and bodily movements by which deaf people naturally make articulate contact with one another. In the United States, these make up American Sign Language (ASL or Sign). Today, proponents of ASL view deaf people as constituting a distinct culture with its own, unique mode of communicating. From this perspective, members of deaf culture function best socially by utilizing their natural facial, gestural, and bodily communicative resources, thereby adapting to their deafness rather than attempting to overcome it.

Dyer demonstrates that the remaining two approaches, oralism and combinism, are grounded in the symbol model. Oralists and combinists view language as a representational system made up of units that can be instrumentally manipulated to meet the user's goals. They treat deaf persons as initially "languageless" and work to equip them with a spoken language and a supplementary system of invented signs in order to "normalize" them. Their goal is to empower deaf people with the means to adapt to and thereby enter, at least to some degree, the hearing world.

Thomas H. Gallaudet imported the bilingual approach to the United States when he returned from a trip to France in 1816 with Laurent Clerc, a profoundly deaf person who had successfully been educated by the Abbé de l'Epée. In 1817, Gallaudet and Clerc founded the first permanent school for the deaf in America.[14] Alexander Graham Bell led proponents of oralism in the United States. In the 1860s he helped a group of parents and educators express their concerns that "no effort was made, or little attention given, to teach articulation" in the "manual" deaf schools.[15] Bell's efforts resulted in the opening of several purely oral schools and the adoption in manual schools of some speech training. The oral philosophy held "out the hope and reassurance to parents that their child can learn to talk and lipread, and that with these tools he or she will fit into a hearing society as a 'normal' person would."[16] Whereas Clerc and other proponents of Sign believed that the ability to use both it and English was a worthy goal for both deaf and hearing people, Bell and the oralists affirmed that "it is important for the preservation of our national existence that the people of this country should speak one tongue"[17] and speak it orally. In 1880 a group of educators of deaf learners attempted to end this dispute by agreeing at the International Congress on Education of the Deaf in Milan to three resolutions designed to eliminate education using ASL or other cultural forms of sign language. The first resolution decreed that the language of each country's deaf classrooms was to be the national oral language, not the manual one; the second proscribed any compromise or combination of oral and manual language; and a third specified how pure oralism was to be phased in and signs phased out.[18]

But the Milan conference did not succeed in resolving the issue. The debate over these approaches continues,[19] and as we noted, the controversy is significant here because proponents of bilingualism, for the most part implicitly, view language as constitutive articulate contact; whereas oralists and combinists, often explicitly, view language as a system of symbols that function representationally and that deaf persons can be taught to use as a tool to enhance their assimilation into the world of the hearing.[20] Because the debate over deaf education embodies these contrasting views, an examination of some of its arguments can amplify this book's articulation of distinctions between the symbol model and a post-semiotic account of language.

Oralist and Combinist Educators' Views of Language

As recently as 1990, a magazine published by the Alexander Graham Bell Association for the Deaf affirmed that it "proclaims in print and from the podium that Our Kids can be taught to listen or to lipread, and to speak."[21] The explicit goals of this association are to encourage deaf people to develop maximal use of residual hearing, speechreading, and speech and language skills, and to collaborate in research relating to auditory-verbal communication. The association and the schools that apply its philosophy proscribe signing, because they believe it operates as a crutch and thereby interferes with oral learning. Documents that describe these programs clarify these educators' central beliefs about the nature of language and the nature of communication.

One is that language is an instrument or tool that must be taught to deaf children who, like feral children, are born without it. For example, one program uses a "Phonetic Inventory" to assess the degree to which a child has successfully *acquired* language. Its literature states that "Our children are equipped with essential language skills as they learn to speak and because they learn to speak."[22] Language is perceived by these oralists as a competency that deaf children are without and skill that they need to acquire, and the degree to which they have acquired language is demonstrated through their ability to speak.

One of the "speech tools" some of these educators advocate to help deaf children acquire language is cued speech. To use cued speech the deaf person must learn to make gestures to accompany specific speech sounds. The resulting combination of vocalization and gesture helps cue the lipreader to distinctions between phonemes that look alike, such as /f/ and /v/ or /b/ and /p/. From the perspective of those who teach cued speech, language can be broken down into discrete sound units that, when appropriately deployed, symbolize intentions, goals or meanings. The deaf person is believed to "have" language when he or she can correctly pronounce appropriate utterances.

This view of language is also manifest in these educators' discussions of cochlear implants, electronic devices that bypass the damage in the inner ear and directly stimulate auditory nerve fibers to create sounds in the brain. Advocates of these implants argue that it is unimportant that implant recipients hear something resembling a "Mickey Mouse voice or a computer voice," so long as the person "learns to make correct associations with certain signals."[23] Here again, the implicit claim is that language is made up of a series of sounds that can be analyzed into discrete phonemic units to which one can then attach meaning. A deaf person who develops the ability to associate phoneme and meaning accurately is viewed as having acquired language.

Harlan Lane suggests the philosophical significance of these educators' view of the nature of language when he notes that "One of the central questions of the Enlightenment was 'What makes us human?' and one of the accepted answers had been, ever since Aristotle and then Descartes, 'Language.' . . . Deaf children and wild children were, however, an embarrassment for this definition of [the hu]man, since the deaf were thought to have no language and feral children were invariably mute."[24] This view that deaf children have no language until they can speak is premised on the assumption that language is a system that is acquired by human subjects at a certain stage of development. In this sense, humans have a subject-object relationship with their language. For persons holding this view, the fact that children who are fluent in their natural signed language but unable to speak may be quite successfully negotiating their way about their social and material worlds (everyday coping) says nothing about their "language" competency. For these educators, the successful acquisition of language is evidenced only by the student's ability to *vocalize*. Oralist literature describes language as "*what* we say. It is the words we use to express meaning." Receptive language is "conversation that is understood," and expressive language is "language (words) used with meaning." Through processes of encoding and decoding sounds, deaf children "learn how to use words—language—*with meaning*."[25]

Accounts of combinist approaches clarify that they hold a similar view of language as they emphasize that "speech is . . . the primary signal in the conglomerate of signing and speaking." For these educators, the goal of the signing that accompanies speech "is to present simultaneous signed and spoken utterances, *both of which are held to be complete representations of English* [italics added]. According to this model, it is these representations of English that serve both as the input for natural language acquisition and as the vehicle for the transmission of curricular material."[26]

As Dyer summarizes it, the oralist-combinist literature embodies the following convictions about the nature of language:

1. Language is a system of sounds and symbols that the human subject acquires, and skill in this language system is demonstrated through an ability either to vocalize or to speak and sign the predominant spoken language simultaneously.

2. Learning language involves a process of encoding and decoding sounds or other symbols between a sender and a receiver. Meaning is subsequently attached to the symbols themselves.

3. Language is a tool that we use for the purpose of communicating.

4. Invented sign or symbol systems can be developed to teach language. These systems manipulate the socially constructed language of deaf people to match the grammatical structure of the predominant spoken language.

5. Language is acquired through oral-aural and visual channels.

6. Language can be studied and understood through scientific investigation, and broken down into analyzable phonemic or gestural units.

7. A culture's native spoken language is superior to the natural signed language of a linguistic-cultural minority.

8. Language and thinking are dichotomized or at least distinct.[27]

Unfortunately, many children educated in programs that subscribe to this philosophy of language are rendered communicatively incompetent. The first systematic evaluation of oralist approaches to education of the deaf concluded in 1910 that "People are mistaken about the practical result of the oral method. . . . It does not enable deaf-mutes to get jobs; it does not permit them to exchange ideas with strangers; it does not allow them even a consecutive conversation with their intimates; and deaf-mutes who have not learned to speak earn their living just as easily as those who have acquired this semblance of speech."[28] Subsequent research has concluded that " 'oralism' has not been successful in teaching English to the majority of prelingually deaf children,"[29] and "almost yearly publications lament the 'failure of [audist establishment[30]] deaf education'."[31] A 1990 study concurred that there have been "A hundred years of extremely unacceptable results of predominantly oralist philosophy in American Education."[32]

Comments by deaf people whose language learning has been frustrated by well-meaning oralist or combinist educators clarify the link between these failures and the philosophies of language underlying these educational programs. One of these persons expresses the impossibility of extending lipreading exercises beyond concrete nouns to actual living conversation: "When young, you build confidence as you guess correctly 'ball,' 'fish,' 'top,' and 'shoe' on your teacher's lips. This confidence does not last. As soon as you discover that there are more than four words in the dictionary, it evaporates. Seventy percent of the words when appearing on the lips are not more than blurs. Lipreading is a precarious and cruel art which rewards a few who have mastered it and tortures the many who have tried and failed."[33] Another, born into a deaf family who communicated in ASL, relished the articulate contact he enjoyed via that modality and anguished over the many hours of speech training he was forced to endure. "The teacher who was so excited about my uttering the letters of the alphabet was deceiving me," he writes. "Even now this deceit is still widely practiced among speech and lipreading teachers who . . . unwittingly encourage [their pupils] to believe that, once they graduate and go out into the hearing world, their speech can be understood. I just cannot tell whether it is deliberate deceit or self-delusion brought on by belief in oralism."[34]

Bilingualist Educators' Views of Language.

At least some of these deaf authors appear to recognize clearly that the problems they experience are anchored in the unwillingness of their teachers to acknowledge that living language is much more a matter of articulate contact than symbolic representation. One manifests this awareness as he describes the typical estrangement of a deaf child in his own home:

> You never forget that frightening experience. When you were Brian's age, you were left out of the dinner table conversation. It is called mental isolation. While everyone is talking or laughing, you are as far away as a lone Arab on a desert that stretches along every horizon. . . . *You thirst for connection* [italics added]. You suffocate inside but you cannot tell anyone of this horrible feeling. You do not know how to. You get the im-

pression nobody understands or cares. . . . You are not granted even the illusion of participation.

You are expected to spend fifteen years in the straitjacket of speech training and lipreading.[35]

Proponents of ASL argue that this deaf person, and others with his experience, could have been aided by educators who acknowledge that language is first and foremost communicative, the accomplishment of the "connection" or contact that hearing children spontaneously achieve oral-aurally. The years these deaf persons spend in the "straitjacket" of instrumental language training, they contend, could be spent much more fruitfully in the enjoyment, development, and application of their natural, gestural modes of articulate contact.

As we noted earlier, in the United States, these modes of contact are embodied in ASL or Sign, the culturally and socially constructed language of deaf persons.[36] ASL is a visual and spatial language with its own semantics, grammar, and structure. Proponents emphasize that it has "evolved among Deaf people and reflects their communication needs and strengths in much the same way that spoken English evolved among hearing persons."[37] Findings from over three decades of research now enable William A. Stokoe, Ursula Bellugi, Edward Klima, and many other scholars to argue convincingly that ASL is a true language, with a unique, spatial organization. In its lexicon, grammar, and syntax it deploys *space linguistically*. As Oliver Sacks explains, "much of what occurs linearly, sequentially, temporally in speech, becomes simultaneous, concurrent, multileveled in Sign."[38] Sacks also highlights data that indicate that growth into ASL by deaf children "bears remarkable similarities to the acquisition of spoken language by a hearing child. Specifically, the acquisition of grammar seems identical, and this occurs relatively suddenly, as a reorganization, a discontinuity in thought and development, as the child moves from gesture to language, from prelinguistic pointing or gesture to a fully-grammaticized linguistic system: this occurs at the same age (roughly twenty-one to twenty-four months) and in the same way, whether the child is speaking or signing."[39]

Some recent work even suggests that ASL- or Sign-like forms are "natural" or biologically determined embodiments of deaf childrens' thinking. One study reported that, "when deaf children are exposed to signed forms of English (manually encoded English), *but not* to ASL, they tend to innovate ASL-like forms with little or no input in that [constructed] language."[40] In this instance, in other words, children who had never seen ASL nonetheless evolved ASL-like forms. Klima concludes from evidence like this that "Sign is closer [than invented forms] to the language of the mind."[41]

A recent working paper from the Gallaudet University Research Institute[42] argues that deaf children should not be denied this genuine first language proficiency by being forced to learn oral language. "The first language of deaf children should be a natural sign language (ASL)." This language is best acquired as early as possible to take advantage of developmentally critical periods for language learning and to best enhance social identity and self-esteem. Primary models should be "deaf signers who use the language proficiently." The authors of this paper argue that sign language and spoken language are distinct and must be kept separate in the curriculum and in use, and that learning a spoken language is, for a deaf person, "a process of learning a second language through literacy (reading and writing). . . . Speech should not be employed as the primary vehicle for the learning of a spoken language for deaf children." Moreover, they insist that deaf children not be seen as "defective models" of hearing children.

Proponents of this approach to deaf education acknowledge that every language, including ASL, is "formed and renewed by constant exposure to basic modeling through the natural process of everyday communicative interchange."[43] In other words, deaf children who cannot speak are not perforce "without language," and language is not a system of signs and symbols that can be given to them as an instrument or tool. A deaf scholar emphasizes this point when she explains, "It is possible to research historical data and discover who invented the finger-spelling method, who invented Cued Speech, who invented the MCE [Manually Coded English] methods and so forth. It is not possible to specifically name who 'invented' ASL because *languages are not invented. They naturally evolve within a community from a variety of sources*" [italics added].[44] These scholars also view language not as a means for associating sounds with meanings but as a competency a child acquires "while making sense of his or her world."[45] This is why language can be *learned* but cannot specifically be *taught*. Like culture, language is acquired by the growing child and "cannot and should not be forced" on him or her.[46]

Harlan Lane's 1992 book, *The Mask of Benevolence: Disabling the Deaf Community,* is an impassioned argument for this perspective. Lane contends that an "audist establishment" of well-intentioned hearing people has dominated the deaf community in the United States, especially by attempting to proscribe their native language. Lane writes, "Hearing authorities commonly view American Sign Language as a crutch, refuse to learn it, and discourage its use; the half million or more deaf Americans for whom this is a primary language believe it is the equal of English as a natural language and clearly superior for instructing and communicating with deaf people."[47] Deaf people have been faced with overpowering paternalism and ethnocentrism, Lane argues, grounded in the conviction that they are "impoverished in language" and thus in culture and social identity. As he puts it, "In hearing people's milieu, languages are spoken; since deaf people rarely speak, hearing professionals have long contended that deaf people command little or no language" (p. 45). Lane continues, "Indeed, teachers of deaf children commonly say they are teaching their charges 'language' when in fact they are trying, and failing, to teach them English: most of the children are already as fluent in their primary, manual language as the teacher is in his or her oral one" (p. 46).

Lane argues that ASL embodies deaf culture in the United States just as integrally as American English embodies hearing culture: "deaf children growing up in the deaf community learn in manual language from older deaf children and adults what it means to be a deaf person, the lives that deaf people have lived before them and therefore the possible lives for them to lead, the wisdom of this minority, peculiar to its situation and accumulated across the centuries" (p. 82).

In fact, although neither Lane nor Sacks claims to be a communication scholar or language philosopher, both appear to sense the same connection between language and human being that Heidegger, Gadamer, Buber, and Bakhtin thematize. Sacks writes of his time spent with members of deaf culture fluent in ASL, "I get an overwhelming feeling, not only of another mode of communication but of another mode of sensibility, another mode of being. One has only to see the students . . . to feel that in their language, their mode of being, . . . "[48] Lane concurs. Deafness, he notes, is "not a disability but rather a different way of being."[49] Dyer's research led her to agree with Sacks and Lane that the way of being of deaf persons fluent in ASL contrasts with the way of being of those confined to oral methods or invented gestural systems. She also believes that these differences manifest or embody distinct views of the nature of language. She concludes her review of the proponents of bilingual approaches to deaf education with this summary of these scholar-educators' views:

1. American Sign Language is a language in its own right.

2. Spoken languages do not hold a privileged status over sign languages.

3. ASL and English coexist.

4. ASL is not a sign representation of English.

5. Language is formed and renewed through everyday communicative interchange.

6. Language is learned and should not be taught.

7. Human existence is linguistic in nature.

8. Culture and language are learned simultaneously, and this happens in face-to-face communication.

9. Language and communication are not distinguishable phenomena in the sense that one is a system and one is a process.

10. Language is not just a tool that humans use.

11. Language evolves within a community. There can be no language without community.

12. The languages of the world are in a constant state of flux and should not, nor can they be, manipulated or controlled.

13. Languages are not methods.

14. Language is a social, cultural, presentational phenomenon.[50]

Clearly much of the current discussion among educators of the deaf about various approaches to language learning can be understood as an embodiment and application of the two contrasting views of the nature of language discussed in earlier chapters. Both oralists and combinists treat language as a representational system that deaf children must be taught to acquire so they can function effectively, preferably in the hearing world. Those who promote ASL do so to a considerable degree because they view it as a full-fledged language, which, like all other languages, is a culturally embedded, socially developed complex of *ways to accomplish articulate contact*. The research and writing of those who promote ASL identify many of the same weaknesses in representational, instrumentalist accounts of language that have been identified earlier in this work. Their arguments for the appropriateness of these spatio-gestural modes of communicating also echo some of the claims made in earlier chapters for a post-semiotic view of the nature of language. Moreover, their analyses of the forms and functions of ASL flesh out this book's description of constitutive articulate contact.

For example, they affirm, from a pedagogical and empirical as contrasted with a philosophical perspective, that language cannot be adequately understood as an instrument or tool. They offer arguments against designing educational approaches around the belief that language is a system with which humans can have a subject-object relationship. They clarify the partial and impoverished nature of the belief that language is representational and that thoughts or other mental contents can be associated with phonemes, words, or other units. And in the writings of scholars who are intimately familiar with deaf persons—and even more clearly in the writings of deaf people themselves—it becomes clear that in the United States, ASL or Sign is the deaf persons' way of being-in-the-world. It is not the case that ASL gestures stand for elements or features of some nonlinguistic world; rather, this language is these persons' mode of constitutive articulate contact, their way of worlding.

The Symbol Model and Artificial Intelligence

There appears to be as much conceptual and methodological distance between deaf education and artificial intelligence scholars as there was between philosophical hermeneuticians and deaf education scholars. But it is again possible to find parallel views of the nature of language in this similarly diverse literature.

The general agenda for artificial intelligence research was defined in 1950 by Alan Turing. Turing proposed a thought experiment involving a game with three players: an interrogator, a second person, and an "intelligent" machine, none in the direct presence of the others. The object of the interrogator is to determine which of the other two is the machine. The interrogator proceeds by interviewing each through some kind of unconstrained though indirect verbal (but nonoral) channel, such as, a computer terminal equipped with appropriate word-processing software. Each player attempts to convince the interrogator of his-her-its humanness. Turing proposed the game as a secure test in response to the question, "Can machines think?" The machine that successfully fooled its interrogator would operationally define *artificial intelligence* (AI).[51]

Literally hundreds of AI researchers have used the Turing machine as a benchmark against which to evaluate their work and the work of others. And for over twenty years, they labeled the primary model of human cognition from which they worked toward this goal, the *symbolic paradigm*. This paradigm began with the mental structures of what AI writers call "folk psychology"—goals, beliefs, concepts and so forth. According to the symbolic paradigm, these mental concepts were formalized as a "language of thought" that purportedly followed "rules of thought." The mental structures were conceived of as supported by a physical symbol system—a computing device for manipulating symbols—which in turn was supported by lower implementation levels in the computing device. As one commentator summarizes, "The idea is that eventually, if we were to get low enough down in the human physical symbol system, we would see something like neurons. In other words, on this account we need only figure out how to relate neural structures and mental structures";[52] they were the entities between which a "symbolic" relationship purportedly existed.[53]

When applied to the task of designing artificial intelligence, the basic hypothesis underlying this paradigm is that the necessary and sufficient condition for a physical system to exhibit general intelligent action is that it be a physical *symbol* system.[54] The term *general intelligent action* means rational behavior; *rationality* means that when an agent has a certain goal and the knowledge that a certain action will lead to that goal, the agent selects that action; and *physical symbol systems* are physically realized universal computers. According to this paradigm, goals, beliefs, and the like are all formalized as symbolic structures built of symbols, each of which is semantically interpretable in terms of ordinary concepts. Symbol-manipulation procedures operate on these structures and, "according to the symbolic paradigm, it is in terms of such operations that we are to understand cognitive processes."[55]

In the early 1980s philosophers began to challenge the assumptions underlying the symbolic paradigm. For example, in 1984 Steve Torrance argued that the paradigm was anchored in "an inadequate metaphysical tradition which has dominated much of Western Philosophy, an inadequacy identified by Heidegger and by Wittgenstein."[56] The inadequacy consisted in this: Because the commonsense knowledge that informs our linguistic productions is essentially openended, it cannot be captured within the predefined limits of any computer program. As a result, Torrance argued, "The procedures underlying human knowledge formation are not just exceedingly difficult to formulate, they are unformulable."[57]

Similarly fundamental weaknesses in this paradigm were displayed two years later when computer scientists Terry Winograd and Fernando Flores wrote *Understanding Computers and Cognition*.[58] Winograd and Flores noted the pervasive influence in talk about computers of the tradition that emphasizes "information," "representation," and "decision making," a tradition that has led to much technological progress. This same tradition, they argued, "has also led to many of the problems created by the use of computers" (p. 8). The aim of their book was to challenge this tradition via "a critique of the current mythology of artificial intelligence and its related cognitive theories." Their ultimate goal was not merely to debunk, however, but to "attempt to create a new understanding of how to design computer tools suited to human use and human purposes" (p. 8).

The first two chapters of the book describe "the rationalistic tradition," which, they emphasize, is distinguished especially by one claim: *It "regards language as a system of symbols that are composed into patterns that stand for things in the world"* (p. 17, italics added). The concomitant "correspondence theory of meaning" supports a view of rational behavior as "a consequence of choosing among alternatives according to an evaluation of outcomes" (p. 20). This view of problem solving, which, at the time, was generally taken for granted in artificial intelligence research, construed problem solving as involving the manipulation of internal representations of a task environment via symbol structures. Thus, from Winograd and Flores's perspective, virtually all the primary artificial intelligence research programs at the time assumed the efficacy of the symbol model of language and a representational analysis of meaning.

The third chapter of *Understanding Computers and Cognition* presents the first of three bodies of work that stand in contrast to this rationalistic, symbolic tradition. It outlines a Heideggerian-Gadamerian perspective on hermeneutics that emphasizes the preference for practical rather than theoretical understanding, the rejection of the claim that humans relate to things primarily through mental representations, and the argument that "meaning is fundamentally social and cannot be reduced to the meaning-giving activity of individual subjects" (p. 33). The following chapter reviews the biological theorizing of Humberto Maturana, which also challenges the rationalistic tradition. Maturana and his colleagues ground their theorizing in empirical evidence, for example, that the elements of seeing involving the optic nerve are not carried out with direct representations of the pattern of light on the retina. Color vision, as they put it, does *not* involve "a mapping of a colorful world on the nervous system, but rather . . . the participation of the retina (or nervous system) in the generation of the color space of the observer" (p. 42). These perceptual processes, in other words, "are the results of patterns of activity which, although triggered by changes in the physical medium, are not representations of it" (p. 43). These empirical studies lead Maturana to conclude that "Learning is not a process of accumulation of representations of the environment; it is a continuous process of transformation of behavior through continuous change in the capacity of the nervous system to synthesize it. Recall does not depend on the indefinite retention of a structural invariant that represents an entity (an idea, image, or symbol), but on the functional ability of the system to create, when certain recurrent conditions are given, a behavior that satisfies the recurrent demands or that the observer would class as a reenacting of a previous one."[59] From this post-representational perspective, language is viewed not as a means for transmitting information or describing an independent universe—as the symbolic paradigm claimed—but, in Winograd and Flores's words, as "the creation of a consensual domain of behavior between linguistically interacting systems through the development of a cooperative domain of interactions."[60]

The third body of work with which Winograd and Flores challenge the rationalistic assumption is John Searle's Speech Act Theory. The authors underscore implications of this theory for listening and develop the argument that "meaning arises in listening to the commitment expressed in speech acts," and that "the articulation of content—how we talk about the world—emerges in recurrent patterns of breakdown and the potential for discourse about grounding"(p. 68). They conclude from their review of this language philosophy that "nothing exists except through language" (p. 68), which, they emphasize, is not an effort to construct a linguistic solipsism. Their point is that to say that something "exists" is to bring it into a domain of articulated objects and qualities that exist in and through language. Part II of their book is dedicated to showing "that this apparently paradoxical view (that nothing exists except through language) gives us a practical orientation for understanding and designing computer systems" (p. 69).

Winograd and Flores begin building this alternative orientation by reviewing Heidegger's and Maturana's arguments against the adequacy of representational views of language and knowledge. "In this view," they emphasize, "language—the public manifestation in speech and writing of this mutual orientation—is no longer merely a reflective but rather a constitutive medium" (p. 78).

The final four chapters of their book argue "that one cannot program computers to be intelligent and that we need to look in different directions for the design of powerful computer technology" (p. 93). One primary reason, they claim, is clarified by Heidegger's distinction between objects as *present-at-hand* and objects as *ready-to-hand*.[61] Heidegger argued that the human's ability to treat experience as involving present-at-hand objects is derived from a preconscious experience of them as ready-to-hand. Whenever we treat something as present-at-hand, for example, by analyzing it in terms of objective features or properties, we inescapably create a blindness. Our understanding is limited to what can be expressed in the terms we have adopted. This is not a thinking flaw we can avoid; in fact, it is a necessary and inescapable feature of thought. But this blindness is not acknowledged in systems that reduce knowledge to representation. This is why artificial intelligence systems grounded in a representational model are inherently incapable of successfully reproducing human thinking. Winograd and Flores celebrate recent developments in robotics, natural language interaction, and cognitive modeling, but they raise questions about the desirability of working toward "intelligent" systems. In Chapter 11 they develop a theory of management and conversation and develop its implications for computer design. And in the final chapter, echoing Heidegger and Gadamer, they argue for "the ontical-ontological significance of [computer] design—how our tools are part of the background in which we can ask what it is to be human" (p. 163).

As will become apparent, Winograd and Flores certainly do not produce the final words about the representational problem in artificial intelligence research or the feasibility of designing "thinking machines." But it is of more than passing interest to notice how they attribute many of the problems experienced by early artificial intelligence researchers to these researchers' inclination to view language as a "system of symbols that are composed into patterns that stand for things in the world" (p. 17). As Winograd and Flores demonstrate, this belief about the nature of language was a logical outgrowth of a more basic conviction that thinking consists essentially of manipulating representations. By 1986 it was clear that representational analyses of thinking and symbolic analyses of language were as inadequate for most AI projects as they have been for analyses of living language. It was also clear to Winograd and Flores that Heideggerian-Gadamerian hermeneutics and Maturanian biology decisively challenged the bedrock assumptions on which these analyses were based and pointed toward an alternative way of modeling language and cognition.

In 1992, artificial intelligence researchers were still struggling with the issues Winograd and Flores highlighted six years earlier.

The vocabulary had changed, however. One prominent version of the dispute had become known as the debate between the "symbolic" and "connectionist" paradigms.[62] In early 1990s writings, the debate was described as having begun in 1984 when there was a significant shift of attention away from models of the mind as a physical symbol system and toward "connectionist architectures," "parallel distributed processing systems," or "neural networks." Researchers continued to differ on the key issues in the debate, the status of GOFAI (good old fashioned artificial intelligence) or CTM (the computational theory of mind) and the extent to which the new paradigm had clearly broken with the old. But some samples of their arguments will show that the center of the dispute continued to be the representational problem and its concomitant symbolic conception of language.

Serious questions about the symbolic paradigm had been raised by certain neurophysiological data that were as revealing as the optical nerve data collected by Maturana and his colleagues. For instance, when sets of neural units were subjected to careful statistical analysis, it could be shown that a certain node is always ON whenever the subject being considered is "dogs," for example, and never ON—or ON very weakly—when the subject is "cats," whereas another node is ON for "cats" and not for "dogs." Originally these data appeared to support the symbolic paradigm, because it seemed that certain neural nodes corresponded with, represented, or symbolized certain semantic features. But, as one author explains, "the best reason for *not* calling the dog-active node the dog symbol is that you can 'kill' or disable that node and the system will go right on discriminating dogs, remembering about dogs, and so on, with at most a slight degradation in performance."[63] Moreover, other nearby nodes that appeared to be operating almost randomly picked up some of the disabled node's functioning, so those "noisy" nodes are also involved in the process. System functions, in other words, overlap, or are distributed in parallel and interconnected networks, not in the simple linear structure prescribed by the symbolic paradigm.

Partly as a result of data like these, critics of early artificial intelligence efforts argue that the "fathers of AI made a bold conjecture, and encountered an equally uncompromising refutation." It has become abundantly clear, Margaret A. Boden contends, that symbolic AI research cannot model either commonsense reasoning or flexible pattern matching. And these are significant failures. In fact, Boden asserts, rarely in the history of science "has there been such an expensive blind alley. The only comfort to be drawn from nearly forty years of AI research is that it has finally been shown to be a dead end. The abject failure of GOFAI has at least spurred the investigation of alternative computational approaches."[64]

Boden believes that these alternative approaches are heavily indebted to GOFAI, and she supports those proponents of parallel distributed processing who believe that it is wrong to see their efforts as a clear *alternative* to representational schemes like semantic networks or production systems. Symbolic and connectionist paradigms are different in degree, not kind, she claims, in that many connectionist models can be seen as one way of implementing the earlier schemes in parallel networks.

Other contributors to this conversation reinforce Boden's view when they argue, contra Winograd and Flores, that *both* symbolic and connectionist paradigms are *representational*. For example, Tim van Gelder asserts,

> Assuming that any remotely plausible theory of mind must be based on manipulation of internal representations of some kind, we need to find some other generic form of representation to play a foundational role in the new theory analogous to that played by symbolic representation in CTM. . . .
>
> The alternative form of representation required by this approach has to satisfy some demanding conditions. It must, of course, be demonstrably nonsymbolic, but it must also be sufficiently general to allow the characterization of a reasonably broad conception of the mind.[65]

For van Gelder, the primary feature that distinguishes a nonsymbolic representational system from a symbolic representational one is superposition. To explain, the most reliable current neurophysiological data indicate that each memory is stored across a wide network of neurons, which means that it is possible in practice to store many memories over the same set of neurons. This is the sense in which the memory is "distributed." Precisely because it is distributed, it is misleading to characterize a memory stored in this way as "symbolic." There is no discrete "symbolized" to correspond with any discrete "symbol." As van Gelder explains, it is as if there were no separate location in a filing cabinet for each discrete item, but that "the whole cabinet would be representing every item without any more fine-grained correspondence of sheets or locations to individual items."[66] Van Gelder's summary of this point clearly demonstrates the parallels between this dispute among artificial intelligence researchers and arguments over the symbol model reviewed in earlier chapters of this book:

> Superposed schemes thus differ fundamentally from more stan-
> dard localist varieties. In general, schemes of representation
> define a space of allowable representations and set up a corre-
> spondence with the space of items or contents to be represented.
> We are accustomed to thinking of such schemes as setting up
> a roughly isomorphic correspondence—that is, there is a dis-
> tinct representation for every item to be represented, and the
> structure of the space of representations systematically corre-
> sponds (in a way that can only be characterized relative to the
> scheme in question) to the structure of the space of possible
> contents. Thus, languages usually define an infinite array of
> distinct expression types, which are then put in correspondence
> with distinct items or states of affairs; and standard methods
> of generating images aim at finding a distinct image for every
> scene. When this kind of discrete correspondence fails to be the
> case. . . we usually think of it as some kind of aberration or
> defect in the scheme. . . .
>
> The notion of superposed representation overthrows this
> whole familiar picture.[67]

Not all artificial intelligence researchers or philosophers of cognition are satisfied with the claim that symbolic and connectionist
paradigms are both *representational*. In fact, at this writing, the construct of representation is being closely scrutinized by these scholars, and some are questioning how universally it should be assumed
to characterize cognitive functioning and thus how central it is to
models of artificial intelligence. This literature is voluminous and
complex, and there is space here to mention only three important
contributions. But a brief review of these essays will emphasize again
how important work on the representational problem and the symbol model is being done by cognitive philosophers and AI researchers.

In a widely cited essay, philosophers Jerry A. Fodor and Zenon
W. Pylyshyn argue for a version of the symbolic paradigm and
against the efficacy of connectionist models, in part because the latter cannot account for the construction of complex representations
from simpler ones.[68] They maintain that human linguistic and mental representations are productive and systematic and that to account for these features in a finite system it is necessary for there
to be a "physical instantiation mapping" process that, as two commentators put it, "maps atomic symbols to simple physical structures
and complex expressions to complex physical structures such that
the causal relations between the physical structures are sensitive
to the syntactic constituency structure of the instantiated symbols."[69]

Connectionist networks in principle, they argue, lack the capability to perform this kind of mapping.

This essay and Fodor's earlier work[70] led Thomas Goschke and Dirk Koppelberg to explore the construct *representation* itself. "It is far from being settled," they note, "what exactly is meant when semantic content or meaning is ascribed to internal states of symbolic or connectionist systems."[71] To develop a connectionist theory of internal representation, they claim that two problems must be addressed: (1) the problem of semantic content, that is, "what it is that makes internal states in connectionist networks representations with a specific semantic content?" and (2) the problem of semantic compositionality, that is, "How can connectionist models account for the combination of simple representations into complex ones?" They first argue with respect to (1) that it is important to distinguish between what a system *represents* and what its elements *indicate* and that not every indication is a representation. They also contend that it is not enough to focus on relations between hidden units and the input patterns they respond to, but that relations among internal states also have to be taken into account. With respect to (2), they offer empirical evidence that pragmatic, semantic, lexical, and psychological aspects of context affect exactly what information is integrated into a given representation of a category and thus that a context-independent theory of compositionality is unsupportable. Against Fodor and Pylyshyn, they argue that it is not the tokening of an internal symbol but "the connectivity of the network and the covariational patterns that are encoded in it that underlie the network's ability to categorize objects. . . . Viewed in this way, there is *no representation of fixed meanings* associated with each word form in the lexicon" (italics added).[72] They conclude that their view challenges the notion that human thought is a logiclike inferential process and that it "considers symbolic operations at best only part of our mental life."[73]

John Haugeland covers some of the same ground in "Representational Genera."[74] Haugeland distinguishes between two genera of representations—*logical* (calculi and computer programming languages) and *iconic* (photographs)—and asks whether *distributed* representation is a separate genus and, if so, what is its "generic essence." Like other analysts, he breaks representation into three elements, that which represents, representing, and that which is represented; and he argues that essential differentia can best be identified in what is represented. He reviews the "canonical accounts" of logical, iconic, and distributed representations and then demonstrates that these accounts do not render the three mutually exclusive and hence "are incapable of supporting principled distinctions among the genera."[75] The reason they fail, Haugeland claims, is that they focus on the relation instead of what is represented. Haugeland's analysis of the "represented" depends on his assertion that there is something he terms "the strict content of a representation, that which is not augmented or mediated by any other, its *skeletal* or *bare-bones* content."[76] He gives an example of a police officer's report of the scene of a crime, arguing that the fact, for example, that the contents of some drawers were strewn about might be in the report, but the fact that the drawers were "searched" would not. "The content of what is strictly said—said in so many words— is intuitively what we mean by *skeletal* content."[77]

Haugeland admits that there are problems with his "skeletal content" notion, perhaps the most serious of which is that it assumes language without any (context-dependent, agenda-driven) interlocutors. But he insists that this notion clears the way for characterizing the essences of the general phenomenon of representing in terms of the natures of their respective *contents*. Logical representation represents atomic sentences, set membership or function application, propositional attitude ascription, and so on, which are always identifiable separately and individually. The contents of iconic representations are not so identifiable; they are "variations of values along certain dimensions with respect to locations in certain other dimensions."[78] Connectionist networks contain two candidates for status as representations, "patterns of activation" and "patterns of connection weight."[79] Haugeland argues that there is a sense in which these function as "stand-ins" for specific features or aspects of the environment to which the system must adjust its behavior and that in this sense they *are* representations. He concludes that "the contents of logical, iconic, and distributed representations are characterized respectively by absolute, relative, and associative elements."[80]

Haugeland's metaphysics is clearly problematic; it is at least uncertain whether he has successfully identified a distinct and characteristic "represented" for each of his alleged representations. But it is equally clear that he is working a familiar set of problems. His final sentences display the connections between his interests and this book's:

> Thus, everyday speech is extraordinarily sensitive to relevance and topical surprise, yet remarkably unfazed by ambiguity, ungrammaticality, and catachresis; it is thoroughly suffused with allusion, trope, posture, and drama; it is biassed [sic], fanciful, opportunistic, emotion charged, and generally fast and

loose; and much the same could be said of thought. Yet these qualities are notoriously resistant to capture in explicit symbolic models. Perhaps, that is because they involve adjustment to contents that cannot be represented logically: sophisticated and intricate abilities that, in symbol processing terms, could only be classified as transductions or basic operations—but are hardly peripheral or primitive. Perhaps natural language is possible only as symbiotic with the distributed representations of the system it is implemented in.[81]

The books and essays reviewed in this section illustrate how, like the philosophers, linguists, and semioticians discussed in Chapters 2 and 3, cognitive philosophers and artificial intelligence researchers are grappling with the commitments that make up the symbol model. For example, with respect to the two worlds commitment, Winograd and Flores claim that "nothing exists except through language"; that is, that there is only one world. On the other hand, some proponents of the connectionist paradigm struggle to distinguish "internal states" from "words in the lexicon," "hidden units" from "input patterns," and "features of the environment" from "patterns of activation weight." Haugeland recognizes the problems created by postulating "skeletal content" divorced from the humans for whom it is "content" at all, but he proceeds nonetheless. Therefore it is still uncertain whether these theorists will be able to work out a coherent connectionist alternative to the symbolic paradigm that is nonetheless *representational*. They have not yet done so.

With respect to the atomism commitment, these authors are puzzling over the significance of connectivity and patterning versus individual elements and the possibility of identifying individual "bones" in "skeletal content." Extended sections of most of the discussions also evidence these scholars' concerns with commitment 3, the central issue of representationalism—consider, for example, Goschke and Koppleberg's distinction between *indication* and *representation*. Haugeland manifests a focal interest in working out this same commitment when he distinguishes among that which represents, representing, and that which is represented and when he comments in his conclusion about the impossibility of "capturing" common features of natural language in explicit symbolic models of language. In 1992, this part of the general project was also unfinished.

Perhaps some of these scholars would be persuaded by the argument in the previous chapter—and in previous sections of this chapter—that the central problem is their continued commitment to representation itself. It may be that the connectionist paradigm will emerge as genuinely paradigmatic only when it is worked out as a non- or post-representational model of cognition. But in any case it is clear that there are fruitful connections between the projects pursued by these artificial intelligence researchers and cognitive philosophers, on the one hand, and communication theorists and philosophical hermeneuticians, on the other.

Conclusion

My goal in this chapter has been to provide some collateral to back up the promissory note about interdisciplinary studies offered in the Preface. I argued there that scholars who read and contribute to a variety of disparate literatures are developing remarkably similar critiques of their disciplines' accounts of the nature of language and remarkably parallel alternative perspectives. Many of these critiques build on ideas first articulated by Heidegger and other postmodern philosophers, and the alternative accounts move in directions these thinkers indicated. Thus it is not surprising that parts of these projects complement mine.

But it does appear significant. Clearly when cadres of careful scholars whose works are published in such as diverse journals as *Cognitive Science, Philosophy of the Social Sciences, American Annals of the Deaf, Artificial Intelligence, Communication Theory, Gallaudet Encyclopedia of Deaf People and Deafness, Human Studies, Philosophy and Phenomenological Research, Memory and Cognition, Cultural Hermeneutics,* and *Quarterly Journal of Speech* raise similar questions and offer similar responses, the parallels and overlaps are worth noting. Consensus is emerging here, although admittedly at a high level of abstraction. It is becoming increasingly difficult to insist that language can most fruitfully be viewed as a semiotic system and increasingly clear that it can be accounted for as articulate contact.

The primary goal of Part I has been to articulate a post-semiotic account of the nature of language anchored in the claim that language is first and foremost not a system of signs or symbols but constitutive articulate contact. The purpose of Part II is to begin to demonstrate the efficacy of this post-semiotic account by using it as a lens to examine three influential philosophies of language.

Part II
The Symbol Model and Three Philosophies of Language

❀ Chapter 6

Semiotics and Dialogue In
Marxism and the Philosophy of Language

Marxism and the Philosophy of Language was first published in Leningrad in 1929.[1] Several translations, including an English one by Ladislav Matejka and I. R. Titunik, appeared in the early 1970s,[2] and in 1986 Harvard University Press reprinted the Matejka and Titunik translation with an introduction and appendices by the translators.[3] The translators' Preface to this edition and related scholarship explain that this work is one of a group of more than a dozen interconnected articles and books published in the U.S.S.R. between 1925 and 1934 whose authorship is disputed. The works emerged from a loosely structured literary circle whose membership included Pavel N. Medvedev, Valentin Nikolaevic Volosinov, and by far the best known of the circle, Mikhail M. Bakhtin. Volosinov is identified as the author of the Harvard Press edition of *Marxism and the Philosophy of Language*, even though many scholars accept V. V. Ivanov's 1973 claim that the work was written by Bakhtin. Bakhtin's American biographers, Katerina Clark and Michael Holquist, agree with Ivanov that Bakhtin was responsible for "ninety percent of the text of the three books in question" (*Marxism and the Philosophy of Language*; *Freudianism: A Marxist Critique*, also published under Volosinov's name; and *The Formal Method in Literary Scholarship*, attributed to Medvedev).[4] There are reports of private

165

conversations in which Bakhtin's authorship was corroborated by Bakhtin himself, his wife, and Volosinov's wife.[5] Clark and Holquist also note that, at least up until the breakup of the Soviet Union, the official Soviet publishing agency (VAAP) required that Bakhtin's name appear on any new edition of the disputed volumes, and they argue that these instances of "reverse plagiarism" may be attributed to Bakhtin's love of conversation, his conviction that "meaning is always a function of at least two consciousnesses," and that "texts are always shared."[6]

On the other hand, although Bakhtin was still alive at the time of Ivanov's original assertion, he never made a public statement accepting or denying it. In addition, when the VAAP urged Bakhtin shortly before his death to sign an affidavit concerning the authorship of these works, he refused. Tzvetan Todorov concludes that Bakhtin probably did not write all the works in question.[7] I. R. Titunik concurs, and argues that there are textual data to refute the argument for Bakhtin's authorship of several works, including a distinct lack of cross-references and important terminological differences among key concepts in the writings attributed to each of the three authors.[8] At least partly as a result of questions raised by Titunik and others, the translators of *Marxism and the Philosophy of Language* conclude that, "fair-mindedness and scholarly integrity dictate that the author of *Marxism and the Philosophy of Language* continue to be identified as Valentin Nikolaevic Volosinov since it has not been conclusively proved otherwise. It is a common practice in countries like the Soviet Union to remake the past by fiat; we see no reason to follow suit."[9]

The authorship question is potentially important here, because there are books and essays attributed to Bakhtin and Medvedev that elaborate and modify some of the claims made in *Marxism and the Philosophy of Language*. Thus one could conceivably argue that any close reading of this book should integrate materials from other works by members of the Bakhtin circle. But this work clearly constitutes a structurally complete, conceptually coherent whole that addresses central questions about the nature of language.

Moreover, the reason I examine *Marxism and the Philosophy of Language* here is that it relies heavily at some points on the symbol model and at others points toward a distinctly post-semiotic view of the nature of language. So regardless of whether the manuscript was produced by Volosinov, Bakhtin, or a collaboration among members of the circle, it can function as a test case of what occurs when semiotic and post-semiotic constructs are juxtaposed. Close reading reveals that this "first extensive Russian prolegomenon to semiotics"[10] embodies a tension between, on the one hand, a Saussurian, binary, representational concept of sign and, on the other, an account of the nature of language that is first social, then communicative, and finally dialogic. When in later chapters the work turns to application, this tension is largely resolved in a post-semiotic, communicative direction. Thus, a symbol model critique of *Marxism and the Philosophy of Language* is warranted by the work's intellectual significance, its Russian and Marxist perspective, its dialogic focus, and its attempt to foreground both semiosis and dialogue.

Overview

The book is divided into three parts, the first of which, according to the author's introduction, is designed "to substantiate the significance of the philosophy of language for Marxism as a whole" and "to *bring out the position that the philosophy of language occupies in the Marxist worldview*" (pp. xiv–xv). In this section Volosinov[11] tightly connects the central Marxist focus on ideology theory with the primary topic of semiotics: "Everything ideological possesses *meaning*: it represents, depicts, or stands for something lying outside itself. In other words, it is a *sign. Without signs there is no ideology*" (p. 9). Part II is an "attempt to resolve the basic problem of the philosophy of language, that of the *actual mode of existence of linguistic phenomena*" (xv). In these four chapters Volosinov moves significantly away from the semiotic focus of his earlier theorizing and toward a communicative view of language, as he argues that linguists have mistakenly treated language either as an abstract *system* or as the product of an *individual* consciousness and have thereby overlooked its inescapably *social* nature. The actual mode of existence of language, he insists, is the concrete utterance, which is "*the product of the reciprocal relationship between speaker and listener, addresser and addressee*" (p. 86). Part III continues the book's progression from general to particular by focusing on one specialized issue, the problem of "reported utterance" or "speech about speech," such as that which occurs in a novel when the narrator reports what a character has said. Although this topic initially might appear marginally important to all but those interested in literary theory, Volosinov explains that he chose it precisely because it embodies the central feature articulated in Part II: reported utterance "interorients" two persons' speech and is thus a concrete instance of language-as-dialogue. Thus the book as a whole is a tightly organized discussion that moves from a general perspective on political philosophy, to a specific account of the nature of language, and then to an application of this account to one issue in literary practice.

From my viewpoint, the most interesting feature of the book is the way it attempts a dialectical synthesis between a Saussurian semiotic and Humboldtian non- or post-semiotic, communicative account of the nature of language. In the reading that follows, I quote extensively from the text to enable the reader to observe where Volosinov echoes symbol model analyses similar to those I reviewed in Chapters 2 and 3, and where he echoes central features of the post-semiotic account of the nature of language outlined in Chapter 4 and further developed in Chapter 5. These quotations illustrate, first, that semiosis is absolutely central to the discussion of the role of philosophy of language in Marxism. Part I is replete with references to several of the five theoretical commitments that make up the symbol model. Meaning is analyzed as representation, words are treated as signs, and a clear distinction is drawn between the "reality of the sign" and the "reality of the outside world." Both "inner" and "outer" speech are treated as signifying processes. Part I also foreshadows the dialogical focus of Part II, as Volosinov discusses the social nature of signs. As the author develops his specific philosophy of language in Part II, however, constructions such as "concrete utterance," the importance of the "listener-understander," and "the practical business of living speech" increase markedly, whereas references to "representation" and "the sign" significantly decrease. The text reveals that the account of the nature of language developed in Part II is much more communicative and post-semiotic than semiotic. Then in Part III, when Volosinov turns to practical application, the symbol model almost completely disappears. His analysis of reported speech is contextual, relational, and communicative; and it clearly does not depend on semiotic constructs or categories. In other words, it appears from the text that the further the author moved away from paying his philosophical and political dues and the closer he got to applying what was genuinely innovative about his philosophical perspective, the less useful he found the symbol model. His insight into the communicative nature of language was difficult to develop within the constraints of his semiotic analysis, especially as he grappled with actual cases of reported speech. So this work appears to be one in which there is a manifest tension between a semiotic and a post-semiotic account of the nature of language, a tension that, insofar as it is resolved at all, foregrounds the post-semiotic.

Some scholars might attempt to account for this tension by questioning the extent to which Medvedev, Volosinov, and Bakhtin were actually committed to Marxism. One might argue, for example, that if the references to Marxism in Part I functioned primarily as a sop to Soviet censors, then any conceptual inconsistencies between that section and the rest of the book could be viewed as relatively inconsequential. In fact, Ivanov, Holquist, and Roman Jakobson make the first half if this argument. All three have characterized Bakhtin's Marxism as "cover," "disguise," or "expedience." Jakobson, for example, claimed that one of the reasons Bakhtin had trouble getting his work published—and therefore might have attributed it to Volosinov and Medvedev—was that "Bakhtine se refusait à faire des concessions à phraséologie de l'époque et à certains dogmes imposés aux auteurs."[12] The terms *la phraséologie de lépoque* and *certains dogmes imposés aux auteurs*, of course, are code words for Soviet Marxist dogma. Holquist takes this position even more strongly. As I noted previously, he believes that Bakhtin wrote the works published under Volosinov's name and, he claims, "Marxist terms are most often present in Bakhtin's books from this period as a kind of *convenient*, in the abstract not necessarily inimical—but above all *necessary*—flag under which to advance his own [orthodox Christian] views."[13] On the other hand, Frederic Jameson, a Westerner with Marxist credentials, claims that the book is not only "quite simply one of the best general introductions to linguistic study as a whole" but also a thoroughly and solidly Marxist work.[14]

As I will illustrate, several features of the text's structure and argument support Jameson's claim about the work's Marxist credentials. I believe it can be shown that there are important inconsistencies in Volosinov's book—which make it much less than "one of the best general introductions to linguistic study as a whole." But these inconsistencies are due much more to the inherent conceptual tension between semiotic and post-semiotic perspectives on language than to any efforts to appease Soviet censors.

Part I: A Semiotic Account of Marxism

The goal of the three chapters making up Part I is to argue that philosophy of language is centrally important to Marxism. The second sentence of Chapter 1 asserts that Marxism "cannot continue to move ahead productively without special provision for . . . [the] investigation and solution" of certain problems in the philosophy of language" (p. 9). The basic connection between Marxism and language philosophy is made in the immediately following sentence which, as I noted earlier, claims that Marxism is first and foremost a theory of ideologies; in fact, ideology provides "the bases for the studies of scientific knowledge, literature, religion, ethics, and so forth." One defining feature of ideology is that "any ideological product is not only itself a part of a reality . . . it also . . . reflects and refracts *another reality outside itself*" (p. 9, italics added). Thus "everything ideological possesses *meaning:* it represents, depicts, or stands for something lying outside itself. In other words it is a *sign. Without signs there is no ideology*" (p. 9).

These initial sentences contain Volosinov's articulation of the defining feature of the symbol model—the commitment to two worlds. A fundamental distinction is made here between the ideological product or sign and something "lying outside itself." This commitment is clarified in the next paragraph which outlines what happens when a physical object is converted into a sign: "Without ceasing to be a part of material reality [World$_1$], such an object, to some degree, reflects and refracts another reality [World$_2$]" (p. 9). The following page also includes a reference to the world made up of "natural phenomena" and a correlative "special world—the *world of signs*" (p. 10).

The initial sentences also manifest the author's commitment to representationalism, and they open the door for an atomistic analysis. Each ideological product is identified as a "sign" which means that it "represents . . . or stands for something lying outside itself." Moreover, the term *any product* and the example of individual "physical bodies" that function as signs suggest that the representational relationships hold between identifiable *units*. As if to remove any ambiguity about his basic perspective, Volosinov emphasizes that "*everything ideological possesses semiotic value*" (p. 10).

Volosinov then elaborates his commitment to two worlds as he emphasizes the materiality of every ideological sign. Idealistic philosophy of culture and psychologistic cultural studies both ignore the fact that "*consciousness itself can arise and become a viable fact only in the material embodiment of signs*" (p. 11). World$_1$, in other words, is not psychological, as Saussure sometimes claimed; it does not consist of some inner, nonmaterial, unembodied realm, but of material reality. Moreover, one important feature of this material reality is that it is interindividual. "Signs emerge, after all, only in the process of interaction between one individual and another" (p. 11). Idealism distorts this fact by treating consciousness as "somewhere above existence," and psychological positivism distorts it by treating consciousness as "just a conglomeration of fortuitous, psychophysiological reactions which, by some miracle, results in meaningful and unified ideological creativity" (p. 12). But "the ideological as such" can be explained only in terms of "the special, social material of signs crated by man," which "arise only on *interindividual territory*" (p. 12). This line of argument leads to the conclusion that "the reality of ideological phenomena is the objective reality of social signs," and *"the word is the ideological phenomenon par excellence"* (p. 13). The word, in short, is the material and ideological reality that arises between persons and is thus the primary unit of semiosis.

In the remaining ten paragraphs of this chapter, Volosinov develops his incipient commitment to atomism as he outlines various features of the word as an ideological materiality. Given his claim that ideological phenomena are inherently social, one might expect that Volosinov was not actually thinking here of the individual word but, perhaps, of the phrase, statement, or, with an eye toward Part II, the utterance. But this position seems to be denied by the text. His commitment to atomism appears to persist as he declares, "A word is the purest and most sensitive medium of social intercourse," "a word . . . can carry out ideological functions of *any* kind—scientific, aesthetic, ethical, religious," and "the material of behavioral communication is preeminently the *word*" (p. 14). He also maintains that the word can become *"the semiotic material of inner life—of consciousness* (inner speech)," and that all ideological manifestations "are bathed by, suspended in, and cannot be entirely segregated or divorced from" words (p. 15).

In sum, this first chapter includes several manifestations of Volosinov's commitment to the symbol model. One is that his concept of the sign is similar in some ways to Saussure's in that, as Clark and Holquist note, it is composed of "a mark that is simply an indicator, the signifier, and a concept that is so indicated, the signified. [Volosinov], however, concentrates on the worldly, sensory aspect of the sign"; that is, on the features of World$_1$.[15] A second is Volosinov's representationalism. In a footnote he praises Cassirer's neo-Kantianism for its claim that "each element of consciousness represents something, bears a symbolic function."[16] Third, he describes language as essentially made up of individual word units.

Chapter 2 shifts focus to one of the fundamental problems of Marxism, the relationship of basis and superstructure. The goal of the chapter is to clarify how philosophy of language can provide one fruitful way to understand this relationship. Marx and Engels claimed that society is generated dialectically, through a process that emerges from material bases and comes to completion in superstructures. Volosinov illustrates this dynamic with the example of how, when the gentry class in a society degenerates, this material event is followed by the appearance in the society's literature of the character the "superfluous man," which then becomes an ideological product. Marxism also asserts that the basis determines ideology *causally*, but, argues Volosinov, this statement is "far too general and therefore ambiguous" (p. 17). Simplistic analyses have treated this causality as mechanical, and Volosinov claims that it is much more complex. The point of the chapter is that this relationship between basis and superstructure "can be elucidated to a significant degree through the material of the word" (p. 19). As Volosinov summarizes, "Looked at from the angle of our concerns, the essence of this problem comes down to *how* actual existence (the basis) determines sign [superstructure] and *how* sign reflects and refracts existence in its process of generation.... The word has the capacity to register all the transitory, delicate, momentary phases of social change" (p. 19).

The communicative life of a society, Volosinov argues, consists of a variety of utterances that make up a multitude of *speech genres*, such as technical on-the-job communication. Because of the close connection between these genres and the ideology, "*A typology of these forms* is one of the urgent tasks of Marxism" (p. 20). These genres or forms, which are superstructure, are conditioned by "*the social organization of the participants involved and also by the immediate conditions of their interaction [basis]*" (p. 21). Here the relationship between basis and superstructure is clearly dialectical. Moreover, "Existence reflected in sign is not merely reflected but *refracted*. How is this refraction of existence in the ideological sign determined? By an intersecting of differently oriented social interests within one and the same sign community, i.e., *by the class struggle*" (p. 23). In this way, "Sign becomes an arena of the class struggle" (p. 23).

Thus a perennial Marxist problem can be solved with the help of philosophy of language in the following way: "The material of the verbal sign allows one most fully and easily to follow out the continuity of the dialectical process of change, a process which goes from basis to superstructures. The category of mechanical causality in explanations of ideological phenomena can most easily be surmounted on the grounds of philosophy of language" (p. 24).

Without foregrounding them, this chapter introduces several constructs that figure prominently in Parts II and III. Despite his earlier comments about "the word" as the preeminent sign, here Volosinov indicates his interest not just in written words or in communicative abstractions but in "*verbal interaction* ... this actual process of verbal communication and interaction"(p. 19). He also characterizes this interaction as made up not only of words but also of nonverbal elements, "the gesture, the act" (p. 19). And he underscores the crucial importance of context to the forms and meanings of these interactions (p. 20). Thus, although his analysis is clearly still semiotic, he introduces constructs that can be expected subsequently to strain any effort to reduce language to a semiotic system.

The plot thickens in Chapter 3, as Volosinov turns to a major task of Marxism, the challenge of constructing "a genuinely objective psychology, which means a psychology based on *sociological* not physiological or biological, principles" (p. 25). This psychology must affirm the materiality of its subject matter without reducing it to an object of natural scientific analysis. The key is to recognize that the subject psyche must be understood and interpreted as *ideological*. This insight allows one to see that *"the reality of the inner psyche is the same reality as that of the sign"* (p. 26). The subjective psyche is located between the organism and the outside world and its material manifestation is as *sign*.

Volosinov uses a ten-paragraph discussion of Dilthey to distinguish between an "idealistic" version of this insight and one consistent with dialectical materialism. He lauds Dilthey's insistence that the human sciences focus on *meaning*, but rejects Dilthey's treatment of meaning as ultimately inhering "in a-temporal, a-spatial Spirit" (p. 28). "Meaning," Volosinov insists, "is the expression of a semiotic relationship between a particular piece of reality and another kind of reality that it stands for, represents, or depicts" (p. 28). So meaning analysis must centrally and simply be sign analysis. There is no need to attempt to explain how "outer experience" expresses a qualitatively different "inner experience," because *meaning* is accessible in signs. Signs not only express experience outwardly but they also constitute the material form of the experience for the experiencer.

What then, Volosinov asks, is the sign material of the psyche? Partly the organic processes of breathing, blood circulation, and so on, but "preeminently the word—*inner speech*. . . . it is the word that constitutes the foundation, the skeleton of inner life" (p. 29). This psychic content is the only proper object for psychology. Volosinov argues that his conception can be clarified by contrasting it with that of functional psychology, which focuses not on the "what" of experience but the "how." Like Dilthey's work, functional psychology is also grounded in idealism, and thus gives preference to the psyche rather than to ideology. Functional psychology can give an account of the experience of a tree or stone, but, because of its Kantian tendency to appeal ultimately to a transcendental realm, it cannot explain the experience of a logical concept, ethical value, artistic image, or other ideological phenomenon.

The history of these questions, Volosinov argues, reveals a "peculiar periodic alternation" between psychologism and antipsychologism. At the beginning of the twentieth century, Husserl, the phenomenologists, and the neo-Kantians of the Marburg and Freiburg schools argued for "the banishment of psychologism from all fields of knowledge and even from psychology itself!" (p. 32). Now, says Volosinov, this wave has begun to abate, and a new form of psychologism is growing under the rubric, *philosophy of life*. What is still missing, however, is a dialectical synthesis of these two perspectives; this is why psychology cannot yet give a suitable account of ideology. The solution to this problem is to acknowledge that "the ideological sign is the common territory for both the psyche and for ideology, a territory that is material, sociological, and meaningful" (p. 33).

This is why Volosinov makes the ideological sign central to his program. It is crucial, he argues, to acknowledge the close connection between the psyche and ideology: "Every outer ideological sign, of whatever kind, is engulfed in and washed over by inner signs— by the consciousness. . . . Therefore, *from the standpoint of content, there is no basic division between the psyche and ideology; the difference is one of degree only*" (p. 33). This move leads Volonisov into one of his central claims; namely, that the individual is a social being or, as a postmodern theorist might express it, the self is decentered. We are led astray, Volosinov claims, by thinking of the "social" in binary opposition with the "individual," and thus concluding that the psyche is individual while ideology is social. "Notions of that sort are fundamentally false. The correlate of the social is the "natural" and thus "individual" is not meant in the sense of a person, but 'individual' as natural, biological specimen. The individual, as possessor of the contents of his own consciousness, as author of his own thoughts, as the personality responsible for his thoughts and feelings—such an individual is a purely socioideological phenomenon. Therefore, the content of the 'individual' psyche is by its very nature just as social as is ideology. . . " (p. 34). Volosinov acknowledges immediately that, despite this correlation, there is still a difference between inner and outer signs, between psyche and ideology, and it has to do with the context of interpretation of each. Inner signs are interpreted in the context of the self's particular life, and outer signs are interpreted in the context of the relevant system of ideology.

In a move that reflects what will become his primary interest in this work, Volosinov dedicates the final section of this chapter to "the problem of the inner sign" (p. 37). A fully elaborated philosophy of language, he argues, would describe the nature of the word as inner sign, the form in which inner speech is implemented, how inner speech ties in with the social situation and with external utterance, and how one can uncover or capture inner speech. But here he addresses—in three relatively brief paragraphs—only the question of the form in which inner speech is implemented. Setting the stage for a central claim he will make in Part II, Volosinov asserts that inner speech cannot be categorized lexically or grammatically, because its units are whole entities that "resemble the *alternating lines of a dialogue*"(p. 38). These units are "*total impressions of utterances*," such as "the aroma of a totality . . . which precedes and underlies knowing the object distinctly" (p. 38). With this brief but intriguing comment, Volosinov turns to his conclusion.

His dialectical synthesis of psychology and antipsychology underscores how psychology must be grounded in Marxist ideological science. This means that "speech had first to come into being and develop in the process of the social intercourse of organisms so that afterward it could enter within the organism and become inner speech" (p. 39). At the same time, the ideological sign "is made viable by its psychic implementation. . . . between the psyche and ideology there exists. . . a continuous dialectical interplay," an interplay that has heretofore "never found proper understanding or adequate expression" (p. 39). "Thus," the chapter concludes, "the psyche and ideology dialectically interpenetrate in the unitary and objective process of social intercourse" (p. 41).

Two features of Part I should be underscored. One is that a close reading of the text does not readily support those who claim that this work's Marxism is simply "cover," "disguise," or "expedience." Although Volosinov was undoubtedly eager to have the work approved by Soviet censors, several authentically Marxist commitments are integral to both the form and the substance of his philosophical argument.[17] The most obvious are the primacy of ideology, the importance of the basis-superstructure relationship, the appeal to materialism, and the importance of dialectically synthesizing an extant thesis and antithesis. These commitments resurface in Parts II and III. It may well have been that this work's brand of Marxism was unpalatable to the mechanists, reflexologists, and Marrists who, according to Matejka, "in the 1930's gained absolute control over all aspects of humanistic studies in the Soviet Union."[18] Clearly the disappearance and apparent deaths of Volosinov and Medvedev and the exile of Bakhtin indicate that Stalinist dogmatists violently disagreed with at least some of the views expressed by these authors. But from a perspective outside Marxism, it is difficult to deny the centrality to this work of both Marxist issues and Marxist modes of argument.

The second notable feature of Part I, as I have already indicated, is its commitment to central features of the symbol model. The text includes explicit affirmations of the first three theoretical commitments: to two worlds, atomism, and representationalism. Both it and the secondary literature affirm Volosinov's conviction that the sign is of absolutely central importance, that it is an ontologically binary phenomenon that links aspects of two distinct worlds, that the relationship between a sign and its meaning is representational, and that the word is the preeminent example of a sign. Importantly, these commitments are attenuated by Volosinov's criticism of the notion that language constitutes a system and the absence of any prominent argument that humans use language as an instrument or tool.

Part II: A Dialogical Account of Language

Volosinov entitled Part II, "Toward a Marxist Philosophy of Language." It begins with a straightforward identification of its central focus:

> What, in fact is the subject matter of the philosophy of language? Where are we to find it? What is its concrete, material existence like? By what method or methods can we come to grips with its mode of existence?
>
> In the first—the introductory—section of our study, we completely eschewed these concrete issues. We addressed ourselves to the philosophy of language, the philosophy of the word. But what is language, and what is word (p. 45)?

As Part II develops, it becomes clear that, in three of its four chapters, Volosinov's method for pursuing this question is Hegelian. After some introductory comments, he reviews what he argues are the two extant responses to this set of questions, *"individualistic subjectivism"* and *"abstract objectivism."* Then he offers his perspective as a dialectical synthesis which is responsive to the shortcomings of each. The heart of Volosinov's philosophy of language appears in the three chapters that develop this synthesis.

After the comments just quoted, Volosinov provides eight paragraphs to frame or contextualize his approach. He acknowledges that he will not provide any "conclusive definition" of language but will proceed empirically, not led so much by "the intellectual faculty for making formulas" but rather by "the eyes and hands attempting to get the feel of the actual presence of the subject matter"(p. 45). He rejects, however, the *"superficial phonetic empiricism"* that dominates linguistic science, partly because such approaches miss "the very essence of the thing we are studying—its semiotic and ideological nature"(p. 46). The phenomenon is much more complex than phonetics acknowledges, he argues, and the primary features of its complexity are that language is *context dependent* and *social*.

Given this frame, Volosinov begins characterizing the "two basic trends," individualistic subjectivism and abstract objectivism. The former is epitomized in Humboldt's works. According to Volosinov, Humboldt considered the basis of language to be "the individual creative act of speech. The source of language is the individual psyche"(p. 48). From this perspective language is an unceasing creative activity (*energeia*), governed by laws of individual psychology. Proponents of this view believe that accounts of the language *system* capture only "the hardened lava of language creativity" (p. 48). Volosinov alludes to the works of various followers of Humboldt, and emphasizes the influence of "one of the most potent movements in contemporary philosophical-linguistic thought," the Vossler school (p. 50). Vosslerites reject phonetic positivism and emphasize the aesthetic dimension of language. For them the basic reality of language is also the individual creative act of speech. Most of the actual studies completed by Vosslerites "stand on the boundary between linguistics (in the narrow sense) and stylistics" (p. 51). The Italian literary philosopher Benedetto Croce's ideas are "close in many respects to Vossler's" (p. 52).

The second trend of thought treats language as a system of phonetic, grammatical, and lexical forms. "If, for the first trend, language is an ever-flowing stream of speech acts in which nothing remains fixed and identical to itself, then, for the second trend, language is the stationary rainbow arched over that stream"(p. 52). From this perspective individual creative features of speech are "totally unimportant. What is important is precisely the *normative identity*" of language forms (p. 53). The insistence on the part of abstract objectivists in studying language synchronically rather than diachronically highlights the contrast between this approach and that of Humboldt and the Vosslerites. From this perspective, the individual acquires the system of language from his or her speech community and the linguist studies language as it manifests itself in this system.

The first point of contrast between the two trends that Volosinov emphasizes is their respective treatments of language history. For the individual subjectivists, "the very essence of language is revealed precisely in its history" (p. 56). This trend views the immutable system of language as only "the inert crust . . . of the true essence of language . . . " (p. 56). "Meanwhile, for the second trend, it is exactly this system of self-identical forms that becomes the essence of language" (pp. 56–57). For abstract objectivists language is a stable, immutable system of forms connected by linguistic laws that have nothing in common with artistic, cognitive or other ideological values. History and the system are "alien to one another" (57).

Abstract objectivism is rooted, says Volosinov, in Cartesianism and in Leibniz's conception of universal grammar. "In somewhat simplified form, the idea of language as a system of conventional, arbitrary signs of a fundamentally rational nature was propounded by representatives of the Age of the Enlightenment in the eighteenth century" (p. 58). The most influential current proponent of this view is, of course, Ferdinand de Saussure.

Especially because Saussure and his followers are "among the most prominent linguists of modern times" (p.58), and more influential among Russian linguists than any other theorists, Volosinov dedicates the next fourteen paragraphs to an overview of the Saussurian approach to the nature of language. He reviews Saussure's *langage-langue-parole* distinction and his preference for *langue*. He emphasizes Saussure's claim that language is social but that utterance is "a thoroughly individual entity" (p. 61). The latter, he indicates, is a significant Saussurian oversight. Volosinov cites Saussure's preference for synchronic study and characterizes this as "extremely characteristic for the [Cartesian] spirit of rationalism . . . " (p. 61). He then concludes the chapter with a call for accepting "the obligation and trouble of thinking in responsible, theoretical, and, consequently, philosophical terms" by avoiding both "academic eclecticism" and "academic positivism" (p. 62). The final paragraph sets up Chapter 3 of Part II by asking what, in relation to the thesis of individualistic subjectivism and the antithesis of abstract objectivism is "the true center of linguistic reality" and "the real mode of existence of language" (p. 63)?

Before responding to this question, Chapter 2 of Part II contains Volosinov's critical analysis of abstract objectivism. As he raises objections to this perspective, he also begins to develop his alternative. Referring back to the goal of Part II to define the concrete material existence of language, Volosinov begins by asking to what degree a language *system* could be considered a "real entity?" Such a system obviously has no concrete material reality. If one views language "in a truly objective way—from the side, so to speak, or more accurately, from above it," Volosinov maintains that one will see that there is no real moment when a synchronic system could be constructed. Because such a system may be said to exist only from the point of view of the subjective consciousness of an individual speaker, this system cannot be the essential mode of existence of language. Unfortunately, "most representatives of abstract objectivism . . . assert *the unmediated reality, the unmediated objectivity of language as a system of normatively identical forms*" (p. 67). But such a system is "a product of deliberation on language" and *in* language. What actually matters to a speaker is not the system but "the particular, concrete utterance he [or she] is making" (p. 67) and the meaning it acquires in its particular context. This point, says Volosinov, can be expressed this way: "*what is important for the speaker about a linguistic form is not that it is a stable and always self-equivalent signal, but that it is an always changeable and adaptable sign*" (p. 68). Linguistic understanding is not a matter of recognizing its acontextual identity but understanding its polysemous and, ultimately, context-dependent novelty.

Volosinov develops this notion in eight paragraphs that use the contrast between a signal and a sign to emphasize the constancy in interpretation of the former and the variability of interpretation of the latter. His point in this section is that, as he summarizes, "the ideal of mastering a language is absorption of signality by pure semioticity and of recognition by pure understanding" (p. 69). That is, one feature of the understanding of a sign is that it varies depending on context, while the recognition of a signal does not; it is context independent. Mastering the task of speaking and understanding reveals that language shares the quality of the sign, not of the signal.

In this section of the chapter, Volosinov is clearly maintaining and to some degree extending the semiotic account of language he developed in Part I. He refers to the linguistic form as a "changeable and adaptable *sign*" and argues for "pure semioticity." Notice, however, that he uses these terms and the constructs "sign" and "signal" to highlight the context dependence of language, a feature that will later become one of the main reasons why Volosinov moves away from a semiotic perspective. In other words, in these paragraphs the distinction between direct ["signality'] and arbitrary ["semiotic"] representation helps Volosinov underscore the importance of context, but as he continues in the rest of Part II and in Part III to explicate and exemplify the basic reality of language as it is *lived* in the utterance, he will move farther and farther away from semiotic terminology and analogues.

In fact, Volosinov begins to move in exactly this direction in the paragraph immediately following the summary statement just quoted, as he discusses for the first time the "linguistic consciousness of the speaker and of the listener-understander, in the *practical business of living speech*" (p. 70, italics added). Four paragraphs later he characterizes his object of study as "language in the process of its practical implementation" (p. 70), which on the next page is paraphrased as "real-life practice in social intercourse" (p. 71) and "living speech as actually and continuously generated" (p. 71). This shift in interest toward concrete communication events has an immediate impact on Volosinov's position regarding the atomism commitment of the symbol model. When focused on actual communicating, he notes, one fact that becomes immediately apparent is that communicators "never say or hear *words,* we say and hear what is true or false, good or bad, important or unimportant, pleasant or unpleasant and so on" (p. 70). As a result, Volosinov concludes, the real mode of existence of language cannot be as a system made up of individual word units.

He makes a second move away from system and toward utterance when he clarifies that the real-life, practical phenomena on which he wants to concentrate are dialogic, not monologic. Monologic utterance, which has been the favored object of inquiry in most Indo-European linguistic thought, is itself a kind of abstraction, for one crucially important reason: it overlooks the discursive context to which it is a *response*. This notion of response becomes pivotal. As Volosinov explains, "Any monologic utterance, the written monument included, is an inseverable element of verbal communication. Any utterance—the finished, written utterance not excepted—makes re-*sponse* to something and is calculated to be *responded* to in turn. It is but one link in a continuous chain of speech performances" (p. 72, italics added). These sentences contend that the central weakness of philological study is that it effaces the *inherently relational or dialogic quality of every utterance.* Volosinov's argument is that no utterance is purely and simply generated *ab initio.* Each is *responsive* to something the utterer has remembered, read, or heard. Gadamer expresses this same insight when he urges the person who would understand a written text to ask what *question* the text is a *response* to. This doctrine of question-and-answer is at the heart of Gadamer's philosophical hermeneutics.[19] It is one feature that distinguishes Gadamer's interpretation theory from its semiotic predecessors.

Volosinov also appears to recognize not only the importance of responsiveness to the nature of language but also how responsiveness challenges semiotic formulations. He concludes his criticism of philological analyses with these words:

> The result of all this is a fundamentally erroneous theory of understanding that underlies not only the methods of linguistic interpretation of texts but also *the whole of European semasiology* [italics added]. Its entire position on word meaning and theme is permeated through and through with the false notion of *passive understanding*, the kind of understanding of a word that *excludes active response in advance and on principle* [italics added].
>
> We shall see later that this kind of understanding, with built-in exclusion of response, is not at all in fact the kind of understanding that applies in language-speech (p. 73).

As we shall see, this claim about the inherent centrality of response is at the very heart of Volosinov's dialogic or "translinguistic" perspective. For him, the "actual mode of existence of language" is dialogic, and this fact emerges as it becomes apparent that the abstract objectivist view that pervades contemporary linguistics almost completely overlooks the importance of *response*.

Volosinov's third move away from system and toward utterance emerges from his criticism of the tendency of philologists and linguists to concentrate on *alien* languages. These scholars "are spellbound and held captive in their thinking about language," argues Volosinov, "by one and the same phenomenon—the phenomenon of alien, foreign-language word" (p. 75). Linguistics is still "enslaved" by this perspective (p. 75). But when one breaks this spell and attends to the mundane event of communicating in one's *native* language, things begin to look remarkably different.

These differences surface as Volosinov summarizes the eight problems he has identified with the abstract objectivists' view of the nature of language. First, individual differences rather than systemic similarities are most important. Understanding one's own, everyday language is not dependent mainly on recognizing identities but on adapting to context-dependent differences. Second, one can understand language best by focusing not on an abstraction but on the concrete. The "finished monologic utterance is an abstraction" (p. 77), because it omits the context of the original implementation, that is, it ignores what the speech is responding to. Third, the formalism and systematicity that characterizes abstract objectivism arrests the dynamism of living language. Fourth, abstract objectivism is oriented toward the isolated, monologic utterance and cannot comprehend the *connections*—with earlier utterances and between speaker and listener—that characterize living language. Fifth, "abstract objectivism supplies the grounds for the reification of the linguistic form," which impoverishes its subject matter. As Vossler argued, this approach is like a history of clothing that only "provides a chronologically and geographically arranged list of buttons, clasps, stockings, hats, and ribbons" (p. 79). Sixth, abstract objectivism cannot account for the fact that "the meaning of a word is determined entirely by its context" (p. 79). Here Volosinov explicitly argues against the atomism manifested in Part I. Abstract objectivism "solidifies" the "unity factor of a word," he contends, which "is exactly opposite [to] that of real-life understanding on the part of the speaker engaged in a particular flow of speech" (p. 80). It isolates a word and fixes its meaning outside any context. But words must be analyzed as they are mundanely understood: in wholes. Seventh, abstract objectivism teaches that language "is handed down as a ready-made product from generation to generation," and it is not. "Language cannot properly be said to be handed down—it endures, but it endures as a continuous process of becoming. Individuals do not receive a ready-made language at all, rather, they enter upon the stream of verbal communication . . . "(p. 81). In a statement that is strongly reminiscent of Heidegger and Gadamer, Volosinov goes as far as to claim that "People do not 'accept' their native language—*it is in their native language they they first reach awareness*" (p. 81, italics added). Finally, abstract objectivism cannot account for the dialectical interplay between synchrony and diachrony, system and evolution.

Volosinov concludes the chapter by reemphasizing that "system cannot serve as a basis for understanding and explaining linguistic facts as they really exist and come into being. On the contrary, this system leads us away from the living, dynamic reality of language and its social functions . . . " (p. 82). This does not mean that all the insights of abstract objectivism must be rejected, however, or that the truth lies somewhere *between* it and subjective idealism, but that there must be a *dialectical synthesis* of the two perspectives.

Chapter 3, "Verbal Interaction" moves in this direction by identifying the strengths and weaknesses of individualistic subjectivism. This trend was first associated with European Romantics, who were "the first philologists of native language" and "the first to attempt a radical restructuring of Cartesian-Kantian linguistic thought" (p. 83). The concept of "expression" was central to these authors. They viewed speech as essentially an outward objectification for others of an inner feeling or belief. This approach presupposed a dualism between inner and outer and treated expression as moving from the former to the latter and understanding from the latter to the former.[20]

Volosinov argues that this theory is "fundamentally untenable," first, because it ignores the fact that "there is no such thing as experience outside of embodiment in signs" (p. 85), so there is no fundamental, qualitative difference between the inner and the outer, and perhaps between World$_1$ and World$_2$. Moreover, experience does not organize expression, but "expression is what first gives experience its form and specificity of direction" (p. 85). For its part, expression is determined by the material conditions of its utterance, and the most important condition is *its addressee*. This is why utterance "is constructed between two socially organized persons" (p. 85). Volosinov emphasizes this point in a paragraph that removes any lingering doubt about his communicative focus and at the same time introduces some additional ambiguity about his positions on the two worlds and atomism commitments: "Orientation of the word toward the addressee has an extremely high significance. In point of fact, *word is a two-sided act*. It is determined equally by *whose* word it is and *for whom* it is meant. As word, it is precisely *the product of the reciprocal relationship between speaker and listener, addresser and addressee*. Each and every word expresses the 'one' in relation to the 'other.' I give myself verbal shape from another's point of view, ultimately, from the point of view of the community to which I belong. A word is a bridge thrown between myself and another. If one end of the bridge depends on me, then the other depends on my addressee. A word is territory shared by both addresser and addressee, by the speaker and his interlocutor" (p. 86).

At this point it has become obvious that the more explicitly Volosinov attempts to describe the dialogic character of the "concrete, material existence" (p. 45) of language, the further he moves away from the claims in Part I that the word is "a sign which represents . . . or stands for something lying outside itself"(p. 9). It has also become apparent that his dialogic conception of language raises important questions about beliefs that are central to "the whole of European semasiology" (p. 73). At this point of the book, Volosinov certainly does *not* completely turn his back on the symbol model; he continues to write, for example, of "the implementation of word as *sign*" (p. 86). But he does emphasize that the view of language that follows from the insight into its fundamentally dialogic nature is much more complicated than either Saussure or Humboldt acknowledged.

To underscore his point about the pervasively *social* reality of language, Volosinov follows the quotation just cited with nineteen paragraphs that explain how virtually all human experiences from what is called *inner sensation* to what is called *outward expression* are determined by their human context. Using hunger as an example, he describes a continuum ranging from the "I experience" to the "we experience." The nearer one approaches the former extreme the closer one gets to "the physiological reaction of the [nonhuman] animal." *Human* reality is characterized by distinctions among, for example, the hunger of the loner, "the man down on his luck, the beggar, or the like" and one who is hungry because he or she is part of a collective or class (p. 88). He also briefly discusses the construct "self-experience," which is related to the individualism of the bourgeois class as elaborated in such works as those by the novelists Rolland and Tolstoy. Volosinov's point here is that "personality. . . turns out to be wholly a product of social interrelations" and that "*consciousness is a fiction*," except insofar as it appears as a material expression in a social context (p. 90).

Volosinov then dedicates nine paragraphs to the definition and development of the term *behavioral ideology*, which he proposes as a substitution to the Marxist label *social psychology*. His point is to avoid the word *psychology*, because of its individualistic connotation and to underscore the centrality of ideology. He argues that there are different "strata" of behavioral ideology and that theorists' and practitioners' understanding of important phenomena could be enhanced were this nomenclature adopted.

But up to this point in the chapter, the primary rationale for each of Volosinov's moves is to display the *social* dimensions of utterance that individualistic subjectivism overlooks. He praises Humboldt and the Vosslerites for recognizing, contra Saussure, that "individual utterances *are* what constitute the actual, concrete reality of language," and he condemns them for "failing to understand the social nature of the utterance" (p. 93). Only recently, he argues, have some scholars recognized that "the basic function of language is not expression but *communication*," and that "the minimal condition for a linguistic manifestation is . . . *twofold* (speaker and listener)" (p. 94). But even these scholars maintain remnants of psychologism. Volosinov summarizes:

Now we are in a position to answer the question we posed at the end of the first chapter of this section of our study. *The actual reality of language-speech is not the abstract system of linguistic forms, not the isolated monologic utterance, and not the*

psychophysiological act of its implementation, but the social event of verbal interaction implemented in an utterance or utterances.
Thus, verbal interaction is the basic reality of language (p. 94).

This emphatic claim substantially effaces a distinction central to semiotics, linguistics, philology, language philosophy, and even much of rhetoric since those disciplines were invented by the Greeks and Romans: the distinction between language and speech communication (for the latter, read "verbal interaction" or "language-speech"). The actual reality of language, argues Volosinov, is the *event of aural-oral articulate contact* ("verbal interaction implemented in an utterance or utterances"). Language consists of events of speech communicating.

In the final section of the chapter Volosinov emphasizes that the concrete form of this actual reality is *dialogue*. By *dialogue* he means "not only direct, face-to-face vocalized verbal communication between persons, but also verbal communication of any type whatsoever," including the reading of a book (p. 95). The essential feature of each instance of dialogue is *response*. "*Any utterance . . . is only a moment in the continuous process of verbal communication*"(p. 95), which, in turn, is "only a moment in the continuous, all-inclusive, generative process of a given social collective"(p. 95). He reiterates his claim that *"language acquires life and historically evolves precisely here, in concrete verbal communication . . ."*(p. 95).

Interestingly, Volosinov admits in passing that his analysis raises "an important problem" that appears to be about the two worlds that purportedly get connected via language. As he puts it, the problem concerns the nature of "the connection between concrete verbal interaction [World$_1$] and the extraverbal situation—both the immediate situation and, through it, the broader situation [World$_2$]" (p. 95). He observes that the forms this connection takes differ across situations, but in the one paragraph containing this discussion, his focus shifts from the connection between "verbal interaction and the extraverbal" to "verbal intercourse . . . and . . . communication of other types," and then to "word . . . and . . . this eternally generative, unified process of communication" (p. 95). So it appears that at the end of this paragraph that he has clearly rejected the system commitment of the symbol model but that he may be maintaining some form of the two worlds commitment.

Before he concludes the chapter, however, he clarifies his claim that *contact* ("social intercourse") comes first; that *in* this contact *"verbal communication and utterance are generated"* (that is, this contact is itself *articulate*); that these utterances generate *"forms of speech performances;"* and that *"finally, this generative process is reflected in the change of language forms"*(p. 96). Marxist philosophy of language, he contends, should focus holistically on the multitude of forms or "genres" of speech performance that characterize dialogue in "the drawing room . . . between husband and wife, brother and sister . . . [in] village sewing circles, urban carouses, workers' lunchtime chats, etc. . . . "(p. 97).

Volosinov concludes the chapter with five propositions that formulate his philosophy of language: (1) the concrete reality of language cannot be apprehended so long as language is viewed as an abstract *system;* (2) *"language is a continuous generative process implemented in the social-verbal interaction of speakers"*; (3) the laws governing this generation are sociological not psychological; (4) linguistic creativity must be understood as historical and ideological not mechanical; and (5) "The utterance, as such, obtains between speakers. The individual speech act (in the strict sense of the word 'individual') is *contradictio in adjecto"*(p. 98).

Thus as he moves into the final chapter of Part II, Volosinov's argument has progressed from the claim that language is *social*, to the more concrete claim that it is *communicative*, and then to the most specific claim that it is *dialogic*. For him, the actual reality of language is something very close to what I would call aural-oral articulate contact between speaker and listener.

Chapter 4 consists of nearly eight pages discussing "Theme and Meaning in Language." Volosinov acknowledges that "meaning is one of the most difficult problems of linguistics" but notes that the scope of his work compels him to treat it in "a very brief and perfunctory" way (p. 99).

After reasserting his decision to focus on the utterance as a whole, he proposes to call "the significance of a whole utterance its *theme"* (p. 99). Even such a simple utterance as "What time is it?" has a different theme each time it is uttered, because the concrete, historical situation that engenders it is always unique. Thus the theme is determined not only by the morphology, syntax, and intonation of its production but also by its situation. Meaning, on the other hand, is all that is *"reproducible* and *self-identical* in all instances of repetition"(p. 100). The theme of an utterance is indivisible, but the meaning breaks down into the meanings of each of the parts. No absolute distinction between them can be drawn, but they do differ. Hence, the theme is the *"upper, actual limit of linguistic significance"* and meaning is "the *lower limit* of linguistic significance" (p. 101).

Volosinov claims that this distinction is vital if the nature of meaning is to be clearly delineated and if the problem of understanding is to be solved. Understanding, as he has argued earlier, "will be active and will constitute the germ of a response"(p. 102). Thus *"Any true understanding is dialogic in nature.* Understanding is to utterance as one line of a dialogue is to the next" (p. 102). This is why meaning is not a feature of words as such but of the "word in its position between speakers; that is, meaning is realized only in the process of active, responsive understanding"(p. 102). In Volosinov's analysis, both language and meaning become relational phenomena.

The chapter then moves to a consideration of the relationship between meaning and evaluation. Volosinov notes that evaluation is pervasive in language, and that it is conveyed in part by intonation. He cites the example from Dostoyevski's *Diary of a Writer* in which the novel's narrator's reports a "conversation" among six drunks who carry on a complex interaction using only one word, a familiar, single-syllable obscenity uttered in a multitude of intonations. With only this resource the drunks communicate disdain, doubt, indignation, rapture, condemnation, and mutual affirmation. Volosinov emphasizes that "in living speech" intonation contributes significantly to evaluation and other important nuances of meaning, and that linguists who focus their attention on the abstract system of language miss these features entirely.

The focus of this chapter is admirable and promising, but it accomplishes little. Volosinov's distinction between theme and meaning is incompletely developed, and these paragraphs contribute little to an understanding of the perennially complex problem of linguistic meaning. From my perspective, however, it is worth noting that Volosinov continues here to work out, however incompletely, his *holistic* analysis of *dialogic utterance* as it manifests in *living speech*.

Part III: A Post-Semiotic Analysis of Speech About Speech

As was noted earlier, the purpose of the four chapters making up Part III is to apply Volosinov's philosophy of language to one problem or issue. The first chapter defines this problem, a "syntactic" one that Volonisov chooses because syntactic forms are *"closest to the concrete forms of utterance"* and because heretofore linguists have reduced syntax to phonetic and morphological categories (pp. 109–110). He also insists on considering an issue having to do with a type of whole utterance conceived dialogically. In passing, he argues that linguists should shift their focus toward this kind of utterance, and that "all the basic categories of linguistics should be closely reexamined" (p. 112).

The problem he chooses is "reported speech," utterances that report other persons' utterances and incorporate them into a monologic context such as a novel. He argues that reported speech is a "pivotal phenomenon," one that has been examined before as a "limited and secondary phenomenon" but that "actually has meaning of fundamental importance" (p. 112). When examined from his sociologically oriented scientific perspective, he contends, reported speech will be shown to have considerable hermeneutic power.

Chapter 2 begins by sharpening the definition of his topic as "speech within speech, utterance within utterance, and at the same time also *speech about speech, utterance about utterance"* (p. 115). Reported speech talks about the themes of one's words—"for instance, 'nature,' 'man,' or 'subordinate clause' (one of the themes of syntax)"—and it also has its own syntactic and semantic autonomy (p. 115). The key feature of reported speech is that it embodies its author's syntax, composition, and style while preserving the syntax, composition, and style of the speech it reports. In this way, reported speech expresses an *"active relation* of one message to another" (p. 116). This is one reason why any complete study of dialogue must seriously consider reported speech.

More specifically, he continues, a study of reported speech can provide responses to such questions as, "How, in fact, is another speaker's speech received? What is the mode of existence of another's utterance in the actual, inner-speech consciousness of the recipient? How is it manipulated there, and what process of orientation will the subsequent speech of the recipient himself have undergone in regard to it?" (p. 117). As these questions suggest, any instance of reported speech integrates three perspectives: that of the original speaker, that of the reporter, and that of the audience to whom the reporter speaks. This is why the study of reported speech can provide insights into the basic processes of understanding and communication, conceived of as social, dialogical processes.

Previous studies of reported speech, Volosinov argues, have overlooked the importance of the connection between the first two perspectives. As the original speaker's words come into contact with the reporter's inner speech, they are framed in "a context of factual commentary" and then a reply is prepared. Earlier studies have also overlooked the second dynamic, the way reported speech is intimately tied to its reporting context. "This dynamism reflects the dynamism of social interorientation in verbal ideological communication between people" (p. 119). Because of the importance of this dynamism, Volosinov spends the remaining fifteen paragraphs of the chapter explaining the two basic directions it can move.

The first direction is to maintain the integrity and authenticity of the original speaker's words, to condense and enhance them, and to preserve them from the reporter's intonations. The "what" is reported and the "how" is not. This "depersonalizing" way of reporting predominates in Old and Middle French and is also found in Old Russian. Volosinov calls it the "linear style" of speech reporting.

The second occurs when the reporting and the context are permitted to infiltrate the original words and provide "commentary in deft and subtle ways" (p. 120). This is the "pictorial" style. It weakens the boundaries of the original utterance, for example by allowing elements in the reporter's context to permeate the reported speech. This type characterizes the Renaissance, the end of the eighteenth century, and "virtually the entire nineteenth century" (p. 121). Another version of this style occurs when the reporter's authority subsumes the original speaker's. This style is characteristic of the narration of Dostoevsky and other recent Russian prose writers. Recently developed mixed forms, such as quasi indirect discourse and quasi direct discourse are examples of this second direction.

Two summaries conclude this chapter. The first restates the four versions of reported speech Volosinov has discussed, "authoritarian dogmatism," characterized by reported speech in the Middle Ages; "rationalistic dogmatism" of the seventeenth and eighteenth centuries; "realistic and critical individualism" prominent at the end of the eighteenth century and early in the nineteenth; and "relativistic individualism," which appears in current works. The second restates the central thesis of Part II, that "it is solely through the utterance that language makes contact with communication, is imbued with its vital power, and becomes a reality" (p. 123).

It would be difficult for a reader of these two chapters and the seven preceding them not to notice the shift that has occurred. The symbol model was clearly focal in Part I and appeared periodically in Part II. But up to this point in Part III, neither Volosinov's definition of his critical object—reported speech—nor his analysis of this phenomenon has utilized semiotic constructs or terminology. Reported speech is not described in semiotic terms, and no semiotic categories or concerns surface in Volosinov's explication of the phenomenon. In fact, the word *sign* appears only once in the first two chapters of Part III, in a list of elements that frame the inner reception of reported speech (p. 118).

More important, all of Volosinov's central claims are anchored in his perception of language as social, communicative, and dialogic. The primary weakness of previous discussions of reported speech is that they overlooked its communicative nature. The "two directions" Volosinov discusses differ not in their modes of representation or semiotic form but in the ways they interorient the original speech, the reporter's inner speech, and the communicative context. The chronological differences Volosinov identifies mark tendencies "in the dynamic interrelationship of reported and reporting speech" (p. 123). In short, Volosinov's analysis up to this point is communicative or post-semiotic rather than semiotic.

It is also worth noting to what degree Volosinov has followed his own implied advice in Part II to concentrate on "the practical business of living speech" (p. 70), or the "real-life understanding on the part of the speakers engaged in a particular flow of speech" (p. 80). One might argue that the reported speech captured on the pages of a novel is an instance of "the social event of verbal interaction implemented in an utterance or utterances" (p. 94), which is how Volosinov defines "the actual reality of language-speech" near the end of Chapter 3 in Part II. But reported speech in a novel consists of crafted, edited, and written prose, which differs from living speech between persons almost as much as the reported speech in a novel differs from the novel's dialogue. Volosinov has chosen to work out his insight into the formative significance of *response* and *contact* by analyzing utterances that interorient perspectives, but that do so from the sole perspective of the novelist. Insofar as all the novelist's speakers are creations of his or her imagination, no actual, concrete otherness is manifested in reported speech. Thus the reader of Volosinov's work has yet to encounter any example of genuine *living speech*. As a result, the author has far from fully exploited the potential of his view of language as social, communicative, and dialogic.

Chapter 3 describes indirect discourse, direct discourse, and their modifications, and Chapter 4 treats quasi-direct discourse in French, German and Russian. As their topics suggest, these chapters contain the most detailed and technical of Volosinov's discussions. For example, Volosinov notes early in Chapter 3 that "A lack of consecut*io temporum* and the subjunctive mood deprives indirect discourse in Russian of any distinctive character of its own" (p. 126).

Volosinov dedicates fourteen paragraphs in Chapter 3 to his criticism of the mechanical formalism of A. M. Peskovsky's claim that the Russian language is uncongenial to reporting indirect speech. The primary weakness of Peskovsky's analysis is that he overlooks the function of reported speech to capture both the "ideational, referential" meaning and the "various stylistic strands that compose its verbal texture" (p. 130). Although the term *referential* suggests that Volosinov may be thinking representationally, he describes the "referent-analyzing" move as one that "provides a wide opportunity for the reporting and commenting tendencies of authorial speech, while at the same time maintaining a strict and clear-cut separation between reporting and reported utterance" (p. 130). He also notes how this move works only at the expense of "a certain depersonalization of the reported speech" (p. 130), that it is "somewhat rationalistic and dogmatic in nature," and that interest in this dimension is "only weakly developed in Russian" (p. 131). In other words, he analyzes even this feature communicatively, not semiotically.

Volosinov offers six examples of reported speech, five from *The Brothers Karamazov* and one from *The Idiot,* to illustrate the "texture-analyzing modification" (p. 131). He summarizes the differences between the "referent-analyzing modification" and the "texture-analyzing modification" as differences in the interorientation between the narrator and the speaker. He also briefly notes a third type, midway between the other two, that reports the internal thoughts of a character; he terms it "the impressionistic modification."

He then turns for seventeen paragraphs to a consideration of direct discourse. Each step of his analysis applies the distinctions worked out in Chapter 2 among the original speaker's words, the agendas and words of the reporter, and the context in which the speech is reported. To cite just one example, Volosinov discusses what he calls *particularized direct discourse* in which "The authorial context . . . is so constructed that the traits the author used to define a character cast heavy shadows on his directly reported speech. The value judgments and attitudes in which the character's portrayal is steeped carry over into the words he utters. The referential weight of the reported utterances declines in this modification but, in exchange, their characterological significance, their picturesqueness, or their time-and-place typicality, grows more intense. . . . Such is the way direct discourse is usually handled by Gogol and by representatives of the so-called 'natural school' (p. 134). As the reader can readily note, the analysis continues to be communicative rather than semiotic.

The chapter ends with a discussion of several types of quasi-direct discourse, including rhetorical direct discourse and substituted direct discourse. He ends the chapter with an example of "real quasi-direct discourse" from Pushkin's *Poltava*.

Chapter 4 branches out culturally to consider instances of this same phenomenon found in French and German literature. Volosinov notes the demands that speech reporting puts on verb tense and pronoun choice. He criticizes other literary theorists' analyses because they have failed to acknowledge how different interorientations distinguish various forms. He comments on an 1887 work by the German Tobler, an 1899 analysis by the German Kalepky, and two responses the Frenchman Bally made to Kalepky, one in 1912 and one in 1914. Because Bally is partly responsible for the *Cours de linguistique générale*, it is not surprising that Volosinov chides him for the way he "hypostasizes and vivifies forms of language obtained by way of abstraction from concrete speech performances" (p. 145).

These comments are followed by a lengthy (thirty-eight paragraph) section discussing the Vosslerites' views of quasi-direct discourse. Because, as has been noted, this group's work is defined in contrast with the semasiology of Saussure, it is not surprising that Volosinov's analysis of their perspective completely ignores semiotic constructs and concerns. Instead, he notes, for example, how the Vosslerites concentrate on "affect in language, fantasy in language, empathy, linguistic taste, and the like" (p. 146). This section is primarily dedicated to reviews of a 1914 volume by Eugen Lerch and a 1921 work by E. Lorck. Volosinov also briefly analyzes the Old French and Renaissance writings that influenced these authors' works.

Again, Volosinov's approach is communicative rather than semiotic. For example, he cites Lerch's argument that "it is empathy *(Einfühlung)* that finds adequate expression in quasi-direct discourse. . . . The author is able to present the utterances of his characters in a way suggesting that he himself takes them seriously, and that what is at stake is not merely something that was said or thought, but actual facts. This is possible, Lerch claims, only on the basis of the poet's empathy with the creations of his own fantasy, on the basis of his identifying himself with them" (p. 150).

Volosinov's final move in the book echoes his dialectical strategy as he argues that both the Vosslerites' individualistic subjectivism and Bally's abstract objectivism are unacceptable accounts of reported speech. Bally misses the material features of language, and Lorck and Lerch fail to take fully into account the social features. Volosinov summarizes Part III by reemphasizing that, when one examines language in which are manifested one person's perceptions of another—reported speech—one can see how "the vicissitudes of utterance and speaking personality in language reflect the social vicissitudes of verbal interaction, of verbal-ideological communication, in their most vital tendencies" (p. 157). Language—Volosinov (or his translators) again calls it *the word*—is the ideological phenomenon par excellence, and it has been studied either by treating it as a reflection, representation, or artifact of "ideas" or "history," or by focusing on "the *generation of language itself, as ideological material, as the medium for ideological reflection of existence*" (p. 158). There is a third route, and that is to study "*the reflection of the social generation of word in word itself,* with its two branches: the *history of the philosophy of the word* and *the history of word in word.* It is precisely in this latter direction that our own study lies" (p. 158).

Volosinov ends with a plea to resist the tendency both in "bourgeois Europe and here in the Soviet Union" to analyze language as a thing and thereby to pass over its thematic value. Formalism must be replaced by an approach that keeps the ideological in language intact and acknowledges how the word is "permeated with confident and categorical social value judgment, the word that really means and takes responsibility for what it says" (p. 159).

Conclusion

Volosinov makes his recap brief, because, as he writes, "the substance of the matter is in the argument itself, and we shall refrain from rehashing it" (p. 157). I will follow his example. Throughout this chapter I have quoted extensively from the text to enable the reader to hear for himself or herself the tension between semiotic and post-semotic accounts of the nature of language present in Volosinov's work, and the post-semiotic quality of the latter pages of the book.

Marxism and the Philosophy of Language outlines an account of the nature of language that strains against its own author's initial assumptions. In Part I, Volosinov makes a coherent argument that Marxism and language philosophy are intimately connected, because ideology is both central to Marxism and essentially linguistic. His rationale is that everything ideological possesses *meaning,* that to be meaningful is to represent something, and that everything which represents something in this way is a *sign.* Thus Part I employs a semiotic analysis to connect Marxism and language philosophy. It prominently asserts the existence of two worlds, describes language representationally, and, at least part of the time, treats language as analyzable into word units. Importantly, the text does not treat language as either a system or a tool.

Part II argues that the concrete material existence of language is the *utterance*, which emerges in the reciprocal relationship between speaker and listener. As the text of these chapters demonstrates, it is virtually impossible to discuss this phenomenon semiotically. Utterance is more event or *energeia* than product or *ergon*. Thus it cannot be segmented into units that can be said to function as signs. Utterance is also inherently *responsive*, which means that it is not only relational but also context dependent. No phenomenon of this sort can be reduced to a *system*, which is precisely what semiotic accounts of language tend toward. Perhaps most important, Volosinov's focus on utterance threatens the commitment to two worlds manifest in Part I. When he declares that *"the actual reality of language-speech is not the abstract system of linguistic forms"* (p. 94), he undercuts the possibility of analyzing language into units ("forms") making up a world of language that represent units in a nonlinguistic world. When he insists that language does not consist of *"the psychophysiological act of"* an individual's speech (p. 94), he rejects the view that language is made up of external (World$_1$) signs of internal (World$_2$) meanings. And when he affirms that the actual reality of language is not *"the isolated monologic utterance"* (p. 94), he opens the door to treating language as a *coconstituting* dynamic, an event of dialogic worlding.[21]

In Part III, he moves, as it were, part of the way through this opened door. He gives an account of reported speech that does not rely on semiotic constructs or terms. Instead, his principal of explication is communicative and his critical stance is dialogic. One can understand reported speech, he argues, only when one recognizes how it embodies a set of relationships among the original speaker's discourse, the linguistic world of the reporter, and the context that constrains the reporting. Reported speech is what it is because of the interorientation among all three elements. In this way it is an essentially, inherently communi*cative* phenomenon. This is why I would question Matejaka's and Ivanov's claims that Volosinov's orientation is consistently semiotic.[22] The constructs and associated vocabulary of signs, symbols, and representation introduced in Part I simply will not permit Volosinov to say what he wants to say in Part III.

Volosinov's account stops short of affirming the view I outline in Chapter 4. Despite his recognition that living language exists as aural-oral contact between persons, he concentrates Part III on a category of written prose. This is one way he misses the opportunity to move completely through the door he opens in Part II. Had he analyzed question-answer sequences in spoken Russian, for example, rather than the literary phenomenon of reported speech, he might have more fully realized the potential of his basic insight. In addition, perhaps because of the prominence of semiosis in Part I, Volosinov's text fails to exploit the fundamental distinction between treating language as representational and treating it as constitutive. Thus there is no development in this work of the ontological implications of this dialogic view of language.

But *Marxism and the Philosophy of Language* is nonetheless a monument of innovative theorizing about the nature of language and a worthy counterpoint to the semiotic accounts that enjoyed such hegemony when it was written. The work also demonstrates in a practical way the incommensurability of semiotic and communicative accounts of the nature of language. One could speculate that its author tried hard to stay within the accepted semiotic frame but found it impossible both to affirm the communicative nature of language and to explicate it as a system of signs or symbols.

❀ Chapter 7

The Symbol Model and the Philosophy of Language: The Case of Kenneth Burke

John Stewart and Karen J. Williams[1]

Among rhetorical theorists and critics, Kenneth Burke has been one of the most highly respected and influential scholars to prominently feature "symbol" vocabulary in his accounts of the nature of language. From *Counter-Statement*,[2] his first major work published in 1931, through his 1984 Afterwords to the new printings of *Attitudes Toward History* [3] and *Permanence and Change*,[4] Burke propounded an approach to language that, to a considerable degree, relied on "symbol" vocabulary. Burke defined the human as "the symbol-using animal," treated language as "symbolic action," and emphasized the foundational importance of his distinction between "the symbolic realm of action" and "the nonsymbolic realm of motion."

Yet some parts of Burke's discussions of language are also consistent with aspects of a post-semiotic account of language. For example, like Heidegger, Burke noted some ways that humans not only "use" language but are also used by it,[5] and in some places Burke argued, as do Heidegger, Gadamer, and others, that language *constitutes* rather than merely "symbolizing" or "representing" the human world. As a result, selected writings by Burke can serve as another fruitful test case for an analysis of some effects "symbol" terminology has on a philosophy of language, in this case one which is frequently referenced by rhetoricians and communication theorists.

This chapter offers such an analysis. We contend that Burke's writings about the nature of language exemplify what can occur when the symbol model functions as what Burke called a *terministic screen*. Therefore we believe that a close reading of Burke can inform one's understanding of the nature of language by illustrating what can occur when semiotic and post-semiotic views collide. In Burke's case we argue that the resulting tension led him to make some questionable claims that are traceable to Burke's basic conviction that language is, in his words, a "conventional arbitrary symbol system."[6] Thus our reading of Burke is meant to support the argument that communication theorists and rhetoricians should revise their commitment to symbolic characterizations of language. After a rationale for our approach to Burke, we develop our analysis with a close reading of four of Burke's most direct expositions of his philosophy of language. We conclude with a review of what is at risk when a theorist attempts to describe language as "symbolic" and some suggestions about how this part of Burke might best be read in light of our examination.

Reading Burke

One may ask whether it is appropriate to interrogate Burke's work philosophically; that is, whether he provides a *philosophy* of language to analyze and critique. He was not trained as a philosopher, did not teach in a philosophy department, and is best known for his contributions to rhetorical theory and literary and social criticism. But Burke himself encouraged the approach we take. In the Preface to *Language as Symbolic Action* (hereafter *LSA*), for example, he described the book's contents as "A theory of language, a philosophy of language based on that theory, and methods of analysis developed in accordance with the theory and the philosophy."[7] He similarly described *The Rhetoric of Religion: Studies in Logology*[8] and confided in a letter to a friend, "I'd like to be recognized as a pretty damned good philosopher of language who every once in a while knocked off a fairly reputable poem. And (psst) I wish people knew how important it is for the world to develop a good philosophy of language, though probably if the world had enough sense to know that much they wouldn't need a philosophy of language."[9]

If internal coherence and logically consistent conceptual development are considered to be the marks of an adequate philosophy, many critics would contend that Burke did not achieve his goal of being "a pretty damned good philosopher of language." Even Burke's friend Wayne C. Booth notes that Burke can easily be quoted against himself, "proving that he is inconsistent . . . , whimsical," or worse.[10] But as many commentators also emphasize, it is important to acknowledge Burke's commitment to speculative thinking and his comedic, ironic stance. At the end of his classic analysis of Burke, William H. Rueckert notes that one substantive effect of Burke's sense of humor is to remind the reader that, whenever one is tempted to apply his principles too literally or thoroughly, one should remember, as the Lord consistently says to Satan in Burke's "Prologue to Heaven," "There's more to it than that."[11]

We hope our reading of Burke is consistent with these caveats. On the one hand, we take him at his word and read some of his explicitly conceptual essays as "philosophy of language." At the same time, we accept Richard Rorty's distinction between "systematic " and "edifying" philosophers, and acknowledge that the latter do philosophy by relying more on "satires, parodies, [and] aphorisms" than on rigorously logical arguments.[12] Parts of Burke's writings are clearly "edifying" philosophy. Yet some essays and sections of essays are just as clearly "systematic," especially when, in Rorty's words, Burke "single[s] out one area, one set of practices, and see[s] it as the paradigm human activity . . . [and] then tr[ies] to show how the rest of culture can profit from this example."[13] In short, we find in Burke's work instances of both systematic and edifying philosophizing. We note that much of Burke's writing about the nature of language is what Rorty would call *systematic* and that at some points Burke is prevented from reaching his systematic goals by his reliance on the symbol model.

To identify how and where this occurs, we closely read four essays: "Lexicon Rhetoricæ," the most explicitly theoretical chapter in Burke's first major work, *Counter-Statement*; "On Words and the Word," the first chapter of *RofR*; "What Are the Signs of What?" an account of the nature of language published first in *Anthropological Linguistics* and then in *LSA*[14]; and "Definition of Man," printed first in the *Hudson Review* and also reprinted in *LSA*.[15]

We do not claim that these essays contain even nearly everything Burke said about language between 1931 and the mid-1980s. But we do believe that they accurately capture the view of the nature of language—and of "the symbolic"—that Burke began working out in *CS* and developed through the most productive forty-five years of this career up to his 1978 "(Nonsymbolic) Motion/(Symbolic)

Action" essay and the two new "Afterwords" published in 1984. Burke's other discussions of his philosophy of language, for example in his article on "Dramatism" in the *International Encyclopedia of the Social Sciences*,[16] are consistent with the views expressed in these essays. Some of his most recent work modified positions taken in the four essays we examine, but the modifications are not substantive. For example, although sometime around 1977 Burke changed the label of his definition of humans to "Bodies That Learn Language," his discussions of this material continued to treat language as an "arbitrary, conventional symbol-system" and to underscore the absolutely fundamental nature of his "motion/action," "nonsymbolic/symbolic" polarity .[17] In short, we focus on these four works because they contain some of Burke's most direct and fully developed explanations of the nature of language and symbolicity, and they reflect his thinking about this topic over the most productive years of his career. None of Burke's other writings that we have examined contradicts or significantly alters the view of the nature of language that he expressed in these works. Moreover, these essays comment on all five elements of the symbol model, so in this sense they constitute a *sufficient* sample of Burke's work. Therefore we believe that the four essays can appropriately be treated as a "test case."

"Lexicon Rhetoricæ"

Counter-Statement, the first of Burke's widely noticed books, announced his theoretical-aesthetic-critical agenda. Although the work reflected the social concerns of U.S. artists of the 1930s, its primary purpose, as indicated in Burke's Prefaces to the first and second editions, was to elucidate a "point of view" about art—especially literary art—each major principle of which "is matched by an opposite principle flourishing and triumphant today" (p. vii); hence *counter*-statement. Burke wrote that the centerpiece is a "theory of form" (p. xi) that, Rueckert notes, later developed into Dramatism and Logology.[18]

"Lexicon Rhetoricæ" outlined this theory of form. It is the book's primary theoretical essay, and Burke called it his "set-piece" (p. ix). It consists of thirty-nine numbered sections discussing the central "principles underlying the appeal of literature" (p. 123). We are interested in the essay because of its focus on such "systematic" elements as central principles, pivotal terms, and critical assumptions; it also contains the first of Burke's treatments of the symbol and the process of symbolizing.

"Lexicon Rhetoricæ" consists of five major divisions: the first analyzes the five aspects of form, the second links form and content, the third introduces the construct "Symbol," the fourth distinguishes scientific from poetic expression, and the fifth discusses "problems of literary excellence" (p. 123). Burke began with his often-cited definition of form in literature as "an arousing and fulfillment of desires" (p. 124). Over the next fifteen pages he distinguished types of form, conflict and interrelation between and among forms, and rhythm and rhyme. He noted that form appeals by gratifying the needs which it creates, and he gave examples of how form functions this way.

In the second major division Burke explained how a work of literary art is an "individuation of formal principles" in that it "re-embodies the form principles in different subject-matter" (p. 143). This move linked form to content. He distinguished between appeal based on information and appeal based on form and noted how form interacts with ideology.

Twenty-six pages into the essay, the third major division begins with a discussion of "patterns of experience." Burke identified the phenomena of "universal experiences," those all people are capable of having—mockery, despair, sang-froid, wonder, and so forth. Then he noted that universal experiences are individuated in "specific modes of experience" (p. 150) that, he argued, get generalized into "patterns of experience." For example, a condition of plenty and confinement may lead to obesity. Burke also noted that once patterns of experience exist, "though they may be in themselves results, they become in turn 'creative'" (p. 152). In other words, during the time a pattern endures, it functions recursively in that "it tends to make over the world in its own image" (p. 152).

Section 20 discusses the Symbol, which Burke defined as "the verbal parallel to a pattern of experience" (p. 152). Burke's approach to this construct was different from the one typically taken in contexts like this one. He did not simply adopt the general definition of a *symbol* as "something which stands for something else." Moreover, his initial definition appears to avoid the two worlds and representational commitments of the symbol model. First, he did not say the symbol "stands for" or "represents" but that it "parallels." Second, that which it "parallels" is a "pattern of experience," which Burke had defined earlier as something akin to what a post-semiotic work might call a dimension of one's (perhaps linguistic) "world."

Each of these differences is potentially important. At this point of Burke's treatment of the symbol, he appeared to have avoided committing himself either to the proposition that there is a fundamental distinction between the world of symbols and the world of designata or to the proposition that the relationship between the symbol and its designatum is representational—and can thus be tested by assessing its correspondence. Instead, he postulated that the two central phenomena were "Symbol" and "pattern of experience," and that the relationship consisted of their being "parallel." If we can conclude from earlier sections of this essay that "universal experiences," "modes of experience," and "patterns of experience" *may* be verbal or linguistic, then Burke was not necessarily asserting any fundamental division between the two realms that a symbol bridges. In addition, since it would appear that a "parallel" relation, unlike a "representational" one, could exist between two phenomena with a similar ontological status, Burke may also have avoided any implicit assumption about a fundamental distinction between World$_1$ and World$_2$. In short, if one were looking for a post-semiotic account of the central construct, "symbol," this definition, first published in 1931, would appear promising.

But Burke's definition is problematic because his terms *parallel* and *pattern of experience* are both ambiguous. The term *parallel* suggests a relationship of similar direction but different location. Although such a relationship would clearly differ from a "representing" one, it is not clear how it would differ. Is a "parallel" phenomenon one with, to use another Burkean term, the same "essence"[19] as that to which it is parallel? Is the similarity between two phenomena that are "parallel" greater or less than the similarity between one that "represents" and another that "is represented"? What, after all, is the nature of a "pattern of experience"? Is it in fact linguistic? Moreover, insofar as such a pattern is constitutive of one's view of reality, does this constitutive dimension also apply to "parallel" phenomena? Obviously we cannot answer these questions by looking only at one sentence of this section; we need to consider how Burke developed and explained this construct.

His first example is of a poet who experiences a pattern of "self-pity," and "converts his [or her] pattern into a plot, 'The King and the Peasant.'" In so doing, says Burke, the poet "has produced a Symbol" (p. 153). So it appears that a "plot" is one kind of Symbol. But, Burke writes, the poet "might have chosen other Symbols to verbalize the same pattern," including "a vigorous biography." At this point it appears that by Symbol Burke meant a literary *work*.

In the next paragraph Burke noted that some symbols are obvious, as in *Don Quixote*, *Tom Sawyer*, or *Madame Bovary*, and some less so, as the Symbol of *The Tempest*. He said of the latter that in this case the Symbol "is a complex attitude which pervades the setting, plot, and characters" (p. 153). Then the next sentence notes that "The Symbol might be called [sic] a word invented by the artist to specify a particular grouping or pattern or emphasizing of experiences—and the work of art in which the Symbol figures might be called a definition of this word . . . The Symbol is a formula" (p. 153). Here he ended section 20.

It is revealing that Burke began this two-paragraph section with a one-sentence definition of his central construct. A definition is clearly a systematic philosophical move in that it is an initial statement about "the nature of X," which arouses the expectation that it will be explained. Thus, if Burke were explicitly to follow his own definition of literary form, one would expect him to fulfill the reader's expectation by clarifying what he meant by "verbal parallel to a pattern of experience." But instead, he indicated that a Symbol is a "plot," that it could also be a work, and that it might be "called" a *word*. He said that "the Symbol figures" in a work of art and that it was "a formula." As a result, at the end of this section, the expectation raised by the first sentence remains incompletely fulfilled.[20]

Section 21 moves to a consideration of the appeal of the Symbol. As Burke discussed how a symbol can "work," he indicated again that the term can label an entire work, the outcry of "people in fright" (p. 154), or a character like Malvolio, Falstaff, or Coriolanus (p. 156). He noted that his discussion was to be taken as illustrative, not exhaustive, and summarized "the entire list by saying that the Symbol appeals either as the orienting of a situation, or as the adjustment to a situation, or as both" (p. 156). This summary suggests that there is an important *distinction* between the Symbol and the "situation" it "parallels." Thus Burke appeared here to move away from the position that both "symbol" and "symbolized" may be linguistic and toward the position he subsequently developed about the fundamental difference between the verbal-symbolic and the non-verbal-nonsymbolic.

In section 22 Burke elaborated the claim about recursivity he introduced regarding "patterns of experience." Section 22, called "The Symbol as Generating Principle," begins, "When the poet has converted his patterns of experience into a symbolic equivalent, the Symbol becomes a guiding principle in itself" (p. 157). At first it appears that Burke was offering an alternative view of a "symbol" as a phenomenon that *generates* rather than merely "represents" a pattern of experience. But the sentence just cited demonstrates that Burke envisioned a temporal process: First comes a pattern of (likely nonsymbolic and nonlinguistic) experience that is then symbolized, and subsequently the Symbol guides the development and elaboration of future patterns of experience. So the basic function of the

Symbol continued to be *representational*, first of the underlying pattern of experience and then of other patterns "with no direct bearing upon the pattern of experience behind the key Symbol" (p. 157). This temporal recursivity became an important theme in Burke's later writing about symbolic action.

In sum, in the first nineteen sections of his "Lexicon," Burke's definition of the Symbol appears to be innovative, heuristic, and perhaps even post-semiotic. But as he developed this construct he seemed to move closer to at least the second (atomism) and third (representational) commitments of the symbol model.

The primary point we want to highlight about the remainder of "Lexicon Rhetoricæ" is that all nineteen of these sections employ the construct "Symbol," and most of them employ it as a central construct. Sections 23 and 24 discuss the "ramifications" and the "power" of a Symbol (pp. 158–161). Section 25 characterizes "ideology" in terms of its central Symbol (pp. 161–163). Section 26 is about the "symbolically and formally 'charged'"(pp. 163–164), Section 27 about "eloquence" as "a frequency of Symbolic and formal effects" (p. 165), and so on. From section 20 through the final section's discussion of the artist's "symbolizing of a protective attitude" and expanding the Symbol "for purpose of appeal" (p. 182), Burke consistently employed the term *Symbol* to describe how literature "produces effects" (p. 123).

The prominence of the term after section 20 illustrates in part how the construct became a *terministic screen*. As Burke explained in his discussion of this phenomenon, terministic screens function like colored filters on a camera lens. "Even if any given terminology is a reflection of reality, by its very nature as a terminology it must be a selection of reality; and to this extent it must function also as a deflection of reality."[21] Because of the ways terministic screens operate, many *"observations' are but implications of the particular terminology in terms of which the observations are made."*[22]

Clearly "The Symbol" operated as a terministic screen in "Lexicon Rhetoricæ;" in fact, this term was the conceptual fulcrum of Burke's remarks. The first nineteen sections of the essay discuss "form" and "experience" without employing "symbolic" vocabulary. Section 20 introduced the Symbol, and then the remaining nineteen sections characterized a variety of the elements of literary appeal *as symbolic phenomena*. The symmetrical structure of this essay is certainly not adventitious. As we noted, Burke was inexact about what a Symbol is, but after he introduced this construct, it explicitly functioned to "select" and "deflect" his discussions of all the essay's remaining topics. In subsequent writings Burke was even more explicit about what he meant by "Symbol" and how the term guided and goaded his accounts of language, literature, and human agency.

"On Words and the Word"

Twenty-five years separate "Lexicon Rhetoricæ" from the first version of "On Words and the Word," which was part of a lecture series at Drew University. During this time, Burke wrote several works that included discussions of his philosophy of language. For example, early in his treatment of "Perspective by Incongruity" in *Permanence and Change*, Burke distinguished between "necessitous and symbolic labor" to clarify the kind of more-than-instrumental devotion that "brings one into the realm of piety."[23] The "Dictionary of Pivotal Terms" in *Attitudes Toward History* included discussions of "Stealing Back and Forth of Symbols," "Symbolic Merger," and "Symbols of Authority."[24] In both *A Grammar of Motives* and *A Rhetoric of Motives*, Burke alluded to the proposed *Symbolic of Motives* which was to deal "with unique individuals . . . primarily in their capacity as singulars, each a separate universe of discourse."[25] In *RM* he also characterized rhetoric as "rooted in an essential function of language itself . . . the use of language as a symbolic means of inducing cooperation in beings that by nature respond to symbols."[26]

The long essay introducing *The Philosophy of Literary Form* also extensively discussed symbolic action. For our purposes, the most important part of this essay is Burke's treatment of "the ways in which a 'symbolic' act is 'representative.' "[27] "This moves us into the matter of synecdoche," he wrote, "the figure of speech wherein the part is used for the whole, the whole for the part, the container for the thing contained, the cause for the effect, the effect for the cause, etc. Simplest example: 'twenty noses' for 'twenty men' " (pp. 25–26). Here Burke implied that a symbolic act may represent synecdochically. This could be a very significant claim, because insofar as synecdoche relates *part to whole*, rather than "something" to "something *else*," it may not manifest the two worlds assumption of the symbol model. But Burke's characterization of synecdoche in this essay blurred the distinction between "something" representing "something else" and "a part of something" representing the "whole" of that same thing. Instead of clarifying the ontological distinction between elements of a synecdoche, Burke emphasized how synecdoche links "equations" or "clusters of what goes with what" (p. 77) rather than "the *polar* kind of otherness" (p. 77). "Polar otherness," he wrote, "unites things that are *opposite* to one another; synecdochic otherness unites things that are simply *different from* one another" (p. 78). This discussion of how symbolic action is representative clearly indicates that Burke's thinking about symbolicity had developed from his early treatment of the Symbol. His commitments to some aspects of the symbol model seemed to be attenuated, but his claim that synecdoche links "container" with "thing contained," "cause for the effect," and "effect for the cause" suggested that central philosophical features of his understanding of symbolicity may still have been semiotic. One way to test this interpretation is by closely reading the much more fully elaborated discussion of these issues in "On Words and the Word."

This first essay in *Rhetoric of Religion* provides a succinct introduction to another important dimension of Burke's view of "the nature of language," an investigation of relationships between words-about-words and words-about-The-Word.[28] The general argument of the book, as explained in the Foreword and Introduction, is that much can be learned about language by comparing how we talk about it with how we talk about God and theological matters.

Burke noted explicitly that "On Words and the Word" presented his "philosophy of language" (p. 38), and this is a major reason why we include it here. The essay consists of a four-page introduction, discussions of six analogies between theological and logological concepts, and a four-page recapitulation of the relationship between "Dramatism" and "Scientism" focusing on his four-part "empirical definition of [the hu]man" (p. 40).

Burke's first move was to illustrate the efficacy of his general argument by tracing the meaning of the word *grace* from the secular sense of favor, esteem, and thanks to its theological use to summarize an element of the relationship between God and humans and then, recursively, back as an aesthetic term used to designate a feature of literary style or "the purely secular behavior of a hostess" (p. 8). After some additional examples of this kind of terminological evolution, Burke argued that an examination of the relationships between the "supernatural references" of words and their "natural" references would illuminate important features of language. He then noted that "The quickest and simplest way to realize that words 'transcend' non-verbal nature is to think of the notable difference between the kind of operations we might perform with a *tree* and . . . with the *word* 'tree'" (pp. 8–9). Verbally, he wrote, we can multiply 1 tree into 5,000 by "merely revising our text," whereas it would take "a wholly different set of procedures . . . to get the corresponding result in nature" (p. 9). In a footnote to this paragraph

Burke acknowledged that this discussion raised the question of what he means by *symbolic*. He wrote that he had in mind the kind of distinction that exists between "the thing tree (nonsymbolic) and the word for tree (a symbol)." He noted that there is another sense of "symbolic" "in which an object possesses motivational ingredients not intrinsic to it in its sheer materiality," but he emphasized that even this alternative sense centers on symbols "standing for" ideas (p. 9). Returning to the text of the essay, Burke concluded his introduction with the argument that "Overly 'naturalistic' views conceal from us the full scope of language as motive, even in the sheerly empirical sense. But such oversimplification of linguistic complexities can be avoided if we approach the subject roundabout, through a systematic concern with linguistic principles exemplified with thoroughness in the dialectics of theology" (p. 10). The scene was thus set for a study of secular-theological analogies designed to illuminate Burke's philosophy of language, especially by explicating language as symbolic.

Burke emphasized that his first analogy was the "master analogy, the architectonic element from which all the other analogies could be deduced" (p. 13). The analogy is, "What we say about words, in the empirical realm, will bear a notable likeness to what is said about God, in theology" (pp. 13–14); in other words, this analogy highlights "the likeness between words about words and words about The Word" (p. 33).

The first fifteen paragraphs of Burke's discussion of this analogy offer the clearest *post*-semiotic treatment of language we have found in Burke's work. These paragraphs do not focus on individual terms or on language as a "conventional, arbitrary symbol system,"[29] but on oral-aural *communicating*. Moreover, they highlight how sacred texts present speech as a mode of making present or *presencing*. Burke began with perhaps the most obvious citation for the Christian reader, the opening sentence of the Gospel of John, "In the beginning was the Word, and the Word was with God, and the Word was God," followed by John 1:14, "The Words was made flesh, and dwelt among us" (p. 11). He cited related Old Testament verses and alluded to Babylonian, Egyptian, and Indian cosmologies that stipulate "that the divine word was the agent of creation" (p. 11). He traced the etymology of the primary name of the deity, noting its roots in words for the oral-aural events of swearing, beseeching, imploring, and addressing. He noted how St. Anselm highlighted the primacy of *hearing* the word in the development of faith and cited Romans 10:17 in support: "So then faith cometh by hearing [*ex auditu*], and hearing by the word of God" (p. 12). He reminded the reader that *logos* means "speech" more than "reason" and appreciatively recalled "an early patristic writer, Irenaeus," who made the Gospel a living force by focusing attention on "the 'voice' with which the Father speaks in the revelation to [hu]mankind" (p. 13). He emphasized that readers should keep in mind the oral and the aural dimensions of the word *logos,* that is, its use to identify what is spoken and heard. Burke concluded these remarks about his first analogy, "So much, then, for our master analogy... what we say about *words,* in the empirical realm, will bear a notable likeness to what is said about *God,* in theology" (pp. 13–14).

One could summarize this part of Burke's account of his first analogy as follows: In much early theology, *logos* as speech (not reason) presences God. In *On the Way to Language* Heidegger argued similarly when he maintained that the Greek terms *semia* and *symbola* should be interpreted not as representational constructs but "in terms of showing, in the sense of bringing about the appearance, which in its turn consists of the prevalence of unconcealment (*aletheia*)."[30] Up to this point in Burke's essay, his account of his "master analogy" emphasizing speech as presencing seems consistent with such post-semiotic accounts as Heidegger's. Gadamer's, and the one developed previously in Chapter 4.

But in this case, appearances are deceiving. The remaining sections of "On Words and the Word" present a view of language that is fundamentally different from the one outlined in these first fifteen paragraphs. After an extra line of white space, Burke wrote, "There are four realms to which words may refer" (p. 14). This sentence introduces an account of how words refer to "the natural," "the sociopolitical realm," "other words," and "the 'supernatural'" (pp. 14–15). In other words, Burke moved without discursive transition from a post-semiotic discussion of the oral-aural nature and presencing power of language to a taxonomy of the ways concrete nouns *refer to* different nonverbal "realms." He moved, in other words, from a nonsymbolic to a symbolic treatment of language without acknowledging the fundamental differences between the two.

Why can Burke not have it both ways? Could one not again argue that a pluralistic view of language is preferable to a narrowly unidimensional one? The problem in this case is that, as we have noted earlier and will emphasize later, the account of "the symbolic" most prominent in Burke's writing commits him to at least the two worlds and representational commitments of the symbol model. But Burke's first description of language in this essay takes a fundamentally different orientation. Insofar as speech (*logos*) brings into presence that-which-is-spoken, the speaking and the that-which-is-spoken occupy the same ontological geography. There are no two realms or two worlds in this analysis; there is only the world of speaking and hearing, which makes present what is spoken—the world, or "worlding" discussed in Chapter 4. Thus there is no representing or standing-for in this account. Constituting, embodying, uncovering, and showing are different from representing. In the first paragraphs of "On Words and the Word," Burke's focus was also on the event of communicating, not on individual words as *atoms* in a language *system*. But then, after fifteen paragraphs the picture changes radically, and Burke's discussion of types of words and their referents manifests a view of the nature of language that is incommensurable with the view manifested in his immediately preceding discussion of speech as presencing.

But is not foolish consistency the hobgoblin of little minds? Could this not be a place where Burke is being an "edifying" philosopher, and is it not inappropriate to require that edifying philosophy be internally consistent? Burke himself forestalled this interpretation. He described *RofR* as a book about *"terminology"* (p. vi), and he characterized this essay as an account "about the nature of language" (pp. 1–2). Issues of definition and accounts of the fundamental constructs of one's philosophy are much more systematic than edifying topics. So although consistency may not be the appropriate criterion to apply to some philosophical writing, it is a legitimate measure for efforts to define central constructs.

The white space after the first fifteen paragraphs of "On Words and the Word" poignantly embodies a tension we notice in all of Burke's discussions of the nature of language. On the one hand, he was clearly aware of the constitutive power of the oral-aural nexus humans experience as language; on the other, his thinking and writing were deflected by the terministic screen of the symbol model. If he were unaware of the primary potential of speech to make present, he could not have drafted the first section of this essay. But if he were unconstrained by the terministic screen of the symbol model, he would not have been drawn to develop his discussion as he did.

Burke's second analogy is, "Words are to the non-verbal things they name as Spirit is to Matter" (p. 16). The first two paragraphs of his discussion of this analogy provide another example of the way Burke's allegiance to the symbol model affected some of his most fruitful insights. Immediately after introducing the analogy he wrote:

> That is, if we equate the non-verbal with "Nature" (using "Nature" in the sense of the less-than-verbal, the sort of sheerly

electro-chemical motion there'd be if all entities capable of using language ceased to exist), then verbal or symbolic action is
analogous to the 'grace' that is said to 'perfect' nature.

There is a sense in which the word 'transcends' the thing
it names (p. 16).

Although these first lines clearly echo the two worlds and tool
commitments of the symbol model, the final phrase of the paragraph
again reflects the tension we identified. When "grace" is said "to perfect nature," the relationship between the two is clearly not simply
representational. Unfortunately, Burke did not clarify what it is. So
the reader is left with an undeveloped hint. And importantly, Burke's
next move was to return to the "words as names" account that he
began a few paragraphs earlier.

As he developed his point about the "duality of realm . . .
implicit in our definition of [the hu]man as the symbol-using animal," he pointed out that "there is also a notable sense in which these
two realms cannot be kept rigidly apart" (p. 16). His example was
of "psychogenic illnesses," where a context of (verbal) "ideas" can directly affect the health of one's (nonverbal) body. He concluded that,
"In all such cases . . . the realm of the natural . . . is seen to be pervaded, or *inspirited*, by the realm of the verbal, or symbolic. And in
this sense the realm of the symbolic corresponds (in our analogy) to
the realm of the 'supernatural'" (p. 17). Thus the second analogy re-
asserted the distinction between words and nonverbal things, but
Burke's development of it emphasized that the distinction is difficult if not impossible to maintain. In some special cases, "matter"
is "inspirited" by language, but Burke's account of how this occurs
stopped with his assertion that "the word" in some sense "'transcends' the thing it names." So the tension we noted previously surfaced again here, and it remained unresolved. Some later works,
especially "(Nonsymbolic) Motion/ (Symbolic) Action," moved toward
resolving this tension in clearly semiotic directions.

The third analogy concerns language and the negative. Burke
summarized, "Language theory, in coming to a head in a theory of
the negative, corresponds to 'negative theology'" (p. 33). He began
his discussion of this analogy with a reminder of what he termed in
other places the *paradox of substance*,[31] namely, as he put it here,
that, "whatever *correspondence* there is between a *word* and the
thing it names, the word is *not* the thing" (p. 18). At this point, the
two worlds orientation of Burke's claim is undoubtedly apparent to
the reader, as is the semiotic perspective apparent in his acceptance

of the possibility of there being a correspondence between verbal name and nonverbal thing.

Burke's development of this analogy also illustrates once more how the terministic screen of the symbol model can introduce difficulties into a discussion of the nature of language. Echoing an earlier example he wrote, "Quite as the word 'tree' is verbal and the thing tree is non-verbal, so all words for the non-verbal must, by the very nature of the case, discuss the realm of the non-verbal in terms of *what it is not*. Hence, to use words properly, we must spontaneously have a feeling for the principle of *the negative*" (p. 18). Here again Burke was working to manage problems created by positing the existence of two worlds, one of which "represents" the other. He clearly recognized the difficulty: How can one (verbal) kind of phenomenon faithfully re-present another essentially different (nonverbal) kind of phenomenon? His solution was to postulate a "principle of the negative," which, rather than solving the problem, simply restated it: One realm is not-the-other (i.e., is its negation). So the representational puzzle remained.

As in the earlier essay, two primary difficulties with Burke's analysis are his distinction between the verbal and the nonverbal and his focus on individual words. First, as Burke himself noted in other places, humans cannot get "out from behind" language; language pervades human awareness and is our *way* of sense making. This is precisely the sense of Heidegger's claim that "Language is the house of Being. In its home [the human] dwells"[32] and of Gadamer's that "Being that can be understood is language."[33] As has been noted in earlier chapters, these claims about the relationship between Being and language do not deny facticity. But they do underscore the central problem with any two worlds analysis: there can be no nonlinguistic human *world*, no humanly meaningful realm completely independent of language. *All aspects of the human world are permeated by language.* Language processes are coterminous with the worlding processes of everyday coping—awareness, perceiving, understanding, and thinking.

Burke appeared at times to make this very point. In *P&C*, for example, he emphasized that "Reality is what things will do to us or for us. It is expectation of comfort or discomfort, prosperity or risk." He highlighted the pervasive presence of morals in human action and characterized morals as "fists" that sometimes violently mold realities (pp. 22, 191–192). In *ATH* he emphasized that "Words are a mediatory realm that joins us with wordless nature while at the same time standing between us and wordless nature" (p. 373).

In addition, several Burke scholars emphasize his powerful treatment of language as constitutive of social reality .[34]

So there is clearly a tension in Burke's corpus, but difficulties arise because it is not possible coherently to embrace both sides of this tension, especially in chapters and essays that treat issues systematically. When Burke maintained his commitment to an explicit articulation of the symbol model and simultaneously treated language as constitutive of human reality, it was at the expense of coherence. It does not work to claim—as he continued to do in his most recent works—that there is a fundamental distinction between the nonverbal world of motion and the verbal world of action, and to insist at the same time that there is, for the human, only one world, the one constituted by language. As we noted earlier, much of his writing leads us to believe that, were he free of the terministic screen of the symbol model, he would have been much better able to characterize language consistently as a "presencing" medium, one constitutive of the human world.

The problematic nature of Burke's second major assumption follows directly. Language cannot most fruitfully be viewed as simply an objective system of word-symbols, but as the activity or process of oral-aural articulate contact. Speaking and listening, or addressing and responding, are the primary and uniquely human linguistic processes, not choosing and using individual terms. An account of the nature of language that begins from or focuses on discrete words inescapably distorts the lived phenomena it attempts to describe. When Burke chose to discuss the nature of language by emphasizing individual words and word combinations, he risked reducing his analysis to only a reductive and derived account of language as humans live it.[35]

Burke's focus moved in exactly this direction in "On Words and the Word." Despite the explication of primal speaking and hearing in the first fifteen paragraphs, a major part of his discussion was an attempt to correlate "realms" with examples of individual terms— *tree, sun, dog, justice, monarchy, moral obligations,* and so on. One problem with this strategy is that it is relatively easy to identify difficulties in the arguments he offers about individual words. For instance, Burke's primary example of the second analogy is a South Pacific islander who "had been hexed by members of his tribe and was dying, despite the efforts of modern medicine to save him" (p. 17). "Hexing" is what Wittgenstein would call a language-game or a way of speaking (and listening).[36] Although hexing consists, in part, of ritual incantations of certain words, this part occurs in the cultural, social, spatiotemporal, and psychological context that surrounds and reinforces the complex of events and actions—all the contextual elements that Volosinov/Bakhtin would say the words *respond* to. In short, "Hexing" is much more than individual word using, but Burke employed it to illustrate an analogy expressed as an insight about individual words. He took a similar word-based approach to the third analogy. This concentration on words led him toward a problematically atomistic analysis.

The fourth and fifth analogies build on the first three and develop ideas tangential to our primary concerns. But the sixth analogy discusses how "the relation between the name and the thing named is like the relations of the persons in the Trinity" (p. 34). Here Burke's topic was the same as that addressed in the third commitment of the symbol model, and he argued against it: the relationship between "word" and "thing," he claimed, is not representational but Trinitarian. He began by contending that in the relation between "tree" and a given tree, "the power is primarily in the thing," just as the first person of the Trinity is said to have the power to "generate" the second (p. 29). Then he suggested that the "correspondence" among terms of the Trinity is not objective but *personal*. "And the word for perfect communion between *persons* is 'Love'" (p. 30). Thus the "technical" correspondence between thing and name is analogous to the "love" relationship between Father and Son in the Trinity. Though Burke did not direct this argument against the symbol model, his discussion of this analogy again indirectly manifested the tension between his representational and his nonrepresentational beliefs.

Burke followed his development of the six analogies with an argument for the appropriateness of thinking that links logology and theology. He concluded his treatment of the analogies with the statement that these were central to his "philosophy of language," and then briefly noted two final important elements of this philosophy. The first element consisted of two contrasts, one between "Dramatism" and "Scientism," and the second between "action" and "motion" (pp. 38–39). Scientism begins with "problems of knowledge, or perception," whereas Dramatism addresses "problems of act, or form" (p. 39). Action, briefly, "is to 'motion' as 'mind' is to 'brain';" there can be motion without action but no action without motion. Thus "meaning" is not reducible to "'information theory,' mechanical 'interpretation' of 'signals,' and the like. . . . *Dramatism assumes a qualitative empirical difference between mental action and mechanical motion*" (p. 40). Of course language, from Burke's Dramatistic perspective, is a special kind of action; namely, symbolic action (p. 30). This central feature of his perspective leads away from some of the commitments of the symbol model. However, this special kind of action was centrally characterized as not-motion; that is, as not reducible without remainder to the processes of the nonverbal realm. In this way, Burke's distinction between motion and action was parasitic on the Cartesian distinction between subjects (who populate the world of action) and objects (that fill the realm of motion). Thus the nonsemiotic direction of Burke's turn toward language as action was in tension with the two worlds view of reality that was a part of his terministic screen.

The final element of his philosophy that he mentiond here was his definition of the human as "The symbol-using animal, inventor of the negative, separated from [the] natural condition by instruments of [one's] own making, and goaded by the spirit of hierarchy" (p. 40). He ended "On Words and The Word" with a brief discussion of this definition, which we analyze in the final section of this chapter.

"What Are the Signs of What?
A Theory of Entitlement"

The tension between semiotic and post-semiotic perspectives apparent in "On Words and the Word" emerges even more strongly in "What Are the Signs of What?" In this essay Burke appeared to test his endorsement of the symbol model, but from a perspective that continued to be constrained by this terministic screen.

According to Dell Hymes, Burke wrote this essay for a lecture series at Boston University in 1956 in which each speaker was asked to take as a theme "the reversal of some common notion."[37] Burke chose to reverse the notion that words are the signs of things. Hymes notes in his introduction to the 1962 version of the essay that Burke was motivated to address the representational issue in order to treat language as "mode of action more than as countersign of thought."[38] In other words, the tension we have noted was present at the outset of this essay, and it surfaced in both his discussion of "words and things" and his explanation of his "theory of entitlement."

The first sentence of the essay asserts, "There are two quite different senses in which we can say that a word has a context," the verbal (the context of other words) and the nonverbal.[39] Burke then elaborated this reassertion of the two worlds commitment by introducing the concept of "scene." He noted that linguistic and nonlinguistic contexts can be very different, and that an "act" can connote different meanings by virtue of the "scene" in which it is located.

For a fuller explication of what he meant by *scene,* Burke referred the reader to the opening essay in *GM,* "Container and Thing Contained." This essay begins with a qualified affirmation of the same two worlds distinction: "Using 'scene' in the sense of setting or background, and 'act' in the sense of action, one could say that 'the scene contains the act.' "[40] Thus verbal action was distinguished from the nonverbal scene that "contains" it. A few paragraphs later in *GM,* however, Burke stated that "The nature of the scene may be conveyed primarily by suggestions built into the lines of the verbal action itself . . . or it may be conveyed by non-linguistic properties" (p. 3). Hence a scene's nature or significance may be expressed linguistically *or* materially. Regarding the relation between scene and act, Burke wrote, "the stage-set [scene] contains the action *ambiguously* . . . and in the course of the play's development this ambiguity is converted into a corresponding *articulacy.* The proportion would be: scene is to act as implicit is to explicit" (p. 7). Thus, action articulates or makes explicit what is inarticulate, that which cannot speak.

But the relationship between action and scene is even more complex. Burke continued, "There is, of course, a circular possibility in the terms [*act* and *scene*]. If an agent acts in keeping with his [or her] nature as an agent (act-agent ratio), [she or] he may change the nature of the scene accordingly (scene-act ratio), and thereby establish a state of unity between himself [or herself] and [the] world (scene-agent ratio). Or the scene may call for a certain kind of act, which makes for a corresponding kind of agent, thereby likening agent to scene" (p. 19). Here Burke saw *act, agent,* and *scene* as necessarily bound up with each other. In this sense, the term *scene* worked for Burke as descriptive of the human situation that entails both the linguistic and the nonlinguistic. Thus when the first two paragraphs of "What Are the Signs of What?" are interpreted in conjunction with his treatment of *scene* in *GM,* it becomes apparent that Burke was arguing that it is possible to differentiate analytically between language and the nonlinguistic world, but that he saw them as inextricably tied together.

To put it another way, although the simplest representational view of language entails the positing of two "contexts," Burke joined them by treating language as "symbolic" action. For Burke, an act always occurred in a scene, so each act simultaneously encompassed both the linguistic "context" and the nonlinguistic one. From the perspective of the symbol model, this move enabled Burke to deemphasize the distinction between linguistic and nonlinguistic contexts without completely abandoning his investment in a nonlinguistic, "objective" reality.

The second notable feature of the early parts of "What Are the Signs of What?" is the hesitancy Burke displayed about his own questioning of the representational view of language. "We tinker with" the idea that words are the signs of things "at our peril," he noted. Yet he proceeded, "if only as a tour de force, if only as an experiment tentatively tried for heuristic purposes" (p. 363). He suggested that he did not want to be understood as advocating that the reversal "should flatly replace the traditional view," but rather that it should be seen as a way of modifying our view of language, "like adding an adjective to a noun" (p. 363).

As he developed these caveats, the tension we have noted surfaced again. Burke acknowledged explicitly that "there is a variant of the Cartesian split" in his accounts of the "world of action" and the "world of motion" (p. 366). But this split is not absolute, he claimed, because "unfortunately, there is an intermediate realm" where motion is affected by action (p. 366). "Regrettably," he continued, the view of language that acknowledges this realm (Dramatism) is grounded more in "rhetoric and poetry" than in "a theory of signs" (p. 367). So although "science" can deal directly with the "relation between the verbal sign and its corresponding nonverbal referent," a Dramatistic approach starts "with problems of terministic catharsis" or "transformation" in meaning (p. 367). In other words, Dramatism "unfortunately" and "regrettably" cannot take for granted the supposition that language is secondary to objective reality, and must attempt, "experimentally at least," to posit the "'transformation' in meaning" as primary (p. 368).

Thus Burke indicated that a reversal of the accepted relationship between words and things violates, in some senses, not only (Cartesian) common sense but also his own "theory of signs." He spent approximately eight pages making this point but noted that this "experiment tentatively tried for heuristic purposes" (p. 363) was nonetheless a fruitful challenge for him, because "insofar as one can encompass such opposition, seeing the situation anew in terms of it, one has dialectically arrived thus roundabout at knowledge" (p. 367).

Ten pages into the essay Burke resumed "the experiment" with an introduction to his theory of entitlement, using the analysis of poetry as his subject matter. He noted that the analyst of poetry or drama looks not for the actual, historical referents of the words, but instead focuses on their internal relationships and their relationship to a "universe of discourse beyond their internal relations" (p. 368). These relationships can best be understood as centrally involving *entitling*, which means summarizing sections or stanzas with "titles."

Titles "sum up" or "infold" all the details for which the title stands, or the details can be seen as the "exfoliations-in-time" of what is "contained" in the title (p. 370). Burke illustrated how a title can be constructed for an utterance and argued that a "title-of-a-title" leads to "universals" like "'man,' 'dog,' [and] 'tree'" (p. 371).

Burke's emphasis on "titles" and "universals" inclined him toward the focus on individual words we noted in his discussions of the second and third analogies in "On Words and the Word." In "What Are the Signs of What?" he maintained a distinction between "titles" and "situations," treated titles as summations of situations or of other titles, and thus "arrived" at singular terms that "infold" or "contain" all the details. So in contrast with Burke's insistence, for example, in *P&C,* that "language be understood to include . . . other such arbitrary, conventional symbol-systems as dance, music, sculpture, painting, and architecture,"[41] here he was comfortable treating language as essentially a system made up of words.

Although such an analytic approach can be useful for written language, it is much less so when one acknowledges speaking as what Michael McGee calls "the regulative ideal" for understanding all discourse.[42] Further, as noted in Chapters 1 and 4, word-based analytics may be applicable to concrete nouns, but are less informative for most other types of speech, including verb forms and syncategorematics. But when Burke argued that "one element of the sentence . . . [is] capable of serving as title for the whole sentence," and that the sentence serves "as the title for its nonverbal context of situation," he offered only concrete nouns as illustrations; he did not contend, for example, that *this, dancing, although of,* or *the* could function as a "title" (p. 371).

Three-quarters of the way through the essay Burke stated that "conditions are now ripe for a shortcut whereby the *summarizing object* can be paired with the *summarizing word*" (p. 372), and that the direction of correspondence could go either way (word to thing or thing to word). To argue for the thing to word reversal, Burke recalled "Plato's theory in which the things of this world are said to be but imperfect exemplars of the perfect forms that have eternal being in the realm of the transcendent" (p. 373). Then, in a single long sentence, Burke offered the heart of his argument for the reversal hypothesis: "For, when you have abbreviated the verbal expression by using one word as its summarizing title, and when you have next abbreviated the nonverbal context of situation by featuring some one object that serves as the material equivalent of a title by standing for the essence of the situation, and when finally you have completed your method of shortcuts by leaping from the word that sums up the expression to the object that sums up the nonverbal situation, then you have a condition wherein the thing can be taken as the visible manifestation of the 'universal form' that resides spiritually in the corresponding word" (p. 373). So the process was again presented as chronological—"when . . . when you have next . . . and when finally . . . then you have a condition. . . . " The *logos* of this chrono-logy moves from a *title* that summarizes verbal expressions to an *object* that summarizes situations and thence to the *object summarizing the title.* "'Things' are now the signs of words . . . " (p. 373). Or more precisely, they "can be taken" this way; it is as possible to argue that things stand for words as to argue that words stand for things.

Elements of the symbol model are clearly apparent here. There is a manifest division between the verbal and the nonverbal and each is analyzable into units—"title" and "object." "Abbreviation" links the two realms and this link is clearly representational—"by standing for the essence of the situation." Although the representation is not simply iconic, nonetheless "the thing can be taken as the visible manifestation of the 'universal form' that resides spiritually in the corresponding word."

At this point in Burke's analysis of this process of entitlement, the factor deciding the direction of the relationship between words and things appeared to be how "context" is construed. If context were treated objectively, then one would be led to see words as signs of things. If context were treated linguistically, then things would become the signs of words. Burke first explored the former, objective account of context and described context as consisting of four "terministic pyramids," each of which is made up of "words for a certain realm, or order" (p. 373): the natural, the verbal, the sociopolitical, and the supernatural. These familiar "realms" were presented as exhaustive but not mutually exclusive, and Burke noted that there was a distinction between the first three and the fourth, because words for the supernatural are all borrowed from the other three contexts; thus, there could be no supernatural "referents."

Treating things as the signs of words, however, requires that each realm be seen as linguistic. To explore the viability of this view Burke asked, "just as the word is said by theologians to be a mediatory principle between this world and the supernatural, might words be a mediatory principle between ourselves and nature" (p. 378)? What we take to be a purely physical world, suggested Burke, may instead be purely a linguistic construction, "a fantastic pageantry" (p. 379).

Burke played argumentatively with this possibility first by granting primacy to the second, linguistic pyramid, because discourse in the verbal order is the "only time when something can be discussed wholly in terms of itself" (p. 375); that is, in this order one uses words to discuss words. Then Burke emphasized that the supernatural realm "cannot be adequately discussed in human terms," because the terms to talk about the supernatural are all borrowed from the other orders (p. 376). The socio-political order is also "inextricably interwoven with [the hu]man's terministic genius" (p. 376). After another brief detour to the "commonsense realistic assumption" that within the "natural order" words correspond to nonverbal entities, Burke asked, "insofar as [the hu]man, the symbol-using animal approached nonverbal nature in terms of his [or her] humanly verbalizing nature, is there not a sense in which *nature* must be as much a linguistically inspirited thing . . . as *super*-nature" (p. 378)? In other words, even if one argued that humans have direct sensory access to nature, if things are seen as the signs of words, this direct perception must be essentially linguistic.

This last move to a treatment of nature as linguistic clearly inclined Burke away from the two worlds commitment of the symbol model. But he did not elaborate this move. Instead, Burke ended the essay by provocatively asking, "*might* it not follow that . . . nature [is perceived] through the fog of symbol-ridden social structures . . . erected atop nature?" and "*might* words be a mediatory principle between ourselves and nature?" (p. 378, italics added) His final sentence reads, "*In this sense* things would be the signs of words" (p. 379, italics added), again suggesting that he preferred a degree of qualification to outright assertion.

Along with Burke's explicit comment that this was an exercise "tentatively tried for heuristic purposes" (p. 373), the fact that he did not develop any implications from his reversal hypothesis indicates that he was not ready to commit fully to a post-semiotic view of language. For example, he did not recast his terministic pyramids into a new model showing "the verbal order" as encompassing the other three realms. He appeared to be intrigued with the notion that reality is linguistically constituted, but he did not use this notion to reframe his own view. Entitling was treated as a process whereby (often single) concrete nouns summarize or stand in the place of more complex discourse, which, in turn, sums up or points to a nonverbal realm.

He also did not reconsider his definition of humans as symbolic in light of his reversal hypothesis. In fact, it appears in this essay that Burke's commitments to elements of the symbol model may have prevented him from seeing the inconsistency between viewing humans as "symbol-users" and viewing language as constitutive of reality, and as we clarify in the next section, we find this same tendency in his "Definition of Man." In "What Are the Signs of What?" Burke treated symbols as "receptacles of personal attitudes and social ratings" which carry these values to the things of nature (p. 361). But right up to the end of the essay, he discussed nature as something that exists objectively, even though it may be "infused with the spirit of words."

In sum, this essay again evidences the tension that Burke apparently experienced which led him both to testify to the efficacy of the symbol model and to explore its limitations. Although he played argumentatively with the view that words and things are "co-eternal," or, even more radically, that things may be constituted by words, he did not develop or apply his reversal hypothesis. A new version of this tension, this time in relation to the tool commitment of the symbol model, surfaces in the final essay we analyze.

"Definition of Man"

This is the first of five papers that make up Part I of *LSA* and that; in Burke's words, "serve as a summation of the book as a whole" (p. viii). It first appeared in 1963 and substantially elaborates several brief comments from earlier works, such as Burke's 1950 characterization of rhetoric.[43] We examine this essay not only because Burke presented it as central to this important book, but also because, like Heidegger and Gadamer, Burke here treated the "nature of humanity" as intimately connected with the "nature of language."

In an introductory note, Burke offered something of a systematic rationale for his topic by observing that because "a definition of [the hu]man is at least implicit in any writer's comments on cultural matters" (p. 2) there is value in making it explicit. The four-paragraph first section of the essay comments "on definition in general," and then offers the following, "in the hope of either persuading the reader that it fills the bill," or of prompting some critical or elaborative response:

> [The hu]*man is*
> *the symbol-using (symbol-making, symbol-misusing) animal*
> *inventor of the negative (or moralized by the negative)*
> *separated from* [the] *natural condition by instruments of. . .*
>   [human] *making*

> *goaded by the spirit of hierarchy (or moved by the sense of*
>   *order)*
> *and rotten with perfection* (p. 16).

Although he admitted that his first clause might not "come as much of a surprise," Burke maintained that this was the first feature that needed explaining. Because he treated symbolizing as primary, and because he focused on symbol *using*, it appears that the now-familiar terministic screen was still functioning here, and that Burke was committed to at least the claims that language is somehow representational, that it constitutes a system, and that this system of symbols is an instrument humans use.

His development of this clause confirmed this inference. Burke began with two stories about birds, one trapped in a philosophy classroom because, without the ability to use symbols, it could not understand the advice, "Fly down just a foot or so, and out one of those windows," and the other a "genius" that figures out a way to get its young out of the nest but cannot share its insight with the rest of birddom because it cannot write or talk about it. Burke observed that without symbols, the "genius" wren might never use its method again, but that, "on the happier side," birds are not susceptible to demagogues (pp. 3–5).

In the next paragraph Burke appeared to shift from a discussion of how symbols can be used to how, in a sense, symbols use humans. He observed that a great deal "of what we mean by 'reality' has been built up for us through nothing but our symbol systems" (p. 5). He acknowledged that we do experience a "tiny sliver of reality . . . firsthand," but emphasized that "the whole overall 'picture' is but a construct of our symbol systems" (p. 5). He further analyzed "the kind of relation that really prevails between the verbal and the nonverbal," employing the analogy of a road map to characterize the relationship (p. 5). Burke repeated his contention from "On Words and the Word" that "[l]anguage referring to the realm of the nonverbal is necessarily talk about things in terms of what they are not" and suggested that the human motivation to talk comes from both "our animality" and "our symbolicity" (p. 6). He averred that the characterization "symbol-making" may be as appropriate as "symbol-using," and that "symbol-misusing" should be added to the formula. After a humorous example about "misuse," and a discussion of Freud's concepts of symbolic "condensation," "displacement," and "substitution," Burke concluded that this clause "parallels the traditional formulas, 'rational animal' and *Homo sapiens*," but that it functions descriptively rather than honorifically (p. 9).

Our initial observation about the twenty-eight paragraphs discussing this first clause is that, despite his introductory comment, Burke did not clarify what he meant by *symbol*. He appeared not to think of it as a problematic term, perhaps because by 1963 it had become so central to his vocabulary that he viewed its meaning as obvious. Or, Burke may have believed that, since he discussed the term directly in other works, there was no need to do so here.

These paragraphs are also consistent with several elements of the symbol model. Despite some reservations, Burke's clearest theoretical commitment here is to the proposition that symbols are instruments humans use and misuse. Burke noted that one can "cut countless corners" by various strategic *uses* of symbols: referring to a person by name, giving a book a title, and translating one expression into another (pp. 7–8). His stories about birds illustrated what they cannot do because they do not possess *instruments* of language, and he discussed the road map as a travel *tool*.

In addition, this section manifests Burke's commitment to the assumption that symbols link the verbal and the nonverbal. The two paragraphs in which Burke discussed the way symbols affect our grasp of "reality" clearly acknowledge the *reciprocal* relationship between words and the world. But they just as clearly embody Burke's now-familiar insistence on the distinction between the verbal and the nonverbal and the role of "words" as both "a link between us and the nonverbal" and "a screen separating us from the nonverbal" (p. 5).

Burke's discussion of symbol "misuse" is especially revealing. When he commented on "demogogic tricks," "psychogenic illnesses," and "hexing" (pp. 6–7), he did not contend that these instances of language create or construct reality but that they alter or distort it. In his words, symbol "misuses" are instances "of the ways whereby the realm of symbolicity may affect the sheerly biologic motions of animality" (p. 7). "Sheerly" was one of Burke's favorite philosophically significant terms. Laura Crowell traced the steady increase in Burke's uses of *sheer* and *sheerly* through eight of his books, noting that he used *sheer* "377 times, and always with the meaning of utter or utterly."[44] Therefore "sheerly biologic motions of animality" can be translated "utterly biologic motions"; that is, those that occur not in the human world but in the "totally" other realm of what might be termed *brute data* or *objective reality*. In his encyclopedia article on Dramatism Burke also emphasized the primacy of this "one overall dramatistic distinction . . . between 'action' and 'sheer motion,'" where *action* refers to the behavior of "a typically symbol-using animal . . . in contrast with the *extrasymbolic* or *non*-symbolic operations of nature."[45]

In "Definition of Man" Burke next explored his second clause, "inventor of the negative." His primary purpose was to reaffirm that the hortatory negative—"Thou shalt not" as contrasted with the propositional "It is not"—was one of the primary and distinctive resources of human language considered Dramatistically. The human, in other words, is distinguished and characterized in part by the ability—and proclivity—to proscribe. In the twenty-one paragraphs of this section, Burke qualified his use of *inventor*, credited Bergson's *Creative Evolution* with the basic insight that "there are no negatives in nature" (p. 9), clarified the distinction between the propositional and the hortatory negative, briefly debunked treatments of "not-being" and "nothingness" by "the Existentialists" (p. 10), distinguished between moralistic negatives and "quasi-positives" (p. 11), maintained the moral priority of the negative over the positive (p. 12), reaffirmed his insistence that words "are *not* the things they stand for" (p. 12), and opined that contemporary life needs more "negativity" to balance the "positives" of the powers that science and advertising promise (pp. 12–13).

The first paragraph of this section illustrates two characteristics of the way Burke philosophized about language. The crucial part of the paragraph reads: "The second clause is: Inventor of the negative. I am not wholly happy with the word, 'inventor.' For we could not properly say that [the hu]man 'invented' the negative unless we can also say that [hu]man[ity] is the 'inventor' of language itself. So far as the sheerly empirical development is concerned, it might be more accurate to say that language and the negative 'invented' [the hu]man. In any case, we are here concerned with the fact that there are no negatives in nature, and that this ingenious addition to the universe is solely a product of human symbol systems . . ." (p. 9).

These sentences again illustrate the tension. Burke was clearly aware of some of the philosophical difficulties inherent in his philosophy of language. His dissatisfaction with the word *inventor* focused precisely on one important problem: *Do humans in fact "make" language and subsequently "use" it, or does language (also?) "make" humans?* Earlier in "Definition of Man," Burke had emphasized the power of language to structure human "reality," and he appeared clearly to recognize the inconsistency between that position and one that treated language as an invention of, and hence subject to the control of, human agents. But although he was aware of the potential inconsistency, he did not attempt to resolve it. Instead, he raised the issue, acknowledged it as important, and then, with only an "In any case," proceeded to his next idea. At this point in his writing Burke was clearly not fulfilling his desire to be "a pretty damned good philosopher of language," because, rather than grappling in any thorough way with the knotty conceptual problem raised by this part of his account of the nature of language, he sidestepped it.[46]

The fourth section of the essay treats the clause, "separated from [the] natural condition by instruments of . . . [human] making." Here Burke made two important claims about the nature of language. The first was that human "symbolizing" is distinguished from the ape's use of sticks to extend its reach and the bees' nectar dance by its reflexivity. Nonhuman beings, to put it bluntly, do not "use words about words" (p. 14). The second was that, to some degree, language is *not* simply an instrument or tool. In his words, "The instrumental value of language certainly accounts for much of its development, and . . . survival . . . but to say as much is not by any means to say that language is in its essence a tool. Language is a species of action, symbolic action—and its nature is such that it can be used as a tool" (p. 5).

Burke's first observations in this section clearly manifest his continuing commitment to the symbol model. But his later comments about "instrumentality" appear, at least in part, to echo the position some philosophers take when they argue against the reduction of language to "instrumental" status. In this section of "Definition of Man," Burke appears to agree with these philosophers, and he was even more explicit in a later interview. Echoing Gadamer's metaphor, Burke commented in 1983, "You can lay a tool down, but you can't lay language down. . . . [Your] own vocabulary hypnotizes you . . . I believe, absolutely, you do get hooked to a vocabulary. If you really do live with your terms, they turn up tricks of their own. You can't get around them. . . . *[They] use you*".[47]

Closer analysis, however, reveals that Burke's position remained at least as semiotic as it was post-semiotic. First, in "Definition of Man," Burke explicitly acknowledged the partial accuracy of an instrumental characterization of language: "The instrumental value of language certainly accounts for much of its development and this instrumental value of language may even have been responsible for the survival of language itself . . . " (p. 15). By contrast, most philosophers who make this point argue that only a misplaced Cartesianism can maintain the conviction that persons live in any way in an instrumental relationship with language.[48] More important, Burke's argument was that language is not simply an instrument because it "is a species of action, symbolic action—and its nature is such that it can be used as a tool" (p. 15). Many postmodern philosophers reject instrumental characterizations of language, not because it is a kind of action, but because language is a kind of *transaction*, an event of contact. In the final sentences of *Truth and*

Method, for example, Gadamer contends that language is fundamentally misunderstood when it is seen "as a stock of words and phrases, of concepts, viewpoints and opinions. In fact," he continues, "language occurs in the infinity of discourse, of speaking with one another, of the freedom of 'expressing oneself' and 'letting oneself be expressed.' Language is not its elaborated conventionalism, nor the burden of preschematization with which it loads us, but the generative and creative power to unceasingly make this whole once again fluent."[49] A key element of this characterization is the receptive moment—"letting oneself be expressed." As has been noted before, this perspective foregrounds the extent to which humans "undergo" language and are used by it.[50]

From this Heideggerian-Gadamerian perspective, Burke's writing illustrates how he "underwent an experience" with symbol terminology. *Burke's account might be that first he chose "symbol" terminology because it accurately represented the reality* of human language and *then* symbol terminology affected subsequent aspects of his philosophy of language. On the other hand, Heidegger or Gadamer would likely contend that Burke's involvement in reflections on language with Kant, Spinoza, Cassirer, Langer, Ogden, Richards, Korzybski, and others immersed him in symbol terminology to the extent that this perspective "overwhelmed and transformed" his insights into the constitutive, generative, and presencing power of speech communicating. Thus there are two important distinctions here between Burke and post-semiotic philosophers. The first is that Burke consistently treated language as a kind of action that people *do*; even when he wrote about "being used by language," he treated this experience as a stage in a temporal series of events in which first one uses words, then one has to cope with the implications of one's earlier choices. Post-semiotic philosophers, on the other hand, see language as an event that humans "suffer" as much as they "enact," so from a post-semiotic perspective, it is fundamentally incomplete to characterize language as a kind of "action." The second important distinction is that Burke consistently treated language as "symbolic," and many post-semiotic philosophers do not.

Section 5 of "Definition of Man" briefly discusses the clause, "Goaded by the spirit of hierarchy." The primary claim of section 6 is that "The principle of perfection is central to the nature of language as motive" (p. 16). Nothing is added in either of these sections to the account of language that Burke has provided in this essay and the works we have considered earlier.

Burke ended "Definition of Man" with an appeal for nuclear disarmament. His point was that, because humans are beings with the five intrinsic features just described, they are especially subject to symbolic "foibles and crotchets" the most extreme of which could literally bring human life to an end. He commented on his need for a "perfect" conclusion to the essay and fixed on a modernizing paraphrase of a "nursery jingle" as an appropriate strategy.

Conclusion

A close reading of some of Kenneth Burke's writings can serve as a second case study in the effects on an influential treatment of language of the conviction that language is symbolic. Our reading of four of Burke's most systematic treatments of language reveals that, from his first introduction of "symbol" vocabulary, Burke's philosophy of language took on aspects of form and substance consistent with the implicit theoretical claims of that vocabulary; namely, (1) that language is made up of identifiable units, most notably terms or words, (2) that these linguistic units are fundamentally and essentially different from nonlinguistic units, (3) that the linguistic units represent the nonlinguistic ones, (4) that the representational units make up a system, and (5) that this system is an instrument humans use to accomplish their goals.[51]

These commitments constituted one pole of a pervasive tension in Burke's philosophy of language. Almost as frequently as he treated language as made up of identifiable, discrete units—terms or words—he acknowledged that it is dynamic and processual. As Chapter 4 clarifies, this latter kind of analysis by units distorts language, because a living event cannot be reduced to its elements—even for analytic purposes—without fundamentally altering the nature of the event.

The tension was also apparent in that, despite Burke's keen awareness of the intimate *connection* between language and human reality, he also insisted that there is an essential *difference* between the "nonsymbolic" world of motion and the "symbolic" world of action. This distinction too is profoundly challenged by philosophers who critique the subject-object polarity on which it is based and who argue, as does Chapter 4, that there is only one human *world* and it is pervasively linguistic.

The tension surfaced again as Burke acknowledged that language can constitute and generate human reality and then, in the same or closely related writings, described the relationship between the two worlds of his analysis as a standing-for or representational relationship. From a post-semiotic perspective these positions are mutually exclusive; if "languaging" is indeed fundamentally constitutive, it cannot also be essentially representational.

A fourth evidence of this tension manifested in Burke's recognition, on the one hand, that humans can be used by language, and his insistence, on the other, that language is primarily an instrument humans employ to enact their motives, induce cooperation, and "dance their attitudes." In short, despite Burke's post-semiotic inclinations, his philosophy of language owed at least as much to Enlightenment as to postmodern thinking. We argue that he was led to this ambivalent position by being caught up in "symbol" vocabulary. In this way Burke's corpus illustrates what is at risk when a language or communication theorist characterizes living human language as an "arbitrary conventional symbol system."

As has been noted before, we do not mean to contend that Burke is uniformly "wrong" and post-semiotic characterizations of language are completely "right." Our primary point is rather that Burke's philosophy of language can fruitfully be seen as an case study of what can happen when a synoptic and innovative view of language is articulated in the terms of the symbol model. Insofar as the tensions between symbolic and nonsymbolic views are resolved in Burke's writings, they tend to be resolved in semiotic directions. We argue that a similar fate threatens other theorists who treat language as symbolic.

We also believe that theorists who wish to adopt aspects of Burke's analysis should be aware of the Cartesianism in his philosophy of language. To say that language is symbolic *action* is to claim that it is engaged in by actors (Cartesian subjects) typically operating with and on objects. This is fundamentally different from the claim that, in Gadamer's words, language is "the generative and creative power to unceasingly make" the human world coherent and "fluent."[52]

How might Burke's work best be read in light of our analysis? First, we agree with Rueckert and other commentators that the fact that there may be inconsistencies and contradictions should not lead one to reject either his theory or his critical insights. The problems we have outlined, however, should give some pause to students of Burke. It may be fruitful to opt for psychologic over logic and to remind the reader playfully that "There's always more to it than that." But problems are created when a writer claims to present a "philosophy of language," focuses explicitly on the most systematic of topics—the definition of one's subject matter—recognizes and raises problematic issues, and then either avoids these problems or presents incomplete arguments to support his position. One cannot thereby generate the kind of philosophy of language that engenders the highest confidence.

It is probably most accurate to view Burke as another of the great theorists whose shoulders provide a vantage from which more is visible than could be seen before. His insights help illumine the path, and where shortcomings exist, they illustrate again that Burke, his progenitors and we who are his descendants all remain "on the way to language."

✤ Chapter 8

The Symbol Model and Calvin O. Schrag's Communicative Praxis

"The speaker is embodied in his gestures, which take on the form of a body language. The author is embodied in his text, present in the *corpus* of his writings."

—Calvin O. Schrag

The reader familiar with philosophy will notice in this epigraph allusions to phenomenology, hermeneutics, and deconstruction. All three traditions figure prominently in Purdue philosopher Calvin O. Schrag's two most recent books, *Communicative Praxis and the Space of Subjectivity*,[1] and *The Resources of Rationality: A Response to the Postmodern Challenge*.[2] In these works and other writings,[3] Schrag draws on his broad knowledge of philosophical history and his intimate familiarity with Kierkegaard, Heidegger, Gadamer, Rorty, Habermas, Derrida, Ricoeur, and other philosophers to work out accounts of language, subjectivity, and reason that both reflect central features of postmodernism and resist several of what he takes to be its excesses. Schrag's anchoring phenomenon in this project is "communicative praxis," by which he means the amalgam of language and speech, discourse and action "that textures the space of human endeavoring, exhibiting a striving for an understanding and explanation of the configurations of experience through which such endeavoring passes."[4] This focus distinguishes Schrag's work

229

from that of many of his progenitors and contemporaries. For example, unlike Heidegger, who at various times interrogated Being or the language of poetry, and Gadamer, who is primarily interested in written texts, Schrag attends closely to living speech communication.

Hence, his writings are generally of interest here because his project and this one draw on some similar literatures to address some similar problems. His focus and mine are different in that I come to philosophy from the perspective of rhetorical and communication theory, whereas Schrag is first a philosopher and then a philosopher of communication. As a result, he is more intimately familiar than I with the philosophical history of the issues we both address, and with, for example, Merleau-Ponty's and Kierkegaard's writings. Moreover, although both his and my programs are motivated by postmodern works, my primary goal is to extend the postmodern critique of representation to semiotic accounts of the nature of language and to outline an approach to language that is responsive to this critique, whereas Schrag is responding to postmodern critiques of subjectivity and rationality and is working out views of of these phenomena that are situated *"between* modernity and postmodernity."[5] Our efforts resemble one another in that both of us are strongly influenced by Heidegger's analyses of epistemology and metaphysics and by Gadamer's hermeneutics. And even more important, the primary goal of Schrag's two most recent books is to underscore the philosophical significance of what I call events of *articulate contact* between and among persons, roughly the events he calls *communicative praxis*. Schrag's works and this one share the conviction that a kind of phenomenology of speech communicating, or an interpretation of the concrete event of living dialogue, can contribute significantly to a contemporary understanding of several issues central to philosophy and communication theory, including the status of the human subject, the role of rationality, and the nature of language.

If these general features were all that connected us, however, it would be most appropriate to discuss Schrag's work in a few laudatory paragraphs or a footnote. But there is a more interesting and potentially fruitful point of contact. I believe it can be shown that Schrag's basic understanding of communicative praxis burdens his analysis with vestiges of the symbol model. This attenuated commitment to some aspects of semiosis creates a problematic tension in what is otherwise an explicitly nonrepresentational, event-focused analysis of speech communicating. I believe this commitment threatens the coherence of the primary argument Schrag makes in the first third of *Communicative Praxis and the Space of Subjectivity*, and introduces ambiguity into some features of his description of "transversal rationality" in his most recent book. I hope to demonstrate in this chapter how symbol model analysis can both clarify the difficulty Schrag encounters and point toward a way of resolving it. Thus, if this chapter achieves its goal, it will show how the approach to language developed in Part I can not only to bring to light problems faced by writers like Volosinov and Burke, who have a foot in both representational and non-representational camps, but also can help tease out the much more subtle ambiguities that can exist when vestiges of a semiotic orientation attempt to share intellectual space with a nonrepresentational program anchored firmly in communicative praxis.

Overview of Schrag's Project

Schrag explains in the Preface and Introduction of *Communicative Praxis* that the book is primarily a response to attempts by deconstruction, critical theory, and hermeneutics to efface the philosophical subject. He characterizes the volume as "an effort to find a new space for subjectivity within the praxical space of discourse and action." The work is divided into three parts, "The Texture of Communicative Praxis," "The New Horizon of Subjectivity," and "The Rhetorical Turn." This structure parallels Schrag's three-dimensional characterization of "the linchpin for the discussion throughout," communicative praxis. As he explains this central term, "Discourse and action are *about* something, *by* someone, and *for someone.* Communicative praxis thus displays a referential moment (about a world of human concerns and social practices), a moment of self-implicature (by a speaker, author, or actor), and a rhetorical moment (directedness to the other). . . . The topical design in the three divisions is to work out plausible notions of hermeneutical reference, hermeneutical self-implicature, and hermeneutical rhetoric" (p. viii). My analysis questions whether the first of these three features is, in fact, "plausible." As I suggested, it is Schrag's commitment to the referential "about something" dimension of communicative praxis that generates a problematic tension in his work.

Schrag begins his analysis with communicative praxis, because he acknowledges the validity of Dewey's critique of the "quest for certainty" and the complementary suspicions about epistemology and metaphysics elaborated by Wittgenstein, Heidegger, Derrida, Rorty, and other postmodern philosophers. After these writers, he notes, the philosopher searching for a proper "starting point" can no longer

begin from an unassailable axiom or unimpeachable epistemological principle, but must rather ponder how best to enter the ongoing
conversation in such a way that its primary themes, directions, and
misdirections can be noted and described. Communicative praxis,
Schrag argues, offers such a starting point. It is a holistic notion,
labeling the ongoing interplay among thought and action, language
and speech, all contextualized in a human world.

Schrag believes that this notion of communicative praxis provides an opening to respond to such influential projects as Foucault's
pronouncement of the "Death of Man," Derrida's deconstruction of
the subject, Rorty's rejection of the subject as an epistemological
foundation for the philosophy of mind, and Fred R. Dallmayr's description of the "twilight of subjectivity."[6] He also explicitly notes the
close connection between traditional accounts of subjectivity and a
traditional view of *representation*. From the Cartesian-Kantian perspective, he writes, the human "becomes the center from which
existence as a whole is viewed. It is thus that a pictorial and representational view of the world travels with the construction of [the
hu]man as subject. The world of nature and history alike are pic-
tured and represented by a representing subject . . ." (p. 9). This tendency, he maintains, must be overcome.

In the first chapter of Part I, Schrag clarifies what he means
by *communication* and *praxis*. He traces an Aristotelian understanding of *praxis* by comparing and contrasting it with *phronesis, theoria,
poiesis*, and *techne*. He rejects definitions of communication that reduce it to codes and emphasizes that it includes "the manner and
style in which messages are conveyed and imparted, always against
the background of the tightly woven fabric of professional and
everyday life, with its shared experiences, participative relationships,
joint endeavors, and moral concerns" (p. 22). Thus understood, "the
space of communication is a space that is shared by praxis"(p. 22).
Echoing Burke, Schrag also distinguishes between the "linguistic"
and the nonlinguistic, "actional" dimension of communication. At the
end of the chapter he notes that he writes of the "texture" (cf. *tex-
tile* and *text*) of communicative praxis to underscore how all its elements are woven together, including everyday speech, the written
word, and the "play and display of meanings" within both perception and human action (p. 30).

The primary function of Chapter 2, "Communicative Praxis as
Expression," is to begin to clarify what Schrag means by "hermeneutical reference." Later I review this chapter in detail. Here it is
enough to note that Schrag attempts to erase the dichotomy between
interior and exterior perpetuated by traditional treatments of ex-

pression to characterize communicative praxis as at the same time linguistic and nonlinguistic, private and public, individual and cultural. The orientation and flavor of the chapter are captured in its final lines: "Never coming to rest as an essential feature of this and that, meaning is stitched into the global and processual texture of communicative praxis in such a way that its holdings can only be determined by taking an inventory of the times. Now the odyssey of this expressive meaning in the life of self and society, when its course is charted by reflection and the designs of understanding and explanation, encounters certain complexities arising from the desire to comprehend the truth of its manifold manifestations. It is to these ensuing complexities that we are forced to turn in the next chapter" (p. 47).

Because Chapter 2 linked meaning and expression so closely, Chapter 3 must raise the same question Ricoeur and Habermas raised with Gadamer: If meaning is embodied in expression, what is the possibility of and the place for distanciation and critique? The question is complex, partly because it invites a representational analysis, and, again, I plan to discuss Schrag's response in more detail later. But one central point is that, whereas traditional accounts treat distanced phenomena as idealized representations and thus underscore the necessity of representation for adequate critique, Schrag proposes an alternative. "The move to a region or field of ideality designed to deliver the needed distanciation from praxis so as to render a trustworthy account of it, if indeed such a move is to be made, cannot profitably follow either the route of a classical doctrine of essence or that of modern epistemologies of meaning" (p. 51). Schrag's alternative begins with a new account of meaning as accomplished and performed in speech and action. When one *reflects* on this meaning, he writes, one "slides into *signitive* meaning" (p. 54). With the help of Merleau-Ponty and Ricoeur, Schrag follows this "slide" to construct a revised notion of the *hermeneutical sign* (p. 57). This leads him to his account of "hermeneutical reference" that he defines as "the taking of something *as* something (be it a perceptual object, a phenomenal property, or a historical event), *as* a figure against a background, *as* a text within a context, *as* a happening within a horizon of happenings" (p. 69). This notion, he argues, provides an account of that which communication is *about* which understands meaning *not as representation but as disclosure.*

The following chapter is prompted because, as Schrag puts it, "The slide of expressive meaning into signitive meaning by way of distanciation opens up the space of the workings of understanding and explanation" (p. 73). He reviews how Dilthey distinguished between these two processes and treated both epistemologically. Dilthey's account perpetuated the interior-exterior and subject-object dichotomies, both of which, says Schrag, need to be set aside. When one attends to communicative praxis, he maintains, one sees how "the sense of the communicated messages is grasped as a whole contextualized within the situation as defined by its purposes and goals" (pp. 78–79). One also notices that "this understanding is never complete, often erratic, and sometimes breaks down. When the achievement of genuine understanding is threatened there is a call for explanation, a request to analyze the elemental units (lexical meanings, grammatical usages, and semantical referents) to supplement the labor of understanding. Comprehension is the play between the grasping of the whole in a unitary act of synthesis and an apprehension of the constitutive elements through regressive analysis" (p. 79). In other words, that which communication is *about* takes on special importance when understanding is incomplete. At this juncture, argues Schrag, a version of the hermeneutic circle begins to come into play as interlocutors turn to explanation, which consists primarily of the *analysis of elemental units*. He emphasizes that understanding is not a matter of achieving a one-to-one correspondence between meaning and author or speaker intent. Cultural, social, and contextual factors are all determinative, so that "understanding and explanation, in our reading, are situated within communicative praxis as moments of interpretive comprehension, penetrating the density of the facticity of our discourse and action" (p. 85). At the end of the chapter he emphasizes again that his account is meant to be "liberated . . . from the alien requirements of epistemological foundations and representational schemata . . . " (p. 93).

The final chapter of Part I discusses "The Illusion of Foundationalism." As Schrag explains, "Foundationalism, as a problem for epistemology, becomes a subject for disputation between those who claim that there is an unimpeachable substratum in our knowledge of the world—be it a direct perception of physical objects, acquaintance with sense-data, experience of 'raw feels,' incorrigibly intuited essences, or whatever—and those who argue that there is no such substratum" (p. 101). Schrag assumes that the anti-foundational nature of his project is apparent, but he admits the possibility that his communicative praxis could be understood as a new sort of foundation. He insists, though, that "the texture of communicative praxis can only be properly displayed after the search for foundations is abandoned" (p. 96). He reviews discussions of foundations in Husserl and especially Rorty, the latter of which lead to a reconsideration of "the philosophical notion of reference" (p. 106).

He resists Rorty's insistence that philosophers should "give up such a fine word [reference] in the English language," however, and attempts again, through a redefinition of *hermeneutical reference,* to rehabilitate it. Why? Because, as I already have noted, Schrag believes that "The need to find a philosophical space for reference arises from the very texture of communicative praxis, in which speech is the saying of something *about* something" (p. 107).

My overviews of the final two sections of *Communicative Praxis* will be brief, primarily because Schrag moves to topics beyond the scope of symbol model analysis. I hope to indicate, however, some of the main similarities between his and my own views of language and communication.

The first chapter of Part II introduces the notion of hermeneutical self-implicature, Schrag's label for the way subjectivity manifests in communicative praxis. Another benefit of dissolving the dichotomy between interior and exterior, he maintains, is to open up a space for a "transvalued subjectivity" to be sketched as that which "is implicated in the discourse and action that limns communicative praxis" (p. 121). Schrag's human subject is neither a pregiven entity nor a postgiven entity but "rather an event or happening that continues the conversation and social practices of [hu]mankind and inscribes its contributions on their textures" (p. 121; cf. Madison's discussion of [inter]subjectivity in Chapter 5.). Schrag cites with approval Émile Benveniste's argument that "it is in and through language that [the hu]man constitutes himself [or herself] as a *subject* . . . (p. 122). In this view, the Saussurian opposition between language and speech is overcome in a way that echoes features of my analysis in Chapter 4: "Language, thusly understood, is not simply *le* [sic] *langue* as a linguistic system, nor is it simply *la parole* as an episodic speech act. It is a third feature, a mediating event of concretion. Language as saying is the epiphany of discourse in which speech intersects with a linguistic tradition of sedimented social forms and grammatical rules" (p. 124). What Schrag calls "the space of subjectivity in which this self-implication eventuates" is, as he puts it, "a space of intersubjectivity" (p. 125). The self is still individual, but its mode of being is "essentially that of being able to speak with other subjects" (p. 125).

The following chapter considers the question of the ontological status of the decentered subject Schrag has resituated. If it is still conceived of as a presence, Schrag notes, then his analysis would be vulnerable to all the criticisms Heidegger and Derrida leveled against such metaphysical formulations. But because the subject is an *implicate* of communicative praxis rather than a *foundation* for it, these criticisms founder. The subject is an interplay of both both presence and absence, and it can be described with the help of three descriptive categories: temporality, multiplicity, and embodiment. Schrag's elaboration of each of these features helps round out his portrait of the decentered subject.

The final chapter in Part II explores contributions to an understanding of this decentered subject that are afforded by the vocabulary of consciousness. Consciousness is another feature of the self that is displaced in its epistemological and metaphysical sense but retained in another form. Briefly, "The move to the praxical and communicative space inhabited by the speaking, writing, and acting subject occasions an accompanying redesign of the texture of consciousness as dialogical rather than monological" (p. 160). This consciousness is both linguistic and actional, and it is experienced as "mine." But Schrag underscores its concretely dialogical nature when he argues, "Yet, being alone is itself a peculiar modality of being with others; soliloquy is carried by a language that belongs to the public; and individual acts have meaning only within the wider context of social practices. One can be alone only because one has already been in communal interaction with others; one can speak 'by' and 'to' oneself only with a grammar that has a social history; and one can act as an individual only as differentiated from others within the body politic. Surrounding all individual manifestations of discourse and action is the space of communicative praxis" (p. 172).

Part III, "The Rhetorical Turn," explores the directedness of discourse and action to the other, hearer, reader, or audience. The first chapter outlines connections among Rhetoric, Hermeneutics, and Communication. As a marker of the persuasive dimension of discourse, rhetoric is integral to all communicative praxis. To discuss the connection between rhetoric and hermeneutics, Schrag turns to an essay by Michael Hyde and Craig Smith, who, following Heidegger, point out that "meaning is derived by a human being in and through the interpretive understanding of reality," and "rhetoric is the process of making-known that meaning."[7] Schrag also cites with approval Henry Johnstone's theory of philosophical argumentation and Walter Fisher's narrative paradigm as movements toward integrating rhetoric, hermeneutics, and communication. These programs, he notes, raise the need for "a new slant on the meaning of rationality" (p. 192). As a general response, Schrag argues that communicative praxis "announces and displays reason" not as formal structure but "as discourse" (p. 193). "In entering discourse the logos is decentered and situated within the play of speaker and hearer as they seek consensus on that which is talked about" (p. 193). Without developing this view of reason in detail, Schrag turns to his final chapter.

"Ethos, Ethics, and a New Humanism" makes explicit the ethical dimensions that arise from Schrag's treatment of communicative praxis as directed toward and engaged with the *other*. "Rhetoric as the directedness of discourse to the other, soliciting a response," he claims, "is destined to slide into ethics" (p. 199). When communicative praxis is the starting point, however, ethical concerns do not focus on the individual valuing subject. "The decentered subject loses its positionality as a center within an abstracted space of ethical and epistemological theory . . . "(p. 201). In its place, the rhetorical event of communicative praxis stays focal, and the ethical question becomes one about "the *fitting response* of the decentered subject in its encounter with the discourse and social practices of the other against the backdrop of the delivered tradition. The ethical requirement within the space of *ethos* is that of the fitting response" (p. 202). Schrag emphasizes, "The language of morality is the language of responsiveness and responsibility, and if there is to be talk of 'an ethics' in all this it will need to be an ethics of the fitting response" (p. 204).

Schrag devotes several pages to an elaboration of what he means by a fitting response, emphasizing that it "should never be reduced to a matter of stylized comportment (Neitzsche) or poetical dwelling (Heidegger)" (p. 211). He does not compare or contrast his notion with the treatment of *response* in Volosinov and Bakhtin. Schrag concludes the book with a sketch of his new humanism. "The phenomenon of *ethos,* as the dwelling site of [the hu]man, shows itself not only in artistic-poetical but also in an explicitly moral horizon of concerns. The integrity of the moral texture of human action needs to be secured not only from the threat of a scientific-technological reductionism but from that of an aesthetic-textual reductionism as well" (p. 214).

In sum, Schrag and I share the strong conviction that careful reflection on and analysis of actual speech communicating, "the play of our quotidian speech and action,"[8] can correct a number of philosophical misunderstandings rooted in reductive accounts of the *system* or *structure* of "language." We agree that even the more recent discussions of "speech acts" (Searle) and "communicative action" (Habermas) fail to take into account adequately the context-dependent, aural-oral, verbal-nonverbal, and dynamic qualities of living communication. We concur that any complete understanding of the human subject must now acknowledge how it is decentered or inter-personal. We agree that Gadamer's philosophical hermeneutics provides what may be the single most fruitful perspective from which to approach the issues of linguisticality, interpretation, meaning, and communication (though Schrag might prefer the continual drive toward compromise in Ricoeur's work). And we also share the belief that all speech communicating is fundamentally responsive, that each utterance, as Bakhtin put it, "refutes, affirms, supplements, and relies on the others, presupposes them to be known, and somehow takes them into account," and that "an essential (constitutive) marker of the utterance is [therefore] its quality of being directed to someone, its *addressivity*."[9]

At the same time, Schrag and I disagree about the value and wisdom of attempting to characterize communicative praxis as fundamentally "about something." We both recognize that this claim is vulnerable to being understood as a representational one, and we acknowledge that if it were, it would be subject to the devastating critiques of representationalism leveled by Heidegger, Gadamer, Derrida, Rorty, and others. But Schrag is convinced that it is possible to formulate a coherent nonrepresentational account of linguistic or discursive reference, and I do not believe it is. With the help of the symbol model, I think it can be shown that there is a fundamentally problematic, unresolvable tension between this ultimately representational and the many other clearly constitutive aspects of Schrag's analysis of communicative praxis.

The Symbol Model and Hermeneutical Reference

As I noted, Schrag's three-dimensional definition of *communicative praxis*—*about* something, *by* someone, *for* someone—appears on the second page of the Preface of his 1986 book, and the five chapters of Part I are designed primarily to explicate the first dimension, which he labels *hermeneutical reference*. If there is any question about whether Schrag is aware of the problems I discuss under the *symbol model* rubric, it should be dispelled by pages 28–29, where he reviews Derrida's and Ricoeur's discussions of the problems of "traditional theories of reference." As he puts it there, these authors accomplish a "dismantling of traditional theories of reference which purport in some way to hook up with what is really there in the world" (p. 29). He also notes, however, that although Derrida lets referential discourse "collapse under its own weight in the rhapsodic play of metaphor, Ricoeur seeks to salvage an intentionality of metaphorical reference"(p. 29). "The undergirding motivation in Ricoeur's project," writes Schrag, "needs to be applauded" (p. 30). Although traditional accounts of representation and reference are to be avoided, he believes, some version of this construct can be retained.

In Chapter 2 Schrag labels this version *hermeneutical reference* and characterizes it as "the reference operative in our conversation about the world and in our being about our everyday activities, displaying variegated patterns of communicative praxis" (p. 32). Here reference is mixed with narration. But the former is "no longer depicted as the mirroring of honest-to-goodness entities in the external world, as the reaching of the real" (pp. 32–33). By way of an extended discussion of the interior-exterior dichotomy and the concept of "expression," Schrag emphasizes that he is not thinking of language as a signifier of an interior mind. Instead, Merleau-Ponty's discussion of embodiment helps frame a new understanding of how discourse is purportedly *about* something.

> The shaking of the fist is not an external sign pointing to anger as a recessed meaning in the mind. The meaning of being angry is inseparable from the gesture itself. The caress is not an atomistic bit of behavior that points to the feeling of affection. The act of caressing is the embodied display of affection. . . .
>
> The spoken word is not an exterior garment that clothes an inner thought. The spoken word is the performance of thought (p. 44).

Up to this point, Schrag's account of the "about something" dimension of communicative praxis appears to be free of symbol model commitments. Although his initial formulation suggests two worlds—the communicative praxis (World$_1$) and what it is "about" (World$_2$)—he follows Merleau-Ponty to an analysis of discourse (or at least of gestures) as *constitutive* of "what they mean" rather than representational and therefore of *one* being, as it were, with their meaning. Up to this point he has also avoided any discussion of communicative praxis as divisible into units—atomism—or analyzable into a instrumentally employed system.

But in Chapter 3, as he addresses questions of "Distanciation, Idealization, and Recollection," Schrag introduces an important qualifier. He reasserts that "the expressivity of a verbal speech act, a gesture, and a form of social behavior is the accomplishment and performance of meaning," and that "reflection will involve not a move to another standpoint but ways of moving about in our everyday engagements" (p. 53). But he insists that the issues he is addressing require a new analysis of meaning, and that "expressive meaning qualified by reflection and distanciation slides into *signitive* meaning" (p. 54). He says that this slide is not to another level; the analysis remains with communicative praxis, but it "enables us to talk about various particularized configurations of expressive speech and expressive action as being in some sense the same" (54).

Schrag acknowledges potential problems raised by his dependence on the construct of "the sign," but he argues that his sense "overflows" the ways linguists discuss signification. The linguistic sign exists in the field of semiology, whereas his version of the sign exists in the field of hermeneutics. "Signification," he writes, "becomes qualified by interpretation. Signs, on whatever level and in whatever context of associations, do not simply indicate a sense. The indicate a sense already infused with interpretation. . . . The sign, inscribed and deciphered, is *taken as* indicating such and such" (pp. 57–58). Rather than highlighting the last four words of this formula ("indicating such and such"), Schrag emphasizes the "taken as." This move, he maintains, enables his account of signitive meaning to exhibit "a texture quite different from that of a representation of a past presence, identified through an act of pure cognition" (p. 68). To give full voice to this part of Schrag's argument, I quote his summary extensively:

> Again, our notion of recollective signitive meaning undermines, at least as a privileged and necessary starting point, this epistemologically laden concept of reference. As a consequence of our reposturing of the sign as hermeneutical, reference is the taking of something *as* something (be it a perceptual object, a phenomenal property, or a historical event), *as* a figure against a background, *as* a text within a context, *as* a happening within a horizon of happenings. The epistemological construct of a region of "pure facts" and untarnished givens is disassembled. That which is recalled in communicative praxis is expressive discourse and action infused with interpretation, bearing the inscriptions of speakers and actors, and the response to this speech and action by the community of inquirers.
>
> Reference as the taking of something as something in their performatives of discourse and action remains unproblematic so long as one desists from requiring of it a representation of reality. One takes something as something by making it a topic of discourse, a motivation for action, a goal to be accomplished, a utensil to be used. . . . The discourse of communicative praxis . . . is geared not to the establishment of a correspondence of word and reality mediated by representation, but rather to a disclosure of patterns of sedimented perspectives and open horizons. The reference of signitive meaning is a performance of disclosure rather than an identification of

things and properties as the basal elements of reality. What is talked about and disclosed is "the world," "work," "experience," or even "being," but not any of these as candidates for metaphysical or transcendental "signifers" and "signifieds." They mark out the topology of communicative praxis and circumscribe the holistic space of our expressive participation and involvement in speaking and acting (pp. 69–70).

Clearly Schrag is attempting to head off to the very kind of examination that is facilitated by symbol model analysis. And his constructive effort here is laudable. If one could develop some sense of "sign" that is actually free of semiotic, representational features, it could indeed make sense of what seems to be an intuitively obvious feature of talk: that it is "about something." But two questions must be raised about this project. First, is semiosis this malleable? Will *the sign, signitive meaning,* and *signification* yield to this treatment without losing their coherence? And can the resulting construct, *hermeneutical reference,* be employed to articulate a clear sense of a genuinely *communicative* referentiality? Second, *is* one dimension of communicative praxis actually the referring by interlocutors to phenomena that their discourse is "about"? Or, to maintain coherence, must one choose *between* an analysis of meaning that is referential and one that is constitutive? Is it possible, in other words, to deploy a unambiguously nonrepresentational sense of *reference* to explain important features of actual speech communicating?

I am much less sanguine about these possibilities than is Schrag. First, notice what happens as one attempts to clarify Schrag's position with respect to the two worlds and atomism commitments of the symbol model. On the one hand, he claims that the shaken fist and the caress *embody* rather than represent their "meanings," and that "the spoken word is the *performance* of thought"(italics added). Here it sounds as if he envisions only one world, the one constituted in communicative praxis. But he also writes of some elements or aspects of communicative praxis—those he calls *hermeneutical signs—referring* to what these elements or aspects are "taken *as.*" When the sign is repostured as hermeneutical, he maintains, it becomes apparent that it can refer to a "perceptual object, a phenomenal property, or a historical event" insofar as it is taken "*as* a figure against a background . . . text within a context . . . [and/or] happening within a horizon of happenings." This formulation sounds more than a little atomistic, and it is difficult to make it coherent without some sense of two worlds.

Regarding the atomism question, when Schrag says hermeneutical reference "is the taking of something *as* something," he raises the question of what might count as the two "somethings" under discussion. Exactly what "is taken as" exactly what? He certainly does not mean that phonemes, morphemes, or words are "taken as" thoughts or things. But this formulation requires that these "somethings" would have to be some sort of units, atoms, or perhaps molecules of communicative praxis. Yet, he does not specify whether or what they are. As he describes praxis, Schrag appears to resist treating it as made up of units. "That which is recalled in communicative praxis," he writes, "is expressive discourse and action infused with interpretation, bearing the inscriptions of speakers and actors, and the response to this speech and action by the community of inquirers." Thus one central problem is that, whereas his account of communicative praxis is holistic, his formulation "the taking of something as something" pushes him toward an atomistic analysis.

On page 69 he indicates that the unit he has in mind is something he calls a *hermeneutical sign*. But, given much of his earlier discussion, it is difficult to determine what he might mean by this term. Again, "communicative praxis" is said to encompass thought and language, speech and action, text and context. But analyses utilizing the constructs *reference* and *sign* are inherently analytic not holistic. For notions of "reference" to be coherent, one needs to give some account of what does the referring and what is referred to. Without a clarification of this transitive relation between subject and object, the notion of "referring" itself becomes amorphous. Moreover, both that which refers and that which is referred to need to be some sorts of units, elements, atoms, or molecules for the transitive relation to be rendered coherent. The same demand is made by "signifying" language. Schrag does not specify either what he means by a hermeneutical sign or to what such a sign stands in its signifying relationship. He insists that by using these terms he does *not* mean to describe any "representation of reality." But what he *does* mean becomes elusive. He writes, "One takes something as something by making it a topic of discourse, a motivation for action, a goal to be accomplished, a utensil to be used." This appears to mean, for example, that one takes a stick *as* a crowbar (utensil) by using it to attempt to move a rock, or that one asks after another's fatigued tone of voice, thereby taking the tone of voice *as* a topic of discourse. But are either of these examples of *referring* or *reference*? If so, exactly what is referring to what? Or, if this is an unreasonable question, one might ask Schrag what phenomena are linked here by the purported referential relationship? Questions like these need to be answered in order to assess the coherence of Schrag's notion of hermeneutic reference.

He responds most directly to them in the final two sentences quoted earlier. What is talked about, he writes, is "the world," "work," "experience," or even "being." But none of these is a metaphysical or transcendental "signifier" or "signified." Rather, *They mark out the topology of communicative praxis and circumscribe the holistic space of our expressive participation and involvement in speaking and acting"* (p. 70, italics added). In other words, *the world, work, experience,* and so on, are examples of objects of reference that are referred to by *talk.* But these objects of reference are not semiotic substantives. They can be understood only functionally, according to what they *do.* And they function to delineate the shape of communicative praxis and provide boundaries for the events of speaking and acting in which we engage.

All this sounds plausible enough, but what has happened here to the concept of hermeneutical *reference*? In the first sentence of this quotation Schrag offers global constructs as examples of what is referred to or talked about in quotidian speech. But one would be hardpressed to cite an example of everyday conversation that could meaningfully be said to be "about" such a general topic as "the world," "work," or "experience." And even if this were a plausible account of a conversation, how useful or informative would be the claim that the "talk" in such a conversation was "about" these constructs? This level of analysis does not begin to tap, much less to interpret, the context-dependent, locally accomplished nature of living communication. Moreover, how in Schrag's description do "topology marking" and "circumscribing" constitute a kind of *referring*? One gets the sense that the construct *referring* has been completely cut loose from its cultural, semantic, and pragmatic moorings. It may well be useful to reflect on the ways general conversational themes circumscribe or bound dialogue. But to discuss this dynamic is clearly not to discuss *referring*.

A similar problem arises as Schrag builds on Rorty and Ricoeur to define hermeneutical reference. "Taking its cues from the metaphorical play of language," Schrag writes, "hermeneutical reference is the display of the work-being of textuality, patterns of human action, institutional designs, and historical trends in the performances of discourse and social practices. Reference as a philosophical term is indeed displaced from its epistemological space, but it returns transmuted and transfigured into the space of communicative praxis" (p. 107). The first, definitional sentence in this quotation has, I am sorry to admit, resisted all my efforts to interpret it. I simply cannot fathom what it might mean that "hermeneutical reference is the display of the work-being of textuality." I clearly understand the

claim made in the second sentence, but I cannot specify in any coherent way the transmuted and transfigured shape in which reference has allegedly returned in this work.

It seems to me that the problem here is similar to, but more
subtle than, the ones encountered by Volosinov and Burke. Like the
other authors, Schrag has a keen sense of the value of attending
closely to living speech communication when responding to philosophical critiques of subjectivity, rationality, and the nature of language. Unlike Volosinov and Burke, he is explicitly aware of the
tension between traditional representational accounts of "language"
and his constitutive-performative one. But Schrag appears to under-
estimate the potency of the semiotic paradigm. His tenacious hold
on the traditional claim that discourse can be meaningfully said to
be "about" something leads him into the representational-referential-
signifying labyrinth. And once he adopts even carefully circumscribed
versions of "signifying" and "reference," he is forced either to own
up to the two worlds and atomism commitments that accompany
them or to settle for accounts of crucial features of communicative
praxis that, as Schrag writes of Husserl, are "characterized by a pervading elusiveness, ever escaping definitive determination" (p. 98).
Schrag claims to have "liberated interpretation from the alien requirements of epistemological foundations and representational schemata, and from the wearisome search for brute facts that might
correspond to clear and distinct ideas of them" (p. 93). In some ways
he is correct. His account of communicative praxis is assertively nonrepresentational. But because it also tries to be referential, at crucial junctures it strains coherence and, thus, plausibility.

These problems resurface in other chapters of *Communicative
Praxis* and some sections of *The Resources of Rationality*. For example, in Chapter 4 of the former work, Schrag argues that the process of comprehending a discourse "swings to and fro between the
moments of understanding and those of explanation" (p. 79). But the
latter, he argues, is principally a semiotic project: "The discourse of
explanation quickly becomes the discourse of signifier and signified"
(p. 86). Semiology stays linked with hermeneutics; the signified remains that which is *"taken as* something signified" (p. 86). But the
elusiveness and indeterminacy of this formulation is not rectified;
Schrag simply argues that the dynamic of explanation consists
mainly in breaking discourse down into its parts and assessing their
referential significance.

In the first chapter of his 1992 book, Schrag repeats his belief
that the displacement of epistemological theories of meaning and
reference does not mean that one must jettison meaning and reference "in all manners conceivable." Instead, he asks, "Can meaning

and reference be in some fashion refigured, circumventing the aporias of epistemological construction and hermeneutical reconstruction whilst rendering an account of the sense of our communicative practices and providing indicators of that which our discourse and action are about" (p. 29)? Later in the book he attempts to answer this question in the affirmative by reasserting much of what he claimed six years earlier, this time with some help from Bakhtin. Schrag's general argument in *Resources of Rationality* is that the logos postmodern philosophers claim is missing in contemporary life is in fact present in communicative praxis. Part of the reason philosophers have missed this point, he argues, is that they have presupposed that the only possible kind of rationality is one anchored in a Cartesian cogito and a theory-based foundationalism. They have overlooked "praxical rationality" that, in Schrag's words, "does not entail a jettisoning of the logos but rather a refiguration of it within an economy of communicative praxis in which the claims of reason become effective by dint of praxis-oriented critique, articulation, and disclosure" (p. 155). In this work, his specific claims about meaning and reference echo and elaborate his argument that:

> In concert with its chronotopal background, dialogic discourse marks out a direction for refiguring the accomplishments of meaning and reference.
>
> This newly won meaning and reference, it should be underscored, is meaning and reference liberated from the strictures of the epistemological paradigm. Meaning is neither the representation of a transparent essence nor a determinate signification; and the refigured reference is not to be confused with a correspondence of word with object. *The "what" of dialogic textuality and the "that" of its referential claims are functions of the play of the moving chronotope in living discourse . It is only through a configuring and refiguring of language, borne by a holistic comprehension solicited by the structure and the dynamics of the text, that events of meaning and reference occur* (p. 88, italics added).

Schrag is obviously reasserting here that his concepts of meaning and reference are not representational. But as the italicized sentences indicate, it continues to be difficult to determine exactly what they *are*. By *chronotope*, Bakhtin meant the sense of time and space that is present in a novel or other large unit of discourse and that defines primary features of the world of the work.[10] Therefore Schrag appears to be claiming that both the text of living dialogue and what it is "about" are "functions" of its world-configured play. As before, I am attracted to the idea that the substance or topical weight—Gadamer's *die Sache*—of a conversation manifests as the world that interlocutors coconstruct in talk. In this, it appears that Schrag and I agree. But I do not believe that this point can be effectively made using the vocabulary of "reference." The nonrepresentational point Schrag appears to want to make here cannot coherently be made in symbol model language, because *it is not possible to purge semiosis of representationalism*. Schrag insists that "a deconstruction of the semiotic model for reference does not entail a jettisoning of reference in every sense you please" (p. 112). But a close reading of crucial sections of his work questions this claim. Schrag's insight could have been expressed more coherently, I believe, had he been willing to forego completely the language of signifying and referring.

Finally, there is in both of Schrag's books an overarching ambiguity involving the two worlds commitment that I have not yet highlighted. On the one hand, he maintains a clear distinction between speech and action, language and action, thought and action. In *Rationality* he expresses this position in contrast to Derrida's claim, "*Il n'y a pas de hors-texte.*"[11] Writes Schrag, "There is indeed something outside the effects of textuality and narrativity. There is perception and there is human action" (p. 113). But given this purported ontological difference, one must ask, What is the relationship between speech, language, or thought, on the one hand, and action on the other? Schrag makes it very clear that he does not believe the relationship is representational; a text is not simply a representation of that which is outside the text. But what then is the relationship? Communicative praxis certainly includes the nonverbal *actions* of gesture, intonation, facial expression, and movement. But, as both Schrag and I argue, all these are inseparable elements of the event of speech communicating itself. The verbal and the nonverbal are elements of the *one* world of aural-oral articulate contact. Schrag indicates as much when he adopts Merleau-Ponty's account of meaning as disclosure or performance—"The act of caressing is the embodied display of affection. . . . The spoken word is the performance of thought."[12] However, the problem is that one cannot coherently describe affection as *embodied in* action while maintaining an ontological distinction between text and action. Insofar as meaning is embodied or performed, it is not referential in *any* sense you please. This, I believe, is why at crucial points in his argument Schrag is driven to make to such abstruse claims as (a) that the references of dialogic textuality "are functions of the play of the moving chronotope in living discourse,"[13] (b) that events of reference occur "only through a configuring and refiguring of language, borne by a holistic comprehension solicited by the structure and the dynamics of the text,"[14] and (c) that the reference of communicative praxis is "a reference elicited by the intrusion of alterity, a reference borne by an incursive disclosure effected by the lifeworld."[15] Each of these claims is decidedly elusive. What can it mean to say (a) that a reference is a (mathematical?) "function" of some space-time dynamic in discourse; (b) that "events of reference" occur in constant flux somehow driven by a gestalt that features of the text "solicit"; and (c) that reference is drawn out by an otherness that the lifeworld somehow "incursively discloses"? I submit that it is Schrag's vestigal commitment to representationalism that leads him to such virtually indecipherable positions.

Conclusion

Schrag's two books illustrate what can occur when a philosophical analysis of living speech communication thoroughly sensitized to the aporias of representationalism attempts to maintain vestiges of the symbol model. On the one hand, his awareness of the value—even the necessity—of attending to everyday talk to respond adequately to questions about subjectivity and rationality is virtually unprecedented among philosophers I have read. Schrag's descriptions of the decentered subject who is implicated in communicative praxis and of the mode of rationality embodied in many forms of quotidian conversation are brilliant and enlightening. He usefully extends some of the most profound discussions of human communication articulated by Wittgenstein, Heidegger, Gadamer, Ricoeur, Benveniste, and Bakhtin. On the other hand, Schrag's conviction that communicative praxis must be understood as "about something" and his willingness at some junctures to appeal to atomistic explanations threaten the coherence of some elements of his account.

The basic problem this reader of Schrag experiences is that of determining which element or feature of communicative praxis performs the function of being "about something" and which (nonlinguistic? actional?) phenomenon this element or feature is "about." When he addresses this question most directly, Schrag argues that "talk" is "about" and d*iscloses* "the world," "work," "experience," or even "being," but *not* as "signifiers" or "signifieds." It thus appears that he may believe, as I argue in Chapter 4, that in verbal-nonverbal talk, a world is negotiated or collaboratively constructed. If this is the case, then I would argue that semiosis does not serve him well to make this point. Had he avoided talk of reference in the first place, his readers would be less inclined to find his accounts of this feature of communicative praxis as "characterized by a pervading elusiveness, ever escaping definitive determination."[16]

Moreover, as Gadamer has demonstrated, Schrag could have made virtually all the points he appears to want to make in Part I of *Communicative Praxis* without the vocabulary of semiosis. He could have foreground the substantive topic or content of conversation as Gadamer does in his discussions of *die Sache*. For example, in *Truth and Method*, Gadamer explains that his primary interest is not in the subjectivities of the dialogue partners but in the issue or subject matter at the heart of their exchange.[17] In his later writing Gadamer also emphasizes how the conversation that is paradigmatic of human understanding develops topical and substantive insights. As he puts it, "In a conversation, it is *something* that comes to language, not one or the other speaker."[18] But this "something" is generated *in* conversation, it is not that which conversation is allegedly "about." Gadamer also addresses the issue Schrag raises in his chapter on "Distanciation, Idealization, and Recollection," when he explains the way in which hermeneutic understanding includes the moments of reflection and critique. To be in this kind of conversation, Gadamer writes, "means to be beyond oneself, to think with the other, and to come back to oneself as if to another,"[19] thereby integrating critique. Like Schrag, Gadamer's effort is to "shake off the burden of an inherited ontology of static substance," which is why he too "started out from conversation and the common language sought and shaped in it."[20] But unlike Schrag, Gadamer relied for the substantive or content features of his analysis not on an adaptation of the semiotic construct of reference but on explications of *die Sache* and the logic of question and answer.

I hope these discussions of Volosinov, Burke, and Schrag have clarified the efficacy of symbol model analysis of accounts of the nature of language. The most informative and enlightening recent treatments of language are those that attempt to attend closely to speech communication as it occurs in living conversation. Unfortunately, however, some of these accounts suffer from tensions, ambiguities, and even inconsistencies because of their authors' attempts to maintain some commitment to semiosis. Volosinov's, Burke's, and Schrag's writings are all marked by some of these problematic features. When these programs are examined for their commitments to two worlds, atomism, representationalism, the systematization of language, and the the claim that language is an instrument or tool, these tensions, ambiguities, and inconsistencies can be brought to light. And the results of this process can lend credence to the argument in Chapter 4 that living human language can more efficaciously be viewed as oral-aural, verbal-nonverbal, constitutive articulate contact.

A companion volume to this one, entitled *Beyond the Symbol Model: Essays on the Nature of Language*, provides an opportunity for several philosophers, linguists, semioticians, and communication theorists to respond to the arguments made in these chapters. The primary goal of *Language as Articulate Contact* and *Beyond the Symbol Model* is to encourage conversations among language theorists of various stripes about their views of the nature of language and especially about the extent to which their accounts of the nature of language are constitutive or representational.

NOTES

Preface

1. John Stewart, "Concepts of Language and Meaning: An Ordinary Language Philosophy Critique," *Quarterly Journal of Speech* 58 (1972): 123–133; cf. John Stewart, "Rhetoricians on Language and Meaning: An Ordinary Language Philosophy Critique," Ph.D. diss., Univ. of Southern California, 1970.

2. William Richardson, *Heidegger* (Oxford: Oxford University Press, 1963).

3. I discuss the impact of some postmodern thinking on communication theory in "A Postmodern Look at Traditional Communication Postulates," *Western Journal of Speech Communication* 55 (1991): 354–379.

4. Michael Reddy, "The Conduit Metaphor: A Case of Frame Conflict in our Language about Language," *Metaphor and Thought*, ed. A. Ortony (Cambridge: Cambridge University Press, 1979), pp. 284–324. Reddy illustrates the incoherence of approaches to communication that construe it as simply a "conduit" for sending and receiving messages. Ten communication theorists critique similarly oversimplified conceptualizations of interpersonal processes in the eight articles making up "Forum: Social Approaches to Interpersonal Communication," ed. Wendy Leeds-Hurwitz, *Communication Theory*, 2 (1992): 131–172; 329–356.

5. Hans-Georg Gadamer, *Truth and Method*, 2nd ed., trans. Joel Weinsheimer and D. G. Marshall (New York: Crossroad, 1989), p. 267. See John Stewart, "An Interpretive Approach to Validity in Interpersonal Communication Research," *Interpretive Approaches to Interpersonal Communication*, ed. Mick Presnell and Kathryn Carter (Albany: SUNY Press, 1994).

251

Chapter 1. The Symbol Model and the Nature of Language

1. Martin Buber reflects similarly on this experience in *I and Thou*, trans. Walter Kaufmann (New York: Charles Scribner's Sons, 1970), p. 145.

2. Hans-Georg Gadamer, "Text and Interpretation," trans. Dennis J. Schmidt and Richard E. Palmer, *Dialogue and Deconstruction*, ed. Diane P. Michelfelder and R.E. Palmer (Albany: SUNY Press, 1989), p. 21.

3. Julia Kristeva, *Language: The Unknown*, trans. A. M. Menke (New York: Columbia University Press, 1989), p. 12.

4. Charles E. Osgood, "What Is a Language," *The Signifying Animal*, ed. I. Rauch and G.F. Carr (Bloomington: Indiana University Press, 1980), p. 12.

5. Norbert Elias, *The Symbol Theory* (London: Sage, 1991), pp. 1–4.

6. Michael T. Motley, "On Whether One Can(not) Not Communicate: An Examination via Traditional Communication Postulates," *Western Journal of Speech Communication* 54 (1990): 1–7.

7. Umberto Eco, *Semiotics and the Philosophy of Language* (Bloomington: Indiana University Press, 1984), p. 7.

8. As noted in the Preface, Michael J. Reddy critiques linear, telementational views of communication in "The Conduit Metaphor: A Case of Frame Conflict in Our Language About Language," *Metaphor and Thought*, ed. A. Ortony (Cambridge: Cambridge University Press, 1979), pp. 284–324.

9. See, e.g., Ernst Cassirer, *Philosophy of Symbolic Forms*, vol. 1, trans. R. Manheim (New Haven, CN: Yale University Press, 1953); Charles Sanders Peirce, *Selected Writings: Values in a Universe of Change*, ed. P. P. Weiner (New York: Dover, 1958); Ferdinand de Saussure, *Course in General Linguistics*, ed. C. Bally and A. L. Sechehaye, trans. R. Harris (LaSalle, IL: Open Court, 1983); Charles Morris, *Foundations of the Theory of Signs* (Chicago: University of Chicago Press, 1938); and D. S. Clarke, Jr., *Principles of Semiotic* (Boston: Routledge and Kegan Paul, 1987).

10. In places, some important writers—e.g., Saussure and Eco—argue that linguistic or psychological units signify or represent other linguistic or psychological units. I address this issue later.

11. Aristotle, *De Interpretatione*, 16a, trans. E. M. Edghill, *The Basic Works of Aristotle* , ed. R. McKeon (New York: Random House, 1941), p. 40.

12. John Locke, *Essay Concerning Human Understanding* (London: Elizabeth Holt for Thomas Basset, 1690), III.8.5.

13. Gilbert Ryle, *Collected Papers* (London: Hutchinson, 1971), vol. 1, p. 49.

14. See, e.g., *The Oxford English Dictionary*, 2nd ed. (Oxford: Clarendon Press, 1989), pp. 451–452; *Dictionary of Philosophy and Psychology*, ed. J. M. Baldwin (Gloucester, MA: Macmillan, 1960), p. 640; *The Encyclopedia of Philosophy*, ed. Paul Edwards (New York: Macmillan), vol. 4, pp. 437–441.

15. And, as I explain in Chapter 3, Saussure ultimately repudiated the *ontological* implication of his claim about system or structure; that is, the implicit claim that units of the system of *langue* are meaningful *only in relation to other system units*.

16. John Horne Tooke, *The Diversions of Purley*, 2nd ed. facsimile reprint (Menston, England: Scolar Press, [1798] 1968), p. 1.

17. Ludwig Wittgenstein, *Philosophical Investigations*, trans. G. E. M. Anscombe (Oxford: Blackwell, 1953).

18. Gilbert Ryle, *The Concept of Mind* (New York: Barnes and Noble, 1949); *Collected Papers*, vol. 1.

19. J. L. Austin, *Philosophical Papers* (Oxford: Clarendon, 1961); *How to Do Things with Words*, ed. J. O. Urmson (Oxford: Oxford University Press, 1962).

20. John Searle, *Speech Acts: An Essay on the Philosophy of Language* (London: Cambridge University Press, 1969).

21. Martin Heidegger, *On the Way to Language*, trans. Peter D. Hertz (San Francisco: Harper and Row, 1971).

22. Hans-Georg Gadamer, *Truth and Method*, 2nd. ed., trans. J. Weinsheimer and D. G. Marshall (New York: Crossroad, 1989).

23. Kristeva, *Language*, p. 295.

24. Ibid., p. 12.

25. "Conversation," write Bavelas and Coates, "is arguably 'the fundamental site of language use.'" Janet Beavin Bavelas and Linda Coates, "How Do We Account for the Mindfulness of Face-to-Face Dialogue?" *Communication Monographs*, 59 (1992): 301–305; citing H. H. Clark and D. Wilkes-Gibbs, "Referring as a Collaborative Process," *Cognition* 22 (1986): 1.

26. John R. Searle, *Intentionality: An Essay in the Philosophy of Mind* (Cambridge: Cambridge University Press, 1983), p. 145.

27. Example from Douglas W. Maynard, "Perspective-Display Sequences in Conversation," *Western Journal of Speech Communication*, 53 (1989): 107.

28. Example from Richard M. Frankel, "I wz wondering-uhm could *Raid* uhm effect the brain permanently d'y know?": Some Observations on the Intersection of Speaking and Writing in Calls to a Poison Control Center," *Western Journal of Speech Communication* 53 (1989): 219.

29. In response to the possible rejoinder that my arguments for the symbol model in these paragraphs are "straw men," I refer the reader to instances of these arguments made by authors whose works are reviewed in Chapters 2, 3, 6, 7, and 8 and to summaries of these arguments in, for example, Roy Harris and Talbot J. Taylor, *Landmarks in Linguistic Thought: The Western Tradition from Socrates to Saussure* (London: Routledge, 1989); and William P. Alston, *Philosophy of Language* (Englewood Cliffs, NJ: Prentice-Hall, 1964).

30. Saussure, *Course in General Linguistics*, p. 66.

31. Émile Benveniste, *Problems in General Linguistics*, trans. M.E. Meek (Coral Gables, FL: University of Miami Press, 1971), p. 44; cf. Kristeva, *Language*, p. 16.

32. Gadamer, *Truth and Method*, p. 267.

33. This is Glen H. Stamp and Mark L. Knapp's term, and my discussion of intent borrows from their article, "The Construct of Intent in Interpersonal Communication," *Quarterly Journal of Speech* 76 (1990): 282–299.

34. Bavelas and Coates, "How Do We Account for the Mindfulness," p. 304.

35. Paul Watzlawick, Janet Helmick Beavin, and Don D. Jackson, *Pragmatics of Human Communication* (New York: Norton, 1967), p. 51.

36. Janet Beavin Bavelas, "Behaving and Communicating: A Reply to Motley," *Western Journal of Speech Communication* 54 (1990): 600.

37. See H. L. Dreyfus, *Being-in-the-World: A Commentary on Heidegger's Being and Time, Division I* (Cambridge, MA: MIT Press, 1991), Chapter 1.

38. Thomas A. McCarthy, "General Introduction," *After Philosophy: End or Transformation?* (Cambridge, MA: MIT Press, 1987), p. 4.

Chapter 2. The Symbol Model from the Ancients to Humboldt

1. See, e.g., Robins' *A Short History of Linguistics,* 3rd ed. (London: Longmans, 1990).

2. Thomas A. Sebeok, ed., *Historiography of Linguistics*, vol. 13, *Current Trends in Linguistics* (The Hague: Mouton, 1975).

3. Norman Kretzmann, Anthony Kenny, and Jan Pinborg, eds. *The Cambridge History of Later Medieval Philosophy* (Cambridge: Cambridge University Press, 1982).

4. Herman Parret, ed., *History of Linguistic Thought and Contemporary Linguistics* (Berlin: Walter de Gruyter, 1976).

5. See, e.g., G. L. Bursill-Hall, "Toward a History of Linguistics in the Middle Ages 1100–1450," *Studies in the History of Linguistics: Traditions and Paradigms*, ed. Dell Hymes (Bloomington: Indiana University Press, 1974), pp. 77–92.

6. See, e.g., Hans Aarsleff, "The Tradition of Condillac: The Problem of the Origin of Language in the Eighteenth Century and the Debate in the Berlin Academy Before Herder," in Hymes, ed., ibid., pp. 93–156.

7. Julia Kristeva, *Language: The Unknown,* trans. Anne M. Menks (New York: Columbia University Press, 1989).

8. Donald S. Clarke, Jr., *Sources of Semiotic* (Carbondale: Southern Illinois University Press, 1990).

9. Roy Harris and Talbot J. Taylor, *Landmarks in Linguistic Thought: The Western Tradition from Socrates to Saussure* (London: Routledge, 1989). Also see Roy H. Harris, *The Language-Makers* (London: Duckworth, 1980); and Roy H. Harris, *The Language Myth* (London: Duckworth, 1981).

10. Walter J. Ong, *Orality and Literacy: The Technologizing of the Word* (London: Meuthen, 1982), p. 86.

11. Thorkild Jacobsen, "Very Ancient Texts: Babylonian Grammatical Texts," in Hymes, ed., *History of Linguistics*, p. 41.

12. J. F. Staal, "The Origin and Development of Linguistics in India," in ibid., p. 63.

13. Robins, *Short History of Linguistics*, p. 15.

14. Ong, *Orality and Literacy*, pp. 28, 90.

15. Robins, *Short History of Linguistics*, p. 16.

16. Ong, *Orality and Literacy*, p. 91.

17. G. B. Kerferd, *The Sophistic Movement* (Cambridge: Cambridge University Press, 1981), p. 69.

18. Ibid., p. 71; see *Euthydemus*, 286a–b.

19. Ibid., pp. 72–73.

20. *Cratylus*, trans. Benjamin Jowett, *The Collected Dialogues of Plato*, ed. E. Hamilton and H. Cairns (Princeton, NJ: Princeton University Press, 1961).

21. Harris and Taylor, *Landmarks in Linguistic Thought*, p. 12. See note 93.

22. Ibid., p. 19.

23. Raphael Demos, "Symposium: Plato's Theory of Language, Plato's Philosophy of Language," *Journal of Philosophy*, 61 (1964): 603.

24. Richard McKeon, "Aristotle's Conception of Language and the Arts of Language, I," *Classical Philology*, 61 (1946): 193.

25. Ibid., p. 202.

26. Richard McKeon, "Aristotle's Conception of Language and the Arts of Language, II," *Classical Philology*, 62 (1947): 22.

27. Jan Pinborg, "Classical Antiquity: Greece," in Sebeok, ed., *Historiography of Linguistics*, p. 77.

28. Harris and Taylor, *Landmarks in Linguistic Thought*, p. 24.

29. Ibid., p. 33.

30. Ibid., p. 25.

31. Aristotle, *Poetics*, trans. Ingram Bywater, *The Basic Works of Aristotle*, ed. Richard McKeon (New York: Random House, 1941), 1456b35–1457a9.

32. Aristotle, *Categories*, trans. E. M. Edghill, in ibid., 1b25.

33. Aristotle, *De Interpretatione*, trans. E. M. Edghill in ibid., 16b6–25.

34. F. H. Sandbach, *The Stoics* (New York: Norton, 1975), p. 20.

35. Harris and Taylor, *Landmarks in Linguistic Thought*, p. 49.

36. Sandbach, *The Stoics*, pp. 16–18.

37. Andreas Graeser, "The Stoic Theory of Meaning," *The Stoics*, ed. John M. Rist (Berkeley: University of California Press, 1978), p. 77.

38. Sextus Empiricus, *Adversus Mathematicos*, VIII 11–12, cited by A. A. Long, "Language and Thought in Stoicism," *Problems in Stoicism*, ed. A. A. Long (London: Athlone, 1971), pp. 76–77.

39. Long, ibid., p. 77.

40. Benson Mates, *Stoic Logic* (Berkeley: University of California Press, 1953), pp. 19–26; Long, ibid., p. 79.

41. C. K. Ogden and I. A. Richards, *The Meaning of Meaning* (New York: Harcourt, Brace, 1923), p. 11.

42. Graeser, "The Stoic Theory of Meaning," p. 81.

43. Ibid., p. 90.

44. Ibid., p. 97.

45. *The Oxford Annotated Bible: Revised Standard Version,* ed. H. G. May and B. M. Metzger (New York: Oxford University Press, 1962) *Genesis* 2: 1; 9–23.

46. Harris and Taylor, *Landmarks in Linguistic Thought,* p. 38.

47. Ibid., p. 38.

48. See, e.g., *Genesis* 5:1–2; 10:25; 12:2, 17:15; 17:19; and 25:29–30; *Numbers* 11:13 and 21:3.

49. St. Augustine, *Confessions,* I, 8., trans. B. Babacz, cited in Bruce Babacz, *St. Augustine's Theory of Knowledge: A contemporary Analysis* (New York: Edwin Mellen, 1981), p. 182.

50. Augustine, *De Dialectica,* ed. J. Pinborg, trans B. D. Jackson (The Hague: Reidel, 1975), 5.7.

51. Augustine, *On Christian Doctrine,* trans. D. W. Robertson, Jr. (New York: Macmillan, 1958), p. 34.

52. Christopher Kirwan, *Augustine* (London: Routledge, 1989), pp. 36–40.

53. Augustine, *De Dialectica,* 5.8.

54. Kirwan, *Augustine,* p. 58.

55. Ibid., p. 38.

56. Ibid., pp. 37–49.

57. Ibid., pp. 39–40. Some kinds of "inner words" may be exceptions. Augustine sometimes indicates that the thoughts a thinker has already formulated in words are verbal, as are thoughts that appear in no specific language but are drawn on in processes of silent vocal formulation. See Ibid., p. 57.

58. Ibid., p. 35.

59. Kirwan attributes to Augustine the principle Gilbert Ryle detected and castigated in Rudolf Carnap's writings, the so-called Fido-Fido principle, which notes that " 'signify' in its modern sense of 'mean' states a relation which holds from every expression to some extra-linguistic correlate to the

expression, like the dog that answers to the name 'fido' " (p. 49), citing Gilbert Ryle, "Discussion of Rudolf Carnap: Meaning and Necessity," in *Collected Papers,* vol. 1 (London: Hutchinson, 1971). But Kirwan appears to believe that this principle applies only to words treated explicitly as names. He does not acknowledge how a version of Ryle's argument critiques not just Augustine's or Carnap's treatment of names but all semiotic analyses of language.

60. Bursill-Hall, "The Middle Ages," p. 189.

61. Robins, *Short History of Linguistics,* pp. 86–87.

62. Thomas of Erfurt, *Grammatica Speculativa,* trans. G. L. Bursill-Hall (London: Longman, 1972), p. 135.

63. Michael Covington, "Grammatical Theory in the Middle Ages," *Studies in the History of Western Linguistics in Honour of R. H. Robins,* ed. T. Bynon and F. R. Palmer (Cambridge: Cambridge University Press, 1986), p. 27.

64. Harris and Taylor, *Landmarks in Linguistic Thought,* p. 76.

65. Covington, "Grammatical Theory," 27.

66. Ibid., p. 28.

67. Jan Pinborg, "Speculative Grammar," *The Cambridge History of Later Medieval Philosophy,* ed. N. Kretzmann, A. Kenny, and J. Pinborg (Cambridge: Cambridge University Press, 1982), p. 258.

68. Covington, "Grammatical Theory," p. 35.

69. Antoine Arnauld and Claude Lancelot, *General and Rational Grammar: The Port-Royal Grammar,* trans. J. Rieux and B. E. Rollin (The Hague: Mouton, 1975), p. 66.

70. Ibid., p. 65.

71. Antoine Arnauld, and P. Nicole, *The Art of Thinking,* trans. J. Dickoff and P. James (Indianapolis: Bobbs-Merrill, 1964), p. 71. This same chapter includes the claim that a sign must be distinct from what it signifies, but that "one state of a thing may be considered as a sign of some other state of that same thing." If developed, this idea would clearly undermine the two worlds assumption. But the example given—"a man in his own apartments [may] be a sign of himself preaching"—is difficult to interpret, and the point is neither extended nor applied.

72. Harris and Taylor, *Landmarks of Linguistic Thought,* pp. 98–99.

73. Arnauld and Lancelot, *Grammar,* p. 72.

74. Harris and Taylor, *Landmarks of Linguistic Thought,* p. 100.

75. Arnauld and Lancelot cited in Harris and Taylor, p. 102.

76. Arnauld and Lancelot cited in Harris and Taylor, p. 105.

77. Norman Kretzmann, "The Main Thesis of Locke's Semantic Theory," in Parret, ed., *History of Linguistic Thought*, p. 331.

78. Hans Aarsleff, *From Locke to Saussure: Essays on the Study of Language and Intellectual History* (Minneapolis: University of Minnesota Press, 1982), p. 121.

79. John Locke, *Essay Concerning Human Understanding,* ed. A. C. Fraser (Oxford: Clarendon, 1894), IV.21.4. Cf. IV. 21.4.

80. Kretzmann, "The Main Thesis," p. 341.

81. John J. Jenkins, *Understanding Locke: An Introduction to Philosophy Through John Locke's Essay* (Edinburgh: The University Press, 1983), p. 161.

82. Jenkins does note some of these very weaknesses in Locke's account and offers a two-page synopsis of Wittgenstein's argument that, in Jenkins's words, "there is no coherent world beyond our language." He also cites Peter Winch's aphorism, "Reality is not what gives language sense. What is real and what is unreal shows itself the sense that language has" (pp. 164–166, citing Peter Winch, "Understanding a Primitive Society," *American Philosophical Quarterly* 1 [1964]).

83. Etienne Bonnot, Abbé de Condillac, *Essay on the Origin of Human Knowledge* , trans. Thomas Nugent (Gainesville, FL: Scholars' Facsimiles and Reprints, 1971), pp. 57–58.

84. Etienne Bonnot, Abbé de Condillac, *Philosophical Writings*, trans. F. Philip and H. Lane (Hillsdale, N.J: Lawrence Erlbaum, 1982), p. 392.

85. Bonnot, *Essay* 1.2.77.

86. Aarsleff, *From Locke to Saussure*, p. 156.

87. Ernst Cassirer, *The Philosophy of Symbolic Forms. Vol. 1 Language,* trans. R. Manheim (New Haven, CN: Yale University Press, 1953), p. 149.

88. Jean-Jacques Rousseau, "Essay on the Origin of Language," trans J. H. Moran, *On the Origin of Language*, ed. J. H. Moran and A. Gode (New York: Frederick Ungar, 1966), p. 17.

89. Johann Gottfried Herder, "Essay on the Origin of Language," in Moran and Gode, eds., pp. 115–117.

90. John Horne Tooke, *The Diversions of Purley*, 1798, 2nd ed., facsimile reprint (Menston, England: Scolar Press, 1968), p. 1.

91. Harris and Taylor, *Landmarks in Linguistic Thought*, p. 148.

92. Hans Aarsleff, "Introduction," Wilhelm Von Humboldt, *On Language*, trans. Peter Heath (Cambridge: Cambridge University Press, 1988), pp. ix–x.

93. Humboldt, ibid., pp. 48–49.

94. Aarsleff, "Introduction," p. xix.

95. Hans-Georg Gadamer, *Truth and Method*, 2nd ed., trans. J. Weinsheimer and D. G. Marshall (New York: Crossroad, 1989), p. 442.

96. Aarsleff, in "Introduction," comments on these criticisms on pp. lxi–lxv.

97. This chapter's basic distinction between representational or semiotic and nonrepresentational approaches to the nature of language is echoed in Pieter A. Verburg, "Vicissitudes of Paradigms," in Hymes, ed., *Studies in the History of Linguistics*, pp. 191–230. Verburg traces paradigms that characterize the study of language from antiquity to the twentieth century. Most of the paradigms he discusses embody the two worlds distinction discussed in this chapter and differ mainly in how or what units of language are said to represent or symbolize.

For example, Verburg diagrams the Platonic paradigm thus (p. 194):

Reality (Things)<—diakrinein:*legein*:didaskein —> Other people

(cognitive)   (communicative)

The paradigm of the speculative grammarians was different, but it still made the distinction between the real world and the world of language (p. 198):

Reality/Things—>Intellect/Thoughts—>Language/Signs

(spoken language—>written words).

The works of sixteenth- and seventeenth-century scholars, especially Hobbes and Descartes, reflected a simple paradigm (p. 204):

REALITY <——— SYMBOLS <——— REASON

Condillac, Rousseau, and Herder introduced a genuine change by focusing not on language as a system of symbols of reality but on language "as inter-subjective communication" (p. 211):

Fellow-man   Human agent,

    <———Speech————

Hearer   Speaker.

Humboldt's main theory, writes Verburg, can be represented as follows (p. 215):

Reality	"Innere Form"	Representative
in ordered<———of national<———Mind of national
perspective	language	community (Volksgeist)

Chapter 3. Twentieth-Century Versions of the Symbol Model

1. Kenneth L. Ketner and Christian J. W. Kloesel, eds., "Preface," *Peirce, Semeiotic, and Pragmatism: Essays by Max H. Fisch* (Bloomington: Indiana University Press, 1986), p. vii.

2. Christopher Hookway, *Peirce* (London: Routledge and Kegan Paul, 1985), p. 3.

3. Charles Morris, appendix to *Signs, Language and Behavior* (New York: Braziller, 1946), cited in Max Fisch, "Peirce's General Theory of Signs," in Ketner and Kloesel, eds., *Pierce, Semeiotic, and Pragmatism*, p. 346.

4. Charles S. Peirce, *Semiotic and Significs*, ed. C. Hardwick (Bloomington: Indiana University Press, 1977), pp. 85–86.

5. For Pierce, there was no more reason to call the inquiry *semiotics* than there is to call related inquiries *logics* or *rhetorics*.

6. Peirce discussed the three as "categories" of the "phaneron," which is, roughly, conscious life. All three categories are present in each phaneron, hence the "-ness" terminology. Firstness is often presented as the a-contextual primary experience of, e.g., freshness, life, or freedom. Secondness is a category that is what it is in relation to one other thing, but independent of any relation to a third entity or category, e.g., "otherness." Existence is a secondness, because it relies on one being "not the other" or "not you." Thirdness is a category marked by the fact that it connects two other somethings. The most important thirds are signs, which, as I clarify later, link object and interpretant. See *Collected Papers of Charles Sanders Peirce*, ed. C. Hartshorne and P. Weiss, 8 vols. (Cambridge, MA: Harvard University Press, 1960), vol. 1, pp. 295–298.

Because these are the three most fundamental categories, one can expect them to be abstract. But when Peirce elaborated and applied them, he often lapsed into indecipherable descriptions and arguments. For example, at one point Peirce explained the three categories in these words: "The first is thought in its capacity as mere possibility, that is, mere mind capable of thinking or a mere vague idea. The second is thought playing the role of a Secondness, or event. That is, it is of the general nature of experience or information. The third is thought in its role as governing secondness. It brings the information into the mind, or determines the idea and gives it body. It is informing thought, or cognition. But take away the psychological or accidental human element, and in this Genuine Thirdness we see the operation of a sign" (*Collected Papers of Charles Sanders Peirce*, vol. 1, p. 537.) About this passage, the generally supportive interpreter Douglas Greenlee comments, "The obscurity of this statement is as great as that of the three categories" (Douglas Greenlee, *Peirce's Concept of Sign* [The Hague: Mouton, 1973], p. 42).

7. D.S. Clarke, Jr., *Sources of Semiotic* (Carbondale: Southern Illinois University Press, 1990) p. 58.

8. Peirce, *Collected Papers*, vol. 5, p. 423.

9. See Hookway, *Pierce*, pp. 20–23, 37–38, 112–117, 262–265, 285–288.

10. Ibid., pp. 285, 287.

11. Charles Sanders Peirce, "Logic as Semiotic: The Theory of Signs," in *Philosophical Writings of Peirce*, ed. Justus Buchler (New York: Dover, 1955), p. 99. Also see Peirce, *Collected Papers*, vol. 2, p. 228.

12. Pierce, *Collected Papers*, vol. 2, p. 92.

13. *Charles Sanders Peirce's Leters to Lady Welby*, ed. Irwin C. Lieb (New Haven, CN: Whitlock's, 1953), p. 29.

14. Peirce, *Collected Papers*, vol. 5, p. 291.

15. Fisch, "Peirce's General Theory of Signs," p. 330.

16. Peirce, *Collected Papers*, vol. 5, p. 253.

17. Ibid., vol. 2, p. 287.

18. Ibid., vol. 2, pp. 298–302, reprinted in Clarke, *Sources of Semiotic*, pp.74, 76.

19. Fisch, "Just How General Is Peirce's General Theory of Signs?" in Ketner and Kloesel, eds., *Pierce, Semeiotic, and Pragmatism*, p. 357.

20. Charles S. Peirce, *The New Elements of Mathematics*, ed. C. Eisele (The Hague: Mouton, 1976), 3.886, cited in Fisch, p. 342.

21. Max Fisch, "The Range of Peirce's Relevance," in Ketner and Kloesel, eds., *Peirce, Semeiotic, and Pragmatism*, pp. 422–446.

22. Julia Kristeva, *Language: The Unknown*, trans. A. M. Menke (New York: Columbia University Press, 1989), p. 13.

23. Ferdinand de Saussure, *Course in General Linguistics*, ed. C. Bally and A. Sechehaye, trans. R. Harris (LaSalle, IL: Open Court, 1986), p. ix; Roy Harris and Talbot J. Taylor, *Landmarks in Linguistic Thought* (London: Routledge, 1989), p. 177. Cf. Roy Harris, *Language, Saussure and Wittgenstein* (London: Routledge, 1988), Chs. 1–3.

24. Harris, "Introduction," in ibid., p. ix.

25. Saussure, *Course*, p. 66.

26. The terms *thinking* and *speaking* allude to the fact that the text I am closely reading is a compilation from Saussure's lectures. Comparison of the text with Saussure's notes has revealed a number of inconsistencies; clearly Bally, Sechehaye, and Riedlinger distorted Saussure at several points. Nonetheless, this text is the one that has been accepted as authoritative, and the current understanding of Saussure's approach is based on it. Moreover, it is unreasonable to assume that Saussure's closest colleagues and sympathizers were not able to understand his thinking, especially on these basic topics. See Roy Harris, "Translator's Introduction," Saussure, *Course in General Linguistics*, pp. xii–xiii.

27. See, e.g., Claude Levi-Strauss, *Structural Anthropology*, trans C. Jacobson and B. Grundfest Schoepf (New York: Basic Books, 1963).

28. Roy Harris, *Language, Saussure and Wittgenstein*, pp. 7–17. I am puzzled why Harris' recognition of the significance of Saussure's commitment to the biplanar character of the linguistic sign did not lead him to moderate his claim about the extent to which the *Cours* is "revolutionary" on this issue.

29. See, e.g., I. M. Copi and R. W. Beard, eds., *Essays on Wittgenstein's Tractatus* (London: Routledge and Kegan Paul, 1966); Henry Le Roy Finch, *Wittgenstein—The Early Philosophy: An Explosition of the "Tractatus"* (New York: Humanities Press, 1971); Allan Janik and Stephen Toulmin, *Wittgenstein's Vienna* (New York: Simon and Schuster, 1973); and Merrill B. Hintikka and Jaakko Hintikka, *Investigating Wittgenstein* (London: Blackwell, 1986).

30. Ludwig Wittgenstein, *Tractatus Logico-Philosophicus*, trans. D. F. Pears and B. F. McGuinness (London: Routledge and Kegan Paul, 1961).

31. Robert J. Fogelin, *Wittgenstein* (London: Routledge and Kegan Paul, 1976), p. 18.

32. Ibid., p. 24.

33. Ibid., p. 29.

34. Edna O'Shaughnessy, "The Picture Theory of Meaning," in Copi and Beard, eds., *Essays*, p.118.

35. Ludwig Wittgenstein, *Philosophical Investigations*, trans. G. E. M. Anscombe (Oxford: Blackwell, 1963), sect. 1–45.

36. Janik and Toulmin, *Wittgenstein's Vienna*, p. 195.

37. Ernst Cassirer, *The Philosophy of Symholic Forms*, 3 vols., trans R. Manheim (New Haven, CN: Yale University Press, 1953–1957; Vol 1, 1923; vol. 2, 1925; vol 3. 1929).

38. Ernst Cassirer, *An Essay on Man* (New Haven, CN: Yale University Press, 1944).

39. Ibid., p. 43.

40. Cassirer, *Philosophy Vol. 1 Language*, p. 158.

41. Ibid., p. 75.

42. Cassirer, *Essay on Man*, pp. 51, 57.

43. Carl H. Hamburg, "Cassirer's Conception of Philosophy," *The Philosophy of Ernst Cassirer*, ed. P. A. Schilpp, (Evanston, IL: Library of Living Philosophers, 1949), p. 78, citing Cassirer, *Philosophie der symbolischen Formen*, vol 3, p. 109.

44. Ibid., pp. 78, 87.

45. Hazard Adams, *Philosophy of the Literary Symbolic* (Talahassee: University Presses of Florida, 1983), pp. 216–217.

46. Cassirer, *Philosophie der symbolischen Formen*, vol. 1, pp. 132ff., cited in Wilbur M. Urban, "Cassirer's Philosophy of Language," Schilpp, ed. in *The Philosophy of Ernst Cassirer*, p. 416.

47. Cassirer, *Philosophy, Vol. 1. Language*, pp. 186–197.

48. Ibid., vol. 1, p. 197.

49. Ibid., vol. 1, p. 159, citing Humboldt, "Über das vergleichende Sprachstudium," *Werke*, vol. 4, pp. 21ff. Cf. Cassirer's distinction between "reproduction" and "production."

50. Ibid., vol. 1, p. 160, citing Humboldt, "Einleitung zum Kawi-Werk," *Werke*, 7, No. 1, 46ff.

51. Cassirer, *The Phenomenology of Knowledge*, vol. 3 of Philosophy of Symbolic Forms, trans. R. Manheim (New Haven, CN: Yale University Press, 1957), p. 15, citing Humboldt, *Einleitung zum Kawi-Werk*, in

Gesammelte Schriften, ed. königliche preussische Akademie der Wissenschaften (Berlin, 1903–22), pp. 7, 46, 60ff.

52. Adams, *Philosophy of the Literary Symbolic*, p. 218.

53. See, e.g., ibid., pp. 221–232.

54. John R. Stewart, "Concepts of Language and Meaning: A Comparative Study," *Quarterly Journal of Speech* 58 (1972): 127–128.

55. Susane K. Langer, *Philosophy in a New Key* (New York: Mentor, 1951), p. 29.

56. John F. Wilson and Carroll C. Arnold, *Public Speaking as a Liberal Art*, 2nd ed. (Boston: Allyn and Bacon, 1968), pp. 274, 299, cited in Stewart, "Concepts of Language and Meaning," p. 127.

Chapter 4. Language as Constitutive Articulate Contact

1. Norman Kretzmann, "The Main Thesis of Locke's Semantic Theory," *History of Linguistic Thought and Contemporary Linguistics*, ed. Herman Parret (Berlin: Walter de Gruyter, 1976), pp. 329–347.

2. Martin Heidegger, *On the Way to Language*, trans. Peter D. Hertz (San Francisco: Harper and Row, 1971), pp. 97, 123.

3. Hans-Georg Gadamer, *Truth and Method*, 2nd. ed., trans. Joel Weinsheimer and D. G. Marshall (New York: Crossroad, 1989), pp. 403–404.

4. Hans-Georg Gadamer, "The Hermeneutics of Suspicion," *Hermeneutics: Questions and Prospects*, ed., G. Shapiro and A. Sica (Amherst: University of Massachusetts Press, 1984), p. 63.

5. Hans-Georg Gadamer, *Philosophical Hermeneutics*, ed. and trans. David E. Linge (Berkeley: University of California Press, 1976), p. 76.

6. Mikhail Bakhtin, "From Notes Made in 1970–71," *Speech Genres and Other Late Essays*, trans. Vern W. McGee (Austin: University of Texas Press, 1986), pp. 135, 147.

7. Mircea Eliade, *Cosmos and History* (New York: Praeger, 1959).

8. John Angus Campbell, "A Rhetorical Interpretation of History," *Rhetorica*, 2 (1984): 236–237.

9. Edmund Husserl, *The Crisis of European Sciences and Transcendental Phenomenology*, trans. David Carr (Evanston, IL: Northwestern University Press, 1970), p. 127.

10. Ibid., p. 381.

11. Martin Buber, "Distance and Relation," *The Knowledge of Man,* ed. Maurice Friedman, trans. Maurice Friedman and Ronald G. Smith (New York: Harper and Row, 1965), pp. 60–61.

12. Ibid., p. 61.

13. Gadamer, *Truth and Method*, pp. 443–444.

14. John Shotter, *Social Accountability and Selfhood* (Oxford: Blackwell, 1984), p. x.

15. Ibid., p. 103.

16. Martin Heidegger, *Being and Time*, trans. J. Macquarrie and E. Robinson (New York: Harper and Row, 1962), p. 195. For Heidegger, Dasein (literally, there-being) is roughly synonymous with "the person," or "human being."

17. Gadamer, *Truth and Method*, p. 259.

18. Heidegger's analysis of "fore-meanings" in *Being and Time* underscores the ways that agendas, culture, and context continually constrain communicating. Gadamer's description of "prejudice" in *Truth and Method* makes this same point.

19. Herbert Dreyfus, *Being-In-The-World: A Commentary on Heidegger's Being and Time, Division I* (Cambridge, MA: MIT Press, 1991), p. 3.

20. Ibid., p. 5.

21. Martin Heidegger, *History of the Concept of Time*, trans., T. Kisiel (Bloomington, IN: Indiana University Press, 1985) p. 161.

22. Ibid., p. 238.

23. Ibid., p. 238.

24. Martin Heidegger, "Letter on Humanism," *Basic Writings*, ed. David F. Krell (New York: Harper and Row, 1977), p. 193.

25. Richard Rorty, *Essays on Heidegger and Others* (Cambridge: Cambridge University Press, 1991), p. 116.

26. "A Nice Derangement of Epitaphs," *Truth and Interpretation: Perspectives on the Philosophy of Donald Davidson,* ed. Ernest LePore (Oxford: Blackwell, 1986), p. 446.

27. Heidegger, *History*, p. 263.

28. Mikhail Bakhtin, "The Problem of Speech Genres," in *Speech Genres and Other Late Essays*, p. 60.

29. Bakhtin, "Notes," p. 138.

30. Richard Palmer, *Hermeneutics: Interpretation Theory in Schleiermacher, Dilthey, Heidegger, and Gadamer* (Evanston, IL: Northwestern University Press, 1969), p. 201.

31. Gadamer, *Truth and Method*, p. 443.

32. It should be clear that for Gadamer, *dialogue* has a different meaning than it had for Martin Buber. See John Stewart, "Speech and Human Being: A Complement to Semiotics," *Quarterly Journal of Speech* 72 (1986): 55–73.

33. Gadamer, *Truth and Method*, p. 446. Occasionally, Gadamer seems to claim that Plato's texts are examples of "living dialogue." See, for example, "Text and Interpretation," in *Dialogue and Deconstruction,* ed. Diane P. Michelfelder and Richard E. Palmer (Albany: SUNY Press, 1989), p. 23. But Gadamer seems more often to have in mind spontaneous, natural conversation rather than the assertively agenda-driven and manipulative exchanges between Socrates and his interlocutors. P. Christopher Smith discusses this and broader issues in "Plato as Impulse and Obstacle in Gadamer's Development of a Hermeneutical Theory," *Gadamer and Hermeneutics*, ed. Hugh J. Silverman (New York: Routledge, 1991), pp. 23–41.

34. One recent persuasive argument for the inseparability of the verbal and the nonverbal is David McNeill's *Hand and Mind: What Gestures Reveal about Thought (*Chicago: University of Chicago Press, 1992). McNeill and his colleagues conclude from their exhaustive analysis of videotapes of individuals engaged in narrative discourse that "the whole concept of language must be altered" to take into account the results of their research. Unfortunately, however, McNeill's conception of communication is drastically oversimplified. He treats gestures as a means of "transferring mental images to visible forms" and "conveying ideas that language cannot always express," echoing John Locke's picture of the relationship between language and thought.

35. Smith, "Plato as Impulse and Obstacle," p. 32.

36. Gadamer, *Truth and Method*, p. 403.

37. Ibid., pp. 403–404.

38. Gadamer, *Philosophical Hermeneutics*, p. 62.

39. The scare quotes mark these verbs as subject-object terms enlisted to help limn a non-subject-object dynamic.

40. Gadamer, *Truth and Method*, p. 474.

41. Ibid., p. 475.

42. Gadamer develops these ideas in ibid., pp. 400–403 and 452–453.

43. Ibid., p. 446.

44. Ibid., p. 401, 452.

45. Ibid., p. 447.

46. Ibid., p. 450.

47. Charles Taylor, "Interpretation and the Sciences of Man," *Review of Metaphysics* 25 (1971): 3–51.

48. Heidegger, *On the Way to Language*, p. 57.

49. Gadamer, *Truth and Method*, pp. 101–103.

50. Ibid., p. 106.

51. Ibid., p. 70.

52. Ibid., p. 357.

53. Ibid., p. 383.

54. Gadamer, "Text and Interpretation," p. 23.

55. Gadamer, *Truth and Method*, p. 446.

56. Hans-Georg Gadamer, "Letter to Dallmayr," *Dialogue and Deconstruction*, p. 98.

57. Gadamer, "Text and Interpretation," p. 36.

58. Ibid., p. 26.

59. Ibid., pp. 29, 31.

60. Ibid., p. 31.

61. Ibid., p. 33.

62. V. N. Volosinov, *Marxism and the Philosophy of Language*, trans. Ladislav Matejka and I. R. Titunik (Cambridge, MA: Harvard University Press, 1973), p. 72. In Chapter 7, I explore the tension between the clearly semiotic and the equally clearly post-semiotic dimensions of Volosinov's work. I also explain my rationale for attributing this work to Volosinov rather than Bakhtin.

63. Bakhtin, "The Problem of Speech Genres," pp. 94, 95.

64. Martin Buber, *I and Thou*, trans. Walter Kaufmann (New York: Charles Scribner's Sons, 1970), p. 53.

65. Martin Buber, *Between Man and Man*, ed. Maurice Friedman, trans. Maurice Friedman and R. G. Smith (New York: Macmillan, 1965), p. 203.

66. Martin Buber, *The Knowledge of Man*, p. 112.

67. Eric V. Voegelin, "Immortality: Experience and Symbol," *Harvard Theological Review* 60 (1967): 272.

68. George Lakoff, *Women, Fire, and Dangerous Things: What Categories Reveal About the Mind* (Chicago: University of Chicago Press, 1987), p. xi.

69. D. B. Chamberlain, "Consciousness at Birth: The Range of Empirical Evidence," in T. R. Verney, ed., *Pre- and Perinatal Psychology: An Introduction* (New York: Human Sciences Press, 1987), pp. 70–86.

70. W. E. Freud, "Prenatal Attachment and Bonding," in ibid., p. 74. Cf. A. Tomatis, "Ontogenesis of the Faculty of Listening," in ibid., pp. 23–35.

71. Eric Havelock, *The Muse Learns to Write* (New Haven, CN: Yale University Press, 1986), pp. 65–66.

72. Walter J. Ong, *Orality and Literacy* (New York: Methuen, 1982), p. 32.

73. Ibid., p. 32.

74. Ibid., p. 34.

75. Adam M. Parry, *The Making of Homeric Verse* (Oxford: Clarendon, 1971).

76. See, e.g., Harlan Lane, *The Mask of Benevolence: Disabling the Deaf Community* (New York: Alfred A. Knopf, 1992); Ursula Bellugi, "Clues from the Similarities between Signed and spoken Language," in *Signed and Spoken Language: Biological Constraints on Linguistic Form*, ed. U. Bellugi and M. Studdert-Kennedy (Weinheim and Deerfield Beach, FL: Verlag Chemie, 1980); William C. Stokoe, *Sign Language Structure* (Silver Spring, MD: Linstok, 1960); and William C. Stokoe, "Sign Writing Systems," in *Gallaudet Encyclopedia of Deaf People*, ed. John Van Cleve (New York: McGraw-Hill, 1987).

77. For a review of these materials, see Oliver Sacks, *Seeing Voices: A Journey into the World of the Deaf* (Berkeley: University of California Press, 1989).

78. Charles Taylor, *Philosopy and the Human Sciences: Philosophical Papers*, vol. 2 (New York: Cambridge University Press, 1985), p. 19.

79. In *I and Thou* and other works, Martin Buber argued that world emerges from contact not only with facticity and other humans but also with the Infinite, which he calls the Eternal Thou. I think he is right. A more complete account of articulate contact would include consideration of the

mysterious or spiritual dimensions of communication. See Craig R. Smith, "Finding the Spiritual Dimension in Rhetoric," *Western Journal of Communication* 57 (1993): 266–271.

80. I clarify the distinction between *interaction* and *transaction* and argue for the appropriateness of the latter term in "A Postmodern Look at Traditional Communication Postulates," *Western Journal of Speech Communication* 55 (1991): 354–379.

81. Gadamer, *Philosophical Hermeneutics*, p. 62.

82. Example from Douglas W. Maynard, "Perspective-Display Sequences in Conversation," *Western Journal of Speech Communication* 53 (1989): 107.

83. Ibid., p. 91.

84. Ibid., p. 107.

85. Ibid., p. 107.

86. A number of philosophers, linguists, semioticians, and communication theorists have agreed to contribute to a second volume, *Beyond the Symbol Model: Essays on the Nature of Language,* which SUNY Press plans to publish in 1996.

87. For example, Dell Hymes, "Linguistic Theory and Functions in Speech," *Foundations in Sociolinguistics: An Ethnographic Approach* (Philadelphia: University of Pennsylvania Press, 1974), pp. 145–178.

88. For example, Clifford Geertz, *Local Knowledge: Further Essays in Interpretive Anthropology* (New York: Basic Books, 1983).

89. For example, John J. Gumperz, and Dell Hymes, eds., *Directions in Sociolinguistics: The Ethnography of Communication* (New York: Holt, Rinehart and Winston, 1972); John J Gumperz, ed., *Language and Social Identity* (New York: Cambridge University Press, 1982).

90. John Darnton, "Accepting Nobel, Morrison Proves Power of Words," *The New York Times* (8 December 1993), p. B1.

Chapter 5. Diverse Friendly Bedfellows

1. G. B. Madison, *The Hermeneutics of Postmodernity: Figures and Themes* (Bloomington: Indiana University Press, 1990), p. v.

2. Ibid., p. 64, citing M. Merleau-Ponty, *The Visible and the Invisible,* trans. A. Lingis (Evanston, IL: Northwestern University Press, 1968), p. 259.

3. M. Merleau-Ponty, *The Primacy of Perception,* trans. J. M. Edie (Evanston, IL: Northwestern University Press, 1964), p. 9, cited in Madison, *Hermeneutics of Postmodernity,* p. 71.

4. G. B. Madison, "The Hermeneutics of (Inter)Subjectivity, or: The Mind-Body Problem Deconstructed," *Hermeneutics of Postmodernity,* pp. 154–177.

5. Ibid., p. 160, citing Roy Schafer, *Language and Insight* (New Haven, CN: Yale University Press, 1978), pp. 84 and 86.

6. Ibid., 161, citing Émile Benveniste, *Problems in General Linguistics,* trans M. Meck (Coral Gables, FL: University of Miami Press, 1971), p. 226.

7. Or, perhaps not.

8. Madison, *Hermeneutics of Postmodernity,* p. 168, citing Hans-Georg Gadamer, "The Problem of Historical Consciousness," *Interpretive Social Science: A Reader,* ed. P. Rabinow and W. Sullivan (Berkeley: University of California Press, 1979) p. 107.

9. H. P. Grice, "Logic and Conversations," *Syntax and Semantics,* ed. P. Cole and J. L. Morgan (New York: Academic Press, 1975).

10. Vito Signorile, "Review of Oliver Sacks', *Seeing Voices,*" *Human Studies* 14 (1991): 371.

11. Jack R. Gannon, *Deaf Heritage: A Narrative History of Deaf America* (Silver Springs, MD: National Association of the Deaf, 1981) p. xxv.

12. There is no one universal sign language for deaf persons. In the United States the natural signed language of deaf persons is American Sign Language (ASL or Sign). In Germany, deaf signers use German Sign Language, in Russia, Russian Sign Language, and so on. Each is as unique as the equivalent spoken language. Invented sign language systems are also operative in many countries. Among English speakers these are called *Signed Exact English* (SEE) systems. There are a number of variations of SEE systems, and educators argue over which is optimal. The same holds true for other languages. For example, in Japan, there are variations of Signed Exact Japanese.

13. Susan K. Dyer, "Hermeneutics and Deaf Education: An Analysis and Critique of Theories of Language and Communication," Master's thesis, University of Washington, 1992.

14. Gannon, *Deaf Heritage,* p. xxv.

15. "Central Institute for the Deaf—Research Departrment," *Gallaudet Encyclopedia of Deaf People and Deafness,* vol. 1 (1987); p. 180.

16. Gannon, *Deaf Heritage,* p. 360.

17. Alexander G. Bell, quoted in Harlan Lane, *When the Mind Hears: A History of the Deaf* (New York: Random House, 1984), p. 341.

18. Ibid., p. 396.

19. Richard Winefield, *Never the Twain Shall Meet: The Communications Debate* (Washington, D.C.: Gallaudet University Press, 1987).

20. Neither oralists nor proponents of ASL make up a completely homogeneous group. For example, some oralists favor auditory teaching methods, others work with several of the senses, and a third group emphasizes cued-speech. See "Oralist Teaching Methods," *Gallaudet Encyclopedia of Deaf People and Deafness*, vol. 1 (1987); p. 289.

21. Phyllist Feibelman, "Editorial," *Our Kids Magazine,* Alexander Graham Bell Association for the Deaf—Parents Section (Spring 1990): 1.

22. Central Institute for the Deaf, *1989 Annual Report* (St. Louis: Author, 1989), pp. 6 and 11.

23. Barbara Craig, "Don't Touch Me, Just Call My Name," *Our Kids Magazine* (Fall 1989): 9.

24. Lane, *When the Mind Hears*, p. 77.

25. Kathleen Collins, *John Tracy Clinic Correspondence Course for Parents of Young Deaf Children,* Part A—*Deaf Babies and Supplemental Papers* (Los Angeles: John Tracy Clinic, 1984), pp. A-11.6, A-1.7.

26. Robert E. Johnson, Scott K. Liddell, and Carol J. Erting, "Unlocking the Curriculum: Principles for Achieving Access in Deaf Education," Gallaudet Research Institute Working Paper 89–3 (Washington, D.C.: Gallaudet University, 1989), pp. 4–5.

27. Dyer, "Hermeneutics and Deaf Education," pp. 52–53, 85–86.

28. A. Binet and T. Simon, "An Investigation Concerning the Value of the Oral Method," *American Annals of the Deaf* 55 (1910): 24, 34, cited in Lane, *When the Mind Hears,* p. 400.

29. Veda R. Charrow and Ronnie B. Wilbur, "The Deaf Child as a Linguistic Minority," in *American Deaf Culture: An Anthgology,* ed. Sherman Wilcox (Silver Spring, MD: Linstok Press, 1989), p. 107.

30. This is Harlan Lane's label for the hearing- and speech-oriented service-providers who wittingly or unwittingly work behind a "mask of benevolence to maintain the view of the deaf as "disabled": "audism is the hearing way of dominating, restructuring, and exercising authority over the deaf community." See Harlan Lane, *The Mask of Benevolence: Disabling the Deaf Community* (New York: Alfred A. Knopf, 1992), pp. 43, 75–77.

31. Hilde S. Schlesinger and Kathryn P. Meadow, *Sound and Sign:*

Childhood Deafness and Mental Health (Berkeley: University of California Press, 1972) 19.

32. Robert Johnson and Scott Liddell, "The Value of ASL in the Education of Deaf Children," *Communiation Issues Among Deaf People, A Deaf American Monograph*, vol. 40 ed. M. D. Garretson (Washington, DC: St. Mary's, 1990), p. 60.

33. Shanny Mow, "How Do You Dance Without Music?" in Leo M. Jacobs, *A Deaf Adult Speaks Out*, 3rd ed. (Washington, DC: Gallaudet University Press, 1989), p. 156.

34. Bernard Bragg, *Lessons in Laughter: The Autobiography of a Deaf Actor* (Washington, DC: Gallaudet University Press, 1989), pp. 13–14.

35. Mow, "How Do You Dance," p. 159.

36. The boundaries of ASL, like the boundaries of Western, English-speaking hearing persons, are imprecise. Deaf persons in Canada, for example, sign a language very close to ASL.

37. Kathee Christensen, "American Sign Language and English: Parallel Bilingualism," in Garretson, *Communication Issues*, vol. 40, p. 28.

38. Oliver Sacks, *Seeing Voices: A Journey into the World of the Deaf* (Berkeley: University of California Press, 1989), p. 87. Cf. E. S. Klima and U. Bellugi, *The Signs of Language* (Cambridge, MA: Harvard University Press, 1979).

39. Ibid., p. 90.

40. James P. Gee and Wendy Goodhart, "ASL and the Biological Capacity for Language," in *Language Learning and Deafness*, ed. Michael Strong (New York: Cambridge University Press, 1988), cited in Sacks, ibid., p. 111.

41. Cited in Sacks, ibid., p. 112.

42. Johnson, Liddell, and Erting, "Unlocking the Curriculum," pp. 15–18.

43. Bernard Bragg, "Communication and the Deaf Community: Where do We Go From Here?" in Garretson, *Communication Issues*, vol. 40, p. 10.

44. M. J. Bienvenu, "Letters from Deaf Americans," in ibid., p. 133.

45. Lil Brannon and Sue Livingston, "An Alternative View of Education for Deaf Children: Part II," *American Annals of the Deaf* 131 (1986): 229.

46. Raymond P. Stevens, "Children's Language Should Be Learned and Not Taught," *Sign Language Studies* 11 (1976): 100.

47. Lane, *The Mask of Benevolence,* p. 44.

48. Sacks, *Seeing Voices,* p. 130.

49. Lane, *Mask of Benevolence,* p. 21. Cf. p. 27.

50. Dyer, "Hermeneutics and Deaf Education," pp. 106–107.

51. Alan Turing, "Computing Machinery and Intelligence," *Mind* 59 (1950): 433–460.

52. Paul Smolensky, "Connectionist Modeling: Neural Computation / Mental Connections," *Neural Connections, Mental Computation,* ed. Lynn Nadel, Lynn A. Cooper, Peter Culicover, and R. Michael Harnish (Cambridge, MA: MIT Press, 1990), p. 51.

53. Hilary Putnam characterizes this model as "the mind as a Cryptographer." It assumes that "the mind thinks its thoughts in Mentalese, codes [symbolizes] them in the local language, and then transmits them (say, by speaking them out loud) to the hearer. The hearer has a Cryptographer in his head too, of course, who thereupon proceeds to decode the 'message.' In this picture natural language, far from being essential to thought, is merely a vehicle for the communication of thought." *Representation and Reality* (Cambridge, MA: MIT Press, 1988), pp. 6–7.

54. A. Newell, "Physical Symbol Sytems," *Cognitive Science* 4 (1980): 170.

55. Smolensky, "Connectionist Modeling," p. 51.

56. Steve Torrance, "Philosohy and AI: Some Issues," *The Mind and the Machine: Philosophical Aspects of Artificial Intelligence,* ed. Steve Torrance (Chichester, England: Ellis Horwood, 1984), p. 22.

57. Ibid., p. 22.

58. Terry Winograd and Fernando Flores, *Understanding Computers and Cognition: A New Foundation for Design* (Reading, MA: Addison-Wesley, 1986). Quotations from book cover by Howard Gardner and Joseph Weizenbaum.

59. Humberto R. Maturana, "Biology of Cognition," in H. R. Maturana and F. Varela, *Autopoiesis and Cognition: The Realization of the Living* (Dodrecht: Reidel, 1980), pp. 2–62, cited in Winograd and Flores, ibid., p. 45.

60. Humberto R. Maturana, "Biology of Language: The Epistemology of Reality," in G. A. Miller and E. Lenneberg, eds., *Psychology and Biology of Language and Thought: Essays in Honor of Eric Lenneberg* (New York: Academic Press, 1978), p. 50; cited in Winograd and Flores, ibid., p. 50.

61. See especially, Martin Heidegger, *Being and Time,* trans. John Macquarrie and Edward Robinson (New York: Harper and Row, 1962), pp. 91–148.

62. See *The Symbolic and Connectionist Paradigms: Closing the Gap,* ed. John Dinsmore, (Hillsdale, NJ: Lawrence Erlbaum, 1992).

63. Daniel C. Dennet, "Mother Nature versus the Walking Encyclopedia: A Western Drama," *Philosophy and Connectionist Theory,* ed. W. Ramsey, S. P. Stich, and D. E. Rummelhart (Hillsdale, NJ: Lawrence Erlbaum, 1991), p. 24.

64. Margaret A. Boden, "Horses of a Different Color?" ibid., p. 11.

65. Tim van Gelder, "What is the 'D' in 'PDP'? A Survey of the Concept of Distribution," Ibid., p. 33.

66. Van Gelder, ibid., p. 45.

67. Van Gelder, ibid., pp. 45–46. Derek Partridge terms the connectionist units *subsymbolic,* and as a result, his account is parasitic on the representational character of symbols. He argues that the symbolic search space paradigm (SSSP) differs fundamentally from the connectionist paradigm (CP), but that both are representational. See Derek Partridge, *A New Guide to Artificial Intelligence* (Norwood, NJ: Ablex, 1991), p. 63.

68. Jerry a. Fodor and Zenon W. Pylyshyn, "Connectionism and Cognitive Architecture: A Critical Analysis," *Cognition* 28 (1988): 3–71.

69. Thomas Goschke and Dirk Koppelberg, "The Concept of Representation and the Representation of Concepts in Connectionist Models," in *Philosophy and Connectionist Theory,* p. 137.

70. Especially Jerry A. Fodor, *Psychosemantics: The Problem of Meaning in the Philosphy of Mind* (Cambridge, MA: MIT Press, 1987).

71. Goschke and Koppelberg, "Concept of Representation," p. 129.

72. Ibid., pp. 152–153.

73. Ibid., p. 155.

74. John Hagueland, "Representational Genera," in *Philosophy and Connectionist Theory,* pp. 61–89.

75. Ibid., p. 66.

76. Ibid., pp. 73–74.

77. Ibid., p. 74.

78. Ibid., p. 79.

79. Ibid., p. 84.

80. Ibid., p. 87

81. Ibid., p. 88.

Chapter 6. Semiotics and Dialogue in *Marxism and the Philosophy of Language*

1. V. N. Volosinov, *Marksizm i Filosofiia Jazyka Osnovnye Problemy Sociologiceskogo Metoda v Nauke o Jazyke* (Leningrad, 1929), cited in I. R. Tutnik, "Bakhtin and/or Volosinov and/or Medvedev: Dialogue and/or Doubletalk?" *Language and Literary Theory,* ed. Benjamin A. Stolz, I. R. Tutnik, and Lubomir Dolezel (Ann Arbor: Dept. of Slavik Languages and Literatures, University of Michigan, 1984).

2. "V. N. Volosinov," *Marxism and the Philosophy of Language,* trans. Ladislav Matejka and I. R. Titunik (New York: Seminar Press, 1973).

3. V. N. Volosinov, *Marxism and the Philosophy of Language,* trans. Ladislav Matejka and I. R. Titunik (Cambridge, MA: Harvard University Press, 1986). Unless otherwise noted, all citations are to this edition.

4. Michael Holoquist, "Introduction," *The Dialogic Imagination: Four Essays by M. M. Bakhtin,* ed. Michael Holquist, trans. Caryl Emerson and Michael Holquist (Austin: University of Texas Press, 1981), p. xxvi.

5. Titunik, "Bakhtin," pp. 535–540.

6. Katerina Clark and Michael Holquist, *Mikhail Bakhtin* (Cambridge, MA: Harvard University Press, 1984), pp. 147, 151.

7. Tzvetan Todorov, *Mikhail Bakhtin: The Dialogical Principle* (Minneapolis: University of Minnesota Press, 1984), p. 8.

8. Titunik, "Bakhtin," pp. 541–546.

9. Matejka and Titunik, "Translators' Preface, 1986," *Marxism and the Philosophy of Language,* p. xi.

10. Ladislav Matejka, "On the First Russian Prolegomena to Semiotics," Appendix I, *Marxism and the Philosophy of Language,* p. 163.

11. Without attempting finally to resolve the authorship issue, I have adopted the English translators' convention of attributing the work to Volosinov.

12. Roman Jakobson, quoted in Titunik, "Bakhtin," p. 547.

13. Michael Holquist, "The Politics of Representation," *Allegory and Representation,* ed. S. J. Greenblatt, (Baltimore: Johns Hopkins University Press, 1979–80), p. 173.

14. Frederick Jameson, "Review of *Marxism and the Philosophy of Language,*" *Style* 8 (1974): 535–543.

15. Clark and Holquist, *Bakhtin* p. 225.

16. Ibid., p. 226. Cf. Volosinov, *Marxism and the Philosophy of Language*, p. 11.

17. Todorov makes this same point on p. 9 of *Mikhail Bakhtin*.

18. Ladislav Matejka, "On the First Russian Prolegomena," p. 173.

19. Hans-Georg Gadamer, *Truth and Method*, 2nd ed., trans. Joel Weinsheimer and Donald G. Marshall (New York: Crossroad, 1989), pp. 362–379.

20. Gadamer makes many of these same points about the romantic theory of expression in Appendix VI of ibid., pp. 502–505.

21. The term *worlding* is introduced and explained in Chapter 4.

22. Matejaka, "On the First Russian Prolegomena," p. 169.

Chapter 7. The Symbol Model and the Philosophy of Language: The Case of Kenneth Burke

1. The authors appreciate significant contributions to this essay made by Walter Fisher, Susan Kline, and Allan Scult.

2. Kenneth Burke, *Counter-Statement*, 2nd ed., (Berkeley: University of California Press, 1968); hereafter *CS*.

3. Kenneth Burke, *Attitudes Toward History*, 3rd ed. (Berkeley: University of California Press, 1984); hereafter *ATH*.

4. Kenneth Burke, *Permanence and Change*, 4th ed. (Berkeley: University of California Press, 1984); hereafter, *P&C*.

5. Cary Nelson comments on this feature of Burke's thinking in "Writing as an Accomplice of Language: Kenneth Burke and Poststructuralism," in *The Legacy of Kenneth Burke*, ed. H. B. Simons and T. Melia (Madison: University of Wisconsin Press, 1989), pp. 156–173.

6. Kenneth Burke, "(Nonsymbolic) Motion / (Symbolic) Action," *Critical Inquiry* 4 (1978): 809.

7. Kenneth Burke, *Language as Symbolic Action: Essays on Life, Literature, and Method* (Berkeley: University of California Press, 1966), p. vii; hereafter *LSA*.

8. Kenneth Burke, *The Rhetoric of Religion: Studies in Logology* (Berkeley: University of California, 1970), p. 2; hereafter *RofR*.

9. Kenneth Burke, cited in R. L. Heath, *Realism and Relativism: A Perspective on Kenneth Burke* (Macon, GA: Mercer University Press, 1986), p. 37.

10. Wayne C. Booth, "Kenneth Burke's Way of Knowing," *Critical Inquiry* 1 (1974): 2.

11. W. H. Reuckert, *Kenneth Burke and the Drama of Human Relations*, 2nd ed. (Berkeley: University of California Press, 1982), pp. 285–287; W. H. Reuckert, "Criticism as a Way of Life or Criticism as Equipment for Living," *Newsletter of the Kenneth Burke Society* 6 (1990): 7–15.

12. Richard Rorty, *Philosophy and the Mirror of Nature* (Princeton, NJ: Princeton University Press, 1979), p. 369.

13. Ibid., p. 366.

14. Kenneth Burke, What Are the Signs of What? A Theory of Entitlement," *Anthropological Linguistics* 3 (1962): 1–23; *LSA*, pp. 359–379.

15. Kenneth Burke, "Definition of Man," *Hudson Review*, 16 (1963–1964); *LSA*, pp. 3–24.

16. Kenneth Burke, "Dramatism," in D. L. Sills, ed., *International Encyclopedia of the Social Sciences* (1968); vol. 4, pp. 445–451.

17. Compare comments in the fourth edition of *P&C*, pp. 295, 298, 300, 308–309, 313, and 331 with his 1978 comments in *Critical Inquiry* on pp. 809–811, 814, 822, 830–831, and 837–838.

18. Reuckert, *Kenneth Burke*, p. 157.

19. See Kenneth Burke, *A Grammar of Motives* (Berkeley: University of California Press, 1969), pp. 430–440, hereafter *GM*; and Kenneth Burke, *A Rhetoric of Motives* (Berkeley: University of California Press, 1969), pp. 13–15, hereafter *RM*.

20. We have not commented on why Burke might have capitalized *Symbol*. Neither does he. The convention obviously suggests that he is discussing what in German might be rendered as Ur-symbol, the "essential," "paradigm," or "generalized" symbol. Our speculation is indirectly supported by Burke's allusion to "the Ur-form" (Kenneth Burke, *The Philosophy of Literary Form: Studies in Symbolic Action,* 3rd ed. [Berkeley: University of California Press, 1973], pp. 103–105), hereafter *PLF.* We have adopted his convention of capitalizing *Symbol* in our discussion of "Lexicon Rhetoricae."

21. Burke, *LSA,* p. 45.

22. Burke, *LSA,* p. 46, italics in original.

23. Burke, *P&C,* p. 83.

24. Burke, *ATH,* pp. 328–336.

25. Burke, *GM,* pp. 21–22.

26. Burke, *RM,* p. 43.

27. Burke, *PLF,* p. 25.

28. Burke, *RofR,* p. vi.

29. Burke, "(Nonsymbolic) Motion / (Symbolic) Action," p. 809.

30. Martin Heidegger, *On the Way to Language*, trans. P. D. Hertz (San Francisco: Harper and Row, 1971), p. 114.

31. Burke, *GM*, pp. 24–25; "Dramatism," p. 10; also see S. B. Southwell, *Kenneth Burke and Martin Heidegger with a Note Against Deconstruction* (Gainesville, FL: University of Florida Press, 1987), p. 37.

32. Martin Heidegger, "Letter on Humanism," in *Martin Heidegger: Basic Writings*, ed. D. F. Krell (New York: Harper and Row, 1977), p. 193.

33. Hans-Georg Gadamer, *Truth and Method*, 2nd. ed., trans. J. Weinsheimer and D. G. Marshall (New York: Crossroad, 1989), p. 474.

34. See, e.g., Jane Blankenship, "'Magic' and 'Mystery' in the Works of Kenneth Burke," in Simons and Melia, *The Legacy of Kenneth Burke,* pp. 128–151; Nelson, "Writing as an Accomplice of Language"; and J. C. Carrier, "Knowledge, Meaning and Social Inequality in Kenneth Burke," *American Journal of Sociology* 88 (1982): 43–61.

35. We acknowledge the obvious point that Burke's discussions of language are unusually wide-ranging, erudite, multidimensional, and polythematic. But we believe that the philosophy of language that grounds them is flawed in the ways we discuss here.

36. Ludwig Wittgenstein, *Philosophical Investigations*, ed. G. H. Von Wright and G. E. M. Anscombe, trans. G. E. M. Anscombe (Oxford: Blackwell, 1953).

37. Hymes reports that during a visit to Burke's home, Burke "rummaged for the manuscript" in response to Hymes's account of the ways some Native Americans talk about raccoons. Burke commented that it sounded to him as if the Native Americans were "good Spinozists," because the words they used to refer to raccoons varied with the situation in which they experienced them. See Dell Hymes, Introduction to "What Are the Signs of What? A Theory of Entitlement," pp. 1–5.

38. Hymes, ibid., p. 2. The 1962 version was apparently commissioned by Hymes, then editor of *Anthropological Lingusitics.* There are very few differences between that version and the one appearing in *LSA.* Our analysis relies on the *LSA* text, unless otherwise indicated.

39. Burke, "What Are the Signs of What?" *LSA* 359.

40. Burke, *GM*, p. 3.

41. Burke, *P&C,* p. 295.

42. Michael C. McGee, "Text, Context, and the Fragmentation of Contemporary Culture," *Western Journal of Speech Communication* 54 (1990): 278.

43. Burke, *GM*, p. 43.

44. Laura Crowell, "Three Sheers for Kenneth Burke," *Quarterly Journal of Speech* 63 (1977): 154–155.

45. Burke, "Dramatism," p. 447, italics added.

46. This is another example of Burke defining a "systematic" philosophical problematic—definition of a central construct—and then, at the crucial and difficult point, turning to "edifying" speculation.

47. Kenneth Burke, "Counter Gridlock: An Interview with Kenneth Burke," *All Area*, 2 (1983): 30–31, cited in Blankenship, "'Magic' and 'Mystery,'" p. 144.

48. See, e.g., Gadamer, *Truth and Method,* p. 452.

49. Ibid., p. 549.

50. Heidegger, *On the Way to Language,* p. 57.

51. We reverse the order of the two worlds and atomism commitments here to reflect Burke's writing more closely.

52. Gadamer, *Truth and Method,* p. 549.

Chapter 8. The Symbol Model and Calvin O. Schrag's Communicative Praxis

1. Calvin O. Schrag, *Communicative Praxis and the Space of Subjectivity* (Bloomington: Indiana University Press, 1986); hereafter *Praxis*.

2. Calvin O. Schrag, *The Resources of Rationality: A Response to the Postmodern Challenge* (Bloomington: Indiana University Press, 1992), hereafter *Rationality*.

3. See, e.g., Calvin O. Schrag, "Rhetoric Resituated at the End of Philosophy," *Quarterly Journal of Speech* 71 (1985): 164–174; "Rationality Between Modernity and Postmodernity," in *Life-World and Politics: Between Modernity and Postmodernity*, ed. Stephen K. White (Notre Dame, IN: University of Notre Dame Press, 1989).

4. Schrag, *Rationality,* p. 9.

5. Ibid., p. 7

6. Fred R. Dallmayr, *Twilight of Subjectivity: Contributions to a Post-Individualist Theory of Politics* (Amherst: University of Massachusetts Press, 1981).

7. Michael Hyde and Craig Smith, "Hermenutics and Rhetoric: A Seen But Unobserved Relationship," *Quarterly Journal of Speech,* 65 (1979): 347–348.

8. Schrag, *Rationality,* p. 168.

9. Mikhail M. Bakhtin, "The Problem of Speech Genres," *Speech Genres and Other Late Essays,* trans. Vern W. McGee, ed. Caryl Emerson and Michael Holquist (Austin: University of Texas Press, 1986), pp. 91, 95.

10. Mikhail Bakhtin, "The *Bildungsroman* and Its Significance in the History of Realism (Toward a Historical Typology of the Novel)," in ibid., pp. 48–53.

11. Jacques Derrida, *Of Grammatology,* trans. Gayatri Chakravorty Spivak (Baltimore: Johns Hopkins University Press, 1976), p. 158.

12. Schrag, *Praxis,* p. 44.

13. Schrag, *Rationality,* p. 88.

14. *Ibid.,* p. 88.

15. *Ibid.,* p. 141.

16. Schrag, *Praxis,* p. 98.

17. Hans-Georg Gadamer, *Truth and Method,* 2nd ed., trans. Joel Weinsheimer and Donald G. Marshall (New York: Crossroad, 1989), p. 489.

18. Hans-Georg Gadamer, "*Destruktion* and Deconstruction," *Dialogue and Deconstruction: The Gadamer-Derrida Encounter,* ed. D. P. Michelfelder and R. E. Palmer (Albany: SUNY Press, 1989), p. 122.

19. Ibid., p. 110.

20. Ibid., p. 111.

REFERENCES

Aarsleff, Hans. "The Tradition of Condillac: The Problem of the Origin of Language in the Eighteenth Century and the Debate in the Berlin Academy Before Herder." *Studies in the History of Linguistics: Traditions and Paradigms,* ed. Dell Hymes, pp. 93–156. Bloomington: Indiana University Press, 1974.

———. *From Locke to Saussure: Essays on the Study of Language and Intellectual History.* Minneapolis: University of Minnesota Press, 1982.

———. "Introduction." Wilhelm von Humboldt, *On Language,* trans. Peter Heath, pp. vii–lxv. Cambridge: Cambridge University Press, 1988.

Adams, Hazard. *Philosophy of the Literary Symbolic.* Tallahassee: University Presses of Florida, 1983.

Alston, William P. *Philosophy of Language.* Englewood Cliffs, NJ: Prentice-Hall, 1964.

Aristotle. *The Basic Works of Aristotle,* ed. Richard McKeon. New York: Random House, 1941.

Arnauld, Antoine, and Claude Lancelot. *General and Rational Grammar: The Port-Royal Grammar,* trans. J. Rieux and B. E. Rollin. The Hague: Mouton, 1975.

Arnauld, Antoine, and P. Nicole. *The Art of Thinking,* trans. J. Dickoff and P. James. Indianapolis: Bobbs-Merrill, 1964.

Augustine. *De Dialectica,* ed. Jan Pinborg, trans. B. D. Jackson. The Hague: Reidel, 1975.

———. *On Christian Doctrine,* trans. D. W. Robertson, Jr. New York: Macmillan, 1958.

Austin, John L. *How to Do Things with Words,* ed. J. O. Urmson. Oxford: Oxford University Press, 1962.

———. *Philosophical Papers.* Oxford: Clarendon, 1961.

Babacz, Bruce. *St. Augustine's Theory of Knowledge: A Contemporary Analysis.* New York: Edwin Mellen, 1981.

Bakhtin, Mikhail. *The Dialogic Imagination: Four Essays by M. M. Bakhtin,* ed. Michael Holquist, trans. Caryl Emerson and Michael Holquist. Austin: University of Texas Press, 1981.

———. *Speech Genres and Other Late Essays,* trans Vern W. McGee. Austin: University of Texas Press, 1986.

Bavelas, Janet Beavin. "Behaving and Communicating: A Reply to Motley." *Western Journal of Speech Communication* 54 (1990): 593–602.

———. and Linda Coates. "How Do We Account for the Mindfulness of Face-to-Face Dialogue?" *Communication Monographs* 59 (1992): 301–305.

Bellugi, Ursula, and M. Studdert-Kennedy, eds. *Signed and Spoken Language: Biological Constraints on Lingusitic Form.* Weinheim and Deerfield Beach, FL: Verlag Chemie, 1980.

Benveniste, Émile. *Problems in General Linguistics,* trans. M. E. Meek. Coral Gables, FL: University of Miami Press, 1977.

Binet, A., and T. Simon. "An Investigation Concerning the Value of the Oral Method." *American Annals of the Deaf* 55 (1910): 4–33.

Bonnot, Etienne, Abbé de Condillac. *An Essay On the Origin of Human Knowledge,* trans. Thomas Nugent. Gainesville, FL: Scholars' Facsimiles and Reprints, 1971.

———. *Philosophical Writings,* trans. F. Philip and H. Lane. Hillsdale, NJ: Lawrence Erlbaum, 1982.

Booth, Wayne C. "Kenneth Burke's Way of Knowing." *Critical Inquiry* 1 (1974) 1–19.

Bragg, Bernard. *Lessons in Laughter: The Autobiography of a Deaf Actor.* Washington, D. C.: Gallaudet University Press, 1989.

Brannon, Lil, and Sue Livingston. "An Alternative View of Education for Deaf Children, Part II." *American Annals of the Deaf* 131 (1986): 229–231.

Buber, Martin. *The Knowledge of Man,* Ed. Maurice Friedman, trans. Maurice Friedman and Ronald Gregor Smith. New York: Harper and Row, 1965.

————. *Between Man and Man,* ed. Maurice Friedman, trans. Maurice Friedman and Ronald Gregor Smith. New York: Macmillan, 1965.

————. *I and Thou,* trans. Walter Kaufmann. New York: Charles Scribner's Sons, 1970.

Burke, Kenneth. "What Are the Signs of What? A Theory of Entitlement." *Anthropological Linguistics* 3 (1962): 1–23.

————. *Language as Symbolic Action: Essays on Life, Literature, and Method.* Berkeley: University of California Press, 1966.

————. *Counter-Statement,* 2nd ed. Berkeley: University of California Press, 1968.

————. *A Grammar of Motives.* Berkeley: University of California Press, 1969.

————. *A Rhetoric of Motives.* Berkeley: University of California Press, 1969.

————. *The Rhetoric of Religion: Studies in Logology.* Berkeley: University of California Press, 1970.

————. *The Philosophy of Literary Form: Studies in Symbolic Action,* 3rd ed. Berkeley: University of California Press, 1973.

————. "(Nonsymbolic) Motion / (Symbolic) Action." *Critical Inquiry* 4 (1978): 798–817.

————. *Attitudes Toward History,* 3rd ed. Berkeley: University of California Press, 1984.

————. *Permanence and Change,* 4th ed. Berkeley: University of California Press, 1984.

Bursill-Hall, G.L. "Toward a History of Linguistics in the Middle Ages 1100–1450." *Studies in the History of Linguistics: Traditions and Paradigms,* pp. 77–92. ed. Dell Hymes. Bloomington: Indiana University Press, 1974.

Bynon, T., and F. R. Palmer, eds. *Studies in the History of Western Linguistics in Honour of R. H. Robins.* Ed. Cambridge: Cambridge University Press, 1986.

Campbell, John Angus. "A Rhetorical Interpretation of History." *Rhetorica* 2 (1984): 227–266.

Carrier, J. C. "Knowledge, Meaning and Social Inequality in Kenneth Burke." *American Journal of Sociology* 88 (1982): 43–61.

Cassirer, Ernst. *An Essay on Man* New Haven, CN: Yale University Press, 1944.

————. *Philosophy of Symbolic Forms,* 3 vols., trans. R. Manheim. New Haven, CN: Yale University Press, 1953–1957.

Clark, H. H. and D. Wilkes-Gibbs. "Referring as a Collaborative Process." *Cognition* 22 (1986): 1–21.

Clark, Katerina, and Michael Holquist, *Mikhail Bakhtin* (Cambridge, MA: Harvard University Press, 1984).

Clarke, D. S., Jr. *Principles of Semiotic*. Boston: Routledge and Kegan Paul, 1987.

———. *Sources of Semiotic*. Carbondale: Southern Illinois University Press, 1990.

Collins, Kathleen. *John Tracy Clinic Correspondence Course for Parents of Young Deaf Children, Part A—Deaf Babies and Supplemental Papers*. Los Angeles: John Tracy Clinic, 1984.

Copi, I. M., and R. W. Beard, eds. *Essays on Wittgenstein's Tractatus*. London: Routledge and Kegan Paul, 1966.

Covington, Michael. "Grammatical Theory in the Middle Ages." *Studies in the History of Western Linguistics in Honour of R. H. Robins, ed. T. Bynon and F. R. Palmer,* pp. 21–43. Cambridge: Cambridge University Press, 1986.

Craig, Barbara. "Don't Touch Me, Just Call My Name." *Our Kids Magazine* (Fall 1989): 7–8.

Crowell, Laura. "Three Sheers for Kenneth Burke." *Quarterly Journal of Speech* 63 (1977): 149–162.

Dallmayr, Fred R. *Twilight of Subjectivity: Contributions to a Post-Individualist Theory of Politics*. Amherst: University of Massachusetts Press, 1981.

Darnton, John. "Accepting Nobel, Morrison Proves Power of Words." *New York Times* (8 December 1993); p. B1.

Davidson, Donald. "A Nice Derangement of Epitaphs." *Truth and Interpretation: Perspectives on the Philosophy of Donald Davidson,* ed. Ernst LePore. Oxford: Blackwell, 1986.

Demos, Raphael. "Symposium: Plato's Theory of Language, Plato's Philosophy of Language." *Journal of Philosophy* 61 (1964): 597–614.

Derrida, Jacques. *Of Grammatology,* trans. Gayatri Chakravorty Spivak. Baltimore: Johns Hopkins University Press, 1976.

Dictionary of Philosophy and Psychology, ed. J. M. Baldwin. Gloucester, MA: Macmillan, 1960.

Dinsmore, John, ed. *The Symbolic and Connectionist Paradigms: Closing the Gap*. Hillsdale, NJ: Lawrence Erlbaum, 1992.

Dreyfus, H. L. *Being-in-the-World: A Commentary on Heidegger's Being and Time, Division I*. Cambridge, MA: MIT Press 1991.

Dyer, Susan K. "Hermeneutics and Deaf Education: An Analysis and Critique of Theories of Language and Communication." Master's thesis, University of Washington, 1992.

Eco, Umberto. *Semiotics and the Philosophy of Language*. Bloomington: Indiana University Press, 1984.

Eliade, Mircea. *Cosmos and History*. New York: Praeger, 1959.

Elias, Norbert. *The Symbol Theory* London: Sage, 1991.

Erfurt, Thomas of. *Grammativa Speculativa*, trans. G. L. Bursill-Hall. London: Longman, 1972.

Feibelman, Phyllis. "Editorial." *Our Kids Magazine*, Alexander Graham Bell Association for the Deaf—Parents Section, (Spring 1990): 1–12.

Finch, Henry Le Roy. *Wittgenstein—The Early Philosophy: An Exposition of the "Tractatus."* New York; Humanities Press, 1971.

Fodor, Jerry A. *Psychosemantics: The Problem of Meaning in the Philosophy of Mind*. Cambridge, MA: MIT Press, 1987.

—— and Zenon W. Pylyshyn. "Connectionism and Cognitive Architecture: A Critical Analysis." *Cognition* 28 (1988): 3–71.

Fogelin, Robert J. *Wittgenstein*. London: Routledge and Kegan Paul, 1976.

Frankel, Richard M. "I wz wondering—uhm could *Raid* uhm effect the brain permanently d'y know?": Some Observations on the Intersection of Speaking and Writing in Calls to a Poison Control Center." *Western Journal of Speech Communication* 53 (1989): 195–226.

Gadamer, Hans-Georg. *Philosophical Hermeneutics*, ed. and trans. David E. Linge. Berkeley: University of California Press, 1976.

——. "The Hermeneutics of Suspicion." *Hermeneutics: Questions and Prospects*. Amherst: University of Massachusetts Press, 1984.

——. *Truth and Method* 2nd. ed., trans. J. Weinsheimer and D. G. Marshall. New York: Crossroad, 1989.

——. "Text and Interpretation," trans. D. J. Smith and R. Palmer. *Dialogue and Deconstruction*, ed. D. P. Michelfelder and R.E. Palmer, pp. 21–51. Albany: SUNY Press, 1989.

Gallaudet Encyclopedia of Deaf People and Deafness, ed. John V. Van Cleve, 3 vols. New York: McGraw-Hill, 1987.

Gannon, Jack R. *Deaf Heritage: A Narrative History of Deaf America*. Silver Springs, MD: National Association of the Deaf, 1981.

Garretson, Mervin D., ed. *Communication Issues Among Deaf People—A Deaf American Monograph*, vol. 40, Nos. 1–4. Washington, D. C.: St. Mary's Press 1990.

Geertz, Clifford. *Local Knowledge: Further Essays in Interpretive Anthropology.* New York: Basic Books, 1983.

Graeser, Andreas. "The Stoic Theory of Meaning. *The Stoics,* ed. John M. Rist., pp. 68–89. Berkeley: University of California Press, 1978.

Greenblatt, S. J., ed. *Allegory and Representation.* Baltimore: Johns Hopkins University Press, 1979–1980.

Greenlee, Douglas. *Peirce's Concept of Sign.* The Hague: Mouton, 1973.

Grice, H. P. "Logic and Conversations," *Syntax and Semantics,* vol. 3, ed. P. Cole and J. L. Morgan. New York: Academic Press, 1975.

Gumperz, John J. ed. *Language and Social Identity* New York: Cambridge University Press, 1982.

———. and Dell Hymes, eds. *Directions in Sociolinguistics: The Ethnography of Communication.* New York: Holt, Rinehart and Winston, 1972.

Hamburg, Carl H. "Cassirer's Conception of Philosophy." *The Philosophy of Ernst Cassirer,* ed. P. A. Schilpp. Evanston, IL: Library of Living Philosophers, 1949.

Harris, Roy. *The Language-Makers.* London: Duckworth, 1980.

———. *Language, Saussure and Wittgenstein.* London: Routledge, 1988.

———. *The Language Myth.* London: Duckworth, 1981.

——— and Talbot J. Taylor. *Landmarks in Linguistic Thought: The Western Tradition from Socrates to Saussure.* London: Routledge, 1989.

Havelock, Eric A. *The Muse Learns to Write.* New Haven, CN: Yale University Press, 1986.

Heath, R. L. *Realism and Relativism: A Perspective on Kenneth Burke.* Macon, GA: Mercer University Press, 1986.

Heidegger, Martin. *Being and Time,* trans. J. Macquarrie and E. Robinson. New York: Harper and Row, 1962.

———. *On The Way to Language,* trans. Peter D. Hertz. San Francisco: Harper and Row, 1971.

———. *Basic Writings,* ed. David Farrell Krell. New York: Harper and Row, 1977.

———. *History of the Concept of Time,* trans. T. Kisiel. Bloomington: Indiana University Press, 1985.

Hintikka, Merrill B. and Jaakko Hintikka. *Investigating Wittgenstein.* London: Blackwell, 1986.

Holquist, Michael. "Introduction." *The Dialogic Imagination: Four Essays by M. M. Bakhtin*. ed. Michael Holquist, trans. Caryl Emerson and Michael Holquist. Austin: University of Texas Press, 1981.

Hookway, Christopher. *Peirce*. London: Routledge and Kegan Paul, 1985.

Horne Tooke, John. *The Diversions of Purley*. 2nd ed. facsimile reprint. Menston, England: Scolar, [1798] 1968.

Humboldt, Wilhelm von. *On Language,* trans. Peter Heath. Cambridge: Cambridge University Press, 1988.

Husserl, Edmund. *The Crisis of European Sciences and Transcendental Phenomenology,* trans. David Carr. Evanston, IL: Northwestern University Press, 1970.

Hyde, Michael, and Craig Smith. "Hermeneutics and Rhetoric: A Seen But Unobserved Relationship." *Quarterly Journal of Speech* 65 (1979): 347–363.

Hymes, Dell. "Introduction to 'What Are the Signs of What?' A Theory of Entitlement." *Anthropological Linguistics* 3 (1962): 1–5.

———. *Foundations in Sociolinguistics: An Ethnographic Approach*. Philadelphia: University of Pennsylvania Press, 1974.

———, ed. *Studies in the History of Linguistics: Traditions and Paradigms*. Bloomington: Indiana University Press, 1974.

International Encyclopedia of the Social Sciences, ed. D. L. Sills. New York: Macmillan, 1968.

Janik, Allan and Stephen Toulmin. *Wittgenstein's Vienna*. New York: Simon and Schuster, 1973.

Jacobs, Leo M. *A Deaf Adult Speaks Out,* 3rd ed. Washington, DC: Gallaudet University Press, 1989.

Jacobsen, Thorkild. "Very Ancient Texts: Babylonian Grammatical Texts." *Studies in the History of Linguistics: Traditions and Paradigms*, ed. Dell Hymes, pp. 37–51. Bloomington: Indiana University Press, 1974.

Jameson, Frederic. "Review of *Marxism and the Philosophy of Language.*" *Style* 8 (1974): 535–543.

Jenkins, John J. *Understanding Locke: An Introduction to Philosophy Through John Locke's Essay*. Edinburgh: The University Press, 1983.

Johnson, Robert, and Scott Liddell. "The Value of ASL in the Education of Deaf Children." *Communication Issues Among Deaf People: A Deaf American Monograph*, 40, ed. Mervin D. Garretson. Washington, D.C.: St. Mary's Press, 1990.

Johnson, Robert E., Scott K. Liddell, and Carol J. Erting. *Unlocking the Curriculum: Principles for Achieving Access in Deaf Education.* Washington, D.C.: Gallaudet University Research Institute, 1989.

Kerferd, G. B. *The Sophistic Movement.* Cambridge: Cambridge University Press, 1981.

Ketner, Kenneth L., and Christian J. W. Kloesel, eds. "Preface." *Peirce, Semeiotic, and Pragmatism: Essays by Max H. Fisch.* Bloomington: Indiana University Press, 1986.

Kirwan, Christopher. *Augustine.* London: Routledge, 1989.

Klima, E. S., and U. Bellugi. *The Signs of Language.* Cambridge, MA: Harvard University Press 1979.

Kretzmann, Norman, Anthony Kenny, and Jan Pinborg, eds. *The Cambridge History of Later Medieval Philosophy.* Cambridge: Cambridge University Press, 1982.

Kristeva, Julia. *Language: The Unknown,* trans. A. M. Menke. New York: Columbia University Press, 1989.

Lakoff, George. *Women, Fire, and Dangerous Things: What Categories Reveal About the Mind.* Chicago: University of Chicago Press, 1987.

Lane, Harlan. *When the Mind Hears: A History of the Deaf.* New York: Random House, 1984.

———. *The Mask of Benevolence: Disabling the Deaf Community.* New York: Alfred A. Knopf, 1992.

Langer, Susanne K. *Philosophy in a New Key* New York: Mentor, 1951.

Levi-Strauss, Claude. *Structural Anthropology,* trans. C. Jacobson and B. Grundfest Schoepf. New York: Basic Books, 1963.

Locke, John. *Essay Concerning Human Understanding* London: Elizabeth Holt for Thomas Basset, 1690.

———. *Essay Concerning Human Understanding,* ed. A. C. Fraser. Oxford: Clarendon, 1894.

Long, A. A. "Language and Thought in Stoicism." *Problems in Stoicism,* ed. A. A. Long, pp. 71–88. London: Athlone, 1971.

Madison, G. B. *The Hermeneutics of Postmodernity: Figures and Themes.* Bloomington: Indiana University Press, 1990.

Mates, Benson. *Stoic Logic.* Berkeley: University of California Press, 1953.

Maturana, Humberto R. "Biology of Language: The Epistemology of Reality." *Psychology and Biology of Language and Thought: Essays in*

Honor of Eric Lenneberg, ed. G. A. Miller and E. Lenneberg. New York: Academic Press, 1978.

———. and F. Varela. *Autopoiesis and Cognition: The Realization of the Living*. Dodrecht: Reidel, 1980.

Maynard, Douglas W. "Perspective-Display Sequences in Conversation." *Western Journal Speech Communication* 53 (1989): 91–113.

McCarthy, Thomas A. "General Introduction." *After Philosophy: End or Transformation?* Ed. K. Baynes, J. Bohman, and T. McCarthy. pp. 1–18, Cambridge, MA: MIT Press, 1987.

McGee, Michael C. "Text, Context, and the Fragmentation of Contemporary Culture." *Western Journal of Speech Communication* 54 (1990): 267–283.

McKeon, Richard. "Aristotle's Conception of Language and the Arts of Language, I." *Classical Philology* 61 (1946): 191–239.

———. "Aristotle's Conception of Language and the Arts of Language, II." Classical *Philology* 6 (1947): 19–49.

McNeill, David. *Hand and Mind: What Gestures Reveal About Thought*. Chicago: University of Chicago Press, 1992.

Merleau-Ponty, Maurice. *The Primacy of Perception,* trans. James M. Edie. Evanston, IL: Northwestern University Press, 1964.

———. *The Visible and the Invisible,* trans. A. Lingis. Evanston, IL: Northwestern University Press, 1968.

Michelfelder, Diane P., and Richard E. Palmer, eds. D*ialogue and Deconstruction: The Gadamer-Derrida Encounter*. Albany: SUNY Press, 1989.

Morris, Charles. *Foundations of the Theory of Signs*. Chicago: University of Chicago Press, 1938.

———. *Signs, Language and Behavior.* New York: Braziller, 1946.

Motley, Michael. "On Whether One Can(not) Not Communicate: An Examination via Traditional Communication Postulates." *Western Journal of Speech Communication* 54 (1990): 1–20.

Nadel, Lynn, Lynn A. Cooper, Peter Culicover, and R. Michael Harnish eds. *Neural Connections, Mental Computation*. Cambridge, MA: MIT Press, 1990.

Newell, A. "Physical Symbol Systems." *Cognitive Science* 4 (1980): 164–180.

Ogden, C. K. and I. A. Richards. *The Meaning of Meaning*. New York: Harcourt Brace, 1923.

Ong, Walter J. *Orality and Literacy: The Technologizing of the Word.* New York: Meuthen, 1982.

Osgood, Charles E. "What is a Language?" *The Signifying Animal,* ed. I. Rauch and G. F. Carr, pp. 9–49. Bloomington: Indiana University Press, 1980.

Palmer, Richard. *Hermeneutics: Interpretation Theory in Schleiermacher, Dilthey, Heidegger, and Gadamer.* Evanston, IL: Northwestern University Press, 1969.

Parret, Herman, ed. *History of Linguistic Thought and Contemporary Linguistics.* Berlin: Walter de Gruyter, 1976.

Parry, Adam M. *The Making of Homeric Verse.* Oxford: Clarendon, 1971.

Partridge, Derek. *A New Guide to Artificial Intelligence.* Norwood, NJ: Ablex, 1991.

Peirce, Charles Sanders. *Charles Sanders Peirce's Letters to Lady Welby,* ed. Irwin C. Lieb. New Haven, CN: Whitlock's, 1953.

———. *Selected Writings: Values in a Universe of Change,* ed. P. P. Weiner. New York: Dover, 1958.

———. *Collected Papers of Charles Sanders Peirce,* ed. C. Hartshorne and P. Weiss, 8 vols. Cambridge, MA: Harvard University Press, 1960.

———. *The New Elements of Mathematics,* ed. C. Eisele. The Hague: Mouton, 1976.

———. *Semiotics and Significs,* ed. C. Hardwick. Bloomington: Indiana University Press, 1977.

Pinborg, Jan. "Speculative Grammar." *The Cambridge History of Later Medieval Philosophy,* ed. N. Kretzmann, A. Kenny, and J. Pinborg, pp. 254–273. Cambridge: Cambridge University Press, 1982.

Plato. *The Collected Dialogues of Plato,* ed. E. Hamilton and H. Cairns. Princeton, NJ: Princeton University Press, 1961.

Putnam, Hilary. *Representation and Reality.* Cambridge, MA: MIT Press, 1988.

Rabinow, P. and W. Sullivan, eds. *Interpretive Social Science: A Reader.* Berkeley: University of California Press, 1979.

Ramsey, W., S. P. Stich, and D. E. Rummelhart, eds. *Philosophy and Connectionist Theory.* Hillsdale, NJ: Lawrence Erlbaum, 1991.

Reddy, Michael J. "The Conduit Metaphor: A Case of Frame Conflict in Our Language About Language." *Metaphor and Thought,* ed. A. Ortony, pp. 284–324. Cambridge: Cambridge University Press, 1979.

Reuckert, William H. *Kenneth Burke and the Drama of Human Relations*, 2nd ed. Berkeley: University of California Press, 1982.

———. "Criticism as a Way of Life or Criticism as Equipment for Living." *Newsletter of the Kenneth Burke Society* 6 (1990): 7–15.

Robins, R. H. *A Short History of Linguistics*, 3rd ed. London: Longmans, 1990.

Rorty, Richard. *Philosophy and the Mirror of Nature*. Princeton, NJ: Princeton University Press, 1979.

———. *Essays on Heidegger and Others*. Cambridge: Cambridge University Press, 1991.

Rosseau, Jean-Jacques. *On the Origin of Language*, trans. and ed. J. H. Moran and A. Gode. New York: Frederick Ungar, 1966.

Ryle, Gilbert. *The Concept of Mind*. New York: Barnes and Noble, 1949.

———. *Collected Papers, vol. I*. London: Hutchinson, 1971.

Sacks, Oliver. *Seeing Voices: A Journey into the World of the Deaf*. Berkeley: University of California Press, 1989.

Sandbach, F. H. *The Stoics*. New York: W. W. Norton, 1975.

Saussure, Ferdinand de. *Course in General Linguistics,* ed. C. Bally and A. L. Sechehaye, trans. R. Harris. LaSalle, IL: Open Court, 1983.

Schafer, Roy. *Language and Insight*. New Haven, CN: Yale University Press 1978.

Schlesigner, Hilde S., and Kathryn P. Meadow. *Sound and Sign: Childhood Deafness and Mental Health*. Berkeley: University of California Press, 1972.

Schilpp, P. A., ed. *The Philosophy of Ernst Cassirer*. Evanston, IL: Library of Living Philosophers, 1949.

Schrag, Calvin O. "Rhetoric Resituated at the End of Philosophy." *Quarterly Journal of Speech* 71 (1985): 164–174.

———. *Communicative Praxis and the Space of Subjectivity*. Bloomington: Indiana University Press, 1986.

———. *The Resources of Rationality: A Response to the Postmodern Challenge*. Bloomington: Indiana University Press, 1992.

Searle, John R. *Speech Acts: An Essay on the Philosophy of Language*. London: Cambridge University Press, 1969.

———. *Intentionality: An Essay in the Philosophy of Mind*. Cambridge: Cambridge University Press, 1983.

Sebeok, Thomas A., ed. *Historiography of Linguistics,* vol 13, *Current Trends in Linguistics.* The Hague: Mouton, 1975.

Shotter, John. *Social Accountability and Selfhood.* Oxford: Blackwell, 1984.

Signorile, Vito. "Review of Oliver Sacks' *Seeing Voices.*" *Human Studies* 14 (1991): 371–373.

Silverman, Hugh J., ed. *Gadamer and Hermeneutics.* New York: Routledge, 1991.

Simons, Herbert B. and Trevor Melia, eds. *The Legacy of Kenneth Burke.* Madison: University of Wisconsin Press, 1989.

Smith, Craig R. "Finding the Spiritual Dimension in Rhetoric." *Western Journal of Communication* 57 (1993): 266–271.

Southwell, S. B. *Kenneth Burke and Martin Heidegger with a Note Against Deconstruction.* Gainesville: University of Florida Press, 1987.

Stamp, Glen H., and Mark L. Knapp. "The Construct of Intent in Interpersonal Communication." *Quarterly Journal of Speech* 76 (1990): 282–299.

Stevens, Raymond P. "Children's Language Should be Learned and Not Taught." *Sign Language Studies,* 11 (1976): 97–108.

Stewart, John R. "Concepts of Language and Meaning: A Comparative Study." *Quarterly Journal of Speech* 58 (1972): 123–133.

———. "Speech and Human Being: A Complement to Semiotics." *Quarterly Journal of Speech* 72 (1986): 55–73.

———. "A Postmodern Look at Traditional Communication Postulates." *Western Journal of Speech Communication,* 55 (1991): 354–379.

———. "One Philosophical Dimension of Social Approaches to Interpersonal Communication." *Communication Theory* 2 (1992): 337–346.

———. "Structural Implications of the Symbol Model for Communication Theory." *Structure in Communication Study,* ed. Richard Conville, pp. 125–154. New York: Praeger, 1994.

———. "An Interpretive Approach to Validity in Interpersonal Communication Research." *Interpretive Approaches to Interpersonal Communication,* ed. Kathryn Carter and Mick Presnell, pp. 45–81. Albany: SUNY Press, 1994.

Stolz, Benjamin A., I. R. Tutnik, and Lubomir Dolezel, eds. *Language and Literary Theory.* Ann Arbor: Dept. of Slavik Languages and Literatures, University of Michigan 1984.

Strong, Michael, ed. *Language Learning and Deafness.* New York: Cambridge University Press, 1988.

Stokoe, William C. *Sign Language Structure*. Silver Spring, MD: Linstok, 1960.

———. "Sign Writing Systems." *Gallaudet Encyclopedia of Deaf People* ed. John Van Cleve. New York: McGraw-Hill, 1987.

Taylor, Charles. "Interpretation and the Sciences of Man." *Review of Metaphysics* 25 (1971): 3–51.

———. *Philosophy and the Human Sciences: Philosophical Papers*, vol. 2. New York: Cambridge University Press, 1985.

The Encyclopedia of Philosophy, ed. Paul Edwards. New York: Macmillan, 1972.

The Oxford Annotated Bible: Revised Standard Version, ed. H. G. May and B. M. Metzger. New York: Oxford University Press, 1962.

The Oxford English Dictionary, 2nd ed. Oxford: Clarendon, 1989.

Todorov, Tzvetan. *Mikhail Bakhtin: The Dialogical Principle*. Minneapolis: University of Minnesota Press, 1984.

Torrance, Steve, ed. *The Mind and the Machine: Philosophical Aspects of Artificial Intelligence*. Chichester, England: Ellis Horwood, 1984.

Turing, Alan. "Computing Machinery and Intelligence." *Mind* 59 (1950): 433–460.

Verney, T. R., ed. *Pre- and Perinatal Psychology: An Introduction*. New York: Human Sciences Press, 1987.

Voegelin, Eric V. "Immortality: Experience and Symbol." *Harvard Theological Review* 60 (1967), 266–289.

Volosinov, V. N. *Marxism and the Philosophy of Language*, trans. Laidslav Matejka and I. R. Titunik. Cambridge, MA: Harvard University Press, 1973.

Watzlawick, Paul, Janet Helmick Beavin, and Don D. Jackson. *Pragmatics of Human Communication*. New York: Norton, 1967.

White, Stephen K., ed. *Between Modernity and Postmodernity*. Notre Dame: Univ. of Notre Dame, 1989.

Wilcox, Sherman, ed. *American Deaf Culture: An Anthology*. Silver Spring, MD: Linstok, 1989.

Wilson, John F. and Carroll C. Arnold. *Public Speaking as a Liberal Art*, 2nd ed. Boston: Allyn and Bacon, 1968.

Winefield, Richard. *Never the Twain Shall Meet: The Communications Debate*. Washington, DC: Gallaudet University Press, 1987.

Winograd, Terry, and Fernando Flores. *Understanding Computers and Cognition: A New Foundation for Design*. Reading, MA: Addison-Wesley, 1986.

Wittgenstein, Ludwig. *Tractatus Logico-Philosophicus,* trans. D. F. Pears and B. F. McGuinness. London: Routledge & Kegan Paul, 1961.

———. *Philosophical Investigations,* trans. G. E. M. Anscombe. Oxford: Blackwell, 1963.

INDEX